Using Past as Prologue

Contemporary Perspectives on African American Educational History

A volume in
Research on African American Education
Carol Camp Yeakey and Ronald D. Henderson, *Series Editors*

Using Past as Prologue

Contemporary Perspectives on African American Educational History

edited by

Dionne Danns
Indiana University

Michelle A. Purdy
Washington University in St. Louis

Christopher M. Span
University of Illinois at Urbana–Champaign

INFORMATION AGE PUBLISHING, INC.
Charlotte, NC • www.infoagepub.com

Library of Congress Cataloging-in-Publication Data

A CIP record for this book is available from the Library of Congress
http://www.loc.gov

ISBN: 978-1-68123-170-9 (Paperback)
        978-1-68123-171-6 (Hardcover)
        978-1-68123-172-3 (ebook)

CONTENTS

PART II

EDUCATION IN THE TWENTIETH CENTURY

PART III

CONTEMPORARY HISTORY AND FUTURE DIRECTIONS

FOREWORD

James D. Anderson
University of Illinois at Urbana-Champaign

In his 1925 essay, "The Negro Digs Up His Past," historian and archivist Arturo Alfonso Schomburg wrote, "the American Negro must remake his past in order to make his future. Though it is orthodox to think of America as the one country where it is unnecessary to have a past, what is a luxury for the nation as a whole becomes a prime social necessity for the Negro. For him, a group tradition must supply compensation for persecution, and pride of race the antidote for prejudice. History must restore what slavery took away, for it is the social damage of slavery that the present generation must repair and offset."[1]

This quote epitomizes the role contemporary historians must play in the discourse and educational policy related to the academic achievement and success of African Americans. Centuries of denied opportunities have shaped the educational experience of African Americans. Slavery denied African Americans the opportunity to attend school; segregation denied African Americans the opportunity for a quality education or to attend school on an equal basis; and contemporary schools attended by African Americans measure their achievement and aptitude to schoolchildren of other races who have neither their historical or current experiences.

Using Past as Prologue is a continuation of the "prime social necessity" of using historical inquiry and methodology to articulate the educational experiences of both the African American past and present. The chapters in

Using Past as Prologue, pages xi–xii
Copyright © 2015 by Information Age Publishing

this book offer new insight and understanding of important questions and developments in the African American educational experience. Similar to the edited volume V. P. Franklin and I published in 1978, *New Perspectives on Black Education*, it is another step toward conveying a written account of the African American past that records the agency, determination, courage, and vision of African Americans to define the meaning of freedom, democracy, citizenship, and education on their own terms.

I have known each editor (and many of the contributors of this volume) from their days in graduate school. I have watched each of them become outstanding historians in their own right and write histories that help to restore the role African Americans played in the advancement of the United States. I am honored by the work of these scholars and the histories they have written in this edited volume. In their own way, each has taken up Schomburg's call to write and remake the African American past in order to make the African American future.

NOTE

1. Schomburg's quote can be found in Nathan Irvin Huggins, *Voices from the Harlem Renaissance* (New York, NY: Oxford University Press, 1995).

PREFACE

Vanessa Siddle Walker noted in *Hello Professor* that although this nation is in a time of resegregation, the era of Jim Crow segregation and the accomplishments Black teachers and school leaders made during that time have passed. As leaders and teachers were dismissed, the world they left behind belongs to history and cannot easily be replicated simply because segregation exists again. Yet, according to Walker this history informs the present and helps us uncover where we have come from to advance our future. In the tradition of Sankofa, we look back to make a way for the future.[1] *Using Past as Prologue: Contemporary Perspectives on African American Educational History* is designed to provide students and scholars in education, history, and African American Studies, along with activists and policy makers, a fresh perspective of the history of American education by elaborating on known and unknown histories, historiography, methodology, and teaching.

Using Past as Prologue broadens the historiography of Black southern schools in the nineteenth and twentieth centuries, in slavery and freedom, in K–12 and higher education. We learn how individuals and communities grappled with the southern context and worked to enhance education through laboratory schools, graduate education, Historically Black Colleges and Universities, Freedom Schools, and Head Start. In northern urban areas, *Using Past as Prologue* highlights how Blacks struggled for quality education through private schools, desegregation, and community control in the postwar era. Finally, the book addresses how contemporary accountability policies and discussions of the achievement gap are shaped by history. These important studies of the past not only extend history, but can also inform the present, and those who plan to transform the future.

Using Past as Prologue, pages xiii–xiv
Copyright © 2015 by Information Age Publishing
xiii

NOTE

1. Vanessa Siddle Walker with Ulysses Byas, *Hello Professor: A Black Principal and Professional Leadership in the Segregated South* (Chapel Hill: University of North Carolina Press, 2009).

ACKNOWLEDGMENTS

This edited volume could not have been completed without the encouragement and support of our contributors, colleagues, families, and friends. We thank each contributor to this volume for their patience, brilliance, and willingness to entertain our countless requests and edits. In addition we would like to thank James D. Anderson and V. P. Franklin for their wonderful words of inspiration in the Foreword and Epilogue. We will forever be indebted to you for your wisdom, scholarship, leadership, call to action, and mentorship. Carol Camp Yeakey helped us shape the contents of this volume, and we appreciate your guidance through the process of publishing with Information Age Press, and for being an absolutely outstanding acquisition editor. We thank Information Age Press for allowing us to publish this important edited work. Additionally, we thank our colleagues at our respective institutions for supporting us in this initiative and affording the uninterrupted time to finalize this volume. A special thanks goes to Kathy Stalter at the University of Illinois at Urbana-Champaign who coordinated every meeting for us, fixed the technology bugs that slowed us down, and kept us on track. Last but not least, we thank our families for their unconditional support, love, wisdom, and guidance throughout the whole process.

Using Past as Prologue, page xv
Copyright © 2015 by Information Age Publishing
All rights of reproduction in any form reserved.

INTRODUCTION

TOWARDS A NEW HISTORY OF AFRICAN AMERICAN EDUCATION

Dionne Danns
Indiana University

Michelle A. Purdy
Washington University in St. Louis

Christopher M. Span
University of Illinois at Urbana-Champaign

> *Historians generally believe that each new generation of scholars
> writes its own history.*
> —Vincent P. Franklin, *New Perspectives on Black Educational History*[1]

In 1978, V. P. Franklin and James D. Anderson co-edited *New Perspectives on Black Educational History*. For Franklin, Anderson, and their contributors, there were glaring gaps in the historiography of Black education that each of the essays began to fill with new information or fresh perspectives from a new generation of scholars.[2] There have been a number of important studies on the history of African American education in the more than three decades since Franklin and Anderson published their volume that has pushed

Using Past as Prologue, pages 1–14
Copyright © 2015 by Information Age Publishing
1

the field forward. Scholars have redefined the views of Black southern schools as simply inferior, demonstrated the active role Blacks had in creating and sustaining their schools, sharpened our understanding of Black teachers' and educational leaders' role in educating Black students and themselves with professional development, provided a better understanding and recognition of the struggles in the North (particularly in urban and metropolitan areas), expanded our thinking about school desegregation and community control, and broadened our understanding of Black experiences and activism in higher education and private schools. While there is a plethora of important books that has broadened our understanding of Black education, below are just some of the books and scholarship that has transformed our field and inspired contributors to this volume, *Using Past as Prologue: Contemporary Perspectives on African American Educational History*.

Scholars such as James D. Anderson, Ronald E. Butchart, Heather Andrea Williams, and Christopher M. Span, have explored the nineteenth century South in new and dynamic ways. Much of the literature has highlighted Black educational efforts as slavery came to a close, after the Civil War, and during and after Reconstruction. Anderson's *The Education of Blacks in the South* influenced countless scholars.[3] His thoroughly researched book established education as a cultural value for African Americans, highlighted the countless acts of Black individuals and communities in the development and maintaining of Black schools even in the worst of times, showed the motives of northern philanthropists, and highlighted the philosophical tensions between Booker T. Washington and W. E. B. Du Bois. Arguing the dual purposes of education—one for second class citizenship and the other for participation in democracy—Anderson captures how the differing purposes of Black education played out in the South and its impact on elementary and secondary schools as well as higher education. Butchart's *Northern Schools, Southern Blacks, and Reconstruction* and more recently *Schooling the Freed People* explored southern education during Reconstruction. *Schooling the Freed People* closely follows who taught Blacks and challenged the view of the northern White teachers with the mission of socially reconstructing the South.[4] In addition, Butchart reveals the role southern White teachers had in educating Blacks. Like Anderson before her, Williams's *Self-Taught* uncovered the role African Americans played in starting the educational movement in the South and how American Missionary Association schools were really schools thought of and organized by freedpeople. Her book also captures education during slavery and the multiple ways in which those enslaved sought and obtained education. Span's *From Cotton Field to Schoolhouse* chronicles Black education during Reconstruction in Mississippi. He follows the complex policies and politics associated with the education of freedpeople. Blacks, wanting control over their education and the independence associated with freedom, had to struggle against the visions and expectations northern and southern Whites had for them. Each of these scholars along with others, have brought to life new histories of the South in the nineteenth century.[5]

Southern Black schools were not given the appropriate resources to thrive through much of the nineteenth and twentieth centuries. The struggle for adequate supplies, buildings, and curriculum, as well as the limited education many Blacks received, has largely left an image of inferior Black southern schools with few redeeming qualities. The arguments put forth in the *Brown v. Board of Education* (1954) Supreme Court case helped to create a belief in the inferiority of these underfunded and segregated schools. Recently, a new set of scholarship has both highlighted the difficult environments in which these schools existed, but also has shown that in the midst of the oppressive environments, Black teachers and school leaders in different schools have created spaces of excellence which challenge notions that all these schools were inferior. These scholars have changed the scholarly understanding of the value of Black schools, and detailed the pedagogies of Black teachers and principals. Vanessa Siddle Walker's *Their Highest Potential* is among the best known of these revisionist histories and more recently, her second book *Hello Professor*, written with and about Ulysses Byas, contributes to our understanding of the role educators played in combating oppressive educational conditions.[6] Scholars such as Faustine Childress Jones, author of *A Traditional Model of Educational Excellence,* and Allison Stewart, author of *First Class,* have written institutional histories about schools with the same name (Dunbar) in different cities (Little Rock and Washington D.C.) which produced excellent education for Black students.[7] Additionally, Sonya Ramsey's *Reading, Writing, and Segregation* and Hilton Kelly's *Race, Remembering, and Jim Crow Teachers* both show the role teachers played in segregated schools in Nashville and North Carolina.[8]

Other scholars have captured twentieth century national and local school desegregation struggles, the desires of Black communities in these struggles, and the experiences of teachers and students in the North, South, and border areas. These struggles show the pervasive nature of racism as the regional lines become blurred with national resistance to desegregation and busing. Though each city, county, or region comes with unique demographics, politics, and social mores, few places easily desegregated, and Whites were typically privileged with most desegregation plans. James Patterson's *Brown v. Board of Education* and Derrick Bell's *Silent Covenants,* provide a national history of school desegregation.[9] Patterson highlights the history before, during, and after the *Brown* decision, while Bell ponders the symbolic nature of the *Brown* decision and wonders if desegregation was the right decision. With time and distance from this historic case, these scholars are more critical of the decision and question the legacy and impact.

David C. Cecelski, R. Scott Baker, Sarah Caroline Thuesen, and a number of other scholars give us a view of the varied local responses to desegregation throughout the South. Cecelski's *Along Freedom Road* captures the desire of Blacks in North Carolina's Hyde County to have desegregation on their terms. Baker's *Paradoxes of Desegregation* highlights the role standardized testing played in South Carolina officials' attempts to limit desegregation and examines the teacher equalization suits in South Carolina.[10] Though much of the focus has been on student desegregation, Black teachers and principals fought for salary equalization, lost their jobs, were demoted, or were also desegregated. Thuesen's *Greater than Equal* makes important ties among the desire for first class citizenship, equalization, and desegregation in twentieth century North Carolina.[11] Michael Fultz has written on the loss of jobs Black teachers and principals in the South experienced as a result of desegregation.[12] Recently, Barbara Shircliffe's *Desegregating Teachers* chronicled teacher desegregation in the South and how faculty desegregation plans reinforced White privilege.[13]

Border states and cities have also received attention. Howell S. Baum's *Brown in Baltimore* shows how a border city with a liberal school board could attempt to desegregate with a freedom of choice plan without addressing race or racial segregation.[14] Two books on Louisville desegregation, Sarah Garland's *Divided We Fall* and Tracy E. K'Meyer's *From Brown to Meredith*, provide compelling histories of how desegregation unraveled in Louisville and Jefferson County, Kentucky leading to the 2007 *Meredith v. Jefferson County* Supreme Court case decision.[15] Brett Gadsden's *Between North and South* disrupts the sectional beliefs about racism and segregation, while providing a history of struggle to successfully desegregate schools in Delaware.[16]

There are also a number of books written about northern desegregation by scholars like Davidson Douglas, Gregory S. Jacobs, and Dionne Danns. Douglas's *Jim Crow Moves North* looks at northern school segregation and pre-*Brown* battles to desegregate those schools in different states. Many other scholars focus on a local view of desegregation in northern cities. Jacob's *Getting Around Brown* highlights the challenges of desegregating Columbus, Ohio's schools. Danns's *Desegregating Chicago's Public Schools* emphasizes the role of federal and state government in implementing the 1964 Civil Rights Act in Chicago, including a chapter highlighting the difficulty the federal government had in trying to desegregate Chicago's teachers.[17]

Research on northern Black education in the nineteenth and twentieth century beyond desegregation studies has expanded. V. P. Franklin's *The Education of Black Philadelphia* focuses on the various institutions where education takes place beyond schools.[18] His social and educational history of the city from 1900–1950 highlights the role education played in the fight against discrimination on various fronts. Community education programs and schooling helped to improve the standing of African Americans. Hilary

Moss's *Schooling Citizens* captures nineteenth century Black education in New Haven, Connecticut; Baltimore, and Boston. Moss fills an important gap in the literature as much of the recent work on northern schooling is focused on the twentieth century. She also highlights Baltimore, a border city, and is able to demonstrate how Black and White views of citizenship impacted the fight for and against Black education.[19]

New York has seen much of the educational focus on the community control struggles in Ocean Hill-Brownsville. Jerald Podair's *The Strike that Changed New York* and Daniel Perlstein's *Justice, Justice* are among the two most popular books on the confrontation.[20] Two newer books, Heather Lewis's *New York Public Schools from Brownsville to Bloomberg* and Glen Anthony Harris's *The Ocean Hill-Brownsville Conflict* have also sought new ways to examine the historical battle to control and enhance Black and Puerto Rican education, the conflicts between Blacks and Jews in New York, and the legacy of the community control confrontation.[21] Beyond community control, Jonna Perillo's *Uncivil Rights* examines how teachers' rights were often at odds with civil rights in New York City, complicating the battle for educational improvement.[22]

Studies on Midwestern cities like Milwaukee and Chicago also add to the literature on Northern urban education. Jack Dougherty's *More than One Struggle*, while examining generational struggles for Black education, also focuses on efforts to desegregate Milwaukee's schools. Michael W. Homel's *Down from Equality* traces the increasing segregation that occurs in Chicago as Blacks migrated to the city prior to the *Brown* decision. Homel provides a view of difficulties Black Chicagoans faced and how they responded. Picking up where Homel left off, Dionne Danns's *Something Better for Our Children* looks at struggles for Chicago school reform in the 1960s and early 1970s. During the Civil Rights and Black Power eras, community members, teachers, and students made demands for educational change focused on desegregation as well as community control.[23]

Other important books include works on secondary education which expand the historiography and methodology of history, biographies of important leaders and their educational philosophies, and edited works which showcase a variety of Black educational thought and other educational endeavors. These studies help to center Blacks in traditional educational philosophies such as progressive education or liberalism, as well as show how Blacks developed their own ideas of racial uplift or radical philosophies based on their lived experiences. In addition, the important role of women is brought to the fore. John L. Rury and Shirley A. Hill's, *The African American Struggle for Secondary Schooling, 1940–1980* uses oral history, archival and quantitative data to detail the efforts to narrow the high school graduation gap.[24] In terms of biographies, Linda Perkins's *Fanny Jackson Coppin and the Institute for Colored Youth, 1837–1902* and Karen A. Johnson's *Uplifting the Women and the Race* showcases the contributions and educational philosophies of women like Fanny Jackson Coppin, Anna Julia Cooper and Nannie Helen Burroughs.[25] Derrick Aldridge's *The Educational Thought of W. E. B. Du Bois*, Patrick J. Gilpin and Marybeth Gasman's *Charles S. Johnson*, and John Spencer's *In the Crossfire* focus on the intellectual contributions of famous scholars like Du Bois and Johnson, and the unknown educational leader Marcus Foster. Like Walker's *Hello Professor*, these studies provide insight into the thinking and actions of these men.[26] A few edited volumes, like William Watkins's *Black Protest Thought and Education*, V. P. Franklin and Carter J. Savage's *Culture Capital and Black Education*, and Karen A. Johnson, Abul Pitre, and Kenneth L. Johnson's *African American Women Educators*, continue to fill the gaps of Black intellectual thought, community struggles, and educational leaders.[27]

Research has also grown on African Americans and private schooling. Edited volumes, such as *Visible Now: Blacks in Private Schools*, includes history of African Americans in historically White elite private schools and Catholic schools.[28] Scholars such as Anderson, Arnold Cooper, Katherine C. Reynolds, Charles Weldon Wadelington and Richard F. Knapp have also detailed private African American educational spaces, including in the South where education pre-*Brown* consisted of a system of public and private schools.[29]

Higher education literature has expanded, particularly the coverage of the Civil Rights era. Combined, Joy Ann Williamson, Martha Biondi, and Ibram H. Rogers provide us with a view of Black activism in the North and South, at Historically Black Colleges and Universities (HBCUs) as well at predominantly White institutions. Williamson's *Radicalizing the Ebony Tower* captures the struggles at Black colleges in Mississippi, expanding the historiography by emphasizing that student activists were students, dispelling the belief that all Black colleges were the same, showing that student status did not protect students, highlighting the important role of Black student activism after Freedom Summer, and demonstrating the difficulties Black colleges faced with academic freedom.[30] Likewise, Martha Biondi's *The Black Revolution on Campus* describes the important role Black students played in transforming college campuses around the country and establishing Black Studies programs. She examines known struggles at San Francisco State and Howard University and little known battles at colleges and universities in Chicago, New York, and HBCUs in the South.[31] Published the same year as Biondi's book, Rogers's *The Black Campus Movement* is also a national study which focuses on both Black and White colleges and universities. Rogers situates what he calls the Black campus movement as part of the long Black student movement (which began prior to the Civil Rights Movement), the student movement in the 1960s, and the Black Power Movement. This Black campus movement helped to transform modern higher education in the United States.[32] Other important studies of student activism of higher education have also emerged. These studies largely focus on individual campuses. Among the most recent is Stefan Bradley's *Harlem vs. Columbia University* and among the pioneering studies was Richard McCormick's *The Black Student Protest Movement at Rutgers*.[33] These and other institutional studies cover a number of higher education institutions around the country.[34]

Beyond student activism, Marybeth Gasman, Cally Waite, and a number of other scholars have examined higher education funding and institutional histories. Gasman's *Envisioning Black Colleges* chronicles the United Negro College Fund's history and contribution to Black colleges.[35] Other scholars including Waite provide institutional histories of higher education. Waite's *Permission to Remain Among Us* examines the experiences of Blacks at Oberlin college at the turn of the twentieth century.[36]

The above listed scholars represent significant contributions to understanding African American educational history, but by no means is the list exhaustive. Yet, it demonstrates the important ways in which the field has grown. *Using Past as Prologue* will highlight and expand upon the changes to the field over the last three and a half decades. In the shadow of the sixtieth anniversary of *Brown v. Board of Education* and the fiftieth anniversary of the 1964 Civil Rights Act, contributors expand on the way Blacks viewed and experienced desegregation, and the other options they chose beyond desegregation. The volume covers both the North and South in the nineteenth and twentieth centuries. Contributors explore how educators, administrators, students, and communities responded to educational policies in various settings including K–12 public and private schooling and higher education. A significant contribution of the book is showcasing the growing and concentrated work in the era immediately following the *Brown* decision. Finally, scholars consider the historian's engagement with recent history, contemporary issues, future directions, historiography, methodology and teaching.

Using Past as Prologue extends the historiography of African American education. In the first section of the volume, contributors explore African American education in the nineteenth and early twentieth century. The first chapter in this section offers a brief historiography of the important shifts in the study of the African American educational experience. Christopher M. Span argues that this shift has come at the expense of asking and answering important questions related to African American education in the nineteenth century. Alisha D. Johnson's chapter follows Span's and illustrates the educational experiences of Free People of Color in antebellum Louisiana. The concluding chapter in this section is by Katrina Sanders. She offers an excellent historiography of the scholarship related to the impact of Catholic schools in the African American experience. Each chapter extends our understanding of the African American educational experience in the era.

In the second section of *Using Past as Prologue,* chapters cover the twentieth century in the era prior to and after the *Brown v. Board of Education* decision. These authors examine new areas such as HBCU laboratory schools, the circular migration of Black educators, the impact of freedom schools and Head Start on Black education, an HBCU president's response to student activism, a private school as a form of historic choice for Blacks, and the role of oral history in school desegregation research. Sharon Gay Pierson adds a neglected topic in African American history. Her chapter on HBCU lab schools brings to the fore another example of the successful educational experiences Black students had in the South during the Jim Crow era and substantiates the dual role of HBCUs as both institutions of K–12 and higher education. Donna Jordan-Taylor's chapter follows Black educators who received advanced degrees in the North, but brought their knowledge home to educate and advance education at Black schools and colleges in the South. While some had options to stay in the North, they saw it was their duty to transform Black institutions in the South. Eddie R. Cole's focus on a college president's speeches at the height of the Civil Rights Movement explores the delicate negotiations Black presidents had to make based on the audiences they addressed. His work explores the larger context of Black education in North Carolina and is a great addition to the literature on Black college presidents. These three chapters subtly address the intersection between higher education and K–12 education.

With a focus on the post-World War II era, one chapter examines the responses of southern Black communities to federal and local education policies. Jon N. Hale explores student activism during the Civil Rights era. Hale shows how students who were impacted by Freedom Summer worked to reconstruct southern education, and how Head Start, though federally funded, carried on important principles of Black education including community control. This chapter adds to the literature the activism of southern high school students. Shifting to the North, Worth Kamili Hayes's chapter discusses the evolution of a Black private Catholic school in Chicago and complicates the way in which Black support of contemporary school choice options is simply viewed as a conservative driven agenda. He argues that Blacks have always exercised choice when financially able. Concluding section two, Danns's chapter focuses on oral historical methodology and highlights how different scholars have used oral history methodology to study school desegregation. In addition, Danns's chapter explores how graduates of Chicago high schools made a choice to attend desegregated high schools for access to better education than neighborhood high schools could provide.

In the third section of *Using Past as Prologue,* scholars offer recent historical antecedents of current educational issues including urban school reform, testing and accountability, the achievement gap, and the relevance of historically Black colleges and universities (HBCUs). The section concludes with considerations of the teaching of African American educational history. Elizabeth Todd-Breland examines how some Black education reformers turned away from the promise of school desegregation to other strategies, including community control and independent Black institutions, to improve Black urban education in the latter part of the twentieth century. R. Scott Baker explores how southern governors in the 1970s advanced a national educational reform agenda that veered from the civil rights agenda and ushered in testing and accountability measures as a means to promote racial equality. In effect, however, these measures have stalled the educational achievement gains African Americans once made. Christopher M. Span and Ishwanzya D. Rivers call for a rethinking of how the achievement gap should be measured. In this chapter, Span and Rivers offer an intergenerational comparison over seventy years to delineate what African Americans have educationally achieved irrespective of comparisons to other groups.

Marybeth Gasman and Felecia Commodore help to complete this section by focusing on historically Black colleges and universities. They discuss HBCUs' major strengths and challenges presently and share the contemporary HBCU story. Michelle Purdy concludes this section by illustrating the importance of including African American educational history in general educational foundation courses; such inclusion fosters students' understanding of race and racism in U.S. education. Together these chapters capture the successes, dilemmas, and challenges of Black education and opportunity in the latter twentieth century and posit considerations for the educational work by and on behalf of African Americans yet to be done.

One perceived limitation of the book is that education is largely focused on schooling. A longstanding debate in the field has been about whether the history of education should just reflect formal schooling or broaden to the other educative and socializing institutions which provide both formal and informal education.[37] While this is certainly an important distinction and one that has marked continuous discussion in the field, we believe the distinction is unnecessary to history of Black education. Without a clear understanding of the larger context for which Black education exists, it is quite difficult to write a history solely focused on Black schools. The schools developed and were taught by those who understood the mis-education of the larger society and sought to provide an alternative message. The fight for better schools and desegregation was not one limited to school buildings, but utilized community organizations, churches, courts, and families. Schooling became in many instances a community endeavor. It is rare that one writes a history of Black education that does not capture the educative process that exists within struggles to transform and reform Black education. *Using Past as Prologue* demonstrates the various ways Blacks have fought for quality education and how intimately schools are tied to the larger struggle for freedom and equality in America.

Though the field of African American history has expanded significantly, there is still more work to be done. Far less is known about Black education in the West, particularly K–12 struggles. In addition, we have reached a point in history where the Black/White binary, though entrenched in this country, has to expand to include interactions among Blacks, Whites and other racial/ethnic groups. More research on the West would assist with this endeavor, but different racial/ethnic groups have lived throughout the country and these histories need to be told. More studies which seamlessly combine higher education and K–12 would also be useful. Furthermore, future studies should highlight northern rural areas, smaller cities and suburban experiences across the nation, class and gender differences, and national and comparative studies to expand our understanding of African American education. In addition, this history needs to intersect with the contemporary national policy conversations. It is our hope that *Using Past as Prologue* will inspire the next generation of scholars to do further work in these areas and write their own histories of African American education.

NOTES

1. Vincent P. Franklin, "Introductory Essay: Changing Historical Perspectives on Afro-American Life and Education." In V. P. Franklin & J. D. Anderson (Eds.), *New Perspectives on Black Educational History* (Boston, MA: G. K. Hall & Co., 1978).
2. Vincent P. Franklin and James D. Anderson (Eds.), *New Perspectives on Black Educational History* (Boston, MA: G. K. Hall & Co., 1978).
3. James D. Anderson, *The Education of Blacks in the South, 1860–1935* (Chapel Hill: University of North Carolina Press, 1988).
4. Ronald Butchart, *Schooling the Freed People: Teaching, Learning and the Struggle for Black Freedom 1861–1876* (Chapel Hill: The University of North Carolina Press, 2010). Butchart has also written *Northern Schools, Southern Blacks, and Reconstruction* (Westport, CT: Greenwood Press, 1980).
5. Heather Andrea Williams, *Self-Taught: African American Education in Slavery and Freedom* (Chapel Hill: University of North Carolina Press, 2005); Christopher M. Span, *From Cotton Field to Schoolhouse: African American Education in Mississippi, 1862–1875* (Chapel Hill: University of North Carolina Press, 2009). See also Robert C. Morris, *Reading, 'Riting, and Reconstruction: The Education of Freedmen in the South, 1861–1870* (Chicago: University of Chicago Press, 1981); Jacqueline Jones, *Soldiers of Light and Love: Northern Teachers and Georgia Blacks, 1865–1873* (Athens: University of Georgia Press, 2004); William H. Watkins, *White Architects of Black Education: Ideology and Power in America, 1865–1954* (New York, NY: Teachers College Press, 2001).

6. Vanessa Siddle Walker, *Their Highest Potential: An African American School Community in the Segregated South* (Chapel Hill: University of North Carolina Press, 1996); Vanessa Siddle Walker with Ulysses Byas, *Hello Professor: A Black Principal and Professional Leadership in the Segregated South* (Chapel Hill: University of North Carolina Press, 2009).

7. Faustine Jones, *A Traditional Model of Educational Excellence: Dunbar High School of Little Rock, Arkansas* (Washington, D.C.: Howard University Press, 1981); Alison Stewart, *First Class: The Legacy of Dunbar, America's First Black Public High School* (Chicago: Lawrence Hill Books, 2013).

8. Sonya Ramsey, *Reading, Writing, and Segregation: A Century of Black Women Teachers in Nashville* (Urbana: University of Illinois, 2008); Hilton Kelly, *Race, Remembering, and Jim Crow's Teachers* (New York, NY: Routledge, 2010). Other important books on Black teachers, their challenges and opportunities to provide excellent education include Vivian Gunn and Curtis L. Morris, *Creating Caring and Nurturing Educational Environments for African American Children* (Westport, CT: Bergin and Garvey, 2000) and Adam Fairclough, *Teaching Equality: Black Schools in the Age of Jim Crow* (Cambridge: Harvard University Press, 2007). In addition, Sharon Gay Pierson's *Laboratory of Learning: HBCU Laboratory Schools and Alabama State College Lab High in the Era of Jim Crow* (New York, NY: Peter Lang, 2014).

9. James T. Patterson, Brown v. Board of Education: *A Civil Rights Milestone and Its Troubled Legacy* (New York, NY: Oxford University Press, 2001); Derrick Bell, *Silent Covenants:* Brown v. Board of Education *and the Unfulfilled Hopes for Racial Reform* (New York, NY: Oxford University Press, 2004).

10. David S. Cecelski, *Along Freedom Road: Hyde County, North Carolina, and the Fate of Black Schools in the South* (Chapel Hill: University of North Carolina Press, 1994); R. Scott Baker, *Paradoxes of Desegregation: African American Struggles for Educational Equity in Charleston, South Carolina, 1926–1972* (Columbia: University of South Carolina Press, 2006). See also Charles C. Bolton, *The Hardest Deal of All: The Battle over School Integration in Mississippi, 1870–1980* (Jackson: University of Mississippi Press, 2005); Karen Anderson, *Little Rock: Race and Resistance at Central High School* (Princeton: Princeton University Press, 2010); Jill Ogline Titus, *Brown's Battleground: Students, Segregationists, & the Struggle for Justice in Prince Edward County, Virginia* (Chapel Hill: University of North Carolina Press, 2011); Liva Baker, *The Second Battle of New Orleans: The Hundred Year Struggle to Integrate the Schools* (New York, NY: Harper Collins, 1996).

11. Sarah Caroline Thuesen, *Greater than Equal: African American Struggles for Schools and Citizenship in North Carolina, 1919–1965* (Chapel Hill: University of North Carolina Press, 2013).

12. Michael Fultz, "The Displacement of Black Educators Post-*Brown*: An Overview and Analysis," *History of Education Quarterly* 44 (Spring 2004): 11–45. Michael Fultz has also written a fantastic historiography of African American teachers, Michael Fultz, "As Is the Teacher, So Is the School': Future Directions in the Historiography of African American Teachers," In W. J. Reese & John L. Rury (Eds.), *Rethinking the History of American Education* (New York, NY: Palgrave MacMillan, 2008), 73–102.

13. Barbarba J. Shircliffe, *Desegregating Teachers: Contesting the Meaning of Equality of Educational Opportunity in the South post Brown* (New York, NY: Peter Lang, 2012).

14. Howell S. Baum, Brown *in Baltimore: School Desegregation and the Limits of Liberalism* (Ithaca, NY: Cornell University Press, 2010).

15. Sarah Garland, *Divided We Fail: The Story of an African American Community That Ended the Era of School Desegregation* (Boston, MA: Beacon Press, 2013); Tracy E. K'Meyer, *From Brown to Meredith: The Long Struggle for School Desegregation in Louisville, Kentucky, 1954–2007* (Chapel Hill: University of North Carolina Press, 2013).

16. Brett Gadsden, *Between North and South: Delaware, Desegregation, and the Myth of American Sectionalism* (Philadelphia: University of Pennsylvania Press, 2012).

17. Davidson M. Douglas, *Jim Crow Moves North: The Battle over Northern School Desegregation, 1865–1954* (Cambridge: Cambridge University Press, 2005); Gregory S. Jacobs, *Getting Around Brown: Desegregation, Development, and the Columbus Public Schools* (Columbus: Ohio State University Press, 1998); Jack Dougherty, *More than One Struggle: The Evolution of Black School Reform in Milwaukee* (Chapel Hill: University of North Carolina Press, 2004); Dionne Danns, *Desegregating Chicago's Public Schools: Policy Implementation, Politics, and Protest, 1965–1985* (New York, NY: Palgrave Macmillan, 2014). Additional studies on northern desegregation include Ronald P. Formisano, *Boston Against Busing: Race, Class, and Ethnicity in the 1960s and 1970s* (Chapel Hill: University of North Carolina Press, 2004); Joyce A. Baugh, *The Detroit School Busing Case: Milliken v. Bradley and the Controversy over Desegregation* (Lawrence: University of Kansas Press, 2011); Joseph Radelet, "Stillness at Detroit's Racial Divide: A Perspective of Detroit's School Desegregation Court Order, 1970–1989," *Urban Review* 23 (September 1991): 173–190; Steven J. L Taylor, *Desegregation in Boston and Buffalo: The Influence of Local Leaders* (Albany: State University of New York Press, 1998); Alan B. Anderson and George W. Pickering, *Confronting the Color Line: The Broken Promise of the Civil Rights Movement in Chicago* (Athens: University of Georgia Press, 1986); John L. Rury, "Race, Space, and the Politics of Chicago's Public Schools: Benjamin Willis and the Tragedy of Urban Education," *History of Education Quarterly* 39 (Spring 1999): 117–142; Stephen Kendrick and Paul Kendrick, *Sarah's Long Walk: Free Blacks of Boston and How Their Struggle for Equality Changed America* (Boston, MA: Beacon Press, 2006).

18. Vincent P. Franklin, *The Education of Black Philadelphia: The Social and Educational History of a Black Community, 1900–1950* (Philadelphia: University of Pennsylvania Press, 1979).

19. Hilary J. Moss, *Schooling Citizens: The Struggle for African American Education in Antebellum America* (Chicago: University of Chicago Press, 2009).

20. Jerald E. Podair, *The Strike That Changed New York: Blacks, Whites, and the Ocean Hill-Brownsville Crisis* (New Haven: Yale University Press, 2002); Daniel H. Perlstein, *Justice, Justice: School Politics and the Eclipse of Liberalism* (New York, NY: Peter Lang, 2004).

21. Heather Lewis, *New York Public Schools from Brownsville to Bloomberg: Community Control and Its Legacy* (New York, NY: Teachers College Press, 2013); Glen An-

thony Harris, *The Ocean Hill-Brownsville Conflict: Intellectual Struggles between Blacks and Jews at Mid-Century* (Lanham, MD: Lexington Books, 2012).

22. Jonna Perrillo, *Uncivil Rights: Teachers, Unions, and Race in the Battle for School Equity* (Chicago: University of Chicago Press, 2012).

23. Michael W. Homel, *Down from Equality: Black Chicagoans and the Public Schools, 1920–1941* (Urbana: University of Illinois Press, 1984); Dionne Danns, *Something Better for Our Children: Black Organizing in Chicago Public Schools* (New York, NY: Routledge, 2003). See also Dougherty, *More than One Struggle.*

24. John L. Rury and Shirley A. Hill, *The African American Struggle for Secondary Schooling, 1940–1980: Closing the Graduation Gap* (New York, NY: Teachers College Press, 2012).

25. Linda Perkins, *Fanny Jackson Coppin and the Institute for Colored Youth, 1837–1902* (New York, NY: Garland Publishing, 1987); Karen A. Johnson, *Uplifting the Women and the Race: The Educational Philosophies and Social Activism of Anna Julia Cooper and Nannie Helen Burroughs* (New York, NY: Routledge, 2000). See also Charles W. Wadelington and Richard F. Knapp, *Charlotte Hawkins Brown and Palmer Memorial Institute: What One Young African American Woman Could Do* (Chapel Hill: University of North Carolina Press, 1999); Linda Perkins, "Lucy Diggs Slowe: Champion of the Self-Determination of African-American Women in Higher Education," *Journal of Negro History* 81 (Spring 1996): 89–105; Stephanie Y. Evans, *Black Women in the Ivory Tower: 1850–1954* (Gainesville: University of Florida Press, 2008).

26. Derrick Aldridge, *The Educational Thought of W. E. B. Du Bois: An Intellectual History* (New York, NY: Teachers College Press, 2008); Patrick J. Gilpin and Marybeth Gasman, *Charles S. Johnson: Leadership Beyond the Veil in the Age of Jim Crow* (Albany: State University of New York Press, 2003); John P. Spencer, *In the Crossfire: Marcus Foster and the Troubled History of American School Reform* (Philadelphia: University of Pennsylvania Press, 2012); Walker, *Hello Professor.*

27. William H. Watkins, *Black Protest Thought and Education* (New York, NY: Peter Lang, 2005); V. P. Franklin and Carter J. Savage (Eds.), *Cultural Capital and Black Education: African American Communities and the Funding of Black Schooling, 1865 to the Present* (Greenwich, CT: Information Age, 2004); Karen A. Johnson, Abul Pitre, and Kenneth L. Johnson *African American Women Educators: A Critical Examination of Their Pedagogies, Educational Ideas, and Activism from the Nineteenth to the Mid-twentieth Century* (Lanham, MA: Rowman and Littlefield, 2014).

28. For example see "Ethnic Diversity: Patterns and Implications of Minorities in Independent Schools," in *Visible Now: Blacks in Private Schools*, ed. Diana T. Slaughter and Deborah J. Johnson (New York, NY: Greenwood Press, 1988) and V. P. Franklin and Edward P. McDonald, "Blacks in Urban Catholic Schools in the United States: A Historical Perspective," in *Visible Now: Blacks in Private Schools*, ed. Diana T. Slaughter and Deborah J. Johnson (New York, Greenwood Press, 1988).

29. For histories of Black private institutions see Anderson, *The Education of Blacks in the South*; Arnold Cooper, *Between Struggle and Hope: Four Black Educators in the South, 1894–1915* (Ames: Iowa State University Press, 1989); Katherine C. Reynolds, "Charlotte Hawkins Brown and the Palmer Institute," in *Founding Mothers and Others: Women Educational Leaders During the Progressive Era*, ed. Alan R.

Sadovnik and Susan F. Semel (New York, NY: Palgrave, 2002); and Wadelington & Knapp, *Charlotte Hawkins Brown & Palmer Memorial Institute.*

30. Joy Ann Williamson, *Radicalizing the Ebony Tower: Black Colleges and the Black Freedom Struggle in Mississippi* (New York, NY: Teachers College Press, 2008).

31. Martha Biondi, *The Black Revolution on Campus* (Berkeley: University of California Press, 2012).

32. Ibram H. Rogers, *The Black Campus Movement: Black Students and the Radical Reconstitution of Higher Education, 1965–1972* (New York, NY: Palgrave Macmillan, 2012).

33. Stefan M. Bradley, *Harlem vs. Columbia University: Black Student Power in the Late 1960s* (Urbana: University of Illinois Press, 2009); Richard McCormick, *The Black Student Movement at Rutgers* (New Brunswick, NJ: Rutgers University Press, 1990).

34. For other sources of student activism see, Jonathan B. Fenderson's "'When the Revolution Comes': New Perspectives on Black Student Activism and the Black Studies Movement," *Journal of African American History* 98 (Fall 2013): 607–622; Wayne Glasker, *Black Students in the Ivory Tower: African American Student Activism at the University of Pennsylvania, 1967–1990* (Amherst: University of Massachusetts Press, 2009); Fabio Rojas, *From Black Power to Black Studies: How a Radical Social Movement Became an Academic Discipline* (Baltimore: Johns Hopkins University Press, 2007); Joy Ann Williamson, *Black Power on Campus: The University of Illinois, 1965–75* (Urbana: University of Illinois Press, 2003); Donald Alexander Downs, *Cornell '69: Liberalism and the Crisis of the American University* (Ithaca, NY: Cornell University Press, 1999).

35. Marybeth Gasman, *Envisioning Black Colleges: A History of the United Negro College Fund* (Baltimore: Johns Hopkins University, 2007).

36. Cally L. Waite, *Permission to Remain Among Us: Education for Blacks in Oberlin, Ohio, 1880–1914* (Westport, CT: Greenwood Press, 2002). Other histories include Bobby L. Lovett, *A Touch of Greatness: A History of Tennessee State University* (Atlanta: Mercer University Press, 2013); and Lovett's *America's Historically Black Colleges: A Narrative History, 1837–2009* (Atlanta: Mercer University Press, 2013 & 2011); and Katrina M. Sanders, *"Intelligent and Effective Direction": The Fisk University Race Relations Institute and the Struggle for Civil Rights, 1944–1969* (New York, NY: Peter Lang 2005). See also, Anderson, *Education of Blacks in the South.*

37. Bernard Bailyn, "Education as a Discipline: Some Historical Notes." In John Walton and James L. Kuethe (Eds.), *The Discipline of Education* (Madison: University of Wisconsin Press, 1963); Lawrence A. Cremin, *American Education: The Colonial Experience, 1607–1783* (New York, NY: Harpercollins, 1970); Richard Storr, "The Education of History: Some Impressions," *Harvard Educational Review 31* (1961); Jennings Wagoner, "Historical Revisionism, Educational Theory, and an Educational Paideia," *History of Education Quarterly* 18 (1978).

PART I

EDUCATION IN THE NINETEENTH
AND EARLY TWENTIETH CENTURY

CHAPTER 1

WHY THE NINETEENTH CENTURY STILL MATTERS

Christopher M. Span
University of Illinois at Urbana-Champaign

Every generation will have to ask and answer questions on their own terms. The study of history is no different. For historians who have studied the specifics of the African American educational experience, there is a noticeable change in the type of questions contemporary historians are asking and answering in relation to their predecessors. In recent years, the study of the educational history of African Americans has significantly shifted from understanding their earliest experiences in the eighteenth and nineteenth centuries to a concentrated focus on mid-to-late twentieth century concerns. In some ways the timing of important milestones has shaped this shift. The anniversaries of *Brown* (1954), Freedom Summer (1964), the Elementary and Secondary Education Act (ESEA) (1965), the Higher Education Act (1965), *Milliken* (1974), and countless desegregation efforts have captured the attention of historians. In addition, attempts to explain contemporary issues and discourse about African Americans have also shaped the questions historians ask and the ways they conduct their research to answer them.

Using Past as Prologue, pages 17–31
Copyright © 2015 by Information Age Publishing
All rights of reproduction in any form reserved.

These new histories have been an enormous contribution to the historiography. They have increased our awareness and understanding of the African American educational experience. They have broadened our range of evidentiary usage and sharpened our methodological and theoretical considerations in historical research. They have complicated the longstanding myth about American education that espouses everyone has equal access to a quality education, particularly after the *Brown* decision. They have documented the long-term cumulative harms inferior and segregated schooling have had on African Americans, and they have been instrumental in serving as much-needed counter-narratives to the pseudo-scientific theories that claim African Americans devalue school and educational success, or possess a genetic or cultural deficiency that inhibit their ability to learn.[1]

Notwithstanding, the histories written over the last two decades are a marked shift from a previous generation of scholarship. A generation earlier, historians devoted much of their scholarly careers to asking and answering questions related to the educational experiences of African Americans in the nineteenth century. The study of how enslaved African Americans acquired the rudiments of literacy to endure or liberate themselves from enslavement, how freed African Americans following the Civil War attempted to use schooling for citizenship and social mobility, and how freeborn African Americans—North and South—sought to use schools to challenge de facto and de jure segregation and achieve equality, served as the central theses proffered by this generation of historians. The most notable historian of this generation, James D. Anderson, and his history, *The Education of Blacks in the South, 1860–1935*, still serves as the standard interpretation in the historiography on the African American educational experience in this time period and has been the evidentiary and theoretical foundation for countless studies within and beyond this era and region.

Most surprising in this paradigmatic shift in the discipline of history of education is how fewer and fewer scholars in the field are expanding or critiquing the central theses of their predecessors. The shift away from research in the nineteenth century to the twentieth century signals a belief—whether real or perceived—that the most important questions related to the African American educational past in this century have been sufficiently answered or are unanswerable because of limitations in archival evidence. Still, the nineteenth century remains extremely influential in helping historians and their readers understand both the chronology of the African American educational experience and their evolution from slavery to freedom in the United States. For other obvious reasons, the nineteenth century remains relevant to historical inquiry as well. Countless states across the nation still rely on school laws established in the nineteenth century and state and federal judiciaries still attempt to understand the original intent of constitutional laws for purposes of determining equity and access in schools and universities.[2]

This chapter contends that despite the thematic and chronological shifts that have occurred in the historiography on African American education, considerable questions remain unanswered from the nineteenth century that would extend our understanding of the African American past and complement contemporary scholarship and discourse on African Americans. It offers historiography and theory on one of the most important questions still virtually unanswered in the history of African American education; a question inspired from the agency and disposition of freedpeople following the Civil War: where and when did African Americans develop a value for schools and knowledge? Numerous histories exist explaining how African Americans developed a value for schools and knowledge and how they expressed it in slavery and freedom, but few have attempted to retrace the origins of this collective value. Can the agency and actions of former slaves in the nineteenth century better inform us of the histories, agencies, and actions of African Americans in the twentieth and twenty-first centuries? Can answers to these questions aid contemporary historians in establishing better connections between the nineteenth and the twentieth and twenty-first centuries? Can this kind of historical inquiry help us rethink why the nineteenth century still matters and needs to be studied?

HISTORIOGRAPHY ON THE ORIGINS AND VALUE FOR EDUCATION IN THE AFRICAN AMERICAN EXPERIENCE

After completing *From Cotton Field to Schoolhouse: African American Education in Mississippi, 1862–1875,* one observation stood out to me more than any other. It did not matter where one went throughout the postbellum South, formerly enslaved African Americans valued literacy and schools for nearly identical reasons. How can this be explained? One of the first to observe this phenomenon was John W. Alvord, the superintendent of schools for the Bureau of Refugees, Freedmen, and Abandoned Lands (better known as the Freedmen's Bureau). Alvord noted:

> The study of books, miscellaneously by the freedmen, to which we have alluded in previous reports, was never so widespread as at the present time.... Thousands of children who have become advanced are teaching parents and older members of the family; so that nearly every freedman's home in the land is a school-house, and instead of scenes of sorrow or stupidity, perhaps of brainless mirth, whole families have become pupils.... To say that half a million of these poor people are now studying the spelling-book, or advanced readers, including the New Testament, who were but lately degraded victims of slavery, would be a low estimate.[3]

Alvord's commentary concerning the proactive initiatives of the South's freedpeople was without question praiseworthy, but it was equally enlightening, especially of the demeanor of formerly enslaved African Africans and the expectations they collectively had for literacy and schools. Alvord deduced that formerly enslaved African Americans, in general, valued literacy and schools for five primary reasons. The first reason was a "natural thirst for knowledge common to all men;" the second was that former slaves had "seen power and influence among White people always coupled with *learning* [original italics]," and it was a sign of that "elevation to which they now aspire." The third reason was that the mysteries of literacy and the study of books excited former slaves in wanting to learn how to read and write. The fourth and fifth reasons (freedom and practicality) were inextricably tied together. In Alvord's mind the newfound freedoms formerly enslaved African Americans were experiencing, combined with the "practical business of life," forced upon many the immediate need of obtaining an education.[4]

While intuitive, this essay posits a reason that Alvord never seriously contemplated; it argues that the common value enslaved African Americans placed on literacy and schools was a value distinct within their culture and past. It was a value born and nurtured during enslavement and was passed on from one generation to the next. Considering the fact that there were no formal lines of communications among enslaved African Americans, it is reasonable to assume that the value enslaved African Americans placed on literacy and schools had to stem from one central source, and thereafter would be transplanted and transmitted from one generation to the next throughout the slave-South until emancipation universally came in 1865. This development was what Alvord witnessed as he toured the South and penned his observations.

Historians who have studied the specifics of this mass movement for universal education in the postbellum South have offered different assessments. While they agree that formerly enslaved African Americans—regardless of where they were held in bondage throughout the South—collectively valued literacy and schools for very similar reasons, none have made a serious attempt to retrace the historical antecedents of this cultural value within the African American experience. The historiography is replete with examples of how former slaves acquired a rudimentary education, or attended their first schools, or how they desired to learn.[5] Missing, however, are in-depth explanations of where and when schools and knowledge came to be distinctively valued among enslaved African Americans.

Only suggestions or inferences have been made. For instance, as early as 1941, historian Henry Swint recognized the tremendous value former slaves had for literacy and schools. While his study concentrated on their teachers and presented an unsympathetic overview of northern-born teachers in the South and their activities among freedpeople, Swint nonetheless postulated without evidence that the value formerly enslaved African Americans placed on learning in the initial years of emancipation had to have been given to them by northerners who trekked across the South with the Union Army.[6] Swint's thesis served as the common interpretation for much of the historical research on schools and teachers for freedpeople until the late 1970s.[7]

Thirty years later, Eugene Genovese in his monumental study, *Roll Jordan Roll: The World the Slaves Made*, would offer a different explanation. He stated with unadulterated confidence that "the roots of black enthusiasm for education lay deep in the slave past." He grounded his contention with a single observation from 1750 of slaves eager to learn reading lessons offered by a minister in Virginia. Albeit, the general tone of Genovese's treatment of African Americans' value for learning specifically, and his publication in general, deduced that enslaved African Americans because of their close proximity to landowning Whites, over time, learned the value literacy and schools could have in their everyday lives.[8]

Historians Thomas Webber and Leon Litwack would offer a similar assessment in their future and respective works, with Litwack being the most forthright.[9] "If black people needed to be persuaded of the compelling importance of learning," Litwack deduced, "they had only to look around them. Power, influence, and wealth were associated with literacy and monopolized by the better-educated class of southern whites."[10] There is a fundamental problem with this contention, however. If the premises of Genovese, Webber, and Litwack were to be accepted, it would assume that all landowning Whites—regardless of their locale or status in the South—valued literacy for nearly identical reasons as well. It would also mean that enslaved African Americans would have had to study and mimic Whites in nearly identical ways. That would be the only way to explain how enslaved African Americans collectively learned to value literacy from those who held them in permanent bondage.

Scholarship, particularly by James D. Anderson, the late Herbert G. Gutman, Christopher M. Span, and Heather Andrea Williams offer interpretations closer to the thesis proffered in this chapter. In his book, *The Education of Blacks in the South*, Anderson recognized the value formerly enslaved African Americans placed on literacy and schools as a deeply ingrained cultural value within the slave experience. As he deduced, "Blacks emerged from slavery with a strong belief in the desirability of learning to read and write. This belief was expressed in the pride with which they talked of other ex-slaves who learned to read or write in slavery and in the esteem in which they held literate blacks."[11] Herbert G. Gutman was just as pronounced. "In examining how men and women fresh from freedom built and sustained schools, Gutman articulated, "we find much more than simply a desire for schooling." Gutman continues, "the freedpeople's early post-emancipation craving for and defense of schooling for themselves, and especially their children, rested in good part on values and aspirations known among them as slaves."[12] This was the overarching thesis in Heather Andrea Williams's significant history, *Self-Taught: African American Education in Slavery and Freedom.*[13]

Christopher M. Span and James D. Anderson's essay entitled, "The Quest for "Book Learning": African American Education in Slavery and Freedom," reinforced the respective arguments of Anderson, Gutman, and Williams and perhaps offers the best speculation of how literacy and schools came to be a distinctive cultural value among African Americans during slavery and a dynamic collective expression upon emancipation. Span and Anderson reasoned that "knowledge and respect for literacy as a way of liberation and protection" arose during the colonial era and amid the earliest years of slavery. This connection between literacy and freedom among enslaved African Americans "was passed down generation to generation, and became a widespread cultural value among African Americans by the American Revolution."[14]

If the assessments made by Anderson, Gutman, Williams, and Span and Anderson are correct, then the value formerly enslaved African Americans placed on literacy and schools was not a practical by-product of emancipation or a natural curiosity, as Alvord deduced. Nor was it a way of mimicking Whites as Swint, Genovese, Webber, Litwack, and others have suggested. Rather, it was a value born and nurtured within a collective Black experience prior to 1800, and thereafter transplanted and clandestinely protected, from one generation to the next, throughout the South. This transplantation was intact well before 1865 when Alvord made his tour throughout the South and identified freed African Americans expressing not a newfound curiosity and respect for literacy and schools, but a distinct longstanding cultural value that was universal, in full expression, and more than a half century old.

But how could this be and where could this value have originated? If one is to retrace this distinct cultural value or theorize its origin, a good place to hypothesize its formation and evolution is to begin where slavery was most pronounced in the colonial era (the Chesapeake—Virginia and Maryland, South Carolina, and Louisiana) and to consider as archival evidence population data of these colonies. While the study of population or demographic data alone will not definitively answer the question of the origins of the value of education in the African American experience (it is after all only one piece in a larger puzzle), it is, nonetheless, a good starting point. Population data offers a quick snapshot of the possible locales that might have had the requisite conditions and time for a people to create, develop, and nurture a cultural value that could be easily transplanted and transmitted from one generation to the next even amid unpredictable displacement and relocation.

Locales

Of the three locales in this study, the Chesapeake has the earliest origin (Virginia and Maryland became colonies respectively in 1607 and 1634). The two colonies were also the first to legally sanction slavery, Virginia in 1661 and Maryland in 1663. South Carolina was founded as a slave colony in 1670. Louisiana was purchased as a territory in 1803 and founded as a state in 1812, but Louisiana as a French province has a much older history and dates back to 1652; slavery began in 1652 as well. Despite its late beginnings in American history, and given the rich traditions and culture that emerged within this region, it should be included in our discussions if we are to consider all the possible locales in retracing this value in the African American experience.

In all three locales, enslaved African Americans had access to learning the rudiments of literacy, but only colonial Virginia repeatedly allowed for the establishment a series of schools for its enslaved population. While Louisiana developed a series of laws, Code Noir, to regulate the lives and opportunities of its inhabitants of African descent, it did not afford any schooling opportunities to the enslaved in any meaningful way prior to statehood. Only the enslaved children of slaveholders could attend school without any fear of reprisal or harm. In 1740, South Carolina became the first colony to establish a law denying African Americans the right to learn; such anti-literacy laws would not be established in Virginia until 1819.[15]

Prior to the American Revolution, and at a time when slavery was not firmly entrenched in the American social order, religious instruction invariably produced these early learning experiences, and countless historians have documented the role religion has played in the education of enslaved African Americans in colonial and antebellum America and how African Americans—enslaved and free—developed a value for education from these experiences.[16] The very fact the enslaved Africans and later African Americans were able to take part in these religious experiences and exercises aided them in their acquisition and appreciation of literacy as a distinct cultural value, disposition, skill, and tool for resistance and freedom. Access meant acceptability, even if this acceptability was only for a limited window of time. In Virginia in particular, White missionaries interest in educating enslaved Africans and African Americans was twofold. For one, it aided them in their mission to preach the Gospel and convert presumed heathens into Christians. In addition, these missionaries deduced that enslaved people learning to read and write to understand the Bible would "have a very good effect upon their [morals?] & make them faithful & honest in their Masters Service."[17]

Origins and Population Data

Access to schooling or educational opportunities is a very important determinant to understanding how African Americans came to value literacy and education as a distinct cultural value, but it is not the only variable of importance. When these regions are studied more specifically to population or demographic data sharp differences occur and further extend our understanding of where and when the value for education developed in the African American past. Identifying a homogenous population that could gain access to educational opportunities and thereafter pass down to their children and grandchildren any acquired literacy skills and an appreciation for the value of learning is just as important as identifying where any early schooling experiences existed for enslaved African Americans.

Allan Kulikoff, Ira Berlin, Philip D. Morgan, Gwendolyn Midlo Hall, Peter Wood, and a perusal of census data illustrate that the Chesapeake established a much more homogenous slave population than South Carolina or Louisiana.[18] Homogenous means that by the 1790 census there was far less diversity of experience or origin in the Chesapeake, than in South Carolina or Louisiana. For instance, in his remarkable study, *Slave Counterpoint: Black Culture in the 18th Century Chesapeake and Lowcountry*, Philip D. Morgan illustrates that the Black population in the Chesapeake in 1700 was 13,000 and half of the Black inhabitants (6,500) were African arrivals who survived the Middle Passage or slavery in the Caribbean, not native-born.[19] By 1790, four generations later, both Virginia and Maryland would have significantly larger slave populations, and ones that were much more native-born and intergenerational (i.e., African American) than African. According to census data there were 293,000 slaves in Virginia and only 4,740 (or 2%) were African.[20] In 1800, there were 346,000 slaves in Virginia with only 678 being African in origin.[21] By 1780, according to Morgan, no African was directly sold into slavery in Virginia. What this means is that by 1780, the only Africans in the colony were survivors from Africa or the Caribbean. What this also means is that the slave population in Virginia was a much more homogenous group than in South Carolina or Louisiana (which will be discussed soon). The same was true in Maryland. In Maryland, by 1790 the slave population was 103,000, and as in Virginia all but a handful were native-born. By 1800, the slave population only increased by 2,000 to 105,000.[22]

The numbers in South Carolina tell a different story. In 1700, there were 2,400 slaves in the colony and half (1,200) were of African origin.[23] By 1750, the slave population would grow to 40,000 and nearly 17,000 (16,858) or 42% would be of African origin. By 1790, the slave population would be 107,000, and those of African origin would be approximately 25,000 (24,884) or 23%.[24] Before the American Revolution, the African population rose each decade. This fact illustrates that South Carolina had a more diverse slave population than the Chesapeake. The continued reliance on an African population to serve as the primary labor of the colony, rather than rely on an African American population that was born within the colony (such as in Virginia and Maryland) limits the possibility that South Carolina would have a somewhat homogenous population that might share a distinct cultural value for literacy by 1790.

The same is true in Louisiana. Gwendolyn Midlo Hall pinpoints that by 1790 nearly 54% of all slaves in Louisiana were African and not African American.[25] Equally important she denotes that most if not all of those who were "American"-born culturally were French-speaking, or creole, or mixed with Native American. In her mind, this population was as diverse as the Africans who were captured and sold into slavery in this region. So Louisiana would not be an ideal location either for the origins of the value of literacy and schools in the African American experience if homogeneity were a prerequisite for its development.

Transplantation

Understanding the movement of enslaved African Americans is just as important as establishing where they originally resided and had access to early educational opportunities or their homogeneity or diversity. Virginia, Maryland, South Carolina, and Louisiana are only four of 17 southern states that would invariably sanction and practice slavery in the South prior to the Civil War. Accordingly, the question must be asked: how did these other southern states obtain their slaves? Where did they come from? And does the movement of enslaved African Americans from one state to another have anything to do with the origins and value for education in the African American experience?

Answers to these questions are all yes. In studying the three main locales, one also gets a sense as to how slavery was practiced in the first half of the nineteenth century. As cotton became the main cash crop in the slave South, many states within the South demanded the need for slave labor. The abolition of the slave trade in 1808 virtually eliminated Africans arriving in the United States in large enough numbers to suffice the need. The answer came in the selling off of slaves from states that abolished slavery (northern states for example) or upper-South states (such as Virginia and Maryland) where slavery was no longer as profitable. By 1840, Maryland's slave population was only 89,000; less than what it was in 1800. By 1860, on the eve of the Civil War its slave population was 87,000. In Virginia, its slave population increases from 346,000 in 1800 to 490,000 in 1860.[26]

There is clearly an increase in Virginia, but not as substantial as in South Carolina and Louisiana. In South Carolina, the slave population increased from 146,000 in 1800 to 402,000 in 1860.[27] There were nearly three times as many slaves in South Carolina in 1860 than there were in 1800. In Louisiana, there were approximately 332,000 slaves in 1860, up from 69,000 in 1820 (the first census that included Louisiana).[28] Slave populations in South Carolina and Louisiana increased at a tremendous rate, which leaves little room for speculation as to whether these states continually sold their slaves to other states in need of slave labor. Virginia demographic suggests a different scenario, however. Virginia's slave population grew by only 145,000 in 60 years or at a rate of about 2,416 a year. Natural selection has a higher rate. As in Maryland, Virginia continued to engage in the practice of slavery, only this time to the extent of an open slave market or the domestic selling of slaves to other territories and states in the Union. In counties where slavery was still profitable, slaves remained; where slavery was not as profitable, enslaved African Americans were sold to the highest bidder or were forced to migrate to new parts of the nation with their slaveholder.

Accordingly as these Black bodies relocated from the Chesapeake to new places throughout the South, they carried with them not only their brawn to be used for labor but their culture and aspirations as well. This research posits that one of the distinct values and aspirations within this culture was a strong appreciation for literacy and schools that expressed itself in its fullest form after emancipation in 1865. If this were the case, it would explain why African Americans throughout the region expressed similar desires and expectations for literacy and schools. It would explain why African Americans well into the twentieth century would continue to equate schooling with freedom.

CONCLUSION

So where do we go from here? How is one to make meaning of these data and the speculation from them? This chapter does not suggest that demographic data alone answers the question of where and when the value for education in the African American past began. In all three locales there were enslaved and freeborn African Americans who obtained literacy, valued it, and passed it on to their children, family, friends, and neighbors. All the same, demographic data provides a good starting point to further investigate the political economy of slavery in the Chesapeake to see how education—as both an idea and practice—developed in the region. Invariably the transcontinental journey (or "Second Middle Passage" as articulated by Ira Berlin) from disproportionately the Chesapeake disrupted the lives of every enslaved African American man, woman, and child forced to make the trek. Most knew it was a one-way trip, which left these transplanted African Americans with only their memories and knowledge of loved ones, traditions, and values; a system of beliefs they would rely upon as they started their lives anew in places like Tennessee, Kentucky, Missouri, Alabama, Mississippi, and Arkansas. As Ira Berlin poetically noted, "Rituals for celebrating marriage, coming of age, breaking bread, and giving last rites to honored elders which had been transferred across the Atlantic and were reconstructed along the coast of mainland North America during the seventeenth and eighteenth centuries were passed on to new ground during the nineteenth century."[29]

As these rituals were held sacred and passed on from one generation to the next, so too was the value for education. A value that may owe its origins, like so many other cultural values and expressions that survived the Middle Passage and were modified amid the Atlantic colonies during enslavement, to the Africans who survived the trip and transplanted their belief systems in places like Virginia, Maryland, South Carolina, and Louisiana. Perhaps, the origins of the value for knowledge and education in the African American experience do not simply begin in the Chesapeake as available demographic data suggests. Perhaps, it is an Africanism that survived the Middle Passage and became the full cultural expression appreciated by Alvord in 1865. If this is the case, a fuller interrogation is needed of all the available evidence and developments of this era and region. Whether this cultural retention is confirmed or not, it affords another reason for historians to continue to ask and answer questions related to the nineteenth century educational experience of African Americans. Just as important, it affords the public another opportunity to better understand and appreciate the long-standing value African Americans have historically placed on education.

NOTES

1. One article that does an excellent job in challenging assumptions that African Americans devalue schools or have inherit cultural deficiencies is James D. Anderson, "Crosses to Bear and Promises to Keep: The Jubilee Anniversary of *Brown v. Board of Education*," *Urban Education* 39, no. 4 (July 2004): 359-373. For sources that articulate the misguided notion that African Americans have or exhibit cultural deficiencies see, Dinesh D'Souza, "Improving Culture to End Racism," *Harvard Journal of Law and Public Policy* 19, no. 3 (Spring 1996): 785; John H. McWhorter, *Losing the Race: Self-Sabotage in Black America* (New York, NY: Free Press, 2000); John H. McWhorter, "What's Holding Blacks Back?," *City Journal* 11, no. 1 (2001): 24–32; John U. Ogbu, *Black American Students in an Affluent Suburb: A Study of Academic Disengagement* (Mahwah, NJ: Lawrence Erlbaum Associates, 2003); Abigail Thernstrom and Stephan Thernstrom, *No Excuses: Closing the Racial Gap in Learning* (New York, NY: Simon & Schuster, 2003).
2. Courts still rely on the expert testimony of historians in important school desegregation cases. For a few examples see, *Brown v. Board of Education*, 347 U.S. 483 (1954); *Brown v. Board of Education II* 349 U.S. 294 (1955); *Knight*

v. Alabama, 14 F. 3d 1534 (1994); *Ayers v. Fordice*, 879 F. Supp. 1419 (1995); *Parents v. Seattle School District* and *Meredith v. Jefferson County Board of Education* 126 S.Ct 2738 (2007).

3. John W. Alvord, *Third Semi-Annual Report on Schools for Freedmen, January 1, 1867* (Washington DC: Government Printing Office, 1868), 5.

4. John W. Alvord, *First Semi-Annual Report on Schools and Finances of Freedmen, January 1, 1866* (Washington DC: Government Printing Office, 1866), 1.

5. Extensive scholarship details the educational motivations of formerly enslaved African Americans during the Reconstruction era. Most notable are the following: James D. Anderson, *The Education of Blacks in the South* (Chapel Hill: University of North Carolina Press, 1988); Ronald E. Butchart, *Northern Schools, Southern Blacks, and Reconstruction* (Westport, Conn., Greenwood Press, 1980); Ronald E. Butchart, *Schooling the Freed People: Teaching, Learning, and the Struggles for Black Freedom, 1861–1876* (Chapel Hill, University of North Carolina Press, 2010); Janet Duitsman Cornelius, *When I Can Read My Title Clear: Literacy, Slavery and Religion in the Antebellum South* (Columbia, SC: University of South Carolina Press, 1991); W. E. B. Du Bois, *Black Reconstruction in America, 1860–1880*, reprint (New York, NY: Free Press, 1999); Eric Foner, *Reconstruction: America's Unfinished Revolution, 1863–1877* (New York, HarperCollins, 1988); 96–102; V.P. Franklin, *Black Self-Determination: A Cultural History of African-American Resistance* (New York, NY: Lawrence Hill Books, 1984); Herbert Gutman, "Schools for Freedom: The Post-Emancipation Origins of Afro-American Education," in *Major Problems in African American History, Volume I: From Slavery to Freedom, 1619–1877*, Thomas C. Holt and Elsa Barkley Brown, eds., (New York, Houghton Mifflin, 2000), 388–401; Jacqueline Jones, *Soldiers of Light and Love: Northern Teachers and Georgia Blacks, 1865–1873* (Chapel Hill, University of North Carolina Press, 1980); Robert C. Morris, *Reading, 'Riting, and Reconstruction: The Education of Freedmen in the South, 1862–1870* (Chicago, University of Chicago Press, 1981); Christopher M. Span, "I Must Learn Now or Not At All:" Social and Cultural Capital in the Educational Initiatives of Formerly Enslaved African Americans in Mississippi, 1862–1869," *Journal of African American History* 87 (Summer 2002): 22–31; Christopher M. Span and James D. Anderson, "The Quest for 'Book Learning': African American Education in Slavery and Freedom," in *A Companion to African American History*, Alton Hornsby Jr., ed., (Malden, MA: Blackwell Publishing, 2005), 295–311; Christopher M. Span, *From Cotton Field to Schoolhouse: African American Education in Mississippi, 1862–1875* (Chapel Hill: University of North Carolina Press, 2009); Heather Andrea Williams, *Self-Taught: African American Education in Slavery and Freedom* (Chapel Hill: University of North Carolina, 2005).

6. Henry Swint, *The Northern Teacher in the South, 1862–1870* (Nashville: Vanderbilt University Press, 1941).

7. In my book, I noticed that a number of historians who made reference to how freedpeople acquired their desire to learn and attributed it to their northern teachers. For an abbreviated list see these reconstruction histories: M. G. Abney, "Reconstruction in Pontotoc County," *Publications of the Mississippi Historical Society*, vol. XI (1910): 240–69; Robert Bowman, "Reconstruction in Yazoo County," *Publication of the Mississippi Historical Society*, vol. VII (1903): 115–30;

W. H. Braden, "Reconstruction in Lee County," *Publication of the Mississippi Historical Society*, vol. X (1909): 135–46; Thomas Battle Carroll, "Historical Sketches of Oktibbeha County," *Historical Publications on Mississippi* (Gulfport, Miss.: Dixie Press, 1930); Rowland Dunbar, "The Rise and Fall of Negro Rule in Mississippi," *Publications of the Mississippi Historical Society*, vol. II (1898): 189–200; Garner, *Reconstruction in Mississippi*; Hardy, "Recollections of Reconstruction in East and Southeast Mississippi,"; J. H. Jones, "Reconstruction in Wilkinson County," *Publication of the Mississippi Historical Society*, vol. VIII (1904): 153–75; Nannie Lacey, "Reconstruction in Leake County," *Publication of the Mississippi Historical Society*, vol. XI (1910): 271–94; Hattie Magee, "Reconstruction in Lawrence and Jefferson Davis County," *Publication of the Mississippi Historical Society*, vol. XI (1910): 163–204; John S. McNeily, "From Organization to Overthrow of Mississippi's Provisional Government, 1865–1868," *Publication of the Mississippi Historical Society*, centenary series I (1918); John S. McNeily, "Climax and Collapse of Reconstruction in Mississippi," *Publication of the Mississippi Historical Society*, vol. XII (1912): 283–474; John S. McNeily, "The Enforcement Act of 1871 and the Ku Klux Klan in Mississippi," *Publication of the Mississippi Historical Society*, vol. IX (1906): 109–72; John S. McNeily, "War and Reconstruction in Mississippi, 1863–1890," *Publication of the Mississippi Historical Society*, centenary series I (1917): 9–403; Irby Nichols, "Reconstruction in DeSoto County," *Publication of the Mississippi Historical Society*, vol. XI (1910): 295–316; Noble, *Forty Years*; E. F. Puckett, "Reconstruction in Monroe County," *Publication of the Mississippi Historical Society*, vol. XI (1910): 103–60; Jesse Thomas Wallace, *A History of the Negroes in Mississippi from 1865 to 1890* reprint (New York, NY: Johnson Reprint Corp., 1970); Ruth Watkins, "Reconstruction in Newton County," *Publication of the Mississippi Historical Society*, vol. XI (1910): 205–28; Ruth Watkins, "Reconstruction in Marshall County," *Publication of Mississippi Historical Society*, vol. XII (1912): 155-213.

8. Eugene Genovese, *Roll, Jordan, Roll: The World the Slaves Made* (New York, NY: Vintage, 1974), 565.

9. Thomas Webber, *Deep Like the Rivers: Education in the Slave Quarter Community, 1831–1865* (New York, NY: W.W. Norton & Company, 1978); Leon Litwack, *Trouble in Mind: Black Southerners in the Age of Jim Crow* (New York, NY: Vintage, 1998).

10. Leon Litwack, *Trouble in Mind*, 53.

11. Anderson, *The Education of Blacks in the South*, 5.

12. Herbert G. Gutman, *Power & Culture: Essays on the American Working Class*, edited by Ira Berlin (New York, NY: The New Press, 1987), 296.

13. Williams, *Self-Taught*.

14. Span and Anderson, "The Quest for "Book Learning," 296.

15. Christopher M. Span, "Post-Slavery? Post-Segregation? Post-Racial?: A Long History of the Impact Slavery, Segregation, and Racism have had on the Education of African Americans," *The National Society for the Study of Education*, *114*(2), (2015).

16. A number of historians have written on the role of religion in the education of enslaved African Americans in these three locales. One of the earliest and most prominent was Carter G. Woodson in 1919, *The Education of the Negro*

Prior to 1861, reprint (New York, NY: A&B Publishers Group, 1998). Other early publications were: C.E. Pierre, "The Work of the Society for the Propagation of the Gospel in Foreign Part among Negroes in the Colonies," *Journal of Negro History* 1 (1916): 349–360; Luther P. Jackson, "Religious Development of the Negro in Virginia 1760 to 1860," *Journal of Negro History* 16 (1931): 168–239; Mary F. Goodwin, 'Christianizing and Educating the Negro in Colonial Virginia," *Historical Magazine of the Protestant Episcopal Church* 1 (1932): 171–212; Martin Luther Riley, "The Development of Education in Louisiana prior to Statehood," *Louisiana Historical Quarterly* 19, no. 3 (1936): 595–613. Other scholarship would become more pronounced after 1960. See, Thad W. Tate, *The Negro in Eighteenth-Century Williamsburg* (Williamsburg, VA: University of Virginia Press, 1965); Carlos Antonio Brossard, "Indians, Economic Development and African Literacy in Colonial Virginia before 1660: A Study in Afro-American Literacy before Absolute Bondage" (PhD dissertation, Harvard University, 1976); Albert Raboteau, *Slave Religion: The "Invisible Institution" in the Antebellum South* (Oxford: Oxford University Press, 1978); Mechal Sobel, *Trabelin' On: The Slave Journey to an Afro-Baptist Faith* (Princeton, NJ: Princeton University Press, 1979); Franklin, *Black Self-Determination*; Charles Joyner, *Down By the Riverside: A South Carolina Slave Community* (Urbana: University of Illinois Press, 1984); Webber, *Deep Like the Rivers*; John C. Van Horne, *Religious Philanthropy and Colonial Slavery: The American Correspondence of the Associates of Dr. Bray, 1717–1777* (Urbana: University of Illinois Press, 1985); Duitsman Cornelius, *When I Can Read My Title Clear*; Janet Duitsman Cornelius, *Slave Missions and the Black Church in the Antebellum South* (Columbia: University of South Carolina Press, 1999); E. Jennifer Monaghan, *Learning to Read and Write in Colonial America* (Amherst: University of Massachusetts Press, 2005); Antonio T. Bly, "In Pursuit of Letters: A History of the Bray Schools for Enslaved Children in Colonial Virginia," *History of Education Quarterly* 51, no. 4 (2011): 429–459.

17. Bly, "In Pursuit of Letters," 432.
18. Allan Kulikoff, *Tobacco and Slaves: The Development of Southern Cultures in the Chesapeake, 1680–1800* (Chapel Hill: University of North Carolina Press, 1986); Ira Berlin, *Many Thousand Gone: The First Two Centuries of Slavery in North America* (New York, NY: Belknap, 2000); Ira Berlin, *The Making of African America: The Four Great Migrations* (New York, NY: Penguin, 2010); Philip D. Morgan, *Slave Counterpoint: Black Culture in the Eighteenth Century Chesapeake & Lowcountry* (Chapel Hill: University of North Carolina Press); Gwendolyn Midlo Hall, *Africans in Colonial Louisiana: The Development of Afro-Creole Culture in the Eighteenth Century* (Baton Rouge: Louisiana State University Press, 1992); Gwendolyn Midlo Hall, *Slavery and African Ethnicities in the Americas: Restoring the Links* (Chapel Hill: University of North Carolina Press, 2005); Peter H. Wood, *Black Majority: Negroes in Colonial South Carolina from 1670 through the Stono Rebellion* (New York, NY: W.W. Norton & Company).
19. Morgan, *Slave Counterpoint*, 81.
20. Census data between 1790 and 1960 can be obtained at: http://mapserver.lib.virginia.edu/php/state.php.
21. Ibid.

22. Ibid.
23. Wood, *Black Majority*, 152.
24. Morgan, *Slave Counterpoints*, 59–61.
25. Midlo Hall, *Slavery and African Ethnicities in the Americas*, 160–161.
26. For census data see: http://mapserver.lib.virginia.edu/php/state.php.
27. Ibid.
28. Ibid.
29. Berlin, *The Making of African America*, 127.

CHAPTER 2

A CLASS ALL THEIR OWN

Economic and Educational Independence of Free People of Color in Antebellum Louisiana

Alisha D. Johnson
University of Illinois at Urbana–Champaign

> *This class was most respectable; they . . . led lives quiet, dignified and worthy,*
> *in homes of ease and comfort . . . it is always to be remembered that in their contact*
> *with white men, they did not assume that creeping posture of debasement—nor did*
> *the whites expect it—which has more or less been forced upon them in fiction[1]*
> —Charles Etienne Gayarré

From the time of French and Spanish rule in the eighteenth century to the onset of the Civil War, relations between Black and White societies in southern Louisiana, particularly in the city of New Orleans, have presented a contradiction to the common narrative characteristic of southern race relations of the period. Due to civil structures and social conditions unique to the region the port town of New Orleans, and its surrounding parishes, came to be home for a sizable population of Free People of Color who, for a time, lived within a particular space of economic and educational freedom. This free class, collectively known as *gens de couleur libres*, or Free

Using Past as Prologue, pages 33–55
Copyright © 2015 by Information Age Publishing

People of Color, consisted of Creoles of Color who were, "the free mixed-blood, French-speaking descendants of immigrants from Haiti" and other French parentage, Creoles of Color with Latin blood, and various other free Blacks.[2] The particular French and Spanish cultural origins of this group established them in a circumstance that treated race quite differently from conceptions exemplified throughout the regions of the nation colonized by the British. In 1866, Nathan Willey pointed out the unique way in which Louisiana's forbearers viewed slavery:

> Among the French and the Spanish settlers and their descendants, the *condition* of the colored people, rather than their *color* as a badge of slavery, has been the subject of popular prejudice. They looked upon a slave and his descendants as an inferior class, simply because they were in a degrading condition of servitude, and not because they bore darker skin. In the North and in States settled by the English the prejudice is one of color rather than a condition.[3]

While Mr. Willey may overstate the extent to which French and Spanish colonists disregarded differences of race, the distinction between their attitudes about race and those of English colonials is an important one. Ultimately, class played a crucial role in race relations for Free People of Color in the region. As a result of this alternate treatment of race, persons of color in New Orleans, while not exempt from southern standards of deference to Whites, were bestowed with certain rights and privileges not granted Black communities throughout the North and South.

As a direct consequence of the privileges enjoyed by Louisiana's Free People of Color, as well as the wealth afforded them, whether through lineage, ingenuity, or both, a three-tiered social structure developed in which scholars have placed Whites at the top, slaves at the bottom, and Free People of Color in the middle.[4] However, the characterization that this community occupied a middling status is misleading. Evidence indicates that although Free People of Color in Louisiana prior to the Civil War did not enjoy the wholesale liberties and protections of citizenship that Whites did; many used their wealth and sophistication to wield power within their own community, as well as, in dealings with Whites. The status of this group existed on a continuum in which a significant representation of this class was positioned considerably above the status of slaves while only moderately below the status of White society as a whole.[5] Many were able to amass substantial wealth, at times matching that of White high-society, and the children of these families were educated in a manner agreeable to that station.[6] Private schools were created, pupils were sent to the North for schooling, and many even felt that an education commensurate with their status could only be acquired through travel to Paris for schooling.[7]

This research utilizes a diverse array of primary and secondary source materials to illustrate how the interplay of civil empowerment, economic autonomy, and unique social norms in antebellum Louisiana enabled, and were strengthened by, the education of Louisiana's Free People of Color. It examines how the confluence of these variables created a space for educational self-determination for Free People of Color, and how education, in turn, supported their ability to take advantage of civil and economic opportunities. On the whole, this research looks beyond the traditional available evidence associated with formal instruction for freeborn African Americans in the nineteenth century in the hopes of detailing a deeper contextual understanding of the rich education obtained by Louisiana's Free People of Color. In the end, this history illustrates the sociocultural and economic autonomy of Louisiana's Free People of Color and how they fostered spaces that progressed their educational development with very little interference from anyone outside their community.

BLACK EDUCATION IN CONTEXT

In his seminal1933 publication, aptly titled *The Mis-Education of the Negro*, Carter G. Woodson clarified the dominant narrative under which the Black community and their educational efforts have been effectually characterized. Woodson's assessment that, "[t]he status of the Negro, then, was justly fixed as that of an inferior . . . Negroes have no control over their education and have little voice in their other affairs pertaining thereto," quickly became the standard interpretation of mid-century historians who researched the agency and control African Americans in the antebellum era—free and enslaved—had over the education of themselves and their children.[8] This precept highlights two notions pertaining to antebellum Blacks and their educational experience. The first is that Blacks were seen as inferior, and the second was that they lacked any meaningful agency to advance their educational aspirations. This early generalization has been complicated by more recent and nuanced historical accounts of Black agency in education. Contemporary scholars have taken up critical analyses of the assumed lack of self-determination in communities of color and have reconsidered the detrimental influences Whites have had on the educational advancement of Blacks in America.[9] Historian Hilary J. Moss probes the antebellum efforts of northern free Black communities to establish their own schooling in the cities of New Haven, Baltimore, and Boston. Even as publicly funded instruction was becoming the norm in northern states, Blacks were still systematically denied access to public schooling in general due to slavery and White aversion to having their children attend schools with children of color. In Baltimore, for example, Moss illustrated "how slavery worked to exclude all people of color, enslaved and free, from the body politic in the white imagination," schools included. [10] Baltimore's Black community's exclusion from the benefits of the public school system was exacerbated by a dearth of private modes of instruction due to the impeding influence of Whites, born of "anxieties over black aspirations."[11] Northern accounts demonstrate comparably greater allowances for communities of Color than granted the majority of Blacks across the South; however, these communities still faced serious obstacles to obtaining education.

Ronald E. Butchart in the preface to his book, *Schooling the Freed People*, also establishes this contention. "Indeed, the efforts of whites in black schools from the dawn of freedom into Reconstruction," Butchart surmised, "were often equivocal and contradictory to the best interests of a truly free people."[12] Similarly, James D. Anderson's investigation of Black education as designed by northern White philanthropists in the post-Reconstruction era further substantiates this argument. Anderson documents how these White benefactors believed Blacks, in culture and development were "at least two-thousand years behind the Anglo-Saxon."[13] Accordingly, they sought to develop schools for Blacks that supported their beliefs of Black inferiority. Despite the limited schooling options for Blacks in the nineteenth century, the scholarship of these historians and others record the ways in which free, enslaved, and freed Blacks fought to claim and obtain an education for themselves and their children from the antebellum era through the post-Reconstruction era.

Historians have also undertaken extensive research on the origins and circumstances of the free Black community in antebellum Louisiana, New Orleans in particular.[14] Several have framed their inquiry around the unique economic and social character of Louisiana's community of Color in the eighteenth and nineteenth centuries. Their work reveals countless examples of ingenuity and exceptional economic success achieved by Free People of Color.[15] Still, very little attention has been given to the importance and implications of educational achievement for this community, as well as the role that economic freedom played in enabling educational opportunity. Indeed, the social mobility and relative economic success of Free People of Color in and around New Orleans afforded them much greater latitude in taking advantage of educational opportunities, unavailable to other free Black communities throughout the nation.

This reality demarcates a crucial point of divergence between most histories that emphasize the oft-times heroic educational efforts of Blacks beleaguered with obstacles by Whites and the experience of Louisiana's Free People of Color. Unlike Louisiana's Free People of Color, most Black communities often lacked the economic resources to pursue education without White assistance. As framed by Carter G. Woodson, these Blacks were "nominally free, but economically enslaved."[16] The common thread woven throughout these narratives is one of adversity; a tale of scholarly knowledge, if obtained, so accomplished despite myriad obstacles. Historical inquiry has pointed overwhelmingly to the fact that Blacks were able to gain literacy and schooling in spite of White resistance and obstruction, but this scholarship in general has yet to deconstruct the all too rare examples of Black education absent paternalism and hardship.

GENS DE COULEUR LIBRES, STEEPED IN CONTEXT

Louisiana's unique treatment of race and slavery was a result of the civil and social standards established by the French government. *Le Code Noir* (The Black Code), enacted by edict of Louis XIV in 1685, outlined a system of slavery and treatment of slaves, laid out a decisive pathway to liberty for the enslaved, and prescribed a standard of citizenship for Free People of Color. With regard to freedom and citizenship, *Le Code Noir* dictated that manumission from slavery bestowed all rights and privileges due a free person. Article LIX reads: "We grant to freed slaves the same rights, privileges and immunities that are enjoyed by freeborn persons. We desire that they are deserving of this acquired freedom, and that this freedom gives them, as much for their person as for their property, the same happiness that natural liberty has on our other subjects."[17] Consequently, Free People of Color in New Orleans were able to enter into civil contracts with Whites and had legally protected property rights which they could pursue and defend in a court of law.[18] The 1802 notarial records of Pedro Pedesclaux reveal multiple transactions between Free People of Color and Whites, including several obligations of mortgage to Free People of Color by Whites, and historian Carl Brasseaux found that the region's Free People of Color won all civil suits brought against White debtors from 1800 to 1820.[19]

The civil tenets of *Le Code Noir* served as a reflection of French and Spanish social dispositions regarding slavery and Free People of Color, and contrasted significantly with the measures adhered to by Louisiana's neighboring states. In fact, as Louisiana courts were apt to uphold civil rights for Free People of Color, the judiciary powers in other slaveholding states were just as inclined to maintain the abject status of free Blacks. The laws of Mississippi, for example, presumed "a negro *prima facie* to be a slave."[20] The laws even went so far as to punish Whites who did not presume and treat all Blacks as if they were slaves. If any White man hired a "negro who claimed to be free," but who "could not produce proof of his freedom," the White man was subject to a fine.[21] Similarly, South Carolina legislation decreed that, "a free African population is a curse to any country ... [and] a dead weight to the progress of improvement."[22] Blacks in Texas were unable to protect their property rights in the collection of debts through the courts as they did not have the right to bear witness against White debtors.[23] By considerable contrast, Louisiana's Supreme Court in 1850 went on record to affirm the ability of the state's Free People of Color to testify. The Court acknowledged:

> free persons of color...are respectable from their intelligence, industry and habits of good order. Many... are enlightened by education, and the instances are by no means rare in which they are large property holders...such persons as courts and juries would not hesitate to believe under oath...No reason has been suggested why a distinction should exist in respect to their competency in civil and criminal cases in which white persons are parties.[24]

Spanish and French social attitudes towards people of color were not only reflected in the *Code*, but were upheld civilly. These regulations established a strong foundation for the rights of Free People of Color in the region.

The social circumstances under which Louisiana's race relations developed were grounded in its early colonization; "In early New Orleans... being black did not necessarily mean being a slave. Nor was whiteness associated with prestige and power. The first African Americans arrived simultaneously with the rejects of French society who had been deported to Louisiana."[25] In early Louisiana, French criminals and outcasts associated with skilled and able Africans; race was not as important as one's utility to the survival of the entire community. Even though Africans were introduced to Louisiana as slave labor, *Le Code Noir* made the manumission of slaves legally sanctioned, binding, and, for a time, commonplace.[26] In these early years, favored bondsmen and bondswomen, and the progeny of French men and African women oftentimes resulted in the emancipation.[27] To this end, 788 acts of manumission were recorded in New Orleans from 1770 to 1803.[28]

Concubinage of African slaves was not uncommon as, in the colony's nascence, a shortage of White women of suitable age and comparable status to White male officers and soldiers removed immediate barriers to intimate unions across racial lines.[29] As *Le Code Noir* determined that a child's condition followed that of its mother, many men who freed their mistresses often did so to ensure the liberated status of their children.[30] The interdependence and social intimacy among Blacks, Whites, and Native Americans, as described by historian Gwendolyn Midlo Hall, was quite unlike the distance maintained between races in rural, as well as more populous areas, across the North and South.[31] The close contact between the races in this region served to literally soften ever-growing rigid color lines and brought about a gradual increase in the free mixed-race population. This increase was further augmented by a mass migration of Free People of Color fleeing the Haitian revolt at the turn of the nineteenth century.[32] The habitual intimate contact between Whites and people of Color consequently evolved into regional social norms that were maintained well after the White male to female ratio had reached relative balance.[33]

Despite the fact that even in Louisiana marriage between the races was illegal, agreements known as *plaçage* became accepted proxy for socially binding, spousal relationships. Plaçage consisted of a "contract" in which a White man agreed to terms to financially support his mistress, or *placée*. These arrangements legitimized, at least to some extent, a level of commitment in unions between White men and women of Color. More than mere liaisons, such arrangements were not completely void of attachment. Historical accounts have characterized Louisiana's Free Women of Color of this period as being quite sought-after. Traveler G.W. Featherstonhaugh noted that "great pains are lavished upon [their] education…" and that these women were described as possessing of, "discernment, penetration and finesse, and as superior to many white girls of the lower classes of society."[34] Again, while these unions were not legally sanctioned, relationships between wealthy White men and Free Women of Color evolved into something beyond that of mistress and benefactor, some to the point of becoming devoted unions that persisted over several decades.[35]

The acceptance of relationships of this sort was indicative of Louisiana's unique social norms; it also legitimized Louisiana's community of Color. It was not uncommon for White men to openly acknowledge their Black mistresses and provide for their mixed-race offspring. Bulletins written in 1831 tell of Maurice Abat who moved to France with his mistress and their two children, intent upon marrying her and legitimizing his heirs.[36] His mistress, Emerile Giraudeau, a Free Woman of Color, was noted to be the daughter of M. Giraudeau, a White man who served as the Justice of the Peace in 1809. In another account, M. Cherbonnier, a former teacher and textbook writer, left for Paris with his mistress, Modèste Fouchet, the daughter of General Lacoste; his intention was to marry her and legitimize their four children.[37] The law banning marriage between the races certainly delimited the extent to which some Free Women of Color could live out their affections. However, natural affection at times led these men and women to circumnavigate statutory precepts, and the broader community's indulgence of these unions extended the space in which they could act upon their affections. Accounts of the passionate betrothals carried out by the men who absconded with these Free Women of Color treated their actions as no more scandalous than worthy of a few months' gossip. Lines written about these attachments certainly painted the affairs as clandestine, but they betrayed no strict disapproval.

The persistence and unabashed acknowledgment of these types of relationships demonstrates a deeper connection in the ties forged between White men, their chosen mates, and their children. Many accounts tell of the generous manner in which wealthy White men ensured the financial security of their illegitimate children. The importance of these attachments cannot be overstated as this parental benevolence introduced a great deal of the initial wealth into the region's community of Color. One notable example is that of Antoine Simien, who in 1800 rendered his 1791 succession null and in its stead had drafted a testament bestowing his wealth to his unsanctioned family. It stated:

> He declares that he has four natural mulatto children which he has had with a free negresse, named Marie, to whom he has granted freedom, these have been baptized free under his name ... and though they are not the issue of a valid marriage, that they have nevertheless in him the same heart, same love of a true father; wishing to give them a visible proof of his love ... He declares that he names ... his natural sons without excluding those that may yet be born of said negresse Marie, their mother by him, and whom he will recognize as his only universal heirs.[38]

In the same vein Barthelemy MaCarty created a stir when his 1832 last will and testament was said to have excluded his legitimate White family from his succession in favor of his *famille de couleur*.[39] The irregularity of this succession was noted, for the most part, by the sizable fortune that was purportedly left to his heirs. Seventy-two year old Pierre Cazelar, a wealthy sugar planter opposite New Orleans, was also cited as having "numerous colored progeny," who would inherit his wealth.[40] Subsequently, the *Seventh Census* enumerated the assets of the household of a twenty-seven year old planter Pierre Cazelar, Free Person of Color, at a substantial thirty-thousand dollars.[41] Like many White men of means who developed romantic bonds across racial lines, the senior M. Cazelar was not remiss in seeing to the future comfort of his mixed-heritage successors.

Generous patronage of well-situated White fathers planted the seeds of wealth in southern Louisiana's community of Color; however, it was the intelligence and entrepreneurial savvy of this class that cultivated those seeds of economic advantage into continued prosperity. Although many Free People of Color were born of White fathers, they routinely married within their own class, reared families, and their wealth was maintained within the proud lineage esteemed by the achievements of these families. Born in 1764 of a White father, Louis Agustin Meullion, and a Mulatto enslaved woman, Marie Jean, Jean Baptiste Meullion reared a family with Free Woman of Color—Céleste Donato, and operated a sizable plantation in St. Landry Parish.[42] Free Men of Color, Albin and Bernard Soulié, worked as builders and commission merchants in New Orleans. Prominent men of business, they owned extensive properties and served as creditors "in considerable sums" to high-ranking New Orleanians such as Leonidas Polk, Episcopal Bishop of Louisiana.[43] The circumstance of this class is most striking when one considers that in 1846 state taxes were paid on Soulié properties valued at $90,200, yet, at this time, the Soulié children would have been unable to utilize Louisiana's foundling public school system. They were barred from enjoying the "free" public education that their family's money so materially contributed to.

Testament to the substantial wealth across this community bears out in the broader records. Historian Loren Schweninger determined Louisiana's Creoles of Color, who at the time possessed over $1.8 million worth of land and claimed 24 percent of the property owned by Blacks in the entire South, to be the wealthiest group of free Blacks in the nation prior to the Civil War.[44] Clearly, this community was adept at accumulating wealth in a society in which class played a prominent role in determining hierarchy. In 1835, G.W. Featherstonhaugh went so far as to deem money "the established religion" of Louisiana. Anyone who possessed wealth could obtain opportunities systematically denied to those without it.[45]

KNOWLEDGE AND A TASTE FOR LEARNING

The confluence of civil empowerment, socially permissive conceptions of race, and economic independence created a particular space of opportunity for the ambitious pursuit of education by Louisiana's Free People of Color. The acquisition of literacy proved the rule rather than the exception for this singular group. In 1850, the total number of illiterate free Blacks and Mulattos in Louisiana was only 3,389. Effectively, of the total population of 17,465 Free People of Color in the state, 14,076 were considered *literate*, a rate of over eighty percent.[46] This is notable as Louisiana's free Black illiteracy rate was 19.4 percent, a full percentage point lower than the national average—20.83 percent—for free Blacks. At the same time, the national average rate of illiteracy for Whites was 4.92 percent, while Louisiana's White population was noted to have an 8.3 percent illiteracy rate. The proportion of Louisiana's White population who could neither read nor write was nearly double that of the national average for Whites.[47]

In order to understand the extent to which this community was able to create spaces for learning, the overall state of schooling during this period must be understood. Education in the United States prior to the Civil War had yet to become synonymous with a uniform system of common schools. While northern cities were moving rapidly in the direction of universal public schooling, the South, most notably Louisiana, obstinately rebuffed the trend.[48] The 1850 *Census* noted that, "In many of the States, particularly the South, there is no general public school system, some counties etc, supporting schools by taxes levied within their own limits, and in other cases the State contributing a proportion towards the support of private schools."[49] Education was not seen as a necessity as during this time period skilled employment could be, and often was, obtained without the necessity of a formal education.

As formal education was not requisite for occupational advancement prior to the Civil War, economic advantage and business acumen required that Free People of Color apprehend more than the rudiments of the grammar book. The competencies necessary for success and independence required an education beyond common schoolhouses, which were few and inconsistent. Louisiana's Free People of Color were able to acquire the training necessary to pursue vocations in the skilled trades despite apparently limited schooling opportunities. In the antebellum era, New Orleans boasted a far greater proportion of Free People of Color employed in the skilled trades than could even be found in the states that did not practice slavery. A mid nineteenth-century comparison of the occupations of Free People of Color in Louisiana to the occupations of their counterparts in the non-slave holding states of Connecticut and New York cited over 1000 laborers in each of the two northern states. Louisiana indicated only 411 of this class employed as such. In other words, in Connecticut and New York 14.4 percent and 2.3 percent, respectively, of their free Black populations were laborers. Like New York, of the entire free population of Color in Louisiana only 2.4 percent worked as laborers, and that number dropped substantially in New Orleans, to just over 1 percent. Despite slavery's stronghold in Louisiana, the state's Free People of Color were of the laboring class on par with those in New York, and in lesser proportion than Connecticut. In fact, Free people of color in New Orleans actually fared better occupationally than those in the Northern states.

On the other hand, Louisiana's Free People of Color had an inordinately high number of its community working in skilled occupations such as carpentry, masonry, and cabinet making.[50] In 1856, the *Western Watchman* reported that, "[o]f the free colored population in New York City, sixty were clerks, doctors, druggists, lawyers, merchants, ministers, printers, and teachers...In New Orleans there were 165...engaged in similar pursuits, which may be considered as requiring education."[51] At the same time, only 1,219 "Free Colored" persons were recorded as attending school during this period as compared to over four times that number in New York.[52] It appears Louisiana's Free People of Color received the training necessary to gain expertise in skilled occupations outside of formal schooling and, in turn, were empowered to openly practice their trades.

For those at the uppermost tier of this class, education proved more than a means to an end; the cultivation of knowledge came to be a reward in its own right. The wealth and subsequent prestige that was augmented and protected by this community's educational attainment perpetuated an expectation that affluent Free People of Color become learned. The upper echelons of polite society necessitated not only business acumen, but also knowledge of classical thought and current events alike. In 1845, Armand Lanusse published an anthology of Creole poetry, *Les Cenelles*, the first such collection published by people of Color in the United States.[53] This volume highlighted the literary talents of New Orleans' accomplished *Gens de Couleur Libre*. The chronicler Rodolphe Desdunes described Lanusse to be "blessed with a studious temperament, he loved the classics... In both his prose and verse, we find adequate proof of his broad education."[54] Moreover, Lanusse's "contemporaries loved such things as literature, painting, music, [and] the theater..."[55] The scholarly and educational interests of this group did not assume education was the means to financial gain, Free People of Color saw education and its continual acquisition as a means in itself. Literary and artistic accomplishments were neither a way to escape a debased condition nor considered wasteful endeavors; they were a realization of higher human potential.

This penchant for literary diversion went beyond the artistic set. The economic autonomy of this well-heeled community was a crucial variable that afforded them the pursuit of knowledge. Their financial comfort fostered the leisurely space for intellectual engagement by which to satisfy the taste for knowledge. In an 1842 diary entry Natchez merchant William T. Johnson relayed a colorful critique of political stump speeches he had observed, noting of one hopeful that, "he made quite a lengthy spectacle... Richard the Third King Lear and several others of ancient time was [sic] represented by him in part."[56] It appears that Mr. Johnson was familiar enough with Shakespeare that his comparison, even now, evokes the melodramatic showmanship he witnessed that day. Absent any practical need for scholarly study, this Free Man of Color took great pleasure in intellectual pursuits. He subscribed to several periodicals and endeavored so far as to create a "reading room" in his home.[57]

This predilection for bookish diversion was handed down from one generation to the next. In a letter from Mr. Johnson's son in New Orleans the youth solicited, "I wish you would tell sis to send me my book called Poetry and Prose of europe and america [sic] and lend me some of her Books to read."[58] The mildly imploring tone of this request suggests that borrowing the books from his sister for his own amusement was of little consequence and would not deprive her of some necessary use. Unlike the struggles faced by the majority of Blacks during this period, and well after slavery ended, Free People of Color in this community possessed the means, occasion, and uninhibited space to enjoy knowledge beyond mere necessity.

This class rarely explicitly mentioned education and schooling, as education was a taken-for-granted aspect of the lifestyle they maintained. Ironically, it is perhaps the silence that is most illustrative of this community's unrestrained pursuit of knowledge. For Louisiana's Free People of Color, opportunity did not hinge entirely upon clawing out a space in which to prove their intelligence. In the easy manner of an indulgent father untroubled about his children's prospects, Mr. Johnson briefly noted, "The Boys commenced to day to say their books again," and then confessed, "I will try and keep them at it for a time if possible, tho I know my failings so well that I am doubtful whether I will keep them at it long."[59] Apparently the young Johnson boys were expected to study, but it is also evident that their overall future success did not hinge upon whether they were compelled to "say their books;" they were at liberty to learn as they chose and, therefore, the need to do so was not an urgent one. In 1844, Phoebe Smith wrote to her sister and, in like manner, stated that her daughter sent love to all of her playmates, "and also she is going to school and as soon as she can write she sais [sic] that she will wrighte [sic] to all the play mates." Not only was this young girl learning to read and write, but the tone of her mother's lines leads to the conclusion that her playmates would have also been educated enough to read the letters sent them. Arguably, education for this well-situated community was not a vocation of mystery, but a mundane circumstance of living out their place in society.

FORMAL SCHOOLING

In the slave states, schooling was a matter of class and racial privilege and Blacks, whether enslaved or free, were for the most part uniformly barred from public schooling. Still, schooling and academics played an important role in the education of Free People of Color in Louisiana. Free People of Color in Louisiana were able to take advantage of religious as well as secular private institutions for their children's formal education. These efforts long preceded free public schooling in Louisiana. Despite earlier efforts to establish a common school system, the state's first free school act was not adopted until May of 1847, and less than fifty percent of the state's eligible (White) children were said to have taken advantage of these schools.[60] By 1850, public school funds in Louisiana totaled just over $349,600, the bulk of which were raised from the taxes of Whites and Free People of Color.[61] During this same period Louisiana's funding for long-established private schooling totaled about $193,000.[62] The fact that Louisianans chose to financially support private schools despite taxation for a new and burgeoning public school system indicated that education was of great value to Free People of Color who could not freely send their children to a public school prior to the Civil War. The financial independence of families of color afforded them the economic agency to still have their children attend school. Louisiana's community of Color possessed not only the desire, but also the capital to ensure their children would attend school and become educated.

The earliest opportunity for formal schooling came to Louisiana's Free People of Color at the beginning of the eighteenth century. The Catholic Church can be credited with establishing the first schools in the region. In 1727, the Jesuits were instrumental in bringing the Ursuline nuns to Louisiana; a girl's school was established promptly upon their arrival. The opportunity to send their daughters to the new school was so favored by colonists that by 1728 the Ursuline school had forty-eight students; twenty-three at the boarding school and twenty-five in the day school.[63] Notably, the Ursulines did not discriminate against those deemed of different class nor on the basis of race. The school opened its doors to Creole, French, Native American, White, and enslaved pupils. The fact that the Ursulines chose to impart education to the enslaved was unprecedented. However, while there was some differentiation within the school, educating young slaves under the tutelage of the Catholic Church was in keeping with the mores of the time.[64] For example, White females attended classes six days a week, while slave and Native American students for only two hours each day and French and Creole students for four. Nonetheless, all were taught reading, writing, some arithmetic, and manual training.[65]

In 1821, almost one hundred years after the arrival of the Ursulines, the Sisters of the Order of the Sacred Heart established the Academy of the Sacred Heart at Grand Coteau in St. Landry Parish, Louisiana. This academy served young women of Color, Native American, and White pupils alike.[66] Subsequent academies under the Order of the Sacred Heart were erected in Natchitoches and Baton Rouge in 1847 and 1851, respectively. Almost 2,600 women were said to have graduated from this institution.[67] In 1823, two years after the founding of an academy in Grand Coteau, Sister Marthe Fortière of the *Dames Hospitalier* opened yet another school for girls. This academy was supported by New Orleans' Free People of Color and catered specifically to young ladies of that class.[68] By 1831, this institution had been placed under the management of the Ursuline nuns, and ultimately came to be cared for by the Sisters of the Holy Family, the second order of Black nuns in the nation, in affiliation with St. Augustine's Catholic Church, the first Catholic Church to be founded by Free People of Color in the United States.[69] Operating as St. Mary's Academy, subsequently St. Mary's Academy for Young Ladies of Color, the course of instruction consisted of:

Reading, Writing, Spelling, Dictation. Orthography, Grammar, Composition, Geography, Arithmetic, Algebra, History, Rhetoric, Natural Philosophy, Astronomy, Science and Etiquette. Sewing, in all of its branches, Embroidery, Crochet, Tapestry, Tarleton Flowers, Artificial Flowers, Drawing, Painting, French and Spanish, (Vocal and Instrumental).[70]

Given a southern woman's place in nineteenth century society, and particularly women of Color, St. Mary's liberally academic course of study is notable. Further, the applied courses of study that did not fall under the academic track speak of greater aspirations for pupils than a life of domestic service or manual labor. This curriculum encompassed the delicate niceties requisite of a life of feminine occupation and refinement.[71] It was to this school that Louis Drouet, a White man of means, sent his mixed-race daughter Louise Drouet.[72] Like many children of her class who were not recognized as legitimate children or heirs of their White fathers, Louise's father nonetheless maintained his parental responsibilities and sponsored her proper education to enhance her life prospects.

Parochial schools were not the only educational institutions for Free People of Color in Louisiana during this period. In 1837, the growing wealth of Louisiana's Free People of Color came to bear fruit in the establishment of a school for the larger community of Color. An act of benevolence by African born former slave Madame Marie Couvent laid the groundwork for a school expressly for free children of Color. Having come to New Orleans by way of Saint Domingue, Haiti, Madame Couvent was the widow of a prominent carpenter and Free Man of Color, Bernard Couvent. Over her lifetime, the widow amassed considerable wealth in real estate, and realizing "that it was necessary that the children of her race should not live without having some advantages of an education," she made a provision in her will to donate a parcel of land "conditionally on the erection of a Colored Orphan Free School."[73] Negligence in the execution of the succession postponed fulfillment of the widow's behest, but after a decade-long delay *L'Institution Catholique des Orphelins Indigents*, also referred to as the Couvent School, was established in 1848.[74] "Scholars of both sexes irrespective of religious creed" were admitted, and the school employed five or six instructors who taught courses up to the eighth grade level; lessons were conducted in both French and English.[75] Laura Ewen Blokker notes of *L'Institution Catholique* that, "Despite its appellation, which served to make the school sound more charity and church based—and therefore less threatening to those who opposed the education of African Americans—the school was neither solely for orphans nor run by the Catholic Church."[76] Although the community of Color was free to operate their school with little outside interference, it was deemed necessary for them to ensure that the achievement of children in the school did not appear threatening to Whites' assumption of their own superiority. Despite the liberties afforded this community, they were still a community of Color, and it was understood by all that any pretense of equality with Whites would jeopardize those liberties. While class afforded them many opportunities, race still dictated the norms of society.

The prestige of this educational space in the community is evident in the prominent figures involved with its success. Many of those named on the Board of Directors were Free Men of Color with appreciable financial means, including Thomy Lafon, Alfred Duhart, and Antoine Dubuclet.[77]

Thomy Lafon's wealth was estimated at a considerable half a million dollars at the time of his death, and, amongst multiple charitable behests, "he left [the Institute] over five thousand dollars in cash and several pieces of real estate, [as well as] the rental for the maintenance of the school."[78] This annuity paid for teacher salaries, custodial services, taxes and insurance, and the general upkeep of the school's properties.[79] In 1850, Alfred Duhart's household included Joseph Bazanae, a forty-six year old Mulatto man from Cuba; Bazanae's occupation was listed as teacher. [80] It is probable that as a part of his commitment to the institution Duhart took on the responsibility of providing room and board for instructors employed there. Brothers Adolphe and Armand Duhart were both instrumental at the school in subsequent years as well. Adolphe held the position of principal and Armand served as director. Board member Antoine Dubuclet's skillful command of business and finance ultimately earned him the opportunity to serve in the distinguished position of State Treasurer during the reconstruction years from 1868 to 1879. It was a post from which, "he retired without leaving behind the least cause for dissatisfaction or any error in his accounts."[81]

The Couvent School illustrates the desire of affluent Free People of Color to not simply maintain their own status, but to also empower Free People with lesser resources to equal aspirations and capabilities. There were many opportunities for the education of Free People of Color in the city of New Orleans during this period, but none that served families of lower means. *L'Institute Catholique* became the most well attended school by Free People of Color in antebellum New Orleans, and, due to its prominence in the community, the school was even periodically granted public financial support from the state legislature as well as the city of New Orleans.[82] *L'Institute* was a testament to the ability of Free People of Color to establish a space for the pursuit of education on their own terms, and without significant assistance or interference from the White community. It was a centralized point of empowerment and pride for a group that had no misgivings about their place or capabilities in society.

In addition to these enduring institutions, other schooling options, including mixed-raced schooling, were available to Louisiana's Free People of Color. The historian Charles Roussève ascertained that, "In New Orleans before the reactionary period free persons of color did not find it difficult to use whatever educational facilities the city afforded. White teachers had no objection to having them as pupils."[83] In an 1834 bulletin, Jean Boze wrote of a boarding and day high school opened for Colored students by Father L'Hoste at 82 Esplanade Street in New Orleans.[84] Similarly, the Grimble Bell School for Free Negroes, an elite private institution in Washington, Louisiana, catered to the educational needs of the youth of wealthy planters. The monthly tuition was fifteen dollars, and four teachers were responsible for the instruction of approximately 125 students.[85]The

Grimble Bell School taught all of the customary subjects, including Writing, Arithmetic, History, Bookkeeping, French, English, and Latin. The school ultimately closed in the 1850s as a result of mounting racial tensions. However, New Orleans contemporary Nathan Willey explained that "since it has been closed many of the youth have been sent to private schools in New Orleans."[86] Apparently the closing of one school did not preclude opportunities for continued studies at another. Likewise, Pointe Coupé Parish was home to many families of Color who had accumulated substantial property, and who, for many decades, had supported their own schools by obtaining rooms in principal houses, hiring teachers of Color, and supporting the operation of the school through a per pupil tuition fee. The result of this education was that, out of nearly two hundred "colored" families in Pointe Coupé who were free before the war, only one was known to be illiterate at the end of the Civil War.[87]

Educational opportunities were routinely advertised in the various newspapers in and around New Orleans. *Le Propagateur Catholique* carried various endorsements for day and boarding schools; and, while it was customary for race to go unmentioned in these advertisements, in February of 1845 *Le Propagateur* announced "*L'École pour les enfants de couleur.*"[88] The advertisement touted that, given the Christian education received there and the progress of its students since its opening, *L'École* "deserves the patronage of the colored people who want to obtain a good education for their children."[89] In addition to this school the paper advertised several institutions, none of which explicitly mentioned race. Nevertheless, given the localities of these establishments, it is likely that many opened their doors to students of Color. Housed in the French Quarter, *L'École* for Children of Color was only one block away from the site at which Father L'Hoste was said to have opened his school for the children of the city's Free People of Color; St. Mary's Academy operated less than two blocks from that location; and *L'Institution Catholique* rested little more than half a mile from these schools. What is striking is that within just over one square mile of these schools, known to cater explicitly to Free People of Color, *Le Propagateur* advertised close to a dozen different learning establishments between 1843 and 1844 alone. Some academies served as boarding schools for young ladies or young men, and there were also day schools, both single sex and coeducational. These various institutions provided instruction in French, Spanish, Latin, Greek, History and Geography, Writing, Mathematics, Physics, and Astronomy.

The *Daily Creole* did its part to inform the community of educational opportunities. The Jefferson Academy located at 53 Bourbon Street in New Orleans, on the edge of the French Quarter, averred: "The plan of this institution comprises a general and extensive system of education... The premises are, perhaps, the best to be found in the city, with ample space for exercise and recreation, every necessary convenience is combined for an institution of learning on a large scale."[90] The St. Charles Institute also "[embraced] all the various branches requisite for a complete English and French education;" exercises were conducted daily in English and French, "there being about as many American as . . . French pupils . . ."[91] Courses tailored to specialized study were also promoted in the *Daily Creole*; instruction conducted in the French Language covered the modern languages of French, German, and English using the "Viva Voce System," as well as writing and bookkeeping.[92]

The absence of a comprehensive, universal system of schooling during the antebellum period allowed parents of means to not only define what constituted a proper education, but to determine where and how it could best be obtained. For Free People of Color, in-state schooling beyond the primary levels was virtually nonexistent. Instead of accepting this circumstance as the inevitable conclusion to their educational progress, the community pursued or created other opportunities to advance their education. It was not uncommon for Louisiana's Free People of Color to send their children out of the South or abroad to obtain an education commensurate with their expectations and station in life. At the time of his death in 1832 the mixed-race heirs of Barthelemy MaCarty, sons aged seventeen and eighteen, were said to be attending college in the North.[93] Many young southern elites such as the children of MaCarty are said to have been educated in northern schools, but many of Louisiana's elite Free People of Color also sent their children abroad to France or other European nations. Some Free People of Color expected a level of educational refinement that they felt could only be achieved in Europe. For instance, in the mid-nineteenth century, the city of New Orleans was home to four of the six physicians of Color in Louisiana. Two in particular, Alexandre Chaumette and Louis C. Roudanez received medical degrees in Paris.

Aspiration of Free People of Color to educate their children abroad was not simply due to their inability to obtain a quality education domestically; deeper consideration of their continued travel abroad for schooling, brings to light something more. In a visit to a lecture at the Sorbonne in Paris, Massachusetts Senator Charles Sumner noted with curiosity young men of Color "dressed quite à la mode, and having the jaunty air of young men of fashion . . . They were standing in the midst of a knot of young men, and their color seemed to be no objection to them." He concluded, "It must be that the distance between free blacks and the whites among us is derived from education, and does not exist in the nature of things."[94] What Sumner observed at the Parisian university was the very reason that this class returned again and again to this space, and it was more than simply education. In Louisiana, they enjoyed liberties and wealth on a scale beyond what the majority of Blacks across the nation could claim, but they were still denied their basic rights to freely be a man or woman due to race and racism. In Paris, they could be acknowledged as the men and women they could never be in Louisiana.

CONCLUSION

French and Spanish underpinnings in Louisiana's colonial culture, for a time, shaped a society that placed nearly as much emphasis on class as it did race. Race relations in antebellum Louisiana developed under circumstances of hardship and mutual dependence, which afforded people of Color recognition as more than simple laborers.[95] This region's unique social beginnings allowed for the introduction of affluence into its communities of Color, and also created a space in which these communities could cultivate the seeds of wealth. *Le Code Noir*, decreed that Free People of Color were deserving of property rights and of equal protection. These civil rights were legally enforceable and Free People of Color made ample use of the privilege. Louisiana's civil and social norms subsequently afforded this community the ability to pursue education on their own terms.

As such, Louisiana's Free People of Color proved to be more than educated; they carried themselves as part of a learned gentry. The knowledge they acquired was taken as a right rather than a privilege. Their educational history is unique in the larger narrative related to Black education during the antebellum era. Their accounts of struggle and triumph diverge from the everyday accounts of Blacks being willfully denied an opportunity to learn, or of Blacks overcoming herculean odds to obtain the rudiments of literacy. While barred from public schooling, they were not denied education. When left to their own devices Louisiana's Free People of Color used their collective and individual wealth to provide for the education of their own. The limits to their educational achievement, in fact, only went so far as their financial means dictated. While race was still a significant factor, its effect was moderated by the role socioeconomic status played in the lives of Free People of Color in Louisiana. Their wealth truly made them a class of their own.

NOTES

1. Quoted in Grace King, *New Orleans: The Place and the People* (New York, NY: The Macmillan Company, 1926), 345. Reprint of 1895 original.
2. Historical documents, and consequently, historians use various terms to describe persons of color in Louisiana during this time period; including Black, Negro, Creole, Creole of Color, and Mulatto. Pinning down one term proves problematic as terms like *Creole* at times refer to people of French and Span-

ish lineage without any African blood, and at other times refer distinctly to those of mixed African and French or Spanish background. *Mulatto* serves to designate all persons of mixed White and African lineage, however this term then excludes those of unmixed blood; and *Creole of Color* proves even more exclusive. Historically, *Negro*, and *Black* have served to designate anyone who contains even a fraction of African heritage, however, these terms do not serve to accurately characterize the unique and culturally mixed population in Louisiana during this time period.

In an effort not to exclude any persons of color, when discussing a free person or group of free people of color within this region I will refer to them as *Free People of Color*, or *Mulatto* in instances in which the literature or historical documentation has done so, as well as cases in which the mixed-race nature of those being discussed is meaningful. When discussing people or groups of Color outside of this region I will use the term *Black* unless otherwise indicated.

Rodolphe Lucien Desdunes, *Our People and Our History: Fifty Creole Portraits*, trans. and ed. Sister Dorthea Olga McCants (Baton Rouge: Louisiana State University Press, 1973), translator's introduction. This work was initially written and published in French in 1911.

3. Nathan Willey, "Education of the Colored People of Louisiana," *Harpers*, July 1866, 246.
4. Carl Brasseaux, *Creoles of Color of the Gulf South*, Ed. James H. Dormon (Knoxville: The University of Tennessee Press, 1996), 72.
5. While it is true that People of Color were unable to vote, and some scholars have held that at times they *did* vote, it is also true that colonial Louisiana existed under imperial control until the Louisiana Purchase in 1803; civic freedom was not necessarily the linchpin of empowerment during this period.
6. Laura Foner, "The Free People of Color in Louisiana and St. Domingue: A Comparative Portrait of Two Three-Caste Slave Societies," *Journal of Social History* 3, no. 4 (1970): 407.
7. John W. Blassingame, *Black New Orleans* (Chicago: The University of Chicago Press, 1973), 11; Harold E. Sterkx, *The Free Negro in Ante-Bellum Louisiana* (New Jersey: Associated University Presses, 1972), 227, 258, 268–274; Willey, "Education of the Colored People of Louisiana," 246.
8. Carter G. Woodson, *The Mis-Education of the Negro*, reprint (Trenton, NJ: Africa World Press, 1990), 19–20.
9. Heather Andrea Williams, *Self-Taught: African American Education in Slavery and Freedom* (Chapel Hill: The University of North Carolina Press, 2005); Christopher M. Span, *From Cotton Field to Schoolhouse: African American Education in Mississippi, 1862–1875* (Chapel Hill: University of North Carolina Press, 2009); Ronald E. Butchart, *Northern Schools, Southern Blacks, and Reconstruction: Freedmen's Education, 1862–1875* (Westport: Greenwood Press, 1980).
10. Hilary J. Moss, *Schooling Citizens: The Struggle for African American Education in Antebellum America* (Chicago: The University of Chicago Press, 2009), 101.
11. Ibid., 54.
12. Ronald E. Butchart, *Schooling the Freed People: Teaching, Learning, and Struggle for Black Freedom, 1861–1876* (Chapel Hill: The University of North Carolina Press, 2010), 3.

13. James D. Anderson, *The Education of Blacks in the South, 1860–1935* (Chapel Hill: University of North Carolina Press, 1988), 85, 134.

14. Sterkx, *The Free Negro in Ante-Bellum Louisiana*; Gary B. Mills, *The Forgotten People: Cane River's Creoles of Color* (Baton Rouge: Louisiana State University Press, 1977).

15. Foner, "The Free People of Color in Louisiana and St. Domingue;" Kimberly S. Hanger, "Origins of New Orleans Free Creoles of Color," in *Creoles of Color of the Gulf South*, ed. James H. Dormon (Knoxville: The University of Tennessee Press, 1996) 1–27; Loren Schweninger, "Socioeconomic Dynamics among the Gulf Creole Populations: The Antebellum and Civil War Years," in *Creoles of Color of the Gulf South*, James H. Dormon, ed. (Knoxville: The University of Tennessee Press, 1996), 51–66; Carl A. Brasseaux, Keith P. Fontenot, and Claude F. Oubre, *Creoles of Color in the Bayou Country* (Jackson: University Press of Mississippi, 1994).

16. Woodson, *The Mis-Education of the Negro*, 14.

17. *Le Code Noir.*

18. For a discussion business partnerships with Whites, see Sterkx, 60 and 178. For legal and contractual privileges, see Sterkx, 54, 88, and 171–173; Mills, *The Forgotten People*.

19. New Orleans Notarial Archives, *Pedro Pedesclaux*, vol. 42, 1802; Brasseaux et al., *Creoles of Color*, 46.

20. Charles S. Sydnor, "The Free Negro in Mississippi before the Civil War," *The American Historical Review* 32, no. 4 (1927): 769.

21. Ibid., 770.

22. James M. Volo and Dorothy Deneen Volo, *Encyclopedia of the Antebellum South* (Westport: Greenwood Press, 2000), 109.

23. Ibid., 99.

24. Quoted in Annie Lee West Stahl, "The Free Negro in Ante-Bellum Louisiana," *The Louisiana Historical Quarterly* 25, no. 2 (1945): 315–316.

25. Ibid., 130.

26. *Le Code Noir*, Article LV. Masters twenty years of age may free their slaves by any act toward the living or due to death, without their having to give just cause for their actions, nor do they require parental advice as long as they are minors of 25 years of age.

27. According to the 1810 census of the Territory of Orleans "Twenty-four of forty white-dominated households (60 percent) contained no white women." Brasseaux et al., *Creoles of Color*, 8.

28. Gwendolyn Midlow Hall, *Africans in Louisiana: The Development of Afro-Creole Culture in the Eighteenth Century* (Baton Rouge: Louisiana State University Press, 1992), 278.

29. In 1721, there were 145 White men, 65 White women and 172 People of Color in New Orleans. Charles Barthelemy Roussève, *The Negro in Louisiana* (New Orleans: The Xavier University Press, 1937), 21. In 1746, New Orleans only had 800 Whites as compared to 3,000 Blacks, and in all of the settlements there were only 1,700 Whites to a Black population of 4,730. Gwendolyn Midlo Hall, *Africans in Louisiana: The Development of Afro-Creole Culture in the Eighteenth Century* (Baton Rouge: Louisiana State University Press, 1992), 177.

30. *Le Code* Noir, Article XIII. We desire that if a male slave has married a free woman, their children, either male or female, shall be free as is their mother, regardless of their father's condition of slavery. And if the father is free and the mother a slave, the children shall also be slaves...

31. Midlo Hall, *Africans in Louisiana*, 238.

32. In 1804, thousands of refugees from the Haitian revolution more than doubled Louisiana's population of Free People of Color; their numbers topped 16,000 by 1830. *Fifth Census of the United States* (1830).

33. See Sterkx, *The Free Negro in Ante-bellum Louisiana*, 61–67, 250–255; Blassingame, *Black New Orleans*, 17–20; and Carl Brasseaux, "Creoles of Color in Louisiana's Bayou Country," in *Creoles of Color of the Gulf South*, James H. Dormon, ed. (Knoxville: The University of Tennessee Press, 1996), 69, Midlo Hall, *Africans in Louisiana*, 238–241.

34. George William Featherstonhaugh, *Excursion through the Slave States: From Washington on the Potomac to the Frontier of Mexico; With Sketches of Popular Manners and Geological Notices*, reprint (New York, NY: Negro Universities Press, 1968), 141. Originally printed in 1844. Berquin-Duvallon quoted in Sterkx, *The Free Negro in Ante-bellum Louisiana*, 62.

35. Nobleman and Spanish Army officer, Augustine Marcarty, lived with Free Woman of Color, Celeste Perrault, for nearly fifty years, Sterkx, *The Free Negro in Ante-bellum Louisiana*, 63.

36. Jean Boze, Bulletin written in 1831, folder 180.7 and 183.5, Ste-Géme Family Papers, Williams Research Center, The Historic New Orleans Collection (New Orleans, LA).

37. Jean Boze, Bulletin, 1831, f. 180 p. 7–8, f. 164, p. 2.

38. Simien Succession, Tureaud Papers, Amistad Research Center at Tulane University (New Orleans, LA).

39. Jean Boze, Bulletin, 1832, Ste-Géme Family Papers, f. 203, p. 2.

40. Jean Boze, Bulletin, Winter 1836, Ste-Géme Family Papers, f. 265, p. 9, "On dit que la fortune qu'il laisse passera par son testatment a ses nombre enfans naturels de couleur..."

41. 1850 Census assets for Free Persons of Color of $250 or greater, Blassingame, John W. Collection, Amistad Research Center at Tulane University (New Orleans, LA).

42. Meullion Family Papers, 1776–1906, Hill Memorial Library, Special Collections, Louisiana State University (Baton Rouge, LA).

43. Soulié Family Ledgers, 1843–1880, Williams Research Center, The Historic New Orleans Collection (New Orleans, LA).

44. Loren Schweninger, "Socioeconomic Dynamics among the Gulf Creole Populations: The Antebellum and Civil War Years," in *Creoles of Color of the Gulf South*, James H. Dormon, ed. (Knoxville: The University of Tennessee Press, 1996), 55.

45. Featherstonhaugh, *Excursion through the Slave States*, 142.

46. *Seventh Census of the United States* (1850).

47. Ibid. Note: The rate of White literacy is suspect as Louisiana had no free public system of schooling until 1847, and only about half of all eligible, i.e., White, children were known to be in attendance in 1848, just two years before the

Census. It is unlikely that, absent widespread access to formal schooling, the White population had attained near complete literacy by 1850. *Seventh Census*, 1850. Edwin Whitfield Fay, *History of Education; Louisiana* (Washington: G.P.O., 1898).

48. Fay, *History of Education*; Carl E. Kaestle, *Pillars of the Republic: Common Schools and American Society, 1780–1860* (New York, NY: Hill and Wang, 1983).

49. *Seventh Census* (1850).

50. *Seventh Census* (1850); "Emancipation at the South—The Tolerance of Louisiana," *The African Repository* September 1856, 276.

51. Ibid.,276.

52. *Seventh Census* (1850), 144.

53. Roussève, *The Negro in Louisiana*, 67.

54. Desdunes, *Our People Our History*, 13.

55. Ibid., 19.

56. Johnson (William T. and Family) Papers, Hill Memorial Library, Special Collections, Louisiana State University (Baton Rouge, LA).

57. Johnson (William T. and Family) Papers, 1837.

58. Johnson (William T. and Family) Papers, 1859.

59. Johnson (William T. and Family) Papers, 1842.

60. In 1849, 6,720 pupils from of a total of 14,258 eligible children attended the new public schools. Fay, *History of Education*, 69–70.

61. *Seventh Census* (1850).

62. *Seventh Census* (1850). Endowment being defined by the Census as a "permanently invested fund or endowment." Pennsylvania's private school endowment was $73,459 at the time, and New York held the third highest at $23,185, less than half of that in Louisiana.

63. Clark Robenstine, "French Colonial Policy and the Education of Women and Minorities: Louisiana in the Early Eighteenth Century," *History of Education Quarterly* 32, no. 2 (Summer, 1992): 199.

64. *Le Code Noir*, Article II. Charles Roussève explained that in this early period religious instruction, "guaranteed the slaves by the Code Noir, brought with it instruction in the rudiments, at least, of reading and writing..." He goes on to call this, "'religion with letters,' as opposed to the scheme, derived by the English colonists for their slaves, of 'religion without letters.'" *The Negro in Louisiana*, 42.

65. Robenstine, "French Colonial Policy," 199.

66. Fay, *History of Education*, 131.

67. Ibid., 131–132.

68. Laura Ewen Blokker, "Education in Louisiana," *State of Louisiana Department of Culture, Recreation and Tourism.* https://www.yumpu.com/en/document/view/4144699/education-in-louisiana-louisiana-department-of-culture-. Accessed 1 February 2013.

69. Ibid.

70. Charles B. Roussève, *Prospectus: St. Mary's Academy for Young Ladies Directed by The Sisters of the Holy Family*, undated, Charles B. Roussève papers, 1842–1994, Amistad Research Center, Tulane University (New Orleans, LA).

71. St. Mary's curriculum bore elements, such as rhetoric, mathematics, and natural philosophy, which were considered suitable only for the education of boys and controversial in girls' education into the nineteenth century. At the same time, these young ladies of Color were given training in elegant crafts that were decried by those pushing for the reform of women's education. On the one hand it was thought that, "learning in men was the road to preferment . . . consequences very opposite were the result of the same quality in women." On the other hand, "Girls were said to need a new kind of education because their traditional training had been superficial and their resulting behavior shallow." These young ladies were afforded *both* forms of education. Linda K. Kerber, *Women of the Republic: Intellect and Ideology in Revolutionary America* (Chapel Hill: University of North Carolina Press, 1980), 199, 203.

72. Justin Nystrom, "In My Father's House: Relationships and Identity in an Interracial New Orleans Creole Family," *Louisiana History: The Journal of the Louisiana Historical Association* 49, no. 3 (Summer 2008): 294.

73. *History of the Catholic Indigent Orphan Institute*, Charles B. Roussève papers.

74. Ibid.

75. Ibid.

76. Blokker, "Education in Louisiana," 13.

77. Roussève Papers, *History of the Catholic Indigent Orphan Institute*.

78. Ibid.; West Stahl, "The Free Negro in Ante-Bellum Louisiana," 319.

79. Persons of Color in Louisiana Possessing More Than $200 in Property at the Time of the 1850, 1860, and 1870 Census, Blassingame, John W. Collection, 1831–1879, Amistad Research Center at Tulane University, New Orleans, Louisiana (New Orleans, LA); Roussève Papers, *History of the Catholic Indigent Orphan Institute*. Also see Desdunes, *Our People and Our History*, 92–93.

80. Desdunes, *Our People Our History*.

81. Ibid. Desdunes also notes Dubuclet's service in this position, 74–75.

82. Desdunes, *Our People Our History*, 104; Sterkx, *The Free Negro in Ante-bellum Louisiana*, 269; Willey, "Education of the Colored People of Louisiana," 248.

83. Roussève, *The Negro in Louisiana*, 42.

84. Ste-Géme Family Papers, f. 238, p. 12, 1834.

85. Sterkx, *The Free Negro in Ante-bellum Louisiana*, 269.

86. Ibid., 270; Willey, "Education of the Colored People of Louisiana," 248.

87. Willey, "Education of the Colored People of Louisiana," 248.

88. *Le Propagateur Catholique*, "École Pour Les Enfants de Couleur," 8 February, 1845.

89. Ibid.

90. "Educational," *The Daily Creole*, 2 July 1856.

91. Ibid.

92. Ibid.

93. Ste.-Géme Family Papers, f. 203 p.1, 1832; f. 238 p. 6, 1834.

94. David McCullough, *The Greater Journey: Americans in Paris* (New York, NY: Simon & Schuster, 2011), 131.

95. Africans actually arrived in America with many useful skills such as shipbuilding, metalworking, and sugar-making. See Midlo Hall, *Africans in Colonial Louisiana*, 133; Roussève, *The Negro in Louisiana*, 32–33.

CHAPTER 3

FORGOTTEN OR SIMPLY IGNORED

A Historiography of African Americans and Catholic Education

Katrina M. Sanders
University of Iowa

Compared to the knowledge we have about the history of public schools in the United States, relatively little is known about the history of Catholic school education. The proliferation of parish schools in major cities such as Boston, New York, and Chicago is well-documented, as are many of the battles waged between Catholics and non-Catholics over the issues of tax-supported schooling. However, relatively little is known about the kinds of teaching and learning that occurred inside Catholic schools or the response of the parents and community to the education their children received. This lack of knowledge doubtless stems from a longstanding lack of interest by the non-Catholic educational research community and from the scarcity of Catholic researchers whose interests lay in educational history.

—Darlene Eleanor York[1]

According to Darlene Eleanor York, relatively little is known about Catholic schools and the education of minority students within those schools as compared to immigrant communities and fights over public educational funds.

Using Past as Prologue, pages 57–83

Although Catholic religious communities have educated African American children since the 1800s, their efforts have been either "forgotten or ignored" by both historians of African American and Catholic education. York attributes this paucity of information to non-interested non-Catholic researchers interested in education. But other factors are also at play. Records on Catholic schools are held in Catholic archives, and the diocesan chancery and/or archivists determine what information researchers can access and utilize.[2] With the exception of sacramental records documenting Catholic baptisms, confirmations, marriages, and deaths within Catholic Church parishes, Catholic records are typically closed to the public. Since the history surrounding African Americans and their education is fraught with racial intolerance, many archives consider their existing material evidence concerning Black Catholic schools sensitive and refuse access or usage. Consequently, researchers are left to "piece together" remaining evidence in the form of former students' personal collections and/or oral interviews.[3] These limited forms of evidence, combined with the obstacles related to researching them can be off-putting and time-consuming. As a result, a more comprehensive knowledge of African Americans in Catholic schools remain elusive as few historians—Catholic or not—attempt to research the topic.

Like York, others have noted the limited research and scholarship on Black Catholic education. In 1988, historian V.P. Franklin pointed out the "wide gaps in our knowledge of the history and development of black Catholic schooling."[4] A year later, the historian Paula S. Fass was more pronounced stating "American education in the twentieth century—and specifically the education of outsiders—is simply incomprehensible, or in the very least incompletely rendered, without an understanding of how Catholic schools have operated within American culture alongside the public schools."[5] Similarly, in the introduction to her co-edited volume, *Growing Up African American in Catholic Schools*, Michelle Foster observed African Americans in Catholic schools were "underresearched and poorly understood."[6]

During the 1980s, research on Catholic school effectiveness concentrated its attention on the relationship between Catholic schools and Black students. In *Inner City Private Elementary Schools: A Study*, authors James Cibulka, Timothy O'Brien, and Donald Zewe found inner-city private elementary schools—most of which were run-down Catholic schools—succeeded when the public schools in the same areas did not.[7] James Coleman, Thomas Hoffer, and Sally Kilgore's book, *High School Achievement: Public and Private Schools*, concluded that when compared to public schools, Catholic schools produced higher cognitive achievement, were less racially segregated, and achievement patterns depended less on family background.[8] In *Minority Students in Catholic Schools*, Andrew Greeley found Catholic school minority student achievement—especially African American and Hispanic—to be greater than public school minority student achievement, and that among the most disadvantaged students, these differences were the greatest.[9] All of these findings, which loosely interpreted can suggest Catholic schools are better for Black students, stirred conversation and debate as social scientists and educational policymakers quickly countered and questioned the methodological limitation of data utilized in each of the studies.

Current educational initiatives and findings also reflect the need to historically understand African Americans in Catholic schools. The most recent data from the National Catholic Educational Association (NCEA) show that the minority population in Catholic schools is growing. Minorities accounted for 10.8 percent of the Catholic school population in 1970, 19.4 percent in 1980, and 29.8 percent in 2010. Black students make up 7.5 percent of the minority population, 7.1 percent of students enrolled in Catholic elementary and middle schools, and 8.7 percent in Catholic secondary schools."[10] In addition to data from the NCEA, popular Catholic school initiatives like the national Cristo Rey Network (CRN) and the Jubilee Schools in Memphis, Tennessee increasingly attract African American and minority students, and further reveal African American interests in Catholic schools. Twenty-six Catholic college preparatory schools located in 25 cities across the country and in the District of Columbia currently comprise the CRN.[11] Ninety-six percent of the CRN's total enrollments were students of color, and 96 percent of students who graduated during the 2009–2010 school year from the then 24 Cristo Rey high schools were students of color. The CRN reported every graduate was accepted to at least one college.[12] In 2003, the Bill & Melinda Gates Foundation, along with venture philanthropists B.J. and Bebe Cassin, provided seed funding to promote the replication of Cristo Rey schools. Similarly in 2012, the Walton Family Foundation announced its investment of $1.6 million in the CRN to accelerate growth, primarily in states that have either vouchers or tax credits.[13]

The Jubilee Schools, also nationally known as the "Miracle in Memphis," are eight previously closed elementary Catholic schools that were reopened in 1999 to serve low-income students living in urban neighborhoods in Memphis, Tennessee. The students are awarded scholarships that follow them to Catholic middle and high schools in Memphis. The Diocese of Memphis reports a nearly 100 percent high school graduation rate.[14] In 2010, the Notre Dame Alliance for Catholic Education (ACE) opened its first Notre Dame Alliance for Catholic Education Academies (NDAA) in Tucson, Arizona. ACE Academies now located in a number of urban areas focus on "putting more children on the path to college and heaven."[15] Their schools report closing the achievement gap per scores on the Spring 2013 Iowa Test of Basic Skills. ACE is also reported that their youngest students are among the highest achieving in the nation, and in some cases, "now outperform the national average."[16] Parental choice scholarships, including vouchers and tax credit scholarship programs, support the ACE Academies. Similar to past research, these current findings also suggest African American students do better in Catholic schools.

Historical examination of the inner-workings of America's second largest school system as it pertains to African American students and their families can inform researchers interested in the history of African American education and school effectiveness for African American students. This essay is a continuation of these considerations and examines the historiography related to African Americans and Catholic education. It is divided into four sections based upon the dominant themes that emerged. The first section titled, "Penance and Proselytization," describes the historical relationship between the Catholic Church and African Americans. It focuses heavily on Catholic involvement in slavery and on the Church's good deeds towards African Americans. The second section, "Agency and Determination," explores the experiences and efforts of African American to achieve parity within the Catholic Church. The third section, "Integration and Change," focuses on the Catholic Church's efforts to end internal practices and policies of segregation. The fourth and final section, "Effectiveness and Mobility," assesses the historiography that advances the belief Catholic schools are more successful in educating African American students than traditional public schools.[17]

BRIEF HISTORICAL CONTEXT

As the Catholic Church took firm root in the United States, three ecumenical councils met in Baltimore, Maryland during the mid-to-late 1800s to decide Church doctrines, administration, and implementation. These councils would ultimately contribute to the creation and support of formalized education for African Americans. Amid debates over a Protestant-based curriculum in the public schools and tax-supported European immigrant Catholic parochial schools, the First Plenary Council in 1852 decreed that each Catholic parish have a school. These schools ensured Catholic children had teachers and a curriculum that valued and cultivated the faith. The Second Plenary Council in 1866 decreed that the Church minister to African Americans—especially newly free People of Color. The mandate intended to grow the Church among southern African Americans. Essentially, the Church feared that newly freed African Americans would join Protestant denominations and by default limit any opportunity of Catholicism expanding in the South. The Third Plenary Council in 1884 mandated Catholic children attend Catholic schools—when possible—and that the schools be free. The decree was especially significant for Black-White relations among Catholics because the directive also established racial segregation within Catholic institutions. Although the Church was interested in growing their numbers among African Americans in the South, and knew schools were the best vehicles to do so, it was not willing to challenge the systemic forms of racial segregation and discrimination that undermined African Americans aspirations for equality. Instead of promoting equality and brotherhood for all, the Church established separate racially segregated schools for African Americans, developed separate religious orders—both priests and sisters—to teach in these segregated schools, and appointed a commission to specifically aid the missions among "Indians and Coloreds."[18] Among these orders specifically developed to work with African Americans, or who had members who agreed to work with African Americans, were The Oblates Sisters of Providence, The Sisters of the Holy Family, The Franciscan Handmaids of the Most Pure Heart of Mary, The Sisters of the Blessed Sacrament, The Mill Hill Fathers, The St. Joseph's Society of the Sacred Heart (Josephites), The Carmelite Sisters, The Holy Ghost Fathers (Spiritans), The Holy Spirit Missionary Sisters, The Sisters of the Holy Spirit and Mary Immaculate (San Antonio), and The Congregation of Divine Providence (San Antonio).[19]

PENANCE AND PROSELYTIZATION

Numerous historians have explored the historical relationship between African Americans and the Catholic Church.[20] Catholic priests wrote most of these initial works and acknowledged the Church's role in the institution of slavery. For example, the Jesuits in Maryland during the 1830s, and the Sisters of Charity of Nazareth, Kentucky at the start of the Civil War, were slaveholders.[21] Although these early publications admitted Catholic participation in slavery, these scholars focused less on the Church's culpability and more on the "good" the Catholic Church had done for African Americans.

There were alternative interpretations, however. In his 1917 article, "Negro Catholics in the United States," the Josephite Joseph Butsch countered claims of a negligent Church by pointing to The Oblate Sisters of Providence and their schools in Boston during the 1830s as an example of the Church's significant missionary efforts towards African Americans in the North and the Third Plenary Council's mandate that Catholic congregations devote themselves to working with African Americans.[22] As for participating in slavery and failing to address the needs of enslaved African Americans, Butsch argued southern legislation hindered Catholic missionary efforts in the region because the Catholics living there already faced discrimination and ostracism for their religion.[23] Butsch advocated dispensation for the Church and Catholic slaveholders because of the legal system, Code Noir—laws that defined the condition of enslavement—established in the French colonies. In many ways his interpretation presumed Catholic slaveholders were better than non-Catholic slaveholders because Catholic slave owners were charged by the Church to follow the Code Noir that mandated that the enslaved be baptized as Catholic, that enslaved Catholics marriages be recognized by law, that enslaved Catholic families not be separated or sold off for the personal gain of a slaveholder, and that enslaved Catholics be taught catechism.[24] In his article in the *Journal of Negro Education*, Butcsh took a more nuanced approach. Instead of rationalizing the Church's past indiscretions against African Americans and blaming southerners, he instead focused on the Catholic Church's charitable kindness towards free and enslaved African Americans. [25] Although his publications did not concentrate specifically on schools, they were among the first scholarship to specifically address African American-Catholic interactions during and immediately following slavery.

Michael Francis Rouse's, *A Study of the Development of Negro Education under Catholic Auspices in Maryland*, also looked at the relationship between African Americans and the Catholic Church. Published in 1935, his book is the first comprehensive work to chronicle Catholic education for African Americans in the Maryland area.[26] Rouse's work discussed slavery in Maryland and the newly freedpeople's efforts to address their own welfare. He explored the Church's contributions to education and highlighted brief individualist efforts tracing back to 1796. Rouse pointed out the Church's attempts to educate African Americans were based on the desire to teach and transmit the Catholic doctrine. He chronicled their endeavors to organize Black Catholic schools, charted where those schools existed, and identified the religious orders and congregations who ran those schools from 1818 to 1933. He even offered the 1932 curriculum of one Black Catholic school. Rouse also discussed the Church's interests in rural education and the growing demands for Catholic vocational secondary schools. In 1936, the *Journal of Negro Education* reviewed Rouse's book and found it to be "carefully done" and "valuable" to African American Catholics and their friends who were "becoming more and more restive and critical of what they believe to be the inadequacies of the current offerings for Negroes in the Catholic educational system."[27] These "inadequacies" will be addressed later in the section "Agency and Determination.".

In 1937, John LaFarge published, *Interracial Justice*, and offered a more theological perspective on African American-Catholic relations.[28] While LaFarge's book spanned issues of humanity, racial differences, segregation, and social programs for African Americans, it also contained a strong slant of Catholic generosity towards the group. Future Morehouse President Benjamin E. Mays reviewed LaFarge's monograph and concluded the book portrayed African Americans solely as takers who contributed nothing to the Catholic Church and the Catholic Church as better for African Americans than other denominations.[29] Mays wrote:

> The Church's educational and religious program is one-sided and paternalistic. One gets the impression that the emphasis is on what the Church does for the Negro rather than placing the emphasis upon a cooperative basis whereby the Negro participates and makes his contribution along with the rest. The Negro seems to be treated as a thing apart from the church, an object from whom something is to be done. The idea of reciprocity is slight. As a Catholic, the author gives the impression that he is biased in favor of the Catholic Church. In places he seems to say that the Catholic Church has more to offer the Negro than other institutions or Churches."[30]

Mays evaluation of LaFarge's work makes a compelling point when one considers LaFarge was a Josephite priest and Catholic publications like *The Colored Harvest*—a Josephite publication—and *Our Negro and Indian Missions* were filled with articles featuring Catholic missionary efforts towards African Americans.[31] Philadelphia's Catholic weekly newspaper, *The Journal*, even carried the phrase "The Catholic Church The Only True Liberator of the Negro" as part of its banner.[32]

John T. Gillard's, *Colored Catholics in the United States* (1941), also highlighted the Church's good deeds towards African Americans in an effort to promote and support racially segregated Catholic institutions. Published in 1941, Gillard (another Josephite) utilized national surveys administered by the Church and chronicled early Catholic educational efforts for African Americans by a number of priests to argue the institutions ultimately benefited African Americans.[33] Many scholars criticized Gillard's work for being racist and patriarchal in nature.[34] Notwithstanding, his publication was valuable for its logistical detailing of the types of Catholic schools offered to African Americans and where they existed, and the religious orders involved in their instruction. Gillard's research also acknowledged how little the Church actually knew about its own relationship with African Americans. While his predecessors attempted to portray a history of solid connections and interactions between the two groups, Gillard revealed the Church had essentially ignored African Americans and did so because it was preoccupied with immigrant European Catholics living in urban areas throughout the United States.

Gillard contended that up until a 1929 national Church survey, "even the best informed were not in a position to give a comprehensive statement of the work of the Catholic Church for the Negroes in this country."[35] He found the survey sparked a Catholic awakening to the existence of African Americans in the Church and increased interests in the welfare of African Americans. As examples, he pointed to African Americans being mentioned in Catholic newspapers, periodicals, social settings, lectures, and conferences. He wrote:

> Since the publication of [the survey], however, it is no exaggeration to state that Catholic interest in the welfare of America's millions of Negroes has increased at least a hundredfold. Even the casually observant must now note the vibrant interest of Catholics in the cause of the colored people living in our midst. Catholic newspapers are giving increased space to news of the Negro; Catholic periodicals are willing, even anxious, to feature him; and several Catholic authors have published books and pamphlets on matters pertaining to him and his problems. Catholic discussion clubs now find the Negro a fascinating topic; study programs are not considered complete without reference to him; while lectures on topics relating to the Negro are much in demand. Catholic classrooms are espousing the cause of the Negro; conventions arrange whole panels on him; and the interracial movement has grown tremendously. Especially significant are the increasingly frequent references to Catholic obligation towards the Negro in official statements from leaders in the Church. There can be no doubt that within the past decade the Catholic conscience has been deeply stirred.[36]

The African American community also took notice of the Church's intrigue with African Americans. For example, William Stuart Nelson, Dean of the School of Religion at Howard University, reviewed *Colored Catholics* in 1942 and noted the Church's growing interest in African Americans was demonstrated by the increasing number of "churches, missions, schools, colleges, and welfare institutions."[37]

Although Catholic scholars seemed to be working hard to absolve the Church from its involvement in slavery, they would be reminded of it yet again in *American Catholic Opinion in the Slavery Controversy*. In 1941, Madeleine Hook Rice analyzed the Catholic Church's position on slavery via an economic framework.[38] Rather than offering reasons to exonerate the Church for turning a blind eye and in some cases being active participants in slavery, Rice theorized the economic and social factors that caused the Church to compromise rather than attack the institution of slavery. She detailed the Catholic Church's relationship with slavery in Latin America to show the connection to the Catholic Church's reactions to enslavement in America. The conclusion of her book argued that "[throughout] the course of the slavery controversy ecclesiastical leaders insisted upon the official neutrality of the Church." Rice deduced that "the American Catholic hierarchy, with a few notable exceptions, [had] not been distinguished for farsighted or courageous leadership in social or economic problems."[39] Her book garnered considerable attention beyond the Catholic community. In 1945, Williston H. Lofton, a Professor of History at Howard University, reviewed Rice's book and made it a point to commend her for being "adversely critical when necessary" and for acknowledging the "compromising attitude of the church" when it came to ending slavery.[40]

The Church's charitable social works towards African Americans continued to be a major theme of scholarly writings during the next 50 years. Amid the social justice and civil rights issues that captured the nation's attention during the 1960s and 1970s, those researching African American Catholics slowly expanded beyond the Catholic scholar priest and religious leader.[41] In his 1970 book, *Of Singular Benefit: The Story of Catholic Education in the United States*, Harold A. Buetow briefly explored the limited interaction between African Americans and the Catholic Church. Buetow, a Brooklyn, New York diocesan Catholic priest himself, discussed brief attempts to educate enslaved and free African Americans in Charleston, South Carolina. Nonetheless, Buetow ultimately conceded there was little connection between the Catholic Church and African Americans.[42] He agreed with Gillard that the disconnect stemmed from the Church being more concerned with immigrant European Catholics in urban areas than with the newly relocated African Americans.[43]

Buetow observed that even when the Church did encounter African Americans in urban areas, its work was "seriously hindered by [a] lack of priests and Catholic teachers, by bigotry, and by prejudice even on the part of some of her own."[44] Buetow considered the development of Black Catholic schools throughout his work and explained when and how Catholic decrees actually impacted the development of the schools and the type of education the schools actually offered African Americans. He noted that the first school, the Oblates established in Baltimore for African Americans, initially focused on industrial work, but later developed into a curriculum which included "English, French, cyphering and writing" as well as "[s]ewing in all its branches, embroidery, [w]ashing and [i]roning."[45]

Scholars who were not priests offered edited works during the late 1980s and mid-1990s on the Church's interactions with African Americans via its schools. In 1988, V.P. Franklin and Edward McDonald argued in "Blacks in Urban Catholic Schools in the United States: A Historical Perspective," most Catholic contact with African Americans in the United States from the colonial era focused principally in Louisiana and Maryland.[46] Instead of presenting the Church as benevolent or absolve past sins against African Americans, Franklin and McDonald focused on the development of Black Catholic schools. They held the Church made no extensive missionary activities among African Americans until after the Civil War when the Church charged the Mill Hill missionaries from England to work with "Negroes" in 1871 and establish their first parish in Baltimore, St. Francis Xavier's Church.[47] They noted that by 1900 there were 144,000 African Americans Catholics attending 45 churches and 109 schools in the United States, and that by 1965 there were 525 African American Catholic congregations in the United States, with 350 of those having schools.[48] They also analyzed policies impacting Catholic education in African American communities during the nineteenth and twentieth centuries and offered educational policy implications. Franklin later explored how the Church utilized the Catholic school to proselytize to Free People of Color in northern and southern communities in "First Came the School: Catholic Evangelization Among African Americans in the United States, 1827 to the Present."[49]

Scholars who were not priests also explored the Catholic Church's presence in Louisiana's African American communities via its schools. For example, the 1993 publication of *Cross, Crozier, and Crucible: A Volume Celebrating the Bicentennial of a Catholic Diocese in Louisiana* edited by Glen R. Conrad, et al., offers insight into African American Catholic education in three of its chapters.[50] It's important to note, however, that Black Catholic schools are not the focus of the chapters, but appear as part of the larger development of Catholic education story. Joan Marie Aycock's chapter, "The Ursuline School in New Orleans, 1727–1771," detailed the growth of the Ursuline community that arrived in New Orleans from France in 1727 and how they taught African American and Native American girls. Aycock's chapter is one of only a few works that offers insight into educational philosophy and pedagogy in a Catholic girls' school; however, she does not clarify if the African American and Native American students were also afforded this curriculum.[51]

Sally K. Reeves's, "The Society of the Scared Heart in New Orleans," is another chapter in *Cross, Crozier, and Crucible*. Reeves examines the efforts of the Society of the Sacred Heart, which arrived in the New Orleans area of Plaquemines Parish in 1818. Reeves' chapter briefly mentioned the Scared Heart's catechetical school for Native American women, the enslaved, and free Black girls, and provides important insight into how the Second Plenary Council of Baltimore impacted the establishment of Catholic education for the freedpeople in New Orleans.[52] Patricia Lynch's chapter, "Mother Katharine Drexel's Rural Schools: Education and Evangelization through Lay Leadership," also illustrates early examples of African American Catholic education in *Cross, Crozier, and Crucible*. The chapter gives insight into Katharine Drexel (now Saint Katharine Drexel) who founded the Sisters of the Blessed Sacrament in 1891 and who played a vital role in evangelization efforts among African Americans. Drexel was also the daughter of Philadelphia financier, Francis Anthony Drexel. Lynch's chapter chronicled the planning and development of schools for African Americans in a number of rural Louisiana communities and demonstrates the different needs of teachers working in these rural schools, such as teacher certification and maintaining a robust teaching force for African American Catholic schools. She also chronicles the development of Xavier University in New Orleans.

Xavier University is the only existing historically Black higher education institution that is also a Catholic institution.[53]

AGENCY AND SELF-DETERMINATION

Scholars and historians also explored the agency and self-determination of African American Catholics. What is unique about African American Catholic agency and self-determination efforts is that the efforts challenged religious and civil structures of oppression. Like general histories concerning African American education, efforts in the larger African American and African American Catholic communities broadly defined the experiences of Blacks in Catholic schools. Two groups must be mentioned here: The Negro Catholic Conferences (NCC) and the Federated Colored Catholics (FCC). The NCC held three national meetings—1889, 1890, and 1892—of representatives from each African American Catholic parish in the United States. The representatives met to give voice to African American Catholics and make their needs known to the larger Church. Securing education, especially in the trades and literary societies, "as a means of completing our young men's training and attainments" was high on the NCC's agenda.[54] The FCC organized in 1924 to "unite black Catholics in a closer bond, to increase the possibility of Catholic education in the black community, to raise the overall position of black Catholics within the church, and to bring about a greater participation of black Catholics in the cause of racial justice."[55]

Numerous journal articles during the 1960s through the 1990s exploring African American Catholic protest efforts detailed the NCC and FCC activities. David Spalding chronicled the FCC and their protest efforts for a space and place within the Church in his 1969 article, "The Negro Catholic Congresses, 1889–1894."[56] Spalding argued the emerging leaders in the FCC who championed rights for African American Catholics did so because they were a "small elite of Negro Catholic leaders" who had "little recollection of the days of servitude . . . were educated, comparatively successful in their professions, and restive under the restraints they encountered at every turn."[57] In 1986, Albert J. Raboteau's article, "Black Catholics and Afro-American Religious History: Autobiographic Reflections," reflectively analyzed discrimination within the Church and how African American Catholics utilized the Black Pride and Black Power movements to self-define what it meant to be an African American Catholic.[58] Raboteau also detailed how these movements inspired African Americans to create the "Black Catholic Clergy Caucus, the National Black Sisters Conference, the Black Catholic Lay Causcus, and the National Office of Black Catholics" between 1968 and 1970 as part of African American Catholics self-definition and affirmation.[59] Marilyn W. Nickels, 1988 article, "Thomas Wyatt Turner and the Federated Colored Catholics," chronicled Turner's vision and efforts to organize the FCC.[60] Nickels offered a more in-depth examination of this group in her book, *Black Catholic Protest and the Federated Colored Catholics, 1917–1933.*[61]

In the seminal work, *Black Catholics in the United States,* Cyprian Davis, an African American Catholic Benedictine monk, also briefly explored early African American protest efforts. Davis highlighted NCC activities to secure Catholic education for African Americans. Davis examined efforts by Dr. William S. Lofton, a prominent African American dentist and one of Howard University's first Dental School graduates, and Charles H. Butler, a well-known employee of the Treasury Department. Both Lofton and Butler spoke at the 1890 NCC. Lofton fiercely supported "manual, industrial and intellectual" education for African Americans recognizing all three areas could allow access to certain trades that were at that time closed to the group.[62] Lofton held industrial education provided African American boys "the most complete control of their faculties, ... [made] them alert, accurate, ready physically as well as mentally for the performance of the duties of life."[63] Lofton argued that the Catholic Church decreed Catholic students should attend Catholic schools, but did not provide opportunities to fulfill the mandate.[64] Butler largely agreed with Lofton and charged "not a single Catholic school in the city of Washington [existed] whose doors are open to the Colored youth after they reach[ed] the age of twelve years."[65] It should be noted that African American Catholic interest in industrial and vocational training was in keeping with thoughts in the larger African American community during the late nineteenth century as many prominent African American leaders such as Booker T. Washington championed vocational training for Blacks.

Agency and self-determination and their connection to African American Catholic education are clearly evident in what is arguably to date the most comprehensive work on a single African American Catholic educational institution. Cecilia Moore's 1997 dissertation, *A Brilliant Possibility: The Cardinal Gibbons Institute, 1924–1934,* explores the Black Catholic high school located in Ridge, Maryland.[66] Moore argued Cardinal Gibbons' mission was "to provide Catholic education to African American youth, Catholic and non-Catholic, to prepare youth for industrial and agricultural work, for teaching careers, and for higher education, and to encourage youth to become leaders in their own communities and churches."[67] Moore noted African American male and female laity staffed and administered Cardinal Gibbons and utilized teaching approaches they learned at Tuskegee Institute. She chronicled the efforts of Mr. and Mrs. Hugo Daniels, the principals of the Institute and Dr. Thomas Wyatt Turner, leader of the FCC, to open the school which was hailed as the "first Catholic co-educational boarding school administered by Negro lay Catholics for young Negro Catholics and non-Catholics."[68] In addition to discussing obstacles like funding issues to establish Cardinal Gibbons, Moore's work identified and critiqued philanthropic organizations that aided the school and other African American Catholic endeavors and their rationale for those contributions. She also provided general information concerning African American Catholic interactions with the larger Church and its European Catholic immigrants. Moore also explored protest organizations including the FCC and intergroup efforts that helped establish the school, and argued The Cardinal Gibbons Institute was the first major interracial Catholic endeavor in the twentieth century and the catalyst for subsequent Catholic interracial efforts.[69]

In 1999, Morris J. MacGregor's *The Emergence of a Black Catholic Community: St. Augustine's in Washington* offered an in-depth look at the development of an African American Catholic community—St. Augustine's—in the nation's capital.[70] Unlike Davis's work, MacGregor focused exclusively on St. Augustine's and explored Washington's free Black community from the late 1700s to 1864. He highlighted the Church and the school and the Federated Colored Catholics involvement with both. In doing so, he provided both a Catholic school history and a brief history of race relations in the school community. MacGregor wove the development of St. Augustine's throughout the book and explored its relationships with local public schools since many of St. Augustine's Catholic School alumni went on to prestigious high schools in the area, namely Dunbar High School and Armstrong High School.[71]

Two other works during the first decade of the twenty-first century also explored the agency and self-determination of African American Catholics. In 2002, Diane Batts Morrow published, *Person's of Color and Religious at the Same Time: The Oblate Sisters of Providence, 1828–1860*. Her book offered the history of the Oblate Sisters during the early 1800s. Morrow situated the Oblates within the Catholic tradition, and showed how the sisters made a place and space for themselves as African American Catholics and educators. Similarly, Donna Porche-Frilot's 2006 dissertation, *Propelled by Faith: Henriette Delille and the Literacy Practices of Black Women Religious in Antebellum New Orleans* also offered a look at African American Catholic education broadly defined via another African American Catholic religious order, The Sisters of the Holy Family. Porche-Frilot provided a theoretical examination of literacy and explored how the sisters understood, displayed, and utilized a multitude of literacies throughout their daily interaction within their community and school.[72]

In 2004, The Cushwa Center for the Study of American Catholicism at the University of Notre Dame in collaboration with Loyola University Chicago organized a national conference on African American Catholics.[73] The conference featured eighteen speakers from various academic disciplines and religious communities. A number of papers delivered at the conference appeared in the 2009 book *Uncommon Faithfulness: The Black Catholic Experience* edited by M. Shawn Copeland with LaReine-Marie Mosely and Albert J. Raboteau. *Uncommon Faithfulness* is ripe with historical, theological, ethical, and pastoral scholarship concerning African Americans in the Catholic Church, but three chapters in particular, illuminate different aspects of agency and self-determination as related to African American Catholics.

The first is Cecilia Moore's essay, "Dealing with Desegregation: Black and White Responses to the Desegregation of the Diocese of Raleigh, North Carolina, 1953." Moore provides incredible insight into the formation of a desegregated Catholic Church in Raleigh.[74] Although I could include this work in the following section on "Desegregation and Integration," I offer it here because Moore stressed that the agency on the part of parishioners was more important than the tactics participants utilized to secure the integrated church. She theorized most of the African Americans and European Americans involved in establishing Raleigh's first integrated parish "were not conscious that they were playing a role in bringing down Jim Crow." Instead, she continues, "[m]ost of these Catholics simply wanted to be faithful to the church and to practice the way of Christ."[75] Moore argued even though African American male participants were especially vulnerable to retaliation, they thought more about their rights as members of the Church than a civil structure. Their agency thus, was rooted in their religious faith.

My own chapter in *Uncommon Faithfulness*, "Black Catholic Clergy and the Struggle for Civil Rights: Winds of Change," examined how approximately 60 African American priests met in secrecy before the start of an already planned 1968 interracial Catholic clergy conference in Detroit to discuss the state of Black America amid violence surrounding the assassination of Dr. Martin Luther King, Jr.[76] The priests challenged the Church to recognize injustices lodged against African Americans. In a statement to the American bishops drafted during the meeting, the African American priests called the Church in the United States a "primarily... white racist institution" which concerned itself primarily with European American society.[77] The chapter also explored how African American clergy and communities made sense of black power and black theology and how the groups demonstrated civil rights agency in overt and covert ways. For example, while some priests organized public demonstrations, others worked quietly as notaries and helped file paperwork for African Americans filing lawsuits.[78]

Diana L. Hayes's, "Faith of Our Mothers: Catholic Womanist God-Talk," also in *Uncommon Faithfulness*, investigates African American female Catholic agency.[79] Although several works explored agency within African American female religious orders, Hayes' work also encompassed the laity. Hayes examines the birth of womanist theology; "a theology of, by, and for black Christian women acting to build (and rebuild) community," and how African American women utilized womanist theology to craft their place within the Church.[80] Hayes identifies and examines challenges facing womanist theology and those specifically facing African American Catholic women. Her interpretation illustrates how African American women have historically been "forgers of new ways of being and speaking in the world" and have "worked to make community" wherever they found themselves. [81]

INTEGRATION AND CHANGE

Historians also explored issues of desegregation and integration in Black Catholic schools and in the larger African American Catholic communities in the North and South. Again, since African American education is rarely confined to formal educational efforts, included in this section are works covering the larger African American Catholic communities. William A. Osborne's, *The Segregated Covenant: Race Relations and American Catholics* (1967) revealed both racial progress and stagnation within the Catholic community.[82] Osborne examined elementary, secondary, seminaries, elder care facilities and hospitals across the country and found that although the Catholic Church did not formally support discrimination against African Americans, the Catholic parishes ostracized the group and practiced de facto segregation.[83] The interpretation offered by Osborne made a significant contribution because it pinpointed the exact location of many Catholic institutions and identified key factors that impacted their success. One factor that stood out to Osborne was the need for more Catholic secondary schools for African Americans because he believed the schools would have a substantial impact on the future opportunities of African American students. Another key factor was integration and its differentiation between urban and rural Catholic schools. Osborne predicted integration in cities or wealthy areas where "affluence and the pace of social change [were] more marked" would happen faster than in rural areas where there was "devastating effects of racial isolation" and a seemingly "lack of necessary leadership" shaped its ideologies and political economies.[84]

In the 1970s and 1980s, as desegregation efforts reshaped the schooling experiences of children across the nation, historians of Catholic education contributed to the growing scholarship on desegregation and its impact. In 1975, historians Steven I. Miller and Jack Kavanagh argued integration of Catholic schools produced re-segregation in urban areas as Whites fled the cities and moved to suburban areas. Fifteen years later, Martin A. Zielinski chronicled the development of the first major Catholic interracial organization, The Catholic Interracial Council of New York (CIC), and how the organization related to other civil rights organizations such as the National Advancement for the Association of Colored People (NAACP), the National Urban League, Congress on Racial Equality (CORE), Southern Christian

Leadership Conference (SCLC) and the Student Nonviolent Coordinating Committee (SNCC).[85]

By the 1990s, new scholarship emerged that assessed the role of African Americans in Catholic leadership, particularly during the Jim Crow era. *Desegregating the Altar: Josephites and the Struggle for Black Priests, 1871–1960* by Stephen J. Ochs explored efforts to ordain African American priests. Ochs chronicles the initial efforts of the Society of the Divine Word and later the Josephites to open St. Augustine Seminary in Bay St. Louis, Mississippi in 1923.[86] *Desegregating the Altar* is particularly useful in understanding the rationale for ordaining African American Catholic priests, and the actual experiences of these priests within the Church. Evident throughout the book are the persistent challenges and racial hostilities African Americans faced as they sought to achieve their aspirations of joining the priesthood, and by default, desegregating Catholic institutions.[87]

In 1994, John B. Alberts's article, "Black Catholic Schools: The Josephite Parishes during the Jim Crow Era," extended our understanding of the challenges faced by African Americans by providing an often overlooked view of segregation in the Catholic Church. Whereas most of the works covered in this essay examine the establishment of Catholic institutions for African Americans and the subsequent integration of White Catholic institutions, Alberts's article illustrated how the Second Plenary Council's 1884 charge to establish segregated Catholic parishes also dismantled long-existing integrated Catholic parishes in New Orleans. Alberts demonstrates New Orleans had never formed all-Black parishes under French and Spanish colonial rule and that African American Catholics in New Orleans were especially resistant to segregated parishes because most could trace their ancestry to French and Spanish colonial settlements in Louisiana or the Caribbean.[88] He noted that even after Americans gained control of the region, French-born priests continued speaking French and did not segregate their congregations.[89] Financial concern was a primary reason parishes opposed Jim Crow policies, because many could not afford to build and operate separate racial facilities. Alberts also examines how the *Plessy vs Feguson* and *Cumming vs. School Board of Richmond County, Georgia* cases eventually served as backdrops to Catholic compliance to the Second Plenary Council's mandate.[90]

In 1998, John T. McGreevy published a book on race and its impact on the Catholic Church in the North. In *Parish Boundaries: The Catholic Encounter with Race in the Twentieth-Century Urban North*, McGreevy examines the impact of desegregation and integration on Catholic parishes in urban cities—Boston, Chicago, Detroit, New York, and Philadelphia—and the racial tensions that developed.[91] McGreevy discusses the racial conflicts that ensued between African Americans and Whites as African Americans migrated into the traditionally European immigrant Catholic communities and schools. He also explored White resentment against the ordination of African American priests, and how civil rights activism and efforts from organizations such as SNCC and CORE impacted African American Catholics and their relationship with the Church.[92]

McGreevy's scholarship is complemented by the work of historian R. Bentley Anderson. In 2005, Anderson published *Black White and Catholic: New Orleans Interracialism, 1947–1956.* The book analyzes African American and White Catholic efforts and challenges to desegregate the New Orleans archdiocese.[93] Amid this dynamic history, Anderson offers an excellent assessment of the processes that shaped the desegregation of Catholic colleges and professional schools in New Orleans. He details the top-down and bottom-up pressures forcing Loyola University's School of Law to admit Norman Francis, an African American Catholic and New Orleans native, to its 1952 class. Anderson, who is a Jesuit, also examined the unsuccessful efforts of those who tried to desegregate Loyola's law school before Francis and the obstacles they faced. He also identified organizations that helped pursue desegregation and the "pressures from above" such as accreditation, tax-exempt status, and leadership, as well as the from "below" such as interracial activities that ultimately ended racial segregation in New Orleans Catholic institutions.[94]

EFFECTIVENESS AND MOBILITY

Scholars have paid the most attention to themes surrounding the effectiveness and benefits of a Catholic education for African American and poverty-stricken students. This body of literature, however, differs from the previous areas discussed in this historiography because scholars from various social science and humanities disciplines also engaged in the research. Discussions on the benefits of Catholic education for African Americans date back to the days following emancipation. Many of the works already discussed in this review also argued this position. For example, in addition to exploring integration, Osborne's *The Segregated Covenant* examined African American parental views and expectations of Catholic schools. Osborne theorized Catholic schools were becoming increasingly important in places like New York as non-Catholic African American parents were often impressed by the "atmosphere in the Catholic school" which they felt was "preserved by social screening processes." Parents found Catholic schools "comparatively clearer and more conducive to learning." Osborne argued the "parochial school parents seem[ed] to have a vague awareness that the continuation of their children in these schools [was] conditioned on not only good behavior but also good academic performance." He concluded that African American parents "therefore tend[ed] to pressure their offspring to live up to the norms."[95] Osborne cited as evidence interviews with parents, Catholic and non-Catholic, whose children transferred from public to parochial schools.[96] Catholic schools became the preferred school of choice because African American parents did not have to deal with bussing or de facto segregation as with the public school counterparts. The only time bussing was utilized in any meaningful way was when schools experienced an under-enrollment from the "marked exodus of the white Catholic population."[97]

Diana T. Slaughter and Deborah J. Johnson's edited socio-historical work *Visible Now: Blacks in Private Schools* offers a wealth of new and diverse scholarship on alternative schools for African American students. In particular, Franklin and McDonald's chapter "Blacks in Urban Catholic Schools in the United States: A Historical Perspective," illustrates that by the 1950s African American parents in large cities became attracted to the Catholic schools' high quality as the "overall deterioration of 'inner-city' public schools was common knowledge among socially aware parents as well as urban educational researchers."[98] In addition, Mary Lynch Barnds' chapter entitled, "Black Students in Low-Income Serving Catholic High Schools: An Overview of Findings from the 1986 National Catholic Educational Association Study," details the findings of a comprehensive study they conducted to explore and define Catholic schools to help educators better understand the inner-workings of these schools.[99] Barnds does an excellent job exemplifying the historical commitment Catholic schools have had to the poor and their current efforts to serve low-income students. She provides great context for how a student's family composition, their use of time and educational expectations, personal and social beliefs, religious values, and individual and familial life skills shape the academic performance of African American Catholic schoolchildren. Lastly, Patricia A. Bauch's chapter, "Black Family Participation in Catholic Secondary Education," delves into the participation of African American families at single-sex male, single-sex female, and co-educational Catholic schools. She re-examines the research of Greely, Coleman, et al., which found African Americans in Catholic schools were more academically successful and offers a framework by which that success could be analyzed.

Similarly, Jordan Irvine and Foster's edited book *Growing Up African American in Catholic Schools* (already mentioned several times in this essay) provides a rich, diverse, and comprehensive exploration of African Americans in Catholic schools. Throughout the volume, noted educational scholars share their firsthand personal experiences as African American students in Catholic schools. The book also addresses other educational considerations such as curriculum, community involvement, and academic achievement. The entire book is a must read for anyone interested in African American education in Catholic schools.

African American parents' belief that Catholic schools were better for their children than the traditional public school is also discussed in Mc-Greevy's *Parish Boundaries*.[100] McGreevy also examined proposals to require non-Catholic parents who had children enrolled in the schools to attend instructional classes or weekly mass. School officials finally dropped those proposals as they began to understand that even though African American parents showed they valued the Catholic schools via their efforts to raise money and hold protests to keep the schools open, they were not willing to convert. He cites research showing African American students in Catholic schools did better academically than those in public schools.[101] He also concluded the Catholic school remained the Church's best missionary instrument as the Church tried to grow its African American community.

Considerable scholarship exists that discuss the benefits of African American children attending a Catholic school. As early as 1971 Harold A. Buetow argued Catholic schools benefited the poor as well as the elite and identified the religious orders that worked extensively with African American communities. Two years later, Sandra N. Smith, in her article, "Parochial Schools in the Black Cities," also concentrated on the benefits African Americans gained by attending Catholic schools in urban areas. According to Smith,

> The primary value of the Catholic high school for Black youth is that it is an educational institution free from the serious problems of the ghetto high school, a place where he can, if he wishes, concentrate on his studies. He may find no real companionship with his white classmates, because he finds their attitudes toward race no different from those of the prevailing society.[102]

The *Journal of Negro Education* was the primary publication outlet for scholarship related to the African American educational experience in Catholic schools. For nearly a half decade, the journal discussed the effectiveness of Catholic schools to educate African American children. By the 1980s, a series of publications from the journal had helped shape the historiography. Two in particular, Theresa A. Rector's "Black Nuns as Educators," and Portia H. Shields's, "Holy Angels: Pocket of Excellence," further extended our understanding of the agency and effectiveness of Catholic schools and its staff and leadership.[103] In the Spring 1992 issue of the *Journal of Negro Education*, African Americans in independent schools were once again highlighted. In that edition, Faustine C. Jones-Wilson, Nancy L. Arnez and Charles A. Asbury provided an essay that explored the question of why African American parents in the greater Washington, D.C. area were choosing private schools over public schools. In "Why Not Public Schools?" the researchers found parents felt traditional public schools lacked discipline and that improved discipline would address many school-related problems. Vernon C. Polite's, "Getting the Job Done Well: African American Students in Catholic Schools," also appeared in this special issue. Among the positives of Catholic schools for African American students, Polite argued Catholic schools achieve high academic outcomes because they "closely resemble the ideal of the common school model" by educating diverse children." Catholic schools also developed close personal relationships with parents and sought to keep them involved in the school, and encouraged students to combat negative peer pressure.

The most recent works that highlight the themes of Catholic school effectiveness and agency are Ethel E. Young and Jerome Wilson's *African American Children and Missionary Nuns and Priests in Mississippi: Achievement Against Jim Crow Odds* and Robert McClory's, *From the Back of the Pews To the Head of the Class.* Young and Wilson's book offers insight into African American parental involvement and expectations of Catholic school education for their children in Meridian, Mississippi. Although the school ran from 1910 to 1975, the book focuses on the 1940s through the 1960s and the school's productivity in spite of a Jim Crow South.[104] McClory's book provides insight into a Black Catholic school founded as an elementary school in 1902 in Mobile, Alabama. The school added a high school curriculum in 1917. McClory's institutional biography interviewed former students, teachers and priests of Most Pure Heart of Mary, which ran for 51 years. The in-depth interviews provided reflections on segregation, desegregation, integration and civil rights. What they revealed most, however, were the great expectations the African American community had for the future of the children who attended the school. Alexis Herman, a Heart of Mary High School graduate and a former U.S. Secretary of Labor, wrote in the book's Foreword:

> Though the students were segregated with inferior resources, they were rich in talent, in community and the gifts of the Spirit.... Despite the odds and with the support and commitment of their teachers and the love and faith of their families and community, many Heart of Mary students rose to unimaginable heights. Many have gone on to become leaders in business, government, medicine, education, church, the military, the arts, and politics.[105]

Excerpts from the interviews with former Heart of Mary students and short biographical sketches of alumni at the end of the book gave life to Herman's comments on the expectations and accomplishments of school's students. While *African American Children and Missionary Nuns and Priests in Mississippi* and *From the Back of the Pews* are not historical accounts, Young and Wilson and McClory widen our understanding of the inner-workings of a Black Catholic school and deepen our understanding of African American education via those who lived the experience. McClory has aided researchers tremendously because of the extensive firsthand accounts and interviews conducted to draft the book. These personal testimonies are archived at Sinsinawa Dominican Motherhouse in Sinsinawa, Wisconsin and the University of South Alabama in Mobile.[106]

CONCLUSION AND IMPLICATIONS

The scholarship included in this historiographical essay is no doubt replete with data from diverse disciplines. From surveys and data sets to secondary sources from journal articles and books, these collective works definitely begin to fill an area of African American education and Catholic education history that has long been missing. However, what is still glaringly obvious is the lack of scholarship from non-religious and ecclesiastical scholars utilizing primary historical documents from Catholic archives. As mentioned at the beginning of this essay, York attributed the lack of information to a disinterested education community and few interested Catholic scholars; however, after conducting research for this historiography, one can firmly contend that the lack of information rests more so on limited access to data in the Catholic archives, and not from a lack of interest. The scholarship covered in this essay, especially since the mid-twentieth century, demonstrates African American scholars are interested in the history of African Americans in Catholic schools, but their interpretations are drawn mostly from secondary, not primary sources. Cyprian Davis' scholarship appears to be the only publication by an African American scholar that has utilized data from a rich variety of archives, including those at the Vatican in Rome, Italy.

So what are the implications for policy and future research? This essay began by noting the continued interest in Catholic schools for African American, Latina/o, and students living in poverty-stricken areas and the research reporting that the Catholic schools are more successful with these students. An historical understanding of what traditionally happened in Catholic schools concerning minorities will provide context to those findings. Those interested in researching African American Catholic educational histories will have to continuously request access to Catholic archives as they continuously search for primary data stored in former alumni's attics, basements, and closets. They will have to continue "visiting" alumni to conduct interviews about their experiences. While some will say no, others will surely say yes; but, immense patience is needed if a more definitive narrative will be crafted on the subject. Time is of the essence in this regard, however. Alumni, teachers, and administrators from the Black Catholic schools, especially those along the Gulf Coast and in the South that date back to the early twentieth century and closed during the 1970s and 1980s, are aging. When they are no longer available to us, we will only be left with the archives.

NOTES

1. Darlene Eleanor York, "The Academic Achievement of African Americans in Catholic Schools: A Review of the Literature," in *Growing Up African American*

in Catholic Schools, Jacqueline Jordan Irvine and Michele Foster, eds. (New York, NY: Teachers College Press, 1996),14–15.

2. A Catholic diocese is a territory led by a bishop. An archdiocese is a combination of territories making up a district, and led by an archbishop. A Catholic chancery can be either diocesan or archdiocesan and is the official and legal business office of the territory.

3. This has been the case for this researcher as I've collected historical data on Black Catholic schools for nearly 20 years.

4. V.P. Franklin, "Blacks in Urban Catholic Schools in the United States: A Historical Perspective," in *Visible Now: Blacks in Private Schools,* Diana T. Slaughter and Deborah J. Johnson, eds. (New York, NY: Greenwood Press), 99. Franklin also discussed Catholic schools for African Americans in V.P. Franklin, *The Education of Black Philadelphia: A Social and Educational History of a Minority Community, 1900–1950* (Philadelphia: University of Pennsylvania Press, 1979).

5. Paula Fass, *Outside In: Minorities and the Transformation of American Education* (New York, NY: Oxford University Press, 1991), 8.

6. Michele Foster, "Introduction," in *Growing Up African American in Catholic Schools,* Jacqueline Jordan Irvine and Michele Foster, eds. (New York, NY: Teachers College Press, 1998), 2.

7. James Cibulka, Timothy O'Brien and Donald Zewe, *Inner City Private Elementary Schools: A Study* (Milwaukee: Marquette University Press), 1982.

8. James Coleman, Thomas Hoffer and Sally Kilgore, *High School Achievement: Public and Private Schools* (New York, NY: Basics Books), 1982. See also James Coleman and Thomas Hoffer, *Public and Private High Schools: The Impact on Communities* (New York, NY: Basic Books), 1987.

9. Andrew Greeley, *Minority Students in Catholic Schools* (Piscataway, N.J.: Transaction Publishers), 2002.

10. The National Black Catholic Congress, 2010; James S. Coleman and Thomas Hoffer, *Public and Private High Schools: The Impact of Communities (New York, NY: Basic Books), 1987*; William N. Evans and Robert M. Schwab, "Finishing High School and Starting College: Do Catholic Schools Make a Difference?", The Quarterly Journal of Economics, 110, no. 4, (November, 1995): 941–974. 1995; Christo Rey website, http://www.cristoreynetwork.org/). Accessed 9/5/2011.

11. Christo Rey website, http://www.cristoreynetwork.org/.

12. Available data do not note the actual percentage of African American students or the actual percentage of African American students graduating from high school and attending college.

13. "Cristo Rey Network: History" http://www.cristoreynetwork.org/page.cfm?p=367 Accessed 9/23/14.

14. Data compiled at the following sites, www.cdom.org; www.bssf.net/schools; www.memphiseducation.org/meet-the-champions/jubliee-schools. Accessed 4/15/2014.

15. About NDAA," http://ace.nd.edu/academies/about-ndaa Accessed 9/23/2014

16. "We're closing the achievement gap", Notre Dame ACE Academies http://ace.nd.edu/files/ACE-NDAA/ndaaupdate-june13.pdf accessed 9/23/2014

17. I reviewed a number of historiographies in preparing this essay. Marybeth Gasman, "Swept under the Rug?: A Historiography of Gender and Black Colleges," *American Educational Research Journal* 44, no. 4 (December 2007): 760–805; Jana Nidiffer, "Poor Historiography: "The Poorest" in American Higher Education," *History of Education Quarterly* 39, no. 3 (Autumn 1999): 321–336; William J. Reese, "Essay on Sources," *America's Public Schools: From the Common School to "No Child Left Behind"*; Eileen Tamura, "Asian Americans in the History of Education: An Historiographical Essay," *History of Education Quarterly* 41, no. 1 (Spring 2001): 58–71.

18. For more on Catholic councils and synods see Neil G. McCluskey, S.J., ed. *Catholic Education in America: A Documentary History* (New York, NY: Teachers College Press, 1964).

19. Orders listed in a variety of works. M.F. Rouse. *A Study of the Development of Negro Education under Catholic Auspices in Maryland.* (Baltimore: Johns Hopkins Press, 1935); John T. Gillard, *Colored Catholics in the United States* (Baltimore: The Josephite Press, 1941); Cyprian Davis, *The History of Black Catholics in the United States* (New York, NY: Crossroad Publishing, 1990); Harold A. Buetow, *Of Singular Benefit: The Story of Catholic Education in the United States* (New York, NY: Macmillan, 1970). The Oblates Sisters of Providence, The Holy Family Sisters, and the Franciscan Handmaids of the Most Pure Heart of Mary were African American religious congregations.

20. Joseph Butsch, S.S.J., John LaFarge, S.J., John T. Gillard, S.S.J., Harold A. Buetow, and Albert Foley, S.J. were all priests. Catholic priests may be members of religious orders, institutes, or dioceses. All have specific ministerial purposes. The letters following a priest's name denotes his order or institute. For example, Butsch and Gillard were Josephites (S.S.J); LaFarge and Foley were Jesuits (S.J.); and Buetow was a diocesan priest for Brooklyn. Diocesan priests commit themselves to certain communities. Order affiliations taken from their works.

21. For more on slaveholding Catholic orders see Anna Blanche McGill, *The Sisters of Charity of Nazareth, Kentucky* (New York, NY: Encyclopedia Press, 1917); Madeleine Hook Rice, *American Catholic Opinion in the Slavery Controversy* (New York, NY: Columbia University Press, 1944); and Randall Miller and Jon Wakelyn, eds. *Catholic in the Old South* (Macon, GA: Mercer University Press, 1999).

22. Joseph Butsch, "Negro Catholics in the United States," *The Catholic Historical Review* 3, no. 1 (April 1917): 33–51.

23. Butsch, "Negro Catholics in the United States."

24. For more on Black Codes/*Code Noir* see Butsch, "Negro Catholics in the United States"; Also see, Rice, *American Catholic Opinion*; Miller and Wakelyn, *Catholic in the Old South.*

25. Joseph Butsch, "Catholics and the Negro," *Journal of Negro History* 2, no. 4 (October 1917): 393–410.

26. Rouse, *A Study of the Development of Negro.*

27. E.A. Clark, Review of *A Study of the Development of Negro Education under Catholic Auspices in Maryland* by M. F. Rouse in *The Journal of Negro Education* 5, no. 2 (April 1936): 269–270.

28. John LaFarge, S.J., *Interracial Justice* (New York, NY: American Press), 1937.

29. Benjamin E. Mays, "A Catholic's View of Race Relations" review of *Interracial Justice*, by John LaFarge. *The Journal of Negro Education* 6, no. 4 (October 1937): 631–634.

30. Ibid., 634.

31. *The Colored Harvest*, a publication from *The Josephites*, ran from 1888 to 1960. *The Negro and Indian Missions*, which were reports from the Bureau of Colored and Indian Missions, ran from 1926 to 1976.

32. *The Journal*, Philadelphia, PA., 9 July 1892. 1. Philadelphia Archdiocesan Historical Research Center, Wynnewood, PA.

33. Gillard, *Colored Catholics in the United States*.

34. See Marilyn W. Nickels, *Black Catholic Protest and the Federated Colored Catholics, 1917–1933*; (New York, NY: Garland, 1988); and Cyprian Davis, *The History of Black Catholics in the United States*, (New York, NY: Crossroad Publishing, 1990).

35. Gillard, *Colored Catholics in the United States*, 1.

36. Ibid.

37. Wm. Stuart Nelson, "Review of Colored Catholics in the United States," *Colored Catholics in the United States* by John T. Gillard, in *The Journal of Negro Education* 11, no. 1 (January 1942): 77–79.

38. Rice, *American Catholic Opinion in the Slavery Controversy*.

39. Ibid., 156.

40. William H. Lofton, "The Church and Slavery" review of *American Catholic Opinion in the Slavery Controversy* by Madeleine Hook Rice in *The Journal of Negro Education* 14, no. 1 (Winter 1945): 63–64.

41. For more on Vatican II see Walter M. Abbott, S.J., ed., *The Documents of Vatican II* (New York, NY: Herder and Herder Press, 1966); John W. O'Malley, *What Happened at Vatican II* (Cambridge, MA: Belknap Press, 2008).

42. Catholic priests may be ordained within a specific religious order, like the Josephites, or they may be ordained within a particular diocese to serve that diocese. Buetow was an ordered priest for the diocese of Brooklyn, New York.

43. Buetow, *Of Singular Benefit*, 206 quoting Gillard, *Colored Catholics in the United States*, 42–43.

44. Ibid.

45. Ibid., 65.

46. V.P. Franklin and Edward McDonald, "Blacks in Urban Catholic Schools in the United States: A Historical Perspective," in *Visible Now: Blacks in Private Schools*, Diana T. Slaughter and Deborah J. Johnson, eds. (New York, NY: Greenwood Press, 1988), 93-108.

47. Ibid.

48. Slaughter and Johnson, *Visible Now*.

49. V.P. Franklin, "First Came the School: Catholic Evangelization among African Americans in the United States, 1827 to the Present," in Jacqueline Jordan Irvine and Michele Foster, eds. *Growing up African American in Catholic Schools* (New York, NY: Teachers College Press,1998), 47–60.

50. Glen R. Conrad, et al., *Cross, Crozier, and Crucible: A Volume Celebrating the Bicentennial of a Catholic Diocese in Louisiana* (New Orleans: Archdiocese of New Orleans, 1993).

51. Joan Marie Aycock, "The Ursuline School in New Orleans, 1727–1771," in *Cross, Crozier, and Crucible*, 203–218.

52. Sally K. Reeves, "The Society of the Sacred Heart in New Orleans," in *Cross, Crozier, and Crucible*, 219–232.

53. Patricia Lynch, "Mother Katharine Drexel's Rural Schools: Education and Evangelization through Lay Leadership," in *Cross, Crozier, and Crucible*, 262–274. Two other chapters in *Cross, Crozier and Crucible* also bear note and were not included because of space limitations. See James N. Grahmann, "The Christian Brothers in Louisiana," 275–288; and James G. Dauphine, "Catholic Education in North Louisiana: The Pre-World War One Foundation of Catholic Life in a Southern Dioces," 289–304.

54. "Three Catholic Afro-American Congresses," 94–104, in *The History of Black Catholics in the United States*, Cyprian Davis, ed., (New York, NY: Crossroad Publishing, 1990), 174.

55. Davis, *The History of Black Catholics in the United States*, 220. The Federated Colored Catholic developed from an earlier group, The Committee for the Advancement of Colored Catholics. See Nickels, *Black Catholic Protest* for more information on the FCC.

56. David Spalding, "The Negro Catholic Congresses, 1889–1894," *The Catholic Historical Review* 55, no. 3 (October 1969): 337–357.

57. Ibid., 339.

58. Albert J. Raboteau, "Black Catholics and Afro-American Religious History: Autobiographic Reflections," *U.S. Catholic Historian* 5, no. 1 (1986): 119–127.

59. Ibid., 126.

60. Marilyn W. Nickels, "Thomas Wyatt Turner and the Federated Colored Catholics," *U.S. Catholic Historian* 7, no. 2/3, Special Issue: The Black Catholic Community, 1880–1987 (Spring-Summer 1988): 215–232.

61. Nickels, *Black Catholic Protest*.

62. Davis, *History of Black Catholics*, 175.

63. *Three Catholic Afro-American Congresses*, 176.

64. Ibid., 175.

65. Ibid.

66. Moore, *A Brilliant Possibility: The Cardinal Gibbons Institute, 1924–1934 (PhD dissertation*, University of Virginia, 1997).

67. Ibid.

68. Ibid., 4.

69. Ibid.

70. Morris J. MacGregor, *The Emergence of a Black Catholic Community: St. Augustine's in Washington* (Washington, D.C.: Catholic University, 1999).

71. Ibid.

72. Donna Porche-Frilot, "Propelled by Faith: Henriette Delille and the Literacy Practices of Black Women Religious in Antebellum New Orleans," (PhD dissertation, Louisiana State University and Agricultural & Mechanical College, 2006). Note that when I went to order Porche-Frilot's dissertation at the Pro Quest Dissertation and Thesis site on 1 May 2014, the site noted the dissertation was no longer available for viewing or purchasing.

73. Uncommon Faithfulness: The Witness of African American Catholics conference was held at Notre Dame University, 11–13 March 2004.

74. Cecilia A. Moore, "Dealing with Desegregation: Black and White Responses to the Desegregation of the Diocese of Raleigh, North Carolina, 1953," in *Uncommon Faithfulness: The Black Catholic Experience*, M. Shawn Copeland, LaReine-Marie Mosely, S.N.D. and Albert J. Raboteau, eds., (Maryknoll, NY: Orbis Books, 2009), 63–77.

75. Ibid., 73.

76. Katrina M. Sanders, "Black Catholic Clergy and the Struggle for Civil Rights: Winds of Change," in *Uncommon Faithfulness: The Black Catholic Experience*, M. Shawn Copeland, LaReine-Marie Mosely, S.N.D. and Albert J. Raboteau, eds., (Maryknoll, NY: Orbis Books, 2009), 78–93.

77. Ibid., 83.

78. Ibid., 78–93.

79. Diana L. Hayes, "Faith of Our Mothers: Catholic Womanist God-Talk," in *Uncommon Faithfulness: The Black Catholic Experience*, M. Shawn Copeland, LaReine-Marie Mosely, S.N.D. and Albert J. Raboteau, eds., (Maryknoll, NY: Orbis Books, 2009), 129–146.

80. Ibid., 145.

81. Ibid., 144–145.

82. William A. Osborne, *The Segregated Covenant: Race Relations and American Catholics* (New York, NY: Herder and Herder, 1967).

83. Ibid., 233.

84. Ibid.

85. Martin A. Zielinski, "Working for Interracial Justice: The Catholic Interracial Council of New York, 1934–1964," *U.S. Catholic Historian* 7, no. 2/3, Special Issue: The Black Catholic Community, 1880–1987 (Spring-Summer, 1988): 233–262.

86. Stephen J. Ochs, *Desegregating the Altar: Josephites and the Struggle for Black Priests, 1871–1960* (Baton Rouge: Louisiana State University Press, 1990).

87. Ochs, *Desegregating the Altar*.

88. John B. Alberts, "Black Catholic Schools: The Josephite Parishes During the Jim Crow Era," *U.S. Catholic Historian* 12, no. 1 (Winter 1994): 80.

89. Ibid., 80–82.

90. Ibid., 84.

91. John T. McGreevy, *Parish Boundaries: The Catholic Encounter with Race in the Twentieth-Century Urban North* (Chicago: The University of Chicago Press, 1996).

92. Ibid.

93. R. Bentley Anderson, *Black, White, and Catholic: New Orleans Interracialism, 1947–1956* (Nashville: Vanderbilt University Press, 2005).

94. Ibid. Norman Francis would go on to serve as president of Xavier University of Louisiana from 1968 to 2015.

95. Osborne, *Segregated Covenant*, 140–141.

96. Ibid.

97. Ibid., 141.

98. Franklin and McDonald, "Blacks in Urban Catholic Schools in the United States," 99.

99. Mary Lynch Barnds, "Black Students in Low-Income Serving Catholic High Schools: An Overview of Findings from the 1986 National Catholic Educational Association Study," in *Visible Now: Blacks in Private Schools*, Diana T. Slaughter and Deborah J. Johnson, eds. (New York, NY: Greenwood Press, 1988), 123–142.

100. McGreevy, *Parish Boundaries*.

101. Ibid., 242.

102. Sandra N. Smith, "Parochial Schools in the Black Cities," *The Journal of Negro Education* 42, no. 3 (Summer 1973): 370–391.

103. Theresa A. Rector, "Black Nuns as Educators," in *The Journal of Negro Education*, 51, no. 3 (Summer 1982): 238–253; Portia H. Shields, "Holy Angels: Pocket of Excellence," *The Journal of Negro Education*, 58, no. 2 (Spring, 1989): 203–211.

104. Ethel E. Young and Jerome Wilson, *African American Children and Missionary Nuns and Priests in Mississippi: Achievement against Jim Crow Odds* (Bloomington, IN: AuthorHouse, 2010).

105. Alexis Herman, "Introduction," in *From the Back of the Pews to the Head of the Class*, Robert McClory, ed. (Chicago: ACTA Publications, 2013).

106. McClory, *From the Back of the Pews to the Head of the Class* (Chicago: ACTA Publications, 2013), 174. I should note that McClory wrote the tapes and transcripts are for scholarly use "as deemed appropriate by archivists." As I stated early in this essay, records relating to Black Catholic education are usually housed in Catholic archives and may not be easily accessible.

PART II

EDUCATION IN THE TWENTIETH CENTURY

CHAPTER 4

NEW PERSPECTIVES ON PROGRESSIVE EDUCATION

HBCU Lab High Schools during Jim Crow

Sharon G. Pierson
Ramapo College of New Jersey

Quiester Craig squared his 12 year-old shoulders, stole a glance at his co-presenter, Jessica Pettus, and readied himself for his part in the 1949 laboratory school commencement program. He looked out among the scores of students, parents, teachers, and professors and began: "I am proud to be a Negro."[1] Every fiber of his being felt the honor of having been selected to recite the poem—a privilege which Craig remembers to this day. A scholarship student at "Lab High," Craig's education at the Alabama State College Laboratory High School gave him the foundation to excel, and that he did. By his junior year he was accepted at Morehouse College on a full scholarship; his education and career continued to climb. Six decades later, Dr. Craig celebrated his retirement as Dean of the School of Business and Economics at North Carolina A&T State University, where more than one thousand professional colleagues and personal friends from across the nation gathered in tribute to his substantial contributions to educational

Using Past as Prologue, pages 87–116
Copyright © 2015 by Information Age Publishing
All rights of reproduction in any form reserved.

progress. Today at seventy-six, the 6'4" former Lab High student leaned forward, intensifying his message, conveying import and purpose, "At Lab High, we were taught to be change agents," he declared.[2]

As Craig and other lab school graduates reflected on their education at Lab High, they noted the absence of "forward thinking" laboratory schools in historical accounts of all-Black schooling in the Deep South. Reflecting on the need to add to our histories the kind of education one receives at a laboratory school, Leonard L. Haynes, III, Senior Director, Institutional Services Postsecondary Education, U.S. Department of Education, and former graduate of Southern University Laboratory High School, shared the "fact" that laboratory schools, such as Southern's were "superior, not inferior."[3] Haynes, recipient of the Congressional Minority Business 'HBCU/MI Leadership Award,' and recognized as a "Game Changer" in 2011, admitted, "When I was in high school, I had contempt for White schools. They didn't measure up to our lab school education."[4] These fully accredited laboratory high schools situated on the campuses of historically Black colleges and universities (HBCUs) were, "highly respected," reform-minded, "prestigious" high schools where students were expected to "keep up" with a rigorous college preparatory curriculum, while at the same time, learn about and celebrate their African American heritage through in-class cultural and literary studies.[5] Challenging the absence of laboratory high schools in historical accounts, Georgette Norman, Director of the Rosa Parks Museum and Alabama State College Laboratory High School Valedictorian, asked, "Where is our history?"[6]

HBCU laboratory high schools were unique educational institutions and their history contributes new historical perspectives on African American education during the era of Jim Crow. Lab schools played an important role in advancing secondary schooling, serving as models of success, not only as schools in which teaching and learning reached high standards set by regional accrediting associations, but also as schools that established a clear bridge to higher educational attainment. An historical analysis of laboratory schools also contributes new perspectives on progressive schooling in the South. Positioned at "the heart" of the college or university campus, these HBCU lab schools were "so situated as to influence the development of other schools."[7]

Classifying HBCU "laboratory schools" is similar to the complicated classification of historically Black colleges and universities themselves. The history of each HBCU lab high school is inexorably tied to the history of its host college or university. Created to educate African Americans during an ethos of overt racism, HBCUs have collectively been categorized as institutions sharing striking characteristics, yet each has an individual history and culture.[8] So, too, is the case for HBCU laboratory high schools. At once, the history of these lab high schools reveals common distinguishing features, and yet each carries its own distinctive traditions, practices, and historical narrative.

During the progressive era, some of these "laboratories of learning" evolved from the original "model," "demonstration" or "practice" schools which were integral to the teacher training institution, as in the case of Alabama State College Laboratory High School, Montgomery, Alabama; while others were formalized during the progressive education movement, as in the case of Atlanta University Laboratory High School, Atlanta, Georgia. This research highlights the HBCU laboratory high schools which were described in the period as "forward thinking," "progressive," and "influential": Alabama State College Laboratory High School, Montgomery, Alabama; Atlanta University Laboratory High School, Atlanta, Georgia; Southern University and Agricultural and Mechanical College Demonstration School, Scotlandville, Louisiana; and D. Webster Davis Laboratory School of Virginia State College for Negroes, Ettrick, Virginia.[9] The histories of these lab schools share common characteristics. Located on an HBCU campus, they were part of the institution's teaching program while also functioning as independent high schools. They participated in the progressive national Secondary School Study for Negroes and were perceived by contemporary students and educators as having an "excellent" college preparatory curriculum with well trained and educated faculty.[10]

Blending the traditional methods of historical research with the testimonies of those who lived this history, this qualitative study captures a more complicated portrait of African American educational history in the era of Jim Crow. Carol D. Lee posits in *Black Education: A Transformative Research and Action Agenda for the New Century* "that it is through everyday practices and institutional social structures ... in African American communities that [the] nexus of interrelated cultural models or belief systems are constructed."[11] The dynamics of those everyday practices and social structures are brought into view through oral histories, which well-nourished this research. Contemporary and contemporaneous scholarship on the development of secondary education for African Americans was analyzed, as well as case studies of "valued" community schooling, studies of "progressive" schooling, and analyses of the expansion of secondary education in the South. More than fifty interviews with former lab school students and teachers were conducted by the author, and multiple state, university, and private archival collections were mined for primary sources, such as school records, accreditation reports, correspondence, newsletters, guidance books, photographs, and the like. These data reveal that these teaching laboratories not only prepared African American teachers for educating America's youth in an increasingly complex world, but also thoroughly prepared its high school students to successfully enter and manage college-level curricula.

Hundreds of historical narratives have captured the plight of African Americans educated under the regime of legal segregation in the South. Reporting on their consequent disadvantage of underfunded schooling and oppressively proscribed and unequal curricula, secondary education was often characterized by ill-trained teachers, narrow curricular offerings, insufficient materials, limited facilities, and impoverished school buildings. For years, *Best Test Preparation for the AP United States History Exam* has provided thousands of high school students an apologetic, succinct description of education for African Americans in the first half of the twentieth century, stating that, "Sadly, most education facilities for Black children were anything but equal. Blacks usually got dilapidated facilities, the worst teachers, and inferior education."[12] While that history lesson has a thick thread of truth, it does not capture the richer, more complex historical narrative that includes the "outstanding quality education ... offered by the laboratory school[s]" and recognized in the period for demonstrating the "best American educational practices."[13]

Among the contributions of scholarly works, Faustine Jones, Vanessa Siddle Walker, Vivian and Curtis Morris, and Sonya Ramsey, among others have added to the historical narrative, writing about their own community schools, presenting studies of academic achievement, "community-valued" schooling, and schools that provided "caring and nurturing environments."[14] More recently, two broad studies were published that addressed the history of African American secondary schools and the preparation of America's teachers, the latter dedicating a chapter to "Preparing African American Teachers in the Segregated South."[15] In both of these surveys the important contribution (or existence) of HBCU laboratory high schools that influenced thousands of teachers and students was missed. Moreover, when historical narrative called for an example of a "teaching school," once again, the oft cited Hampton-Tuskegee model was highlighted instead of Alabama State Teachers College, the largest teacher institution that granted more Rank I teacher certificates to African American teachers than any other institution in Alabama and among the highest producer of certified teachers in the South.[16]

In other words, this research is not about bringing to light another case study of a well-regarded community school that embraced a liberal arts curriculum (although, such important case studies are still called for). It aims to present evidence of the historical importance of these "laboratories of learning" as distinctive contributors to the advancement of education for African Americans through their "pioneering" and "innovative" approaches to educational achievement.[17]

PROGRESS LABORATORIES OF LEARNING

As the nation entered the twentieth century, leading educators were fervently engaged in improving their progressive educational theories, wrestling with which type of educational system and pedagogical approach might best address the nation's diverse citizenry, fulfill America's promise and serve its future. Philosophical and methodological approaches to creating the most effective public school system were almost as diverse as the citizens they were designed to educate. As renowned historian David Tyack concluded, even into the twentieth century, it was evident that there was not "one best system," and as methods were applied to actual classrooms, competing theories overlapped and, occasionally, actually contradicted one another.[18]

Against the backdrop of transformative scientific discoveries and technological inventions, there seemed to be universal agreement that education was the key to social progress. Men and women such as John Dewey, Jane Addams, William H. Kilpatrick, George Counts, and Harold Rugg grappled with theories of progressive educational reform. So, too, did African American progressive education leaders such as W. E. B. Du Bois, John Hope, Carter Woodson, W.A. Robinson, George W. Trenholm, and H. Councill Trenholm, among other lesser known African American reformers.

Attempting to nail down an accurate definition for the term "progressive education" conjured well-supported debate, Lawrence Cremin noted in the introduction to his monumental study *The Transformation of the Schools*.[19] In its simplest form it could be characterized by the notion of reform, and in the case of African American education, reform aimed at challenging a subordinate position in a dual society.[20]

Progressive education for Southern Blacks echoed the malleability of the Progressive education era, as the laboratory high school directors molded their own curricular ideologies. The social reconstructionist ideas of democracy, emanating from the most prominent leaders in education, provided African American educators a welcome mantle in which to clothe their initiatives for educational advancement.[21] It offered Black educators public entry into discussions of recognition, equity, and fairer historical portrayals of African American contributions to American society, one that reflected the nation's public cry for democratic change. As William A. Robinson, Atlanta University Laboratory High School director, declared, progressive education had "set up the tenets of democracy as the guiding principles of the education for *all* people."[22]

African American laboratory school leaders believed there was a "source of new hope for a better day in social thinking."[23] For example, as director of the Alabama State College Laboratory High School, H. C. Trenholm had long encouraged the pedagogical approaches that readied his students to be future leaders and activists in a society that proclaimed, but often failed to practice, democracy.[24] Through a combination of building strategic alliances, collaborating with other reform-minded educators, conducting research projects, and taking advantage of opportunities to attend and participate in national education workshops and studies, "a new age of collectivism" emerged as African American educators seized the opportunity to position their laboratory high schools as centers of influence for Southern Black education.[25] "Progressive education," proclaimed lab school director Robinson, had "already begun the task of reemphasizing and reinterpreting the democratic way of life."[26]

While "democratic rhetoric permeated educational literature and the position papers of the National Education Association," Black leaders of laboratory schools, such as Robinson, Trenholm, John W. Davis, and John F. Gandy, donned the cloak of democracy and carefully advanced their position in the Deep South.[27] Aaron Brown noted in his evaluation of accredited Black secondary schools that laboratory high school directors accepted the "obligation to assume a leadership" role in curricular reform, advancing high school education.[28] This is to say, these educators molded their own approaches to teaching and curriculum, grounded in sound progressive educational theory.

To date, historical accounts that have highlighted progressive high schools have not included examples of all-Black segregated schools in the South. There seems to be a contradictory stance that African American educators who adopted progressive theories championed by renowned White progressive educators while holding fast to their commitment to a liberal arts college preparatory education were not original in their thinking and thus have not been included as examples of "progressive" schools; whereas, other schools that adopted a blend of these same theories have long since been a part of the progressive conversation.[29] Historian Ronald Goodenow noted that laboratory high schools such as those at Alabama State College, Atlanta University, and Virginia State College, to name a few, "advocated progressive education's methodology and theory" and the associated "prime virtues" of "democratic philosophy;" yet, "even though black journals contained innumerable references to it," the work of these Black progressives was "totally ignored" by academe at large.[30]

Qualities of "progressive" education have commonly included such characteristics as experiential learning, problem solving and critical thinking, lifelong learning and social skills, project oriented collaborative and cooperative learning, consideration of the needs of the community, and, perhaps most central, democratic teaching and learning for social responsibility. Research brings to light that these qualities were evident in a number of HBCU laboratory high schools.[31]

HBCU LABORATORY HIGH SCHOOLS:
STRATEGICALLY POSITIONED TO INFLUENCE REFORM

HBCU laboratory schools "held strategic places" in education for African Americans and were among the schools which "exercise[ed] wide influence on secondary schools."[32] In 1940, in the era of controlled curriculum experimentation, President of Fisk University, Thomas Elsa Jones, described the laboratory high schools—among the selected high schools of the influential Secondary School Study for Negroes—as "pioneers" in education; their administrators represented among "the most promising . . . Negro educational leaders" in the South.[33] For the student-teachers who came through the school as part of their core program, the teachers and principals from other schools who visited as part of workshops, and for the lab school pupils themselves, these schools served their mission to educate at the highest level and inspire emulation and achievement. Among the leaders in education, HBCU laboratory high schools accepted the responsibility "to influence" other schools in the state, region, and nation.[34]

One common characteristic that made these lab high schools particularly extraordinary was their setting. Positioned on the college or university campus, lab school students could take advantage of the expanded educational services within arms-reach. While lab schools were not exempt from the documented history of decades of unequal funding for White and Black segregated schools, the profile of lab high schools did not reflect the commonly reported meager facilities of the all-Black segregated community high schools.[35] This was especially advantageous given Jim Crow laws which often prohibited African Americans from using community recreation and sports facilities. For example, at Alabama State College Laboratory High School, students who demonstrated and expressed proficiency and interest in pursuing extended study in science, foreign language, or music, beyond that which was required as part of the core high school curriculum, were able to seek additional tutelage from the college professors.[36] Access also translated to use of facilities, such as the college library, music room, Olympic-sized pool, and gymnasium.[37] "Since we were associated with the university, we had certain privileges," recalled a former lab school student from Virginia State College; "every year we staged an operetta that served as a unifying element for the curriculum."[38] "We would use the University library and see educational films," offered another lab high school graduate.[39] Moreover, because laboratory high schools were part of a teachers college, they largely escaped the scrutiny of the typically racist all-White community boards of education. Proximity to White school board members was distant, both geographically and in the fact that the laboratory school was a "protected" school within a higher education institution.[40]

In this protected environment lab school students benefitted from the cultural environment of being schooled among college students, learning in a well-supported and intellectually nurturing environment.[41] "Being among college students added so much for our education," recalled a 1940s D. W. Davis Laboratory High School graduate.[42] Parents of Lab High students "bought into" the notion that the classrooms were "learning laboratories.[43] This meant that Lab High families supported the concept of not only maintaining an open mind to approaches to teaching and learning, but expected reform-minded classroom experiences. "We were considered a 'progressive' school at the time, stated an Atlanta University Lab High graduate.[44] "Our parents" expressed respect and support for the Laboratory School, which, in their view, provided the rare opportunity for "outstanding" and "quality education."[45] They understood that student teachers were part of the classroom experiences and different methods of teaching would be explored and studied by others.[46]

Students were expected to demonstrate consistent dedication to school as seen in such behaviors as regular attendance, engagement in classroom activities, and responsible homework performance and practices.[47] "You had no doubt that you were a part of a bigger community and you were expected to live up to [the ideals] of that community," declared Kathy Jackson a former Lab High graduate who went on to earn her doctorate and enjoy a career as a college professor.[48] Jackson reflected on the absence of educational experiences at laboratory schools in the historical narrative. Working outside of the South, Jackson was often met with utterances of "poor dear" when she revealed that she was educated in the Jim Crow South. "The assumption was that I had a terrible education. I had a great education," Jackson stated; "I was very privileged" to "go to school at Lab High."[49] The description of a "privileged education" was a common theme among the former HBCU laboratory school students. "We had" the opportunity to go to school "on a college campus and learn from the best teachers," stated former Atlanta University lab student, Rose Palmer, who went on to earn her BA from Smith College and MBA from Stanford University, "it was a privilege," and recognized at the time.[50]

Perhaps most importantly, attending an accredited lab high school was a virtual guarantee that one would go on to earn a college degree. Of the more than fifty interviews conducted with former laboratory school graduates (Alabama, Georgia, and Louisiana), to a person, each stated that graduating from high school was a certainty and entering and succeeding in college was a given.[51] Highlighting the Alabama State College Laboratory High School as an example of laboratory schools' pattern of high graduation rates, it is illuminating to examine the *Historical Statistics of the United States* for graduation rates of White students in a side-by-side comparison to those of ASC Lab High in Table 4.1.

These data may be compared further by looking at the graduation and college entrance statistics for the "highly thought of" local, segregated all-White public schools. Robert E. Lee High School reported 41 percent of its 1958 graduating class expressed intentions to enter college, with an additional 10 percent indicating interest in attending a professional or business school.[52] "The Million Dollar" Sidney Lanier High School reported that

TABLE 4.1 Comparison of Years of School National Census of Persons Ages 25 and Older by Race—1960 and ASC Laboratory School Seniors—1952

	High School 4 years	College 1 to 3 years
Lab School Students	100%	81.8%
National Census "Negro and Other" Students	12.1%	8.8%
National Census White Students	51.4%	18.6%

for the graduating class of 1950, 54.8 percent indicated intentions to enter college, with an additional 2.9 percent expressing interest in enrolling in a professional or business school.[53] This may be compared to the 1952 findings for Alabama State College Lab High of 100 percent of its students intending to enroll in higher education: approximately 80 percent in a four year degree-granting college or university and approximately 20 percent in a "professional" higher education institution.[54]

An evaluation of academic achievement as measured by graduation rate and college entrance statistics clearly distinguished Montgomery's Lab High from schools for African Americans described in most historical accounts of Black secondary schooling during this period. Lab High's characteristic of high graduation and college enrollment rates validated the recollections of former students who praised the academic excellence of their laboratory school education and its college preparatory curricula. Alfred C. Henry, a physics teacher who started teaching at the laboratory school in 1943, remarked about the strength of the curriculum: "Our graduates never had to take remedial classes when they went to college," he stated, which had been a common occurrence for Black students coming from the Black public schools.[55]

Another characteristic of HBCU laboratory high schools that further speaks to its sphere of influence was the students' opportunity to be exposed to and inspired by the intellectual debates and presentations that occurred on many campuses. While inspired by the national "lyceum movement" of the nineteenth century, largely dedicated to (White) adult education, the lyceums held on HBCU campuses in the twentieth were an answer to a segregated South. In a hostile environment where Black higher education, intellectualism, and advanced learning were frowned upon, the privacy of the Black college campuses allowed unpopular messages and messengers a safe venue for "extracurricular" educational enrichment. Over the decades, HBCUs served as hosts for lyceums which provided a public venue for such "celebrities" as Mary McLeod Bethune, E. Franklin Frazier, and Adam Clayton Powell.[56] High school students were expected to attend lyceums and, on some campuses, Lab School students enjoyed "front row" seating.[57] As young members of "this larger university community," former Southern University lab high school student Dorothy Lee Early Davis reflected, the "Lab School students were part of and expos[ed] to … many cultural events and activities of the university."[58]

As part of a higher education institution, unlike a singular community school, the laboratory schools were under the supervision of the college or university president.[59] Accordingly, as leaders of HBCUs, these African American intellectuals held consortia for other principals and presidents, hosted workshops for HBCU and community teachers, and generated scholarly articles and research for and about African Americans.[60] Furthermore, these educators personally hosted professional colleagues, exchanging ideas in less formal gatherings.[61]

An integral part of a teacher education program, the laboratory school's liberal arts curriculum was designed to demonstrate "best practices" in curriculum and teaching.[62] It was not uncommon for the majority of its full time teachers to hold master's degrees, often having earned these degrees at prestigious universities.[63] Intended as a laboratory for teaching and learning, lab school teachers and principals were open to exploration and self-evaluation, employing methods learned at nationally renowned institutions such as Teachers College, Columbia University; New York University, Ohio State University, and the University of Chicago.[64] As members of the Secondary School Study for Negroes, also known as the Black High School Study, lab schools evidenced "an intelligent approach to educational problems" and a promise to enthusiastically commit to welcoming experimentation and, if deemed appropriate, embrace reconstruction of their curriculum and teaching methods.[65]

LABORATORY SCHOOLS' COMMITMENT TO EXPERIMENTATION AND REFORM

"Find[ing] teachers who are themselves capable of assuming the experimental attitude," John Dewey asserted in "Experiment in Education," was "the most difficult single condition to realize."[66] And, yet, archival data reveal lab schools' active engagement in curricular and collaborative experimentation in math, science, literature, social studies, and guidance. African American lab school teachers and students living and learning in a segregated society consciously addressed the complicated and peculiar place of African Americans as they endeavored to achieve full democratic citizenship within the contradictory social policies of the South and nation.67 This "meant that Black experimentation would be geared to the economic, social, and political reality for Blacks of that time period."[68]

C. M. Colson, principal of Virginia State College's lab high school, conveyed his commitment to experimentation and reform at the "Proceedings of the Secondary School Study Conference, November 30—December 2, 1942." Colson reported of his lab school's "modifications in such things as teacher practices, administrative policies, curriculum offerings, [and] school and community relationships." Included in the conference was "definite evidence of how these modifications [had] brought about improvements." These included "new courses or new content in old courses ... improvements in teaching techniques, effective guidance practices [and] ... school-community relationships."[69] Among the progressive approaches of Virginia State's lab high school was its "long-term planning for school development." It framed the teacher and student as "collaborators" in curriculum development, "understanding the influence of home, school, environment, and physical and emotional health [on] the adolescent."[70]

In 1945, New York University professor, Lou LaBrant reported on the six week intensive workshop that NYU hosted for African American English teachers; among the small cohort of eleven were teachers from Alabama State Teachers College, Southern University, and Virginia State College. In addition to attending "a regularly assigned classroom," listening to "morning lectures," observing the "experimental Negro theatre in Harlem," and spending "some time at the Schomburg collection," the teachers worked together in a learning "laboratory where an abundance of pamphlets and books and illustrative materials were at their disposal." This was intended to encourage experimentation and leadership among the participants. LaBrant, noted that the high school teachers, "were among the most promising [he had] met in the English field."[71]

Known for its "academic excellence," the laboratory high school at Atlanta University graduated some of the nation's prominent Black leaders.[72] It was recognized among African American educators nationally, and by schoolmen and community members regionally, as a progressive laboratory of learning. It implemented educational methods that were grounded in scientific study used to guide students toward self-expression. The lab school served as a frequent host for visiting educators from other districts and states. Among its leading-edge methodologies was its progressive approach to evaluating students' achievements where students' performance evaluations did not rely on letter grades, but, instead, used detailed written assessments.[73] It was not uncommon for college presidents, after having visited the laboratory high school, to request permission to send their teachers for further observation.[74]

Alabama State College Lab High's Principal, T. A. Love, working with lab school principals W. D. Gray and C. M. Colson from Talladega College and Virginia State College, respectively, explored curriculum reform that would "discover and take account through the educative process the additional needs of Negro children in the social setting of American life … to find out what is involved in democratic living."[75] Considered to be "one of the most pressing needs of the schools [was] help in planning a curriculum" that provided "for more realistic teaching in science and social studies."[76] Investigation included provocative questions that challenged the perceptions and role of African Americans in science, politics, social science, and the economy from a historical perspective and in contemporary society. Such "problems" to be explored included: "Does the Negro's racial inheritance incapacitate him for significant achievement in a world civilization?" "How is the effort of the Negro to achieve security in the American social order related to the efforts of other minority groups?" and "Can participation by the Negro in labor organizations result in desirable improvement in his social, economic, and political position?"[77] These were courageous questions coming from high school teachers and administrators located in the Jim Crow South.[78]

Inspired by the "discontent about the American economic and social system," the pedagogical theory of "social reconstructionism," championed by Harold Rugg and George Counts of Teachers College, Columbia University, was aimed at preparing students to grapple with the preponderance of social injustices by persistently and responsibly challenging ideals of democracy in American society.[79] Archival evidence shows that theories adapted from these distinguished educators, among other esteemed scholars, such as W. E. B. Du Bois, Carter G. Woodson, and John Dewey, were woven throughout lab schools' curricula.

Curriculum at Alabama State College Lab High reflected a social reconstructionist methodology.[80] The culture of the school was captured in the statement of educational philosophy, as establishing a "mode of social life" that cultivated individual intellectual discovery and personal self-realization within a democratic classroom.[81] The lab school's social studies text, *The Challenge of Democracy,* was a text that enjoyed a strong circulation in high school social studies classes across the nation, although was not used in Alabama public schools. *The Challenge of Democracy* received rave reviews by *The School Review,* which called it "an outstanding textbook in American problems."[82] It was organized in twelve units, thirty-five chapters, and "probed the areas of sociology, economics, and government."[83] The book was written to problematize concepts and ideals of building a democracy. Chapters were written to attract teens' perspectives with titles such as "You and Your Problems" and "Youth Faces Problems of Democratic Society." The opening lines of the latter chapter challenged the very core of Southern White supremacy: "One of the most dangerous doctrines let loose in the modern world is that of racial superiority … The Ku Klux Klan … appeal[s] to the ignorant, the disgruntled, the low-income groups, and the unemployed."[84] This was not a book that couched the challenges of democracy in patriotic lore. It confronted such societal issues as prejudice, fear, economic instability, and oppression head on.

In short, Lab High students were encouraged to actively engage in their democratic society in an effort to develop pathways for change, for the betterment of themselves, their race, and their country.[85] These topics, methodologies, lesson plans, and the like, directly reached over "one hundred Black secondary schools" in a "cooperative attempt to upgrade their programs."[86]

Accepting a leadership role in education, laboratory high schools at such schools as Alabama State Teachers College, Atlanta University Lab High, Southern University, Talladega College, and Virginia State College, consciously undertook responsibility "to influence" other schools in the state, region, and nation.[87] They aimed to develop respect, appreciation, and responsibility for creative collaboration, not only with other HBCUs and all-Black segregated community schools, but also with secondary and higher education institutions throughout the nation.[88] Fred McCuistion of the General Education Board noted that the schools' reformist work would ultimately "improve living through secondary education" and offer "hope" for "improved programs" to African Americans throughout the South.[89]

Leaders of lab schools pioneered educational collaboration among their respective schools, communities, and broader constituency—as participants in workshops held at leading graduate programs in education, collaborators with fellow lab schools in curriculum exploration, or hosts of hands-on workshops for study participants and community educators. In Cynthia Gibson Hardy's PhD dissertation of the Black High School Study, she concluded that "these faculties organized educational procedures and content to incorporate innovative yet useful procedures to educate the Southern Regions' Black secondary school student." They were consciously committed to influencing and advancing educational reform.

RETHINKING PERSPECTIVE

Writing more than fifty years ago, Edgar Knight offered a timeless observation: "Education history, if properly understood, gives the educational past of any community, state or region meaning for the educational present and future."[90] Knight's reflection was part of his evaluation of the "economic, political and social influences in education" for African Americans. His caveat, "if properly understood," begs the question of perspective and the importance of considering the historical context in the analyses. In a 1934 study entitled The Control of State-Supported Teacher-Training Programs for Negroes, Felton Clark observed that laboratory schools in teacher training institutions were excluded from most research studies due to "ignorance [of] or indifference to" these programs' achievements.[91] Consequently, the growing impact of these schools, and the progressive teaching methods practiced in them, were not recognized or simply ignored by White educational leaders of the period.

W. A. Robinson, principal of Atlanta University Laboratory High School, Director of the Secondary School Study of the Association of Colleges and Secondary Schools for Negroes, and President of the National Association of Teachers in Colored Schools (1926–28) asserted that "it was quite understandable that the Negro high school was so frequently not taken into account at the outset."[92] While several of the teacher training institutions had developed laboratory schools that kept up with the latest trends in teaching and curriculum, "the so-called 'Tuskegee Idea,'" Robinson stated, was perceived as the "definite philosophy with regard to the education of Negroes," largely based on the "rather strong belief in the inferior intellectual equipment of the Negro masses." [93]

This is not to say that, as some scholars have argued, where progressive educators failed to remake society through the school, the laboratory school directors succeeded.[94] It is to argue that laboratory high schools were far from being "underdeveloped," "deplorable," or an "embarrassment."[95] The laboratory school directors "agreed that one of their purposes was the provision of the best type of educational experiences for pupils."[96] They were forward-thinking, reform-minded challengers of the contemporary models of Black education, committed to exploration, experimentation, and self-evaluation, and dedicated to preparing students to enter college.[97] They "studied the ideas of" leading educators and fashioned their own progressive approach that addressed their lived experiences.[98]

Robinson observed that "the South fairly generally assumed that the Negro high school, whatever it was, bore little resemblance to similar institutions for white children."[99] Similarly, in 1928, William Brewer claimed that the Jesse Jones *Negro Education Study* had been based on preconceived assumptions and set out to "substantiate those assumptions," resulting in many inaccuracies. Typical of the era, African Americans "were isolated from the mainstream of American research and scholarship, [and] their data were ignored" in national educational journals.[100]

The absence of positive portraits of education during the era of legal segregation was also noted by James A. Banks, professor of education and director of the Center for Multicultural Education at the University of Washington. "The mainstream academic community and its journal editors had little interest in research and work on communities of color prior to the 1960s," Banks argued, "especially work that presented positive descriptions of minority communities ... that was oppositional to mainstream racist scholarship."[101] Even more troublesome, he noted, was the fact that "student after student has been content to repeat propositions concerning

... the Negro past without critical analysis."[102] Banks argued for a keener understanding of the social and political context of the period and its effect on the studies of the period. In a related vein, Melville Herskovits noted in his study, *The Myth of the Negro Past*, that the "study of the Negro's past is important in developing better race relations, because such study shapes attitudes toward Negroes on the part of white persons and attitudes of Negroes themselves."[103] In 2014, historian Charles M. Payne argued that it is time to puncture the stereotype of "the wounded Negro."[104]

For decades, historians have based their analyses of African American educational history on the studies that described inferior quality and victimization.[105] Even today, after considerable work of scholars to bring to fore the valued community schools and importance of African American culture in understanding a "paideia" of African American education, laboratory schools, which served as the exemplar in the period for secondary education, have not been included in education profiles.[106] With a few exceptions, the perspective of the "privileged" educational experiences reported by former students of HBCU laboratory high schools has been absent from the historical accounts of progressive educational initiatives in the South.

CONCLUSION

The notion of a "privileged" laboratory high school experience of which Jackson speaks and the "excellent" academic education reported by Georgette Norman and other lab school graduates, begins to sculpt a more multifaceted historical perspective. Students of these lab schools went on to build careers in government service, law, medicine, and, most commonly, education. Being educated in a "lab high school" still carries a sense of pride and respect for those who were former students. "Even though the lab school was far away, we knew about it," remembered 1940 Southern University Lab School graduate, Bertha Stewart. "Lab School had a big influence on the kids. . . . It was a privilege," Stewart added with conviction, "and we knew it at the time."[107] Ms. Stewart went on to earn her BA in Education at Southern University and had a long career as a teacher. Her daughter also graduated from the laboratory school and went on to earn her B.S., MBA, and PhD, enjoying a career as a university professor.

As Dr. John W. Davis asserted in his address at the National Association of Teachers in Colored Schools annual conference in 1931, "We join all true scientists as well as other seekers after truth in believing that progress is evident when humanity is studied historically."[108] This research strives to document a "truth" about laboratory schools' influential and distinctive role in African American educational history in the first half of the twentieth century, while seeking to remember the humanity of those who lived this history.

As we struggle today with the ever growing challenge of adopting "effective" teaching and curriculum models for our nation's public schools and discerning education policies, especially for the historically disenfranchised, it is vital to consider the history of secondary schooling for African Americans—its challenges *and successes.* The history of regionally accredited, progressive laboratory schools on segregated all-Black college campuses has been overlooked. Education scholars have agreed that the history of teacher education programs have been "understudied;" however, none more so than these HBCU laboratory high schools whose "pioneering innovations and dynamic approaches . . . resulted in recognition and national prestige" during the era of Jim Crow.[109]

Might we benefit from listening to the echoes of past problems and models of success?[110] Writing in 1969, when the trend was to close laboratory schools across the nation, William Van Til posited that "historians of the year 2000" would analyze the rich experiences, "vision," and "brave dream" of the laboratory school model and "learn from the past" to "build" an even "better laboratory school."[111] The challenge is ours to add analyses of HBCU laboratory schools to our educational histories—the "excellent schooling" experiences of thousands of African Americans during Jim Crow and a model that paved a sure pathway to success in higher education.

NOTES

1. Léopold Sédar Senghor, "A l'appel de la race de Saba," "I Am Proud to Be a Negro" (Circa 1936).
2. Quiester Craig (Lab High graduate, MBA, PhD, Dean Emeritus, School of Business and Economics, North Carolina A&T State University), interview with the author, May 2008/March 2012; Craig, interview with the author, 2011.
3. Leonard L. Haynes, III (Southern University Lab High graduate, Senior Director, Institutional Services Postsecondary Education U.S. Department of Education, former Executive Director of the White House Initiative on Historically Black Colleges and Universities and Executive Vice President of Southern University Systems), interview with the author, August 2011.
4. Ibid.; "41st Congressional Black Caucus Foundation Annual Legislative Conference, 2011 Congressional Minority Business Awards," "Game Changers," (Washington, D.C., September 23, 2011); Department of Navy, Office of Naval Research Science & Technology, http://www.onr.navy.mil/Education; U.S. Army Research Laboratory's HBCU/MI, http://www.arl.army.mil.
5. Vanzetta Penn McPherson (Lab High graduate, Columbia University Law School graduate, appointed United States Magistrate Judge), interview with the author, March 2011; Richard Jordan (former Lab High graduate, teacher, MA, career educator, civil rights activist), interview with the author, July 2009; William Winston (Lab High graduate, MA, Veterans Administrator, leader in the community), interview with the author, March 2011; Henry Johnson (Lab

High graduate, M.D.), interview with the author, September 2008/March 2011. This was a common theme reported in multiple interviews.

6. Georgette Norman (Lab High graduate, MA, Executive Director, Rosa Parks Museum, Montgomery, Alabama), interview with the author, September 2008/March 2011.

7. *Catalogue of The Faculty of Students for 1924–1925 and Announcements of Courses for 1925–1926;* W. A. Robinson, "A Co-operative Effort Among Southern Negro High Schools," *The School Review* 52, no. 9 (Nov., 1944): 532–542, 533.

8. Marybeth Gasman, Benjamin Baez, Noah D. Drezner, Katherine V. Sedgwick, Christopher Tudico and Julie M. Schmid, "Historically Black Colleges and Universities: Recent Trends," *Academe* 93, no. 1 (Jan.–Feb., 2007): 69–77, 69.

9. W. A. Robinson, "Progressive Education and the Negro," in *Proceedings Association of Colleges and Secondary Schools for Negroes* (1937), 62–64; and "A New Era for Negro Schools," *Progressive Education,* 7 (December 1940): 541–565. This is not to suggest that these laboratory schools (those that were selected to participate in the Secondary School Study for Negroes, discussed later in this chapter) were the only segregated all-Black high schools or lab schools that were perceived as reform-minded and could boast a sense of pride, prestige, and "excellence" as part of their educational histories.

10. Funded by the General Education Board, the "Secondary School Study for Negroes" began in 1940, six years into the "Eight-Year Study" and three years into the Southern Association's high school study, having sixteen schools across the Southern region as "members." Criteria for selecting member high schools for the study included high school's demonstration of "intelligent and promising" administrative leadership "from the standpoint of training, energy, capability, and general alertness to educational progress." See W. A. Robinson, "A Secondary School Study," *Phylon (1940–1956)* 5, no. 2 (2nd Qtr. 1944): 145–158, 148.

11. Carol D. Lee, "Intervention Research Based on Current Views of Cognition and Learning," in Joyce E. King, ed., *Black Education: A Transformative Research and Action Agenda for a New Century* (Mahwah, N.J.: Lawrence Erlbaum Associates, 2005), 96.

12. J. A. McDuffie and others, *The Best Test Preparation for the AP United States History Exam,* 7th ed. (Piscataway, N.J.: Research & Education Association, 2011), 532.

13. W. A. Robinson and W. H. Brown, *To and From Our Schools—A Newsbulletin of The Secondary School Study of The Association of Colleges and Secondary Schools for Negroes,* No. 2 (1942): 1–10, 1–2; W. A. Robinson, Association of Colleges and Secondary Schools for Negroes, *Proceedings of the Fourth Annual Meeting* (New Orleans, La., 1937): 57–65, 60; "The Cooperative Negro College Study: Office of the Executive Office, State Teachers College," *Montgomery, Ala, Bulletin #1 The 1943–44 Service Project of Dr. Ambrose Suhrie, 8/15/43,* in Association of Colleges and Secondary Schools for Negroes, Reports and Pamphlets, folders 4095–4098, box 391, series 1, subseries 3, Rockefeller Archive Center, hereafter RAC.

14. Faustine Jones, *A Traditional Model of Educational Excellence: Dunbar High School of Little Rock, Arkansas* (Washington, D.C.: Howard University Press, 1981);

Vanessa Siddle Walker, *Their Highest Potential: An African American School Community in the Segregated South* (Chapel Hill: University of North Carolina Press, 1996); Vivian Gunn and Curtis L. Morris, *Creating Caring and Nurturing Educational Environments for African American Children* (Westport, Conn.: Bergin and Garvey, 2000); Sonya Ramsey, *Reading, Writing, and Segregation: A Century of Black Women Teachers in Nashville* (Urbana: University of Illinois, 2008).

15. John L. Rury and Shirley A. Hill, *The African American Struggle for Secondary Schooling, 1940–1980* (New York, NY: Teachers College Press, 2012); James W. Fraser, *Preparing America's Teachers: A History* (New York, NY: Teachers College Press, 2007), 95–113.

16. Fraser, *Preparing America's Teachers*, 98; H. C. Trenholm, "Some Measures of Progress in Alabama's Educational Program for Negro Pupils," *1948 Association Yearbook* (Montgomery: The Alabama State Teachers Association through State Teachers College, Montgomery, March, 1948), 42, 50, Alabama State University Archives, Montgomery, AL, hereafter noted as ASU Archives; "Alabama's Teacher-Progress Efforts of 1932," *Alabama State Teachers Association Fiftieth Anniversary Convention*, "Report on the 'Present State of Professional Progress," ASU Archives; J. D. Messick, "Negro Education in the South," *Journal of Educational Sociology* 21, no. 2 (Oct. 1947): 88–96; H. C. Trenholm to General Education Board, 8 March 1951, folder 4007, box 383, series 1, subseries 3, RAC.

17. Correspondence from L. F. Palmer [on the letterhead of Secondary School Study, W. A. Robinson, Director, with Palmer listed as Members of the Control Committee as Chairman] to Fred McCuistion, Assist. Director, GEB, January 5, 1943, folder 4098, box 391, series 1, subseries 3; *To and From Our Schools* (1942), 8; *Study of The Association of Colleges and Secondary Schools for Negroes, The Secondary School Study Conference Held at D. Webster Davis High School,* Etrick, Virginia,1942, 13–14; V. W. Sims, E.A. Waters, and W. A. Robinson, "Experimental Programs in the Southern Associations," *The High School Journal,* XXVIII (May, 1945), 142, 148]; Purpose of the School," in *Catalogue of Faculty and Students, 1920–1921*, 13; Sharon G. Pierson, *Laboratory of Learning: HBCU Laboratory Schools and Alabama State College Lab High in the Era of Jim Crow* (New York, NY: Peter Lang Publishing, 2013).

18. David B. Tyack, *The One Best System: A History of American Urban Education* (Cambridge, Mass.: Harvard University Press, 1974), 197, 127–128, 11–203; David Tyack, and Elisabeth Hansot, *Managers of Virtue: Public School Leadership in America, 1820–1980* (New York, NY: Basic Books, 1982), 114; Herbert M. Kliebard, *The Struggle for the American Curriculum, 1893–1958,* 3rd Edition (New York, NY: RoutledgeFalmer, 2004), 195.

19. Lawrence A. Cremin, *The Transformation of the School* (New York, NY: Random House, 1961), x.

20. Alan Sadovnik, ed., *Knowledge and Pedagogy: The Sociology of Basil Bernstein* (Westport: Greenwood Publishing, 1995), 339–340, 356; Manning Marable, *How Capitalism Underdeveloped Black America: Problems in Race, Political Economy, and Society* (Cambridge, MA: South End Press, 2000), 217, 219, 227; Gary Nash, "The History Standards Controversy and Social History," *Journal of Social History* 29 (1995): 39; Worth Kamili Hayes, "The Very Meaning of Our

Lives: Howalton Day School and Black Chicago's Dual Education Agenda, 1946–1985," *American Educational History Journal* 37. ½ (2010): 75–94; Nancy Bertaux and Michael Washington, "The 'Colored Schools' of Cincinnati and African American Community in Nineteenth Century Cincinnati, 1849–1890," *The Journal of Negro Education.*74. 1▪ (Winter 2005): 43–52, 43.

21. Considered "social reconstructionists," George Counts and Harold Rugg argued for social justice and recognition of the undemocratic circumstances that produced educational disparities. Rugg argued for a new approach for teaching children how to think about their society and history, specifically through a new social studies curriculum that interrogated social inequality. While John Dewey has often been placed in a class by himself, he has also been included among the "social reconstructionist" theorists of Counts and Rugg. Dewey and Counts argued that education called for a curriculum that taught "tolerance," "equality," "brotherhood," and "fair-mindedness"—key concepts in realizing America's democratic ideals in the classroom. Counts and Rugg believed that a social reconstructionist curriculum, inspired by the "discontent about the American economic and social system," would prepare students to grapple with the preponderance of social injustices. See Kliebard, *Struggle for the American Curriculum,* 184; George S. Counts, *The Selective Character of American Secondary Education* (Chicago: University of Chicago Press, 1922), 3; George S. Counts, *Schools Can Teach Democracy* (New York, NY: John Day Co., 1939); John Dewey in "Democracy and Human Nature" in Debra Morris, Ian Shapiro, *The Political Writings by John Dewey* (Indianapolis, Ind.: Hackett Publishing Co., 1993), 227–228; Harold O. Rugg, "How Shall We Reconstruct the Social Studies Curriculum? An Open Letter to Professor Henry Johnson Commenting on Committee Procedure as Illustrated by the Report of the Joint Committee on History and Education for Citizenship," Historical Outlook 12 (1921): 184–89.

22. W. A. Robinson, *Serving Negro Schools* (Atlanta, Georgia: The Association of Colleges and Secondary Schools for Negroes, 1945), 62–64, RAC. (emphasis added)

23. Ibid.

24. Archival materials, such as catalogues, newsletters, conference minutes, and the like, evidence Trenholm's support of such approaches as student debates (tackling issues and complexities of being an African American citizen living in a America's democracy), experiential field-trips for students, a broad range of nationally renowned guest speakers, intercollegiate academic meets, and teacher workshops and exchanges. The school's culture of encouraging social responsibility was a frequent theme expressed by former students in interviews collected by the author. In addition to the texts used at Lab High, such as, Theodore P. Blaich, Joseph C. Baumgartner, and Richard J. Stanley, *The Challenge of Democracy* (New York, NY: Harper & Bros., 1942), the social studies teacher, Mrs. Faustine Dunne opened her class with the declaration, "Class, we are living in a changing society," requiring students to be current on local, state, and national news. R. Jordan, interview. Pierson, *Laboratory of Learning,* 204–211.

25. American Historical Association, *Conclusions and Recommendations of the Commission on the Social Studies* (New York, NY: Charles Scribner's Sons, 1934), 16, in Kliebard, *Struggle for the American Curriculum,* 165; Pierson, *Laboratory of Learning,* 49–88.

26. W. A. Robinson, "Serving Negro Schools," 62–64.

27. Ronald Goodenow, "The Progressive Educator, Race and Ethnicity in the Depression Years: an Overview," *History of Education Quarterly* 15, no. 4 (Winter 1975): 365–394, 370.

28. Aaron Brown, "An Evaluation of the Accredited Secondary Schools for Negroes in the South," *The Journal of Negro Education* 13, no. 4 (Autumn 1944): 488–498, 491.

29. Susan F. Semel and Alan R. Sadovnik, *"Schools of Tomorrow," Schools of Today: What Happened to Progressive Education* (New York, NY: Peter Lang Publishing, 1999); Semel's new edition, expected 2014, will include an example of African American progressive initiatives in education, see Sharon G. Pierson, "A 'Laboratory of Learning': Alabama State Teachers College Laboratory High School in *"Schools of Tomorrow," Schools of Today: What Happened to Progressive Education* (New York, NY: Peter Lang Publishers. 2014).

30. Ronald Goodenow, "Paradox in Progressive Educational Reform: The South and the Education of Blacks in the Depression Years," *Phylon* 39, no. 1 (1st Qtr., 1978): 49–65, 60.

31. W. H. Brown, Staff Associate, *Secondary School Study of The Association of Colleges and Secondary Schools for Negroes, C A T A L O G, Partial Directory of Developmental Programs in Schools Cooperating with the Secondary School Study,* 1943; Brown and Robinson, *Serving Negro Schools;* Christy Folsom, *Teaching for Intellectual and Emotional Learning (TIEL): A Model for Creating Powerful Curriculum* (New York, NY: Rowman and Littlefield Education, 2009), 17, 35.

32. W. A. Robinson, Director, Secondary School Study for Negroes to L. M. Lester, Assistant Director of Negro Education, State Department of Education, Atlanta, Georgia, 23 February 1940, folder 4088, box 468, subseries 3, series 1, RAC; W. A. Robinson to Members of the Control Committee of the Secondary School Study of the Association of Colleges and Secondary Schools for Negroes, April 1940, folder 4088, box, 468, subseries 3, series 1, RAC; A. R. Mann, GEB to Dean George A. Works, University of Chicago, October 4, 1938, folder 5125, box 481; W. A. Robinson to F. McCuistion, GEB, 2 April 1940, folder 4088, box 468, subseries 3, series 1, RAC; W. A. Robinson, "Report of Progress of the Secondary School Study of the Association of Colleges and Secondary Schools for Negroes," to GEB, May 1940; Thomas Elsa Jones, President, Fisk University to Fred McCuistion, GEB, 30 December 1939, folder 4088, box 391, subseries 3, series 1, RAC; Laboratory high schools that distinguished themselves as part of the progressive Secondary School Study for Negroes included: Drewry Practice High School of Talladega College, Alabama; State Teachers College Laboratory School, Montgomery, Alabama; Atlanta University Laboratory School, Atlanta, Georgia; Louisiana; Southern University and Agricultural and Mechanical College Demonstration School, Scotlandville, Louisiana; D. Webster Davis Laboratory School of Virginia State College for Negroes, Ettrick, Va., and Lincoln High School, Tallahassee, the

latter considered a laboratory school by Robinson, as it was used as a training school for Florida A & M.

33. J. Minor Gwynn, "Trends in Curriculum Development," in Will Carson Ryan, J. Minor Gwynn, and Arnold K. King, eds., *Secondary Education in the South* (Chapel Hill: University of North Carolina Press, 1946), 115–125; Thomas Elsa Jones, President, Fisk University to Fred McCuistion, Assistant Director, GEB, January 5, 1940, folder 4088, box 391, subseries 3, series 1, RAC.

34. J. W. Davis, address at the American Teachers Association Annual Meeting in Perry, *History of ATA,* 245; Clarence A. Bacote, *The Story of Atlanta University: A Century of Service, 1865–1965* (Atlanta, Ga.: Atlanta University Press, 1969), 291; "Catalogue 1931–32: Announcements," *The Atlanta University Bulletin,* 18, Atlanta University Center Archives and Special Collections; See also Brown, "Accredited Secondary Schools," 491; W. H. Brown, "Report of Two Years of Activity of the Secondary School Study," *Journal of Negro Education* 12, no. 1 (Winter 1943): 121–130, 121, 129; A. R. Mann to Dean George A. Works, University of Chicago, 4 October 1938; Geo. A. Works, Department of Education, University of Chicago to Leo Favrot, GEB, 4 October 1938; Fred McCuistion, GEB Internal Memo, 19 December 1941; Brown and Robinson, *Serving Negro Schools,* 36–38.

35. Of a total of 7,059 high schools nationwide and "1,400 Negro secondary schools of all kinds in the region, only 77 were approved by the Southern Association of Colleges and Secondary Schools," 26% were laboratory-type schools—high schools that were "laboratory," "training," or "demonstration" schools associated with a higher education institution. See Southern Association of Colleges and Secondary School, Committee on Approval of Negro Schools, *The Southern Association of Colleges and Secondary Schools: Approved List of Colleges and Schools for Negro Youth* (Memphis, Tenn., 1939), 2–6; U.S. Department of Education, Office of Education Research and Improvement, *120 Years of American Education: A Statistical Portrait,* Thomas d. Snyder, ed. (Center for Education Statistics, 1993), 37; Brown and Robinson, *Serving Negro Schools,* 3.

36. Alma Dacus Collier (Lab High graduate, MA, EdD, psychometrist, higher education administration), interview with the author, September 2008/ March 2011. Alma Dacus Collier graduated from Lab School in 1958 and, inspired by her thorough preparation in foreign languages, went on to earn her undergraduate degree in French and German from Fisk University. This allowed her to return to Lab School to teach foreign languages at Lab High in 1963 and 1964. Collier continued her graduate studies, earning an EdD in Higher Education Administration from George Washington University in Washington, D.C. While Collier praised her foreign language readiness, she emphasized the positive influence Lab High's comprehensive, liberal arts curriculum had on her academic success.

37. Robert C. Hammock, Coordinator, Reviewing Committee, University of Alabama, "An Administrative Statement of Setting, Role, Function and Philosophy of a College-Operated Teachers-Education Laboratory School," *Report of the Evaluating Committee,* (1953), The Commission on Colleges and University Southern Association of Colleges and Secondary Schools, Southern

Association of Colleges and Secondary Schools (SACS), 7, hereafter cited as *SACS Report of Evaluating Committee;* Brown and Robinson, *Serving Negro Schools,* 25; President H. C. Trenholm included access to college resources as one of the advantages of being a Laboratory High School Student in the "Laboratory School Student Handbook," 5, ASU Archives; "The Alabama State College Laboratory School Student Handbook" (1954–1955); "The Alabama State College Laboratory High School Homeroom Guidance Program" (1947, 1948, 1952, 1955); *The Atlanta University Bulletin,* "Catalogue Number, 1936–1937," 11–12, Atlanta University Archives, Atlanta, Georgia; The remembrances of students taking "advantage of using college professors as resources" were repeated by multiple Lab High graduates in interviews with the author; Rosalyn King (Lab High graduate, teacher, principal, and assistant superintendent), interview with the author, September 2008; among many others.

38. Laureta Matthews (D. W. Davis Laboratory High School graduate), interview with Craig Kridel, Curator, Museum of Education Project, http://www.ed.sc. edu/museum/second_study.html.

39. Brenda Birkett (Southern University Laboratory High School graduate, and professor of accounting at Louisiana State University), interview with the author, September 2011.

40. Helen Smith (Lab High graduate), interview with the author, September 2008. Multiple students at Alabama State College Lab High, Atlanta University Laboratory High School, and Southern University Laboratory High School spoke of the sheltered environment.

41. Jeanne E. Nesbitt Moore Smiley (Lab High graduate), written communication to the author, September 2008/March 2011; McPherson, interview with the author, March 2011; Considering the issue of learning from the past and evaluating the benefits of a supportive environment in contemporary scholarship see James Earl Davis, "College in Black and White: Campus Environment and Academic Achievement of African American Males" in "Pedagogical and Contextual Issues Affecting African American Males in School and Society," *The Journal of Negro Education* 63, no. 4, (Autumn, 1994): 620–633; Jacqueline Jordan Irvine and Leslie T. Fenwick, "Teachers and Teaching for the New Millennium: The Role of HBCUs" in "Preparing Black Students to Become Teachers," *Journal of Negro Education* 80, no. 3 (Summer 2011): 197–208, 198, 200; Shirley E. Faulkner, "Letters to Young High School Students: Writing and Uniting an Academic Community" in "Reflections: Writing, Service-Learning, and Community Literacy" 10, no. 2 (Spring 2011): 1–197, 63–107.

42. Viola Bouldin Maniego (D. W. David Lab High graduate), Interview with Craig Kridel, Curator, Museum of Education Project, http://www.ed.sc.edu/ museum/second_study.html.

43. W. Winston, interview; Bertha Steward (1940 Southern University Lab High School graduate, career educator), interview with the author, September 2008; Mirian Chibers (1942 Atlanta University Lab High School graduate, career medical doctor), interview with the author February 2013; Margaret Aiken Jacobs (1940 Atlanta University Lab High School graduate, BA, MA, Business Administration, teacher and school principal), interview with the

author February 2013; William Van Til, "The Laboratory School: Its Rise and Fall," Address to the National Meeting of the Laboratory School Administrators Association in Chicago, February, 1969.

44. Jacobs, interview.

45. Letter from Parents, Patrons and Friends of Atlanta University Laboratory Schools to President and Board of Trustees of Atlanta University, April 24, 1942; Bertha Stewart (1940 Southern University Laboratory High School graduate, career teacher), interview with the author, October 5, 2011; Rose Palmer (Atlanta University Lab High student, BA Smith College, MBA Stanford University), interview with the author, April 10, 2012; V. McPherson, interview; Jordan, interview.

46. Jordan, interview with the author, September 2008; Robert Clinton Hatch, "A Program of In-Service Teacher Education: A Report of a Type B Project" (EdD diss., Teachers College, Columbia University, 1946); William Webster Clem, Jr., "Administrative Practices in Laboratory Schools Connected with Land-Grant and State Teachers Colleges for Negroes," (PhD diss., University of Wisconsin, 1949); Brown and Robinson, *Serving Negro Schools,* 4.

47. Regular, consistent attendance and completed homework was the absolute expectation, as voiced in virtually every interview conducted by the author; "Laboratory School Student Handbook, 1953–1954," 10.

48. Kathy Dunn Jackson (Lab High graduate, MA, EdD, University Professor), interview with the author, September 2008, September 2009/March 2011.

49. Ibid.

50. Rose Palmer, interview with the author April 2010.

51. Brenda Birkett (Southern University Laboratory High School graduate), interview with the author, October 9, 2011; John Winston, Jr. (Lab High graduate, MD, leader in the community), interview with the author, March 2011; Mirian Chibers (Atlanta University Lab High School graduate), interview with the author, February 28, 2013; Trenholm and Robinson, "Proposal To The General Education Board By The Secondary School Study And The Cooperative Negro College Study," folder 4102, box 392, subseries 1, series, 1, RAC.

52. The Southern Association for Colleges and Secondary Schools, *Report of Evaluative Criteria Committee, Robert E. Lee High School, Montgomery, Alabama, April 7–11, 1958,* box 3, SG11937, Alabama Department of Archives and History, Montgomery, Alabama, hereafter ADAH.

53. *Report of Reviewing Committee Applying The Evaluative Criteria In Sidney Lanier High School, Montgomery, Alabama, April 1950,* "School Plant," 63–69; Alison L. Murphy, "Fifty Years of Challenges to the Colorline, Montgomery, Alabama," (master's thesis, Georgia State University, December 2009); SACS *Report of Sidney Lanier High School,* "Educational Intentions," 23, 16, box 1, SG11935, ADAH.

54. *SACS Report of Evaluating Committee,* 16–19. A follow-up study was done to determine the actual outcomes of students' intentions, and it revealed that "81.5 percent of the class of 1952 entered four year colleges." The SACS evaluation team concluded that the data indicated a "consistency in educational intentions, what happens to graduates, and purpose of the school," for the class of 1952 and for years prior.

55. Alfred C. Henry (Lab High physics teacher, 1945–1969), interview with the author, September 2010.

56. Lyceum programs at Alabama State College began under G. W. Trenholm and continued through the decades, welcoming such luminaries as: U.S. President William Howard Taft, George Washington Carver, Dr. Benjamin E. Mayse, Dr. Samuel Nabrit, Dr. John W. Davis, Dr. Horace Mann Bond, Charles H. Wesley, Lorenzo Green, E. Franklin Frazier, Adam Clayton Powell, Jr., Honorable Benjamin Hooks, Carl T. Rowan, Honorable Kweisi Mfume, Ralph David Abernathy, Reverend Jesse Jackson, Duke Ellington, Joe Louis Barrow, and Mohammed Ali, among many other celebrities and entertainers. See Charles Varner, Jr., "Luminaries and Orators of Renown at ASU" (lecture, Alabama State University, 2001); *State Normal Courier-Journal,* 1926, 12, ASU Archives.

57. Alice Wimberly (ASC Lab High graduate, BA and MA in Education, 32 year career teacher), interview with the author, September 2008.

58. Dorothy Lee Early Davis (Southern University Demonstration School graduate), Interview with Craig Kridel, Curator, Museum of Education Project, http://www.ed.sc.edu/museum/second_study.html.

59. See Jacqueline Jordan Irvine and Leslie T. Fenwick, "Teachers and Teaching for the New Millennium: The Role of HBCUs" in "Preparing Black Students to Become Teachers," *Journal of Negro Education* 80, no. 3 (Summer 2011): 197–208, 197.

60. For example, W. A. Robinson, "A Secondary School Study," *Phylon (1940–1956)* 5, no. 2 (2nd Qtr., 1944):145–158; H. C. Trenholm, "Some Background and Status of Higher Education for Negroes in Alabama," in *The 1949 ASTA Yearbook* (Montgomery: Alabama State Teachers Association through State Teachers College, Montgomery, March, 1949), 35, 46; H. C. Trenholm, "The Accreditation of the Negro High School," *Journal of Negro Education* 1, no. 1 (1932): 34–43; John W. Davis, "The Negro Land-Grant College," *Journal of Negro Education* 2, no. 3 (1933): 312–28; Ellen Swartz, "Stepping Outside the Master Script: Re-Connecting the History of American Education," *The Journal of Negro Education* Vol. 47, No. 2 (Spring , 2007): 173–186, 178–179; Felton G. Clark, *The Control of State-Supported Teacher-Training Programs for Negroes* (New York, NY: Teachers College, Columbia University Press, 1934).

61. Chibers, Interview; W. Winston, Interview; V. McPherson, Interview; W. A. Robinson to H. C. Trenholm, 9 June 1937; Folder 15, Box 179–22, Manuscript Division Moorland-Spingarn Research Center, Howard University; Robinson to Trenholm, 8 August 1962, Folder 15, Box 179–22, Howard University; H. C. Trenholm to Dr. Jerome Davis, Yale University Divinity School, 11 April 1935, Folder 2, Box 179–14, Manuscript Division, Moorland-Spingarn Research Center, Howard University.

62. Archival materials support the claim that lab high schools were intended to "...develop an adequate and thoroughly modern laboratory-school service so as to insure the effective embodiment of our best educational theories (as taught in college classes) in the actual practices of the campus demonstration school," as stated in "The 1943–44 Service Project of Dr. Ambrose Suhrie," *Bulletin* 1, "The Cooperative Negro College Study: Office of the Executive Office, State Teachers College," (Montgomery, Ala.: August 15, 1943), 2; Bacote,

Story of Atlanta University, 291; Cynthia Gibson Hardy, "A Historical Review of the Secondary School Study of the Association of Colleges and Secondary Schools for Negroes, 1940–1946," (PhD diss., Ohio State University, 1977), 33; Association of Colleges and Secondary Schools for Negroes, *Fourth Annual Meeting,* 60.

63. See "The Alabama State College Laboratory School Student Handbook" (1954–1955); "The Alabama State College Laboratory High School Home-room Guidance Program" (1947, 1948, 1952, 1955); *The Atlanta University Bulletin,* "Catalogue Number, 1936–1937," 11–12, Atlanta University Archives, Atlanta, Georgia; Museum of Education Project, Secondary School Study for Negroes, http://www.ed.sc.edu/museum/second_study.html.

64. See multiple issues of *The Crisis* for references to Atlanta University Laboratory High Schools teachers and others having attended workshops at Teachers College, Columbia University, University of Chicago, University of Michigan, etc.; Jerome A. Gray, Joe L. Reed, and Norman W. Walton, *History of the Alabama State Teachers Association* (Washington, D.C.: NEA, 1987), 161–164.

65. "Purpose of the School," in *Catalogue of Faculty and Students, 1920–1921,* 13, ASU Archives; *The* Alabama *State College Laboratory High School at Montgomery, Alabama Home Room Guidance Program,* (1947), 3; "The Alabama State College Laboratory School, Montgomery, Alabama, Student Handbook, 1953–1954"; "The Newsletter," *Commission on Teacher Education of the American Council on Education* 2, no. 6 (March 1942), 2, 4–5; Trenholm and Robinson, "Proposal To GEB," RAC; V. W. Sims, E.A. Waters, and W. A. Robinson, "Experimental Programs in the Southern Associations," *The High School Journal,* XXVIII (May, 1945), 142; Brown and Robinson, *Serving Negro Schools, passim; The Cooperative Negro College Study: Office of the Executive Office, State Teachers College,"* *Montgomery, Ala, Bulletin #2* "Some Administrative Proposals Incident to of Dr. Ambrose Suhrie, 9/30/43," folder 4095, box 391, subseries 1, series 1, RAC; "Report from the Cooperative Negro College and the Secondary School study of the Association of Colleges and Secondary Schools for Negroes on the Workshop on Evaluation Direct by Dr. Louis E. Raths at Ohio State University, June 12–july 27, 1944," folder 4104, box 392, subseries 3, series 1, RAC; Robinson, to State Agents and Others, March 3, 1942, RAC; Hardy, "Secondary School Study," 9; 37, 89, 113.

66. John Dewey, "Experiment in Education," *The New Republic,* February 3, 1917, 16. For more on the histories of progressive curriculum experimentation in schools, see Susan F. Semel and Alan R. Sadovnik, eds., *"Schools of Tomorrow, Schools of Today": What Happened to Progressive Education* (New York, NY: Peter Lang, 1999; and Alan R. Sadovnik and Susan Semel, eds., *Founding Mothers and Others: Women Educational Leaders During the Progressive Era* (New York, NY: Palgrave, 2002).

67. On the issue of contemporary concerns of increasingly "complicated" issues challenging adolescents see Progressive Education Association, "The Reorganization of the Curriculum of the Secondary School, Exhibit C" in "Progressive Education Association Commission on Secondary School Curriculum 1933–1934" (April 12, 1934), folder 2911, box 279, RAC; On the issue of how racial discrimination and subordination shaped the complicated society in

which these students learned and lived (and continue to challenge students) see James D. Anderson, "Race-Conscious Educational Policies Versus a 'Color-Blind Constitution': A Historical Perspective" *Educational Researcher* 36, no. 5 (June/July 2007): 249–257; Also see Sharon G. Pierson, "'Living in a Changing Society': A Case Study of the Challenge of Democracy in Segregated Schooling at Alabama State College Laboratory School," *American Educational History Journal, 37,* no. 1 & 2, 2010: 187–205.

68. Hardy, "Secondary School Study," 37.
69. "Proceedings of the Secondary School Conference, Ettrick, Virginia, November 30—December 2, 1942; folder 4015, box 392, RAC.
70. W. H. Brown, *Partial Directory of Developmental Programs in Schools Cooperating with the Secondary School Study* (Atlanta, Georgia: Secondary School Study of the Association of Colleges and Secondary Schools for Negroes, 1943), 4.
71. Lou LaBrant, New York University, English Workshop Chairman to Rhind, August 3, 1945, folder 4103, box 392, RAC; Thomas Clark Pollock, Chairman, Dept. of English Education, NYU to W. A. Robinson, January 15, 1945, folder 4103, Box 392 RAC.
72. "Hope Report, 1933–1934," 54–58, in Clarence A. Bacote, *The Story of Atlanta University: A Century of Service, 1865–1965* (Atlanta, Ga.: Atlanta University Press, 1969), 291.
73. Jacobs, interview; Hardy, "Secondary School Study," 35;
74. Bacote, *Story of Atlanta University,* 291; "Catalogue 1931–32: Announcements," *The Atlanta University Bulletin,* 18, Atlanta University Center Archives and Special Collections. See also Brown, "Accredited Secondary Schools," 491.
75. "Report of the Committee on Evaluation of the Conference," "Secondary School Conference at Fisk University, Nashville, Tennessee, January 26–29, 1942," 1, folder 4088, box, 391, subseries 3, series 1, RAC.
76. Robinson, "Co-Operative Effort," 536, 538.
77. Ibid.
78. For more detailed analysis of the Secondary School Study for Negroes, see S. Pierson, "A 'Laboratory of Learning' in Historical Context," (PhD diss. Teachers College, Columbia University, 2012).
79. This phrase, "discontent about the American economic and social system," has been quoted in multiple book length studies of progressive education. See especially, Kliebard, *Struggle for Curriculum,* 154; Counts, *Schools Can Teach Democracy,* 19–20.
80. Alabama State College Laboratory High School's text was *The Challenge of Democracy,* see Blaich et al., *Challenge of Democracy;* Harold O. Rugg, *Man and His Changing Society* (Boston, MA: Ginn and Company, 1929); Elmer A. Winters and Harold Rugg, "Man and His Changing Society: The Textbooks of Harold Rugg, *History of Education Quarterly* 7, no. 4 (Winter 1967): 493–514; American Historical Association, *Conclusions and Recommendations of the Commission on the Social Studies* (New York, NY: Charles Scribner's Sons, 1934), 16, in Kliebard, *Struggle for Curriculum,* 165; *The* Alabama *State College Laboratory High School at Montgomery, Alabama Home Room Guidance Program,* (1947), 3.
81. "Philosophy," *Laboratory High School Home Room Guidance Program,* 3–4; John Dewey, *Democracy and Education* (New York, NY: Macmillan Co., 1916), 101.

82. R. Edgerton, "The Future Belongs to Youth," Review of *The Challenge of Democracy* by T. Blaich and J. Baumgartner, *The School Review* 51 (March 1943): 188.
83. Ibid.
84. T. Blaich and J. Baumgartner, *The Challenge of Democracy* (New York, McGraw-Hill, 1947), 623, 633.
85. Q. Craig, written communication to the author, October 2008; Phrasing of "democratic" teaching and learning appeared in other editions found in the archives, including the 1948, 1953, 1955; it was repeated in the *Catalogue of the Faculty and Students and Announcements of Courses, 1947–48,* and in other catalogue editions; The challenge of teaching democracy and understanding the challenge of democracy in the nation were a key part of the Secondary School Study and central to curricula at other lab schools; See W. H. Brown and W. A. Robinson, "Serving Negro Schools," *Proceedings of the Association of Colleges and Secondary Schools for Negroes* (1937), 62–64; W. H. Brown, "Report of Two Years of Activity," 121–130;To the point of diverse learning environments, see Gasman, et al., "Race and Equality in the Academy: Rethinking High Education Actors and the Struggle for Equality in the Post-World War II Period," *The Journal of Higher Education* 82, no. 2 (March/April, 2011): 121–153, 136–138.
86. W. H. Brown, *Partial Directory, Secondary School Study,* 1; Robinson, *Secondary School Study,* 155; Hardy, "Secondary School Study," 162;
87. George A. Works, Dean, Department of Education, University of Chicago to Leo M. Favrot, GEB, October 4, 1938, folder 5125, box 481, subseries 3, series 1, RAC; Fred McCuistion, GEB Internal Memo, December 19, 1941, folder 4998, box 468, subseries 3, series 1, RAC: J. W. Davis, address at the American Teachers Association Annual Meeting in Perry, *History of ATA,* 245; Bacote, *Story of Atlanta University,* 291; "Catalogue 1931–32: Announcements," *The Atlanta University Bulletin,* 18, Atlanta University Center Archives and Special Collections; W. H. Brown, "Accredited Secondary Schools," 491; W. H. Brown, "Report of Two Years of Activity," 121, 129; To the point of sphere of influence, see Philo Hutcheson, Marybeth Gasman, Kijua Sanders-McMurtry, "Race and Equality in the Academy: Rethinking High Education Actors and the Struggle for Equality in the Post-World War II Period," *The Journal of Higher Education,* 82, no. 2 (March/April, 2011): 121–153, 134.
88. Robinson, "Co-Operative Effort"; "Report of Two Years of Activity," 121–130; Robinson and Trenholm, "Secondary School Study And The Cooperative Negro College Study."
89. Fred McCuistion, General Education Board Interoffice "Interview" Memo, July 18, 1942, Durham, NC, GEB, RAC.
90. Edgar W. Knight, "Some Economic Political, and Social Influences in Education in the South," in Will Carson Ryan, J. Minor Gwynn, and Arnold K. King, eds., *Secondary Education in the South* (Chapel Hill: University of North Carolina Press, 1946), 4.
91. Clark, *Control of State-Supported Teacher-Training Programs for Negroes* (New York, NY: Teachers College, Columbia University Press, 1934), 1.
92. W. A. Robinson, "Some Problems of Secondary Schools," in "The Negro Adolescent and His Education," *The Journal of Negro Education* 9, no. 3 (July 1940):474–481, 465.

93. Clem, "Administrative Practices in Laboratory Schools," 2, 126.

94. For more discussion on this see Sonia E. Murrow's work on the Teachers College, Columbia University's New College, an "undergraduate laboratory school," that based its philosophy and methods on George Counts, John Dewey, and other social reconstructionists; Murrow, "Preparing Teachers to Remake Society," 54; David F. Labaree, "Progressivism, Schools and Schools of Education: An American Romance," *Paedagogica Historica* 41, nos. 1&2 (February 2005): 275–288, 276.

95. For negative descriptions of Black high school education, see, for example, Michael Fultz, "African American Teachers in the South, 1890–1940: Powerlessness and the Ironies of Expectations and Protest," *History of Education Quarterly* 35, no. 4 (1995): 401–422, 402–403; Louis R. Harlan, *Separate and Unequal: Public School Campaigns and Racism in the Southern Seaboard States, 1901–1915* (New York, NY: Atheneum, 1968), 39–40; Charles H. Thompson, "The Status of Education *of* and *for* the Negro in the American Social Order," *The Journal of Negro Education* 8, no. 3 (1939): 489–510, 493; Edward E. Redcay, *County Training Schools and Public Secondary Education for Negroes in the South* (Washington, D.C.: John F. Slater Fund Studies in Negro Education, 1935), 65; U. W. Leavell, "Trends of Philanthropy in Negro Education: A Survey," *Journal of Negro Education* 2, no. 1 (Jan 1933): 38–52.

96. Clem, "Administrative Practices in Laboratory Schools," 55.

97. See Brown and Robinson, *Serving Negro Schools, passim*; W. H. Brown, Associate Director of the Secondary School Study (address, Association Annual Meeting, 1941): 45–46.The premiere laboratory high schools (designated by the author in this paper as "premiere" because of their participation in the progressive national Secondary School Study for Negroes and their high graduation and college enrollment rates), primarily emphasized a liberal arts curriculum; however, some of these high schools also offered a dual track of college prep with vocational classes, as in D. Webster Davis Lab High and Southern University Laboratory High School. Archival data from Alabama's Lab High and Atlanta University's Lab High, such as accreditation reports, school philosophy statements, objectives, and student handbooks asserted that lab schools considered a strong liberal arts education to best prepare students for success in college and professional careers. Curricula sometimes included "business" classes, such as accounting. For more on the strength and history of hybrid curricula see Marybeth Gasman & Tryan L. McMickens, "Liberal or Professional Education?: The Missions of Public Black Colleges and Universities and Their Impact on the Future of African Americans" in "Souls: A Critical Journal of Black Politics, Culture, and Society" 12:3 (2010): 286–305; W. T. B. Williams, "State Normal School, Montgomery, Alabama (May 10, 1906), Folder 100, Box 13, GEB, RAC; Van Til, "Laboratory School: Its Rise and Fall," 2; Bacote, *Story of Atlanta University,* 291.

98. Brown, "Accredited Secondary Schools," 491.

99. Robinson, "Some Problems," 465.

100. William B. Thomas, "Black Intellectuals' Critique of Early Mental Testing: A Little-Known Saga of the 1920s," *American Journal of Education* 90, no. 3 (May 1982): 258–292, 258.

101. James A. Banks, "Multicultural Education and Curriculum Transformation," *Journal of Negro Education* 64, no. 4 (Autumn 1995): 390–400, 395.
102. Melville Herskovits, *The Myth of the Negro Past* (New York, NY: Harper and Brother, 1941), 374.
103. Ibid.
104. Charles M. Payne, as part of the "inaugural Edmund Gordon Lecture," at Teachers College, Columbia University, "Research Publications," http://www.tc.columbia.edu/news.htm?tid=3.
105. Banks, "Multicultural Education and Curriculum Transformation," 395; V.P. Franklin and Bettye Collier-Thomas, "Biography, Race Vindication, and African-American Intellectuals: Introductory Essay," in "Vindicating the Race: Contributions to African-American Intellectual History," *Journal of Negro History* 81, no. 1/4 (Winter-Autumn, 1996) 1–16, 1.
106. V. P. Franklin, "Education in Urban Communities in the United States: Exploring the Legacy of Lawrence A. Cremin," *Paedagogica Historica: International Journal of the History of Education* 39, no. 1, (2003): 153–163; Lawrence A. Cremin, *American Education: the National Experience, 1783–1876* (New York, NY: Harper & Row, 1980).
107. B. Stewart, interview.
108. Dr. John W. Davis, address at the NATCS 1931 Annual Meeting, as quoted in Thelma D. Perry, *History of the American Teachers Association* (Washington D.C.: National Education Association, 1975), 245.
109. David Imig, Review of Fraser, *Preparing America's Teachers,* back cover; H. C. Trenholm to State Board of Education, January 1951.Laboratory schools have been mentioned in biographical accounts of individuals who attended them. A total of six dissertations and master theses written over a period of 22 years, 1936 to 1958, examined aspects of laboratory schools. Faustine Jones, Vanessa Siddle Walker, Vivian and Curtis Morris, among others have written about their alma maters, presenting studies of academic achievement, "community-valued" schooling, and schools that provided "caring and nurturing environments." See Faustine Jones, *A Traditional Model of Educational Excellence: Dunbar High School of Little Rock, Arkansas* (Washington, D.C.: Howard University Press, 1981); Vanessa Siddle Walker, *Their Highest Potential: An African American School Community in the Segregated South* (Chapel Hill: University of North Carolina Press, 1996); Vivian Gunn and Curtis L. Morris, *Creating Caring and Nurturing Educational Environments for African American Children* (Westport, Conn.: Bergin and Garvey, 2000). More recent historical surveys of African American education and Teacher training institutions missed including or referencing laboratory schools, which were often the only high school in the area for decades and whose attendance, graduation, and college entrance rates exceeded state and national norms. See John L. Rury and Shirley A. Hill, *The African American Struggle for Secondary Schooling, 1940–1980* (New York, NY: Teachers College Press, 2012); James W. Fraser, *Preparing America's Teachers: A History* (New York, NY: Teachers College Press, 2007), 95–113; also see Tyack and Hansot and their discussion of the underrepresentation of scientific research of African American education during this period. D. Tyack, and

E. Hansot, *Managers of Virtue: Public School Leadership in America, 1820–1980* (New York, NY: Basic Books, 1982), 88, 127–28.

110. Ladson-Billings, G., *The Dreamkeepers: Successful Teachers of African American Children* (San Francisco, CA: Jossey-Bass, 1994); Derrick Bell, *Silent Covenants: Brown v. Board of Education and the Unfulfilled Hopes for Racial Reform* (New York, NY: Oxford University Press, 2004); V. P. Franklin, "American Values, Social Goals, and the Desegregated School: A Historical Perspective, in V. P. Franklin & J. D. Anderson (Eds.), *New Perspectives on Black Educational History* (Boston, MA: G. K. Hall, 1978), 193–21, 1

111. Van Til, "Laboratory School: Rise and Fall," 1, 15.

CHAPTER 5

GRADUATE STUDY AND JIM CROW

The Circular Migration of Southern Black Educators, 1945–1970

Donna Jordan-Taylor
University of Washington, Tacoma

"And what are you going back to Mississippi for?"... I got asked that a lot of times. I didn't even entertain the thought of going anywhere else... And I said, "I'm going back because they need me, and because it's home.[1]

—Lottie Thorton

Mrs. Lottie Thornton recalled this conversation on a train while traveling home to Jackson, Mississippi from The Ohio State University where she was a graduate student during the late 1940s. A Jackson State College graduate and teacher in Florence, Mississippi, Mrs. Thornton was encouraged to attend Ohio State by colleagues at Jackson State College, including President Jacob Reddix, and by an Ohio State alumnus with whom she taught. Thornton graduated from Ohio State in 1948, and while she spoke very highly of the program, campus, and faculty, she had no intentions of staying away from Mississippi for the long term. After returning to Florence,

Using Past as Prologue, pages 117–139
Copyright © 2015 by Information Age Publishing
All rights of reproduction in any form reserved.

she continued teaching, was promoted to principal, and eventually helped found the Early Childhood Education Center at Jackson State University. As she noted, "I knew where the need was, I was right in the midst of it, so I just never entertained the idea of going anywhere else."[2]

For Thornton and thousands of other Blacks with graduate school aspirations during this period, migrating to colleges and universities outside the South was their most practical option. Like other members of the Great Migration, various push and pull factors influenced their decision making. For Black educators, expanded opportunities to pursue graduate study in diverse environments free of legalized discrimination pulled them north, while a segregated educational system with few graduate programs for Blacks served as a major push factor. Like so many other migrants, Black educators weighed their options and found the northern context to be a place where the pursuit of academic and professional goals was possible, with fewer restrictions on their choice of institutions, programs, and fields.

While these push and pull factors encouraged millions of African Americans to permanently relocate during the first half of the twentieth century, the particular case of Black educators differs from the broader migration narrative, as these individuals made very conscious, purposeful decisions to leave temporarily, returning to the South after graduate school where they made concrete contributions to Black education at home. As Historian James Gregory explains, while large-scale return migration surged in the mid-1970s, the example of Black teachers and academics provides an exception to this trend.[3] Their circular migration enabled them to meet the immediate demand for qualified educators in the South, where they contributed their research and credentials to Black schools and colleges. In the process, these educators built upon previous forms of social and cultural capital they experienced as children to become more potent agents of change, creating new educational opportunities for students, and providing access to diverse professional networks and contacts.

SEGREGATION, MIGRATION, AND SOCIAL CAPITAL

Traditionally, the terms social capital (memberships, networks and personal contacts which can help facilitate access to jobs and institutions), and cultural capital (tastes, values, and preferences, including academic qualifications) have been used to describe resources that can be exchanged for material or economic gain, such as jobs, money, or inclusion in high status groups.[4] Yet, in studies of segregated school communities, these terms are also useful in analyzing the ways resources were used to advance educational efforts. In their studies of institutions, historians V. P. Franklin, Adah Ward Randolph, Christopher Span, and Carter Julian Savage utilize social and cultural capital to describe how Black communities capitalized on their own resources to develop and expand schools for Black students in the face of myriad economic and political barriers erected by Jim Crow.5 According to Historian Nancy Beadie, "In this formulation, social capital is a collective resource that a community uses to achieve its own ends. Economic development and opportunity may be among those ends, but so might education itself."[6]

In addition, social and cultural capital also explains what happens within these schools, at the personal or individual level. Several researchers have described the unique forms of social and cultural capital present in all-Black, segregated schools in the American South.[7] In these school communities, networks and personal contacts consistently expressed the value of education, and communicated these messages to children. Parents, teachers, and community members, in their words and actions, emphasized educational attainment as an important goal. In some cases, parents expressed these views vehemently, leaving children with no input in the matter. As one participant of this study described the college selection process, "I didn't choose anything; the decision was already made,"[8] while another explained how her mother went to campus to confirm her daughter had a work study position "before I arrived" so that the family could cover all costs. [9] For others, teachers and other community members encouraged them to continue their education. One participant described being called "Senator" by a church member, which he interpreted as recognition of his leadership and academic potential. In addition, the presence of Tougaloo College alumni in his community meant that Tougaloo "was the only college I ever heard about . . . I was destined to come to Tougaloo, even before I knew it."[10] Here, the participants' contacts and networks, even those who were not members of the educated class, expressed clear preferences for advanced education, values which influenced their academic pursuits.

As beneficiaries of these forms of capital, these educators completed bachelor's degrees, moved away for their graduate work, and returned to the region with the credentials necessary to serve as more powerful agents of change. As highly educated professionals, these individuals not only encouraged students *to attend school*, they made quantifiable improvements *to the schools* through the creation of educational programs and departments, the expansion of graded education, and enhanced subject matter knowledge. They also developed social capital that was more potent, due to the particular memberships and contacts acquired during graduate school, and more diverse because of the geographic location of their graduate institutions. While their early contacts and networks were invaluable in directing their future educational and professional paths, these educators' own subsequent accomplishments facilitated their contributions to improved education and their service as more powerful agents of change via their direct involvement in the academy. They also brought experiences in desegregated environments, a particularly valuable form of knowledge as the nation was embroiled in the highly contested political fight over school desegregation.

THE RETURN TRIP

While all of the study participants spoke highly of their academic experiences away from the South, they were also very clear about their intent to return home after graduation. This is consistent with other research on the pursuit of graduate education by southern Black educators during this period. Margaret Smith Crocco and Callie Waite's study of over 1,200 Black graduate students at Columbia during the early twentieth century traced several graduates to leadership positions roles in southern education, including numerous teachers, college presidents, deans and department chairs.[11] Scott Baker's examination of desegregation efforts in South Carolina includes profiles of three Black high school principals in Charleston, all of whom were South Carolina natives who earned graduate degrees at Columbia, and all of whom played important roles in improving Black education in the state.[12] Another Columbia graduate, Georgia native Ullyses Bias, is the subject of a book-length examination of Black school leadership during segregation recently completed by Vanessa Siddle Walker.[13] Dissertations by Lowell Kent Davis, Madgetta Dungy, and Darnell Larkin focused on students from various southern states studying at a range of northern institutions. While Dungy's work focused on Black students from various southern states at the University of Iowa, Larkin interviewed Kentucky natives who studied at five different Midwestern universities. Davis selected women from three different states who matriculated at five northern universities. While each author approaches this work with a different focus (i.e., sending states and receiving institutions), taken together they highlight a pattern of Black educators from various parts of the South directing their northern training and credentials back to Black institutions in the South.[14]

Primary sources allow one to trace larger samples of southerners who engaged in this circular migration. The names of dozens of Mississippi out-of-state scholarship aid recipients from the 1960s match those of teachers at "Negro" primary and high schools tracked by the Mississippi Sovereignty Commission during its operation.[15] While the data from these documents are limited to the names of teachers and their schools, the scholarship folders indicate that teachers from across the state, from Claiborne and Forest counties in the south, to Pontotoc and Grenada counties in the north, took advantage of funds created by the state to encourage Blacks to study outside of Mississippi. At the post-secondary level, college catalogues more clearly outline the movement of Black faculty, tracing their routes from the southern

Black colleges where most earned their first degrees, to northern graduate institutions, and then back to work in various HBCUs across the region.

An examination of the Jackson State University and Tougaloo College bulletins over three decades illustrates this pattern. Between 1942 and 1970, the percentage of Black faculty at these schools whose educational profiles include HBCUs and northern universities steadily increased. While some faculty profiles indicate graduate degrees completed, others noted "additional study" or "graduate work" at a northern college or university. At Tougaloo, many faculty members were alumni who returned to serve their alma mater, suggesting a pattern of networking based in the institution. Others were graduates of Alcorn, as well as Tuskegee, Hampton, Howard, Arkansas Baptist (Arkansas Pine Bluff) and Tennessee A&I (Tennessee State) University, and they pursued graduate work at a range of institutions, including Columbia University, University of Wisconsin, University of Minnesota, Northwestern University, Harvard, Cornell, and Indiana Universities. At least 19 Tougaloo faculty and administrators completed graduate work at Columbia during this period, including Tougaloo College Library namesake, L. Zenobia Coleman, who directed the library there for 36 years.[16] The emergence of Columbia as a common institution for Tougaloo faculty points to a different form of networking, where faculty returned from study and recommended their graduate institution to colleagues back at home.

During the same period, several Jackson State College faculty members either attended or completed graduate programs at northern institutions, including Northwestern, Michigan, Pennsylvania, Illinois, Cornell, the University of Chicago, and Wisconsin. Eight earned master's degrees from Ohio State University, including Mrs. Thornton. Seventeen others attended graduate school at Columbia University, including education professor Dr. Jean Ellen McAllister. Over forty Black members of the Jackson State University faculty attended or graduated from Indiana University during this period. These include study participants Mrs. Effie Clay (Education), Drs. Dora and George Washington (Speech and Hearing and Biology, respectively), as well as Dr. Beatrice B. Mosley (Professor of Special Education), and other faculty in music, physical education, history, and political science. Like the Tougaloo example, the predominance of Jackson State faculty attending Indiana, Columbia, and to a lesser degree, Ohio State, suggests that as faculty returned from these campuses, they were sharing their experiences with their colleagues, and encouraging them to attend programs at these institutions.[17]

The study participants, all retired educators living in Jackson, Mississippi and Tuscaloosa, Alabama, shared similar experiences, with several choosing graduate programs based on recommendations from fellow teachers, faculty, advisors, principals, or college presidents, and all stating their intention was to return to the South for work.[18] They served as teachers and administrators in early childhood education, K–12, and higher education in fields ranging from English to Bio-Chemistry. Eight of the nine began their careers as K–12 teachers in Mississippi and Alabama; six of these eventually transitioned to higher education. One was a part-time college instructor while teaching full-time in the public schools before moving to higher education exclusively. Six of the eight participants completed master's degrees and three earned a PhD Six of the nine graduated from Indiana University, and all but one returned to the South immediately upon graduation. In order to understand their career choices, it is important to examine the opportunity structures for African Americans in the North and South.

OPPORTUNITIES FOR BLACK EDUCATORS IN THE NORTH AND SOUTH

For the majority of the study participants, returning home for work in the South was a foregone conclusion. While all spoke favorably of their graduate experiences outside the region, most noted the only reason they left was because most graduate programs in the South were either closed to or had just recently opened to Blacks, and they were either barred from enrolling in graduate programs, or simply not interested in studying at these historically White institutions during the process of desegregation. As O.E. Jordan noted, "The reputation, the history, that was still stuck in a lot of people's craws [sic] . . . they knew that all of those people who were prejudiced hadn't been cleared out."[19] A variety of reasons for returning were cited, including family, community, and other commitments to home. In addition, all had jobs awaiting them at home in K–12 or in higher education, resulting from a combination of various professional and personal networks, as well as the demand for highly trained African American teachers in southern education. This demand at home sharply contrasted with barriers to employment many African American teachers faced in the North during this period.

An examination of the opportunity structures for educators in the North and South provides a useful context for understanding the options available to Black teachers and professors during the period. While higher education and K–12 institutions were different, the dynamics of the opportunity structures were similar and related in important ways. For Black faculty, the overwhelming majority of teaching opportunities were within the system of southern, Black colleges. As James Allen Moss reported, until 1938 fewer than twelve Black teachers were employed in White institutions nationally. Between 1948 and 1958, 78 Blacks served on the faculties of northern universities, but only 29 of these were in continuing capacities. As Moss explained, this state of affairs resulted from a variety of factors, including reluctance on the part of both Blacks and Whites, as well as inertia on the part of White institutions in recruiting Black candidates.[20] A few philanthropic organizations, including the American Friends Service Committee, the Rosenwald Foundation, and the General Education Board (GEB), sought to improve this situation during the 1940s by encouraging northern colleges to consider minority candidates, but with limited results. Some administrators explained that the dearth of Black faculty on northern campuses was not "because of any design," and that their campuses held "no prejudice against Negroes."[21] Yet, when presented with a list of highly qualified African American scholars with credentials from various northern institutions, few chose to contact scholars on the list. One president even wondered, "Why I should go out of my way to indicate any special bias in favor of Negroes, unless I were willing to merit the accusation of unwarranted discrimination against white applicants?"[22]

The impact of these attitudes was borne out in the hiring records of many northern universities. Of the nation's flagship institutions, only three (Massachusetts, Minnesota, and Wisconsin) brought Blacks onto their faculties in the 1940s. Nine flagship institutions hired their first Black academics in the 1950s. Finally, in the 1960s, twenty-four northern flagship universities hired their first African American faculty members, but by this time eight of these universities were in the South. The fact that these northern universities hired their first Black scholars at the same time as southern universities finally acquiesced to desegregation supports Anderson's claim: regardless of the presence or lack of manifest racial prejudice on the part of university officials, predominantly White institutions in the North and the South effectively blocked opportunities for Black faculty for the first half of the twentieth century.[23]

Opportunities to teach in northern K–12 schools were also impacted by institutional racism. Blacks encountered a variety of obstacles to employment in the North, most stemming from the increased racial animosity that developed in the years surrounding the two major waves of Black migration to the North. As Black populations increased, Whites in many northern areas began insisting on residential, and hence, school segregation, factors that impacted Black teachers, students, and families. Officials in Pittsburgh, Dayton, Cleveland, and Indianapolis refused to hire Black teachers in any of its schools until the late 1930s. Later, when these districts did begin hiring Blacks, they were limited to Black schools or to teaching non-academic subjects. Although some districts like New York City, employed Black teachers in racially mixed schools, for the most part, opportunities for Black teachers were confined to segregated schools.[24]

And these opportunities were far less numerous. By 1956, the Milwaukee district employed only 1.1 Black teachers per 1,000 Black students. Other Midwestern cities reported similar statistics, including Chicago (2.4 per 1000), Cleveland (4.0 per 1000), Flint (4.7 per 1000), and Gary (6.0 per

1000). Meanwhile, opportunities to teach in mixed schools were negligible. In the 13 cities surveyed by the National Urban League in 1956, less than 2 percent of the Black teachers hired in these districts had been assigned to schools with mixed or mostly White enrollments. Given these factors, the prospects for Blacks to teach in these districts were very limited.[25]

In contrast, the demand for credentialed public school teachers was growing, particularly after state departments of education began increasing requirements for teachers. In addition to the bachelor's degree, many states began requiring continuing education. For teachers with normal school certificates, enrolling at local Black colleges to complete bachelor's programs became the goal, while teachers with degrees were encouraged to obtain continuing education credits, also at local Black colleges. But out-of-state graduate school subsidies for Blacks provided an incentive to pursue graduate degrees instead of merely accumulating hours, and Black teachers' associations encouraged their members to take advantage of these funds. As Vanessa Siddle Walker explained, "Pursuing degrees at no greater cost to them than if they had stayed home certainly provided a powerful financial incentive to acquire this education and may also explain the desire for graduate degrees."[26] As most southern states operated similar out-of-state tuition aid programs, Black teachers in Mississippi and elsewhere were encouraged by their associations to take advantage of these and other opportunities to meet or exceed state requirements for licensure. While it was surely unintended, the same state governments that increased teaching requirements while barring Blacks' admission to state-run universities were indirectly encouraging Black teachers to exceed these requirements through outside study, and to bring these valuable forms of social capital back to the region.

The need for Black college faculty was also growing, fueled in part by rising demand for education by Black veterans after World War II. This demand soon outpaced the supply of available faculty. As *Journal of Negro Education* editor Charles Thompson wrote in 1947, "For the first time since World War I we have an appreciable number (of Blacks) who, because of the G.I. Bill and savings from high wages during the war, are economically able to go to college."[27] While spaces for these students increased, as the number of Black colleges doubled between 1900 and 1947, the supply of qualified Black faculty failed to keep pace with demand. According to Thompson, only 300–400 Blacks were earning the master's degree each year during the 1940s, barely enough to keep up with growing Black demand for faculty, and many of these graduates were choosing to work in different fields. These factors led to what Thompson described as a "totally inadequate supply" of candidates for available teaching positions in Black colleges.[28] These conditions gradually improved, but demand remained high in the mid-1950s, when many of the study participants were starting their careers. In a 1954 survey of Black college administrators, the most urgent concerns facing Black colleges were accreditation, along with the closely related "sub-problem" of the employment of qualified teachers.[29]

Inadequate supply, combined with steadily rising accreditation standards meant an intense demand for professionally trained teachers in Black schools and colleges. Black educators with advanced degrees were sought not just to fill spaces, but because their credentials were desperately needed for accreditation purposes. As Margaret Crocco, Callie Waite and Vanessa Siddle Walker described, for much of the first half of the twentieth century, Black colleges were regularly denied full membership in the Southern Association of Colleges and Schools (SACS). A multi-tiered system of approval and accreditation effectively banned Black colleges and schools from full membership. Even institutions with previous Class A approval were routinely denied full membership with SACS, a designation which gave institutions a sense of legitimacy.[30] Crocco and Waite explain that Black schools worked hard to remove the stigma of being designated as "second class" institutions through revisions to their curricula and through preparation of their faculty. As they noted, SACS Standard Five stated, "The training of faculty of professorial rank should include at least two years of study in their respective fields of teaching in a fully organized and recognized graduate school."[31] The presence of faculty members with graduate degrees completed or in progress, was invaluable to accreditation, and in raising the profile and legitimacy of their institutions. In addition, the fact that faculty were earning their degrees at a variety of prestigious institutions outside the region only enhanced this legitimacy, as they were connecting with scholars from across the country, and bringing a diversity of ideas and research back to their home institutions. These ideas were redirected back to southern schools and colleges in various forms, and included expanded educational programs, increased subject matter expertise, expanded spheres of influence.

EXPANDED PROGRAMMING

O. E. Jordan completed his bachelor's degree at Tougaloo in 1956, and a master's in administration at Indiana University in 1961, a program that provided him with the leadership skills necessary to expand graded education and educational programming at the schools he led in Mississippi. His graduate program was specifically designed for school principals in Indiana, which exposed him to educational trends from outside his home region. Although he received an offer to stay and work in the Indianapolis school district, he chose to return to the South, and introduce these new ideas to schools in Mississippi. In addition, his advanced degree helped to distinguish him from his professional colleagues at home. "At that time there weren't a lot of Blacks in administration with master's degrees. There weren't a lot of whites, either."[32]

While having an advanced degree solidified his credentials for school leadership, Jordan's professional development and networking included participation in a combination of integrated, as well as all-Black educational organizations, including the National Educational Association (NEA), the National Association of School Principals (NASSP), as well as the Mississippi Teachers Association (MTA) and the Principal's Conference. The latter two organizations comprised of Black educators in the state. According to Wayne Urban and Vanessa Siddle Walker, Black educators' participation in both segregated and integrated professional organizations was important to their work in different ways. Membership in the integrated NASSP and NEA provided valuable information to leaders on current educational trends from across the country for improving secondary schools. But these organizations did not specifically address the needs of Black children, nor did they provide leadership opportunities for Black members, or encourage interracial cooperation amongst members. According to Walker's informant, Georgia educator Ulysses Bias, his presence at these meetings was tolerated, but not his ideas.[33] In contrast, regional meetings of Black educators provided opportunities to actively engage in issues of institution building and professional development. The combination of current research on effective practices from across the nation, along with the opportunity to participate in discussions of how to apply this knowledge to the specific context of all-Black schools was typical of the Black educational leadership experience during this period.[34]

Jordan's professional membership reflected a similar combination of segregated and integrated organizations, and his administrative work reflected these organizational goals, placing him in a position to lead an expansion of graded schools for Blacks in Lawrence, Carthage, and Rolling Fork, Mississippi. Jordan had first-hand knowledge of the need to improve Black schools, dating back to his first year of teaching in the 1940s, noting the long hours and limited resources. "That one year I taught, I was also the principal because my first teaching job was in a one-room school house. I was principal, the janitor, and everything else."[35] As late as 1951, Mississippi still operated over 1,400 one-room school houses, primarily for Black pupils.[36] After a year away from teaching, Jordan was recruited back to education by one of his earliest teachers, then serving as the Supervisor of the County Schools. He was hired to be a principal of an elementary school in Lawrence, Mississippi. Jordan worked there for five years, developing the school from an elementary to a junior high school. This work caught the attention of administrators in Carthage, who recruited him to take over the Black junior high school, which he expanded to a high school. According to Jordan, "They had never had a high school for Blacks in Carthage, Mississippi."[37] The school was eventually re-named in his honor.

His work at Carthage drew the attention of administrators in Rolling Fork, who recruited him to lead Henry Weathers High School in 1962. Under his leadership, the school was approved by SACS. At the time, SACS was still an all-White organization, and Black educators operated within a parallel organization, The Association of Colleges and Schools. While is it not certain whether Jordan was active with The Association, his work in Rolling Fork suggests that he was. Guided by an overall philosophy of institution building and professional development, members of the all-Black Association insisted on the same evaluation standards as the regional organization. According to Walker, this move was calculated by Black teachers as they strove to improve their institutions. As she stated, "The thrust to assure measurement by a comparable standard was a covert mechanism to advocate for equality of resources."[38] Under Jordan's leadership, Weathers High School met the standards needed for accreditation through improved resources and teaching, which in turn improved offerings for Black students. "We had one of the finest schools in the state. I had a microscope in the biology laboratory for each student. I had developed a language laboratory where each kid had a microphone, where the teacher could talk to each individual student. And we had a library out of this world. And we had kids who graduated from that school and went on to places like Yale."[39] In addition, in his capacity as principal and as the president of the Mississippi Teachers' Association, Jordan promoted the importance of higher education in his interactions with teachers and students, noting that a number of graduates of the schools in Carthage and Rolling Fork went on to college and graduate school. He also pushed teachers toward higher education, as well. "I encouraged many of my teachers to get their degrees. I was responsible for encouraging a lot of them."[40] During its 54th convention, the MTA reported that the percentage of Black teachers with college degrees had increased from 20 to 70 percent over the previous eight years, progress which surely aided in the accreditation of schools, and quality of instruction for Black students.[41]

While K–12 professionals like Jordan worked to improve academic offerings to prepare students for college, teachers and administrators in higher education prepared to receive these students, and to enroll them in a growing number of departments and fields. A graduate of Alabama Agricultural and Mechanical University and Northwestern University, Dr. Dora Washington came to Jackson State University in 1957 where she began teaching English, speech, drama courses, and directing the theater program. Later, she and two colleagues, also Northwestern graduates, wrote a proposal to expand the school's language offerings and started the Department of Speech Communication, where they taught the spectrum of basic speech, public speaking, persuasion, theater, interpretation, and drama. While her master's program (Oral Interpretation) was more closely aligned with her undergraduate study of English, she was interested in all ranges of communicative ability, from the highest levels of oratory to individuals with communicative difficulties.

While Speech Communication broadened the field in which she worked, she was still interested in work addressing communicative disorders. Even after starting the Speech Communication Department, she noted, "Still, in the back of my mind I wanted speech pathology."[42] In 1969, she and her husband took leave from Jackson State to pursue doctorates at Indiana University in speech pathology and biology, respectively. As she neared the end of her studies, she was encouraged to apply to numerous other colleges, but the couple chose to return to Jackson State, where she and her colleagues developed the undergraduate program in Speech Pathology, followed shortly by the master's program. According to Washington, many of the program's master's graduates have gone into private practice as Speech Pathologists, diagnosing and treating a variety of communicative disorders. Others graduates had earned doctorates in the field, and held faculty positions where they taught and conducted research on a various communicative topics. Still others completed programs in early childhood education, special education, and psychology, writing and researching on various K–12 issues. As one of the founding members of the Speech Pathology Department, her specific training was crucial to introducing Jackson State students to a vitally important field. She also deployed social capital as she helped students in negotiating their educational and professional journeys.

When Jackson State President Jacob Reddix recruited Washington from Northwestern in 1957, surely he was pleased to learn that her husband, George, was a high school science teacher with a master's degree in biology. He made offers to both educators and George began teaching in a program that had just been launched the year before, when the science faculty shared space in an old army building with two other departments. With the completion of the Just Science Building, the department had its own space, and began the work of building its faculty and program offerings.[43]

Washington joined founding faculty members Bolton Price (Clark, Iowa), Herman Nixon (Howard, Teachers College), A.C. Coleman (Alcorn, Michigan), and Shirley Hardy (Spelman, Columbia) in teaching courses in general biology, general zoology, bacteriology, anatomy and physiology.[44] Early on, Washington found this work to be a welcoming challenge, noting, "If you're going to teach . . . I knew when I came here there was fertile ground. . . If you're going to teach, go where it's needed."[45] The need for science education allowed the faculty to grow and develop in a variety of directions, quickly adding courses in genetics, botany, embryology, microbiology, and comparative anatomy, and additional faculty from programs at Iowa and Michigan State. As enrollments grew, graduates began gaining entry to doctoral and medical programs. Other advancements came in the form of clubs and grants, when Washington and two colleagues won the first National Science Foundation (NSF) grant awarded to the institution. Later, he served as director of an NSF earth science grant, and in 1968, was instrumental in establishing one of the first chapters of the Beta Beta Beta National Biological Honor Society in the state, serving as counselor for the group. The 1960s also saw the addition of graduate programs, as well as science teacher education to the department, adding to the academic, research, and networking opportunities in a department only a decade from its formation.

Early on, the department showed success in preparing students for professional degrees, and over time, pre-professional education became a major focus of the department. It consolidated with the departments of engineering and technology, and added pre-professional programs in medicine, dentistry, veterinary, pharmacy, and environmental and marine science. Today, the department boasts being one of the top five programs in the country in granting biology degrees to African Americans, many of whom continue on to professional programs in health related fields. "I can't count the students I've turned out for medicine, dentistry. One of them was just hired down here as a maxillofacial surgeon, just got hired this past August (2008), grew up here in Mississippi."[46]

In retirement, Washington is still active with the department, serving as an adjunct member of the faculty, teaching and offering academic and career advising to graduate and undergraduate students. With many graduates going on to professional school, he tries to encourage sound decision making as students plan for their graduate education. "Let me tell you something, I try to tell these students, anyone who wants to go to a high profile school, they're looking at name. You've got to look at the professors, through the years, for who has produced what. You know Harvard is a good school, because they have a lot of money, but a lot of schools are superior to Harvard."[47] His experience is informed by his time at Indiana University (IU). While not an Ivy League institution, IU was growing its research program under the leadership of long-time President Herman B. Wells, giving Washington the opportunity to witness a variety of ground breaking work. "They were testing Crest, it wasn't called Crest then, later they named it Crest, Colgate, Palmolive. That chemist just died less than a year ago, that chemist, Dr. Day . . . these things evolved."[48] Washington's social capital comes in the form of connecting students to various graduate programs, as well as providing networking opportunities through clubs and organizations, while his particular subject matter expertise was crucial to building the academic program during the infancy of science education at Jackson State University.

SUBJECT MATTER EXPERTISE

While teaching in Biloxi, Mississippi, Mrs. Effie Clay was encouraged by a teaching colleague to attend Indiana University in order to meet the continuing educational requirements for maintaining her license. This move, promoted by Black principals and teaching associations across the South, allowed her not only to meet licensing requirements, but to earn a master of science in elementary education with specialties in special education and reading. This training enhanced her teaching skills and prepared her work in higher education. While she spoke highly of the entire program, she felt she particularly benefitted from her work in reading under Dr. Leo Fay, whose research on diverse learning groups influenced her work in the classroom. As she stated, "An elementary teacher needs to have two or three plans ready to deal with the variety of learning needs of students."[49] This emphasis on preparation for working with a broad range of learners allowed her to better anticipate the needs of students she encountered in her classrooms.

As she finished graduate school, her family relocated to Jackson, where she was recruited to join the Jackson State University teacher education faculty. There, she joined Dr. John Hall, chair of the Reading Department (Rust, NYU), and several other long-time Mississippi educators with graduate degrees from a wide range of northern institutions. As a teacher educator, her sphere of influence expanded greatly as she taught special education and introduction to teaching courses to all entering education majors. She also supervised elementary education candidates during their student teaching experiences, linking her to hundreds of teachers throughout Mississippi and the region.

Her work was informed by sixteen years of experience teaching across the state, as well as by her graduate work. As she described, elementary teachers were required to teach a variety of subjects, including reading, science, social sciences, and math, areas which she herself had taught, then studied further at IU. Here again, she felt that studying under Fay was particularly beneficial to her work at Jackson State. The director of the Indiana University Reading Laboratory, Fay was a nationally recognized reading theoretician who also emphasized hands-on approaches, including various methods of decoding and pronunciation, and the importance of recognizing the individual, as well as the group needs of reading students. Fay's work was influential both nationally and internationally, and the breadth of his influence was evident to Clay as she supervised elementary teaching candidates at Jackson State.[50] There she recognized similar approaches in Hall's reading students. Although Hall was a graduate of the reading program at NYU, Clay detected the influence of Fay through the students both she and Hall taught at Jackson State. Her graduate work enabled her to be an agent of new ideas while also reinforcing the latest methods in the teaching of reading for the next generation of Mississippi teachers.

Mrs. Ester Rigsby completed a master's in English Education at Indiana University in 1957, a move that facilitated her ability to make valuable contributions to the field of English Literature. At Indiana, changes to the literature curriculum were implemented during her time there, specifically revisions in English Literature, American Literature, Writing, Folklore, and English Language. The Writing Laboratory opened in 1954, and the honors program began in 1955, along with various poetry and lecture series on American and English literature. These revisions provided Rigsby with a variety of resources which she introduced into her high school English courses over her thirty years of teaching in public schools, enlarging the knowledge and resources she brought to her teaching.

With a master's degree, Rigby not only improved her own teaching and exceeded state licensing requirements, she also qualified for college teaching at a time when English educators were in high demand on Black college campuses. In the mid-1950s, Black college administrators listed English and education as the top two instructional areas requiring additional faculty.[51] Rigsby taught part-time at Hines Community College, Jackson State, and Alcorn State throughout her 30 years of public school teaching, simultaneously filling the need for English educators at the secondary and postsecondary levels. She spent another fourteen years as a full-time member of the English faculty at Tougaloo, teaching grammar, writing, U.S. and British literature, specifically the works of Shakespeare and John Milton, writers she focused on during her graduate program.[52] Her work helped to fill a growing demand for English faculty in secondary and higher education.

In essence, the social and cultural capital Clay and Rigsby brought with them benefitted their communities in three ways. First, their coursework reinforced their subject matter knowledge as teachers of reading and English literature. Second, their degrees qualified them for college teaching, and served to strengthen the case for accreditation of their institutions. Finally, by transitioning in to higher education, they greatly expanded their spheres of influence as they worked with students from numerous communities around the state. The networks they developed from teaching in several communities, as well as those garnered through their graduate programs, positioned them to recommend students for jobs or additional educational opportunities. Other educators used these spheres of influence to support student success, as well.

EXPANDED SPHERES OF INFLUENCE

Arguably, increased networking is a natural outcome of graduate training, as one is automatically exposed to a variety of students and faculty through their classes, internships, and other practical experiences. Yet, for some individuals, the role of networking is not just a byproduct of the educational process, but an essential feature of their work. For Mr. Amos Hubbard, retired Dean of Student Affairs at Stillman College in Tuscaloosa, Alabama, recruitment and outreach were a major focus in his work. Hubbard was still greeted on campus as "Dean" more than a decade after his retirement, a testament to the reverence the community holds for his work in opening doors and creating opportunities for students. Hubbard spent his entire career in education in Alabama, and over time has built a web of networks which has been vital not only to his own career, but also for connecting several hundred students to an array of opportunities during his career and in his retirement.

Hubbard is a self-described 'people person', and showed a penchant for creating new opportunities for students early in his career as a high school teacher. A graduate of Alabama State College in Montgomery, Hubbard's first teaching job was in Union Springs (Bolivar County), Alabama in 1955. There, he was approached about establishing an athletic program. "One of my students came to me and said, 'Mr. Hubbard, let's start a football team!' They didn't have football there, in this county, and they wanted it. I started a football team in a school system that never had a Black football team before."[53] This provided students with the opportunity for extra-curricular participation, athletic competition, as well as for some to travel outside of their immediate communities, experiences which likely enhanced their personal and social development.

Hubbard taught high school in Union Springs and in North Ford, Alabama until the late 1960s. During that time, he started graduate school at Michigan State University in 1956, and then transferred to Indiana in 1957, where he completed a master's degree in Health and Safety Education, with a specialization in administration and supervision in 1960. This credential qualified him not only for high school administrative work, but also for work in higher education. In 1968, while under consideration for a principal position, he was approached by the academic dean at Stillman College about heading up a new program on campus. According to Hubbard, "Dr. B.B. Harding was an educational pioneer around here."[54] Harding, who was at Michigan State when Hubbard studied there, encouraged Hubbard to apply for a position directing the newly created Education Achievement Program, a college preparatory program designed to assist students who may not had been admitted through the college's normal admissions process. Hubbard's student advocacy work would take on a much broader role. "I was like the principal of the program here, I had two counselors, three English teachers, a math teacher, the whole bit. And we served 100 students."[55] The program, funded by SACS in 1968, brought one hundred students to campus from seven southern states, Ohio, and New York, and enrolled them in pre-college level speech, English, writing, and mathematics. Designed to parallel the regular freshman curriculum, the program participants took electives and extra-curricular courses with the rest of the freshman class. After the first semester, students whose test scores improved were admitted to the regular freshman class, providing them with the foundation needed for success in college.[56]

In November of the program's first year, Stillman received approval for a second year of operation, and in the spring of 1969 Hubbard and his staff began recruiting for the following year's entering class. Hubbard's hands-on approach to recruiting often involved personal visits to rural communities across the state. While visiting his home town of Dora, Alabama, Hubbard stopped through a nearby community called Paris:

> I was going through there, and there's a little place where people would sit out. So one Sunday morning I was going through and I inquired if they knew of anybody who wanted an opportunity to go to college. And somebody referred me to this guy's house, and I went up to his house, a guy named Bernie. I got Bernie, and talked with him. I said 'You want an opportunity to go to school?' He said 'Yeah!' He had graduated in the last couple of years, wasn't doing anything; he didn't know what to do with his life. I gave him the application, and said 'Get it back to me!' which he did. . . . We spent many hours doing course work, remediation for the most part. To make a long story short, Bernie came down and finished, got his degree in four years. He left here, went to University of Alabama and got his master's, and he's in Atlanta now, and doing well! He thinks I'm the best thing that ever happened to him!

Hubbard's commitment and belief in Bernie's abilities surely impacted his academic trajectory, and opened a path to higher education and graduate study that he probably had not considered.

Later, as the Director of TRIO Programs, Hubbard continued creating opportunities for students by serving as a liaison for students not traditionally targeted for college admission. TRIO, a group of programs funded by the Department of Education, emerged from the 1965 Higher Education Act, and includes Upward Bound, Talent Search, and Student Support Services. Together, these programs target potential first generation college students with tutoring services, workshops, college visits, and other information designed to encourage them to apply for, and graduate from college. This work involved academic remediation, motivating students to graduate, and providing networking opportunities for students to connect with alumni, graduate school officials, and employers. Each year, TRIO alumni return to Stillman and talk with students about their college and professional journeys, emphasizing the importance of staying on track for graduation. These talks provide students with concrete examples of the benefits of persevering through the challenges of college. He described one program alumnus who returns every year to share his stories with current students:

Another guy, very bright boy, was in Upward Bound for four years. He was enrolled in engineering at the University of Alabama, and I had heard he wasn't doing well. So he transferred here, and got his degree, I think in math, but he's an air traffic controller now in Cleveland, Ohio. He comes back every year. And he tells the story that I'm the one who caused him to be as successful as he is. He's an air traffic controller.[57]

These programs allow students to imagine a future for themselves they may not have considered otherwise. Students developed their own contacts with alumni and other professionals in positions to help facilitate opportunities after graduation. In addition, Hubbard's resources and contacts are often needed in opening some doors for students. Through his work with the Student Achievement Program and later with TRIO, Hubbard was a member of SACS, and networked with numerous college officials from across the region. Through these connections, as well as through his fraternity, and his Indiana alumni network, Hubbard was able to place students in contact with other college administrators who in turn facilitated connections and introductions for students. His graduate degree provided the credentials needed to enter higher education, where he contributed social capital in the form of vast networks of contacts he used to help open doors for college students.

Mrs. Jean Jordan's graduate program also enabled her to enlarge her sphere of influence within her current school, as she transitioned from social studies teacher to school counselor after completing a master's degree in counseling. In the summer of 1967 Jordan, along with her husband, enrolled in graduate programs at Idaho State University, where she completed the M.S. in Guidance and Counseling in 1969, and gained a variety of practical knowledge from both inside and outside the classroom. In addition to the theories and methods of counseling she gained in her program, her time in Idaho allowed her to observe a variety of differences and similarities between these two geographically and culturally distinct regions. For example, both were essentially rural spaces. "I don't think there was a lot of difference, I really don't, because they were both rural, and they had to use what they had, so far as the environment that they were in. They may have done different things, but they both were very rural. For instance, in the South, where I came from, the crops were different, the topography of the land was different, but they were still rural, just their agriculture was something else."[58] Still, a host of cultural differences counterbalanced the similarities she observed between these regions. The predominance of the Mormon faith was one difference. "But they would always tell you they were reformed Mormons; they were not with the old church. They seemed pretty fair minded."[59] In addition, the racial composition was decidedly different. "For me, I think the most surprising thing was that their minorities were Indians and Mexicans; there were very few Blacks that lived in the community. And even the Blacks who lived there, they called them Natives;

they didn't even see them as being Black."[60] In Jordan's counseling she interviewed Native American and Mexican students, an experience she noted aided in her work with ethnically and socially diverse students. "I think it helped me in being able to relate to students from various social, economic, and academic levels... and through that, I learned not to try to change a person's perspective, but rather to try to help them understand new things, but through their own frame of reference."[61] Her advanced knowledge in counseling theory and methods, combined with the practical training she completed with diverse students, aided the work in which she would soon engage, as school desegregation would become a reality just as she completed her program.

When Jean Jordan completed her master's degree in 1969, desegregation of public education was just beginning in Mississippi. Local school officials effectively resisted and delayed implementing desegregation measures until the U.S. Supreme Court, in *Alexander v. Holmes Country Board of Education*, ordered non-complying districts to merge separate schools by December 31, 1969.[62] While late to the Magnolia State, the arduous process of replacing dual school systems with unitary ones had already proven devastating to the ranks of Black teachers and principals across the South. According to Michael Fultz, "From the mid-1950s to the mid-1970s, African-American school staff at all levels—teachers, principals, coaches, counselors, band directors, even cafeteria workers—were fired, demoted, harassed, and bullied as White communities throughout the South reacted... to the reality of court-ordered desegregation. No one was exempt." Teacher 'displacement' took these and other forms, including "forced resignations, non-hiring, token promotions, reduced salaries, diminished responsibility, and coercion to teach subjects or grade levels other than those for which individuals were certified or had experience."[63] Because of this experience, the U.S. Court of Appeals promptly followed the *Alexander* decision with mandates in *Hamilton v. Jackson*, directing districts to provide protections to teachers displaced specifically due to the process of desegregation, and requiring that district-wide teacher-to-student ratios of both races be maintained in any employment decisions resulting from the specific process of desegregation. Desegregation had devastated the ranks of Black teachers in other parts of the South, but because Mississippi resisted for so long its eventual capitulation coincided with federal mandates that reduced the extensive displacement experienced in earlier experiments in desegregation.

Mississippi's staunch resistance to the *Brown* decision may have benefitted some Black educators in an additional way. As news of desegregation-related job losses surely spread through formal and informal networks during the early phases of desegregation, the delay in implementation in Mississippi may have provided educators there with the time necessary to make alternate career plans should they face the same fate. Although the timeframe for this study ends in 1970, and this question was not addressed, such contingencies may have been on the minds of Black teachers. Of the nine educators interviewed for this study, eight began their careers as K–12 teachers, but only two retired from primary or secondary schools. While the acquisition of graduate degrees definitely enhanced their work in public school classrooms, these credentials also qualified them for work in colleges and universities, benefitting these individuals with an additional avenue for work, as well as institutions looking for qualified Black faculty and administrators.

Each of these educators impacted their institutions in unique ways. Through expanding middle schools into high schools, initiating new academic departments, bringing advanced knowledge in their fields, or by introducing students to their broad networks, these educators helped to improve schools for Black students in numerous ways. While their social and cultural capital took varying, sometimes overlapping forms, taken together, their work made significant differences to the experiences of students at their institutions. In addition, their social capital was more diverse than that of the previous generation, as their credentials were earned in a broad range of institutions, institutions that were racially desegregated. Experience in multicultural environments meant that these educators were better prepared to participate in, and to groom students for the eventual desegregation of education in the South. As leaders and role models in their communities, the cross cultural experiences they gained were perhaps the most important form of social capital these teachers brought with them, as the region prepared for the volatile political period that lay ahead.

NOTES

1. Lottie Thornton, Interview with author, Jackson, MS, September 11, 2008.
2. Ibid.
3. James Gregory, *The Southern Diaspora: How the Great Migrations of Black and White Southerners Transformed America* (Chapel Hill: University of North Carolina Press, 2005), 322–323.
4. Pierre Bourdieu, "Distinction: A social critique of the judgment of taste: The forms of capital," in *Handbook of Theory and Research for the Sociology of Culture*, ed. John Richardson (New York, NY: Greenwood Press, 1986), 241–259. Retrieved from http://econ.tau.ac.il/papers/publicf/Zeltzer1.pdf.
5. V. P. Franklin, "Introduction: Cultural Capital and African American Education," *The Journal of African American History* 87 (2002): 175–181; Adah Ward Randolph, "Building upon Cultural Capital: Thomas Jefferson Ferguson and the Albany Enterprise Academy in Southeast Ohio, 1863–1886," *The Journal of African American History* 87 (2002): 182–195; Christopher M. Span, "'I Must Learn Now or Not at All': Social and Cultural Capital in the Educational Ini-

tiatives of Formerly Enslaved African Americans in Mississippi, 1862–1869," *The Journal of African American History* 87 (2002): 196–205; Carter J. Savage, "Cultural Capital and African American Agency: The Economic Struggle for Effective Education for African Americans in Franklin, Tennessee, 1890–1967," *The Journal of African American History,* 87 (2002): 206–235.

6. Nancy E. Beadie, "Education and the Creation of Capital, or What I have Learned by Following the Money," *History of Education Quarterly* 48 (2008): 1–29.

7. Vanessa Siddle Walker, *Their Highest Potential: African American School Community in the Segregated South* (Chapel Hill, University of North Carolina Press, 1996).

8. George Washington, Interview with author, Jackson, MS, September 11, 2008.

9. Dora Washington, Interview with author, Jackson, MS, March 21, 2007.

10. Edgar Smith, Interview with author, September 12, 2008.

11. Callie Waite and Margaret S. Crocco, "Fighting Injustice Through Education," *History of Education* 33 (2004): 573–583.

12. R. Scott Baker, *Paradoxes of Desegregation: African American Struggles for Educational Equity in Charleston, South Carolina* (Columbia: University of South Carolina Press, 2006), 39–40.

13. Vanessa Siddle Walker, *Hello Professor: A Black Principal and Professional Leadership in the Segregated South* (Chapel Hill: University of North Carolina Press, 1996).

14. Madgetta T. Dungy, "African American graduate school experiences at the University of Iowa, 1937–1959: An Oral History" (PhD diss., University of Iowa, 1997); Vernell D. Larkin, "Dreams Fulfilled and Dreams Denied: The Ironies and Paradoxes of being a Student under the Anderson Mayer State Aid Act, 1936–1950" (PhD diss., University of Kentucky, 2001); Lowell K. Davis, "A story untold: How five African American women used state aid acts to attain advanced degrees, 1940–1959" (PhD diss., Indiana University, 2007).

15. Scholarship folders, 1955–1968; Mississippi Department of Archives and History; Mississippi Sovereignty Commission Online, Name Search, http://mdah.state.ms.us/arrec/digital_archives/sovcom/#basicname

16. Tougaloo College Catalogues, 1942–43 through 1969–70.

17. Jackson State College Bulletins, 1942–43 through 1969–70.

18. One participant, O.E. Jordan, died in April, 2010.

19. O.E. Jordan, Interview with author, Jackson, MS, September 9, 2008.

20. James Allen Moss, "Negro Teachers in Predominantly White Colleges," *The Journal of Negro Education* 27 (1958): 459.

21. James D. Anderson, "Race, Meritocracy, and the American Academy during the Immediate Post-World War II Era," *History of Education Quarterly 33* (1993); 158.

22. Herbert G. Espy to Fred G. Wale, January 24, 1947. Cited in Belles, "College Faculty, Negro Scholar," 388.

23. James D. Anderson, "Race, Meritocracy, American Academy," 153; Anonymous, "The First Black Faculty Members at the Nation's 50 Flagship State Universities," *Journal of Blacks in Higher Education* 39 (2003): 118–126.

24. Davison Douglas, *Jim Crow Moves North: The Battle over Northern School Segregation, 1865–1964* (Cambridge: Harvard University Press, 2005), 174–175.

25. Douglas, *Jim Crow Moves North, 178;* Jack Dougherty, "That's When We Were Marching for Jobs": Black Teachers and the Early Civil Rights Movement in Milwaukee. *History of Education Quarterly* 38 (1998): 121–141.

26. Walker, "African American Teaching, South," 767.

27. Charles H. Thompson, "Editorial Comment: The Improvement of the Negro College Faculty." *Journal of Negro Education* 16 (1947): 2.

28. Thompson, "Editorial Comment, Negro Faculty," 2; Moss, "Negro Teachers, White Colleges," 453.

29. R. Grann Lloyd and George H. Walker, "Teacher Supply and Demand in the Negro College," *The Journal of Negro Education* 23 (1954): 421–427.

30. Walker, *Hello Professor,* 81, 85.

31. Waite and Crocco, "Fighting Injustice Through Education," 581.

32. O. E. Jordan, Interview with author, Jackson, MS, September 9, 2008.

33. Walker, *Hello Professor,* 116.

34. Wayne Urban, *Gender, Race, and the National Education Association: Professionalism and its Limitations.* (New York, NY: Routledge Falmer, 2000): 212–215.

35. O. E. Jordan, Interview with author, Jackson, MS, September 9, 2008.

36. Biennial Report and Recommendations of the State Superintendent of Public Education, 1953–1955, 645. Cited in Charles C. Bolton, "Mississippi's School Equalization Program, 1945–54: 'A Last Gasp to Try to Maintain a Segregated Educational System.'" *The Journal of Southern History* 66 (2000): 804.

37. O. E. Jordan, Interview with author.

38. Walker, *Hello Professor,* 86.

39. O. E. Jordan, Interview with author.

40. Ibid.

41. "O. E. Jordan heads Mississippi Teachers Group" *Jet Magazine,* April 14, 1960, 19.

42. Dora Washington, Interview with author, Jackson, MS, March 21, 2007.

43. Jackson State University, Department of Biology history, http://www.jsums.edu/cset/biohistory.htm.

44. Department of Biology History, Jackson State University, http://www.jsums.edu/cset/biohistory.htm

45. George Washington, Interview with author, Jackson, MS, September 11, 2008.

46. Ibid.

47. Ibid.

48. Ibid.

49. Effie J. Clay, Interview with author, September 10, 2008.

50. See Leo C. Fay "What Research Has to Say about Reading in the Content Areas," *The Reading Teacher* 8,(1954): 68-112; Leo C. Fay, "How Can We Develop Reading Study Skills for the Different Curriculum Areas?" *The Reading Teacher* 6(1953): 12-18; Leo C. Fay, "The Relationship between Specific Reading Skills and Selected Areas of Sixth Grade Achievement." *The Journal of Educational Research* 42 (1950): 541–547; Leo C. Fay. "Trends in the Teaching of Elementary Reading" *The Phi Delta Kappan* 41 (1960); 345–348; "Indiana

Study Affirms Reading Skills." *Wilmington Star News*, April 16, 1978; "Reading Skills Found to be Same as 30 Years Ago," *The Dispatch*, April 15, 1978.

51. Lloyd and Walker, "Teacher Supply and Demand," 422, 424

52. Philip R. Wikelund, "Attracting English Majors at Indiana University." *College Composition and Communication* 7 (1955): 80–84; Stanton Millet and James L. Morton, "The Writing Laboratory at Indiana University," *College English* 18 (1956): 38–39.

53. Amos Hubbard, Interview with author, Tuscaloosa, AL, March 22, 2007.

54. Ibid.

55. Ibid.

56. Ibid. "College Doors Opening for College Shut Outs," *The Tuscaloosa News*, 6, November 17, 1968.

57. Amos Hubbard, Interview with author.

58. Jean Jordan, Interview with author, September 13, 2008.

59. Ibid.

60. Ibid.

61. Ibid.

62. *Alexander v. Holmes Country Board of Education* 396 U.S. 19 (1969); *Singleton v. Jackson Municipal Separate School District* (426 F2d 1364, 1970); "*Singleton v. Jackson Municipal Separate School District*," in *Encyclopedia of African American Education*, ed. Kofi Lomotey (New York, Sage, 2010), 578–81 Sage (2010), 578–81.

63. Michael Fultz, "The Displacement of Black Educators Post *Brown*: An Overview and Analysis" *History of Education Quarterly* 44, (A Special Issue on the Fiftieth Anniversary of the *Brown v. Board of Education* Decision) (2004): 25–26.

CHAPTER 6

WORDS OF ACTION

The Speeches of President Alfonso Elder and the North Carolina Student Movement

Eddie R. Cole
College of William and Mary

To the amazement of many persons, we have seen our students achieve through social action what was thought to be impossible. It is, therefore, past the time in which they must achieve what some may now think is impossible in the area of intellectual achievement.

—Alfonso Elder, faculty and staff address,
North Carolina College, September 10, 1962.

By 1960, Dr. Alfonso Elder had been in office for twelve of the fifteen years he would serve as president of the historically Black North Carolina College in Durham (now North Carolina Central University). Yet, during the same year, Elder and other college presidents in North Carolina faced a new challenge—student-initiated demonstrations against legalized racial segregation. Despite many presidents' years of administrative experience, they

Using Past as Prologue, pages 141–165
Copyright © 2015 by Information Age Publishing
All rights of reproduction in any form reserved.

were mere novices to the student unrest that seemingly appeared out of no-where.[1] In fact, one president considered the demonstrations "unusual."[2]

The first demonstration was small. It started in Greensboro on February 1, 1960, when four students from the historically Black North Carolina A&T State University sat at a segregated lunch counter at the downtown F. W. Woolworth, the local five and ten cent store, refusing to leave until served. The store management refused to serve the students, and eventually, the store closed for the day at its normal hours. Peacefully, the four students returned to the North Carolina A&T campus.[3] Seemingly small, and perhaps even harmless, the first day of protests ended. Yet, news of the demonstration spread quickly, and within a month, similar student-led demonstrations had occurred in ten cities in North Carolina. The same happened across the South in seven cities in Virginia, three in Florida, four in South Carolina, two in Alabama, one in Kentucky, one in Maryland, and two in Tennessee.[4]

With much of the attention on North Carolina, where the student demonstrations started, college presidents, whether leading a historically Black or a predominately White college, were faced with students participating in support of or fighting against desegregation. Many presidents sat quietly on the issue of student protests, and archival findings demonstrate that alumni and other campus constituents pleaded with some presidents in North Carolina to reprimand student demonstrators.[5] Yet, Elder stands out as a vocal leader, not only in support of college students' participation in the Civil Rights Movement but overall issues of race and Blacks in the South.

This chapter examines Elder's public speeches between the initial demonstration in Greensboro on February 1, 1960, and when the Civil Rights Act was signed into law on July 2, 1964. There is research focused on the educational experiences of Blacks in segregated southern schools during the Jim Crow era, such as James D. Anderson's *The Education of Blacks in the South, 1860–1935*, and Vanessa Siddle Walker's *Their Highest Potential: An African School Community in the Segregated South*. These books, among others, focused on the extraordinary work of Black educators during legalized segregation and offer a counter-narrative to previous historical research that portrayed Blacks' education during this era as "inferior."[6] However, little is known about how Black educators have communicated messages of support and racial uplift in the midst of student protests against legalized racial segregation. This chapter complements the existing literature by exploring the complex public disposition Black leaders had to exhibit to satisfy both White leaders' desires and serve the Black community. Previous research has focused primarily on Black college presidents' private correspondence to governors, legislators, and other White leaders as a backdrop to public actions.[7] Yet, these presidents' public speeches before Black and White audiences have not been explored. The case of Elder invites scholars to critically assess how Black leaders historically strategically used words and how the words used help us understand their actions.

Elder believed students had the right to protest segregated public spaces because students were also private citizens. His speeches outlined that it was not the responsibility of the college to impede upon citizens' rights. If students did not violate campus policies, the protests were acceptable. Elder also demanded Black students accept academic responsibility and excel in the classroom. These views were further complicated by his approach of being more critical of Black people when speaking to Black audiences as opposed to when he spoke before Whites. To fully understand Elder's speeches, this chapter first uses the historical context of the social standing of Blacks' educational attainment in America, as well as Elder's personal background, to set the stage for analysis of Elder's public speeches and his formal and informal use of speech to address issues of race.

BLACKS' ACCESS TO HIGHER EDUCATION

Blacks' entry into American higher education as students plays out like an afterthought with opportunities for Whites and Native Americans prioritized. For instance, in the summer of 1619, 20 Africans held captive were released to colonists in Jamestown, Virginia.[8] Two years later, in 1621, settlers moved forward with plans to establish two collegiate schools in the Virginia colony—one as a seminary and the other for "an Indian college."[9] In the spring of 1622, this attempt to establish a college for the "improvement of the Indians" failed when some 340 settlers were attacked by Native Americans, which nineteenth century historians described as an "insurrection of savages."[10] In Virginia, in 1693, the College of William and Mary would become the second attempt in the colony to invite Native Americans into formal education. For the most part in Colonial America, the first colleges were only open to White men interested in training to become ministers and "to convert the Indians."[11] Simultaneous to the growing number of slaves was the building of more colleges in early America. Throughout the following decades, alongside repeated attempts to colonize more than educate Native Americans, populations besides affluent White men eventually gained access to higher education by the late 1700s.[12]

It was not until roughly 200 years after the 1621 plan to establish a college in Virginia that a minuscule number of Blacks were even considered for enrollment at American colleges. In 1823, Alexander Lucius Twilight was the first Black to earn a college degree at Vermont's Middlebury College.[13] In 1833, Oberlin College was founded, and Blacks and women were openly and freely admitted. About the same time, White missionaries and abolitionists spearheaded efforts to open schools with the intended purpose of educating Blacks in substantial numbers. Today, Cheyney University in Pennsylvania (1837), Lincoln University of Pennsylvania (1854), and Wilberforce University in Ohio (1856) function as a testament to the early, pre-Civil War efforts to establish Black colleges.[14]

During the Civil War, the 1862 Morrill Act was passed. This legislation, known as the Land-grant Act, provided federal land to states for the establishment of colleges. The initial academic programs were agriculture, engineering, and home economics, among other vocational-focused subjects. Although this act expanded the purposes and goals of higher education to a broader student demographic, it initially had little impact on Blacks' education. Among the colleges established following the Morrill Act of 1862, Alcorn College in Mississippi (now Alcorn State University) is the only Historically Black College and University (HBCU) founded under this act.[15] With the passage of the Thirteenth Amendment in 1865, which deemed slavery unconstitutional, several northern churches and abolitionist groups funded the start of more than 500 small schools for Blacks throughout the South.[16] To a less widespread extent, Blacks founded their own schools.[17] Yet, regardless of being founded by Blacks or Whites, these schools were mostly elementary level with little educational focus beyond basic literacy skills. It was the 1890 Morrill Act that catalyzed the establishment of several more state-owned HBCUs.[18] With seventeen state-supported HBCUs opening after the 1890 act, educational opportunity expanded for Blacks, although more studied and trained in agriculture and home economics, among other practical areas.[19]

However, the majority of HBCUs were private, and as historian James D. Anderson noted, White missionary societies "were also largely responsible for sustaining the leading Black colleges."[20] The children of the era's Black elite attended these private-supported HBCUs. Howard and Fisk universities are notable omissions from the list of fiscally strapped HBCUs, as both had better equipped campuses; however, "with a few exceptions from the Black upper crust, all students at HBCUs worked" to keep these institutions open.[21]

As stated earlier, most HBCUs opened in the late 1800s and early 1900s. Yet, these normal schools were colleges in name only.[22] This is because the schools only offered curriculums on elementary and high school levels, and as a result of being "founded with haste and limited financial backing, many (HBCUs) ceased to operate following 1900."[23] Limited elementary and secondary schooling also played a part. The longstanding lack of societal inclusion and limited aid from the federal and state governments for HBCUs are among the reasons why, in 1917, only the state-funded Florida A&M College enrolled college-level students, although it was only twelve students.[24]

Notably, and similarly, these challenges regarding higher education opportunities in the South were not limited to HBCUs. In the South, the academic development of all-White colleges paled in comparison to higher education in northern states. For instance, founded in 1848, the state-supported University of Wisconsin strived "to gain national stature as full-fledged modern universities" that educated the state's residents in "a range of fields, including accounting, public health, geography, medicine, law, and engineering."[25] In southern states, on the other hand, South Carolina College (now the University of South Carolina) was established to preserve political power in the South, and by the mid-1800s, its students were being educated in debate, which focused on "the arguments in favor of slavery."[26] This evidence reveals southern White institutions' lack of a robust collegiate curriculum compared to northern institutions, although not for lack of resources like Black colleges.

It is this understanding of all of southern higher education that demonstrates how after 200 years of complete denial to higher education and another 100 years of scant aid in support of state-supported HBCUs, several Black colleges stood as impoverished testaments to the state of Blacks' education in America by the early 1900s. Yet, under the leadership of several politically savvy Black college presidents, many state-supported Black colleges still built collegiate level curricula that soon became among the best in southern states despite the lack of comparable resources to southern White institutions. This is evident at North Carolina College in Durham. Originally chartered as a private institution, it opened in 1910 as the National Religious Training School and Chautauqua. In 1923, the state of North Carolina purchased the Durham school. After several name changes—Durham State Normal School, North Carolina College for Negroes, and eventually North Carolina College—the institution became the first state-supported liberal arts college for Blacks in the nation.[27] James E. Shepard, who served as president from 1910 to 1947, moved from pleas for more support from state legislators during the college's early years to North Carolina College eventually being "positioned as the Black counterpart to the University of North Carolina" by the end of presidency.[28] Shepard's foundation set the stage for Alfonso Elder to take over as president of North Carolina College in 1948.

Elder: A Product of Segregated Schools

As many Black schools pulled together a curriculum on a shoestring budget, in the rural middle Georgia town of Sandersville, Alfonso Elder was born February 26, 1898. Born to Thomas and Lillian Elder, the younger Elder attended his father's school, the Thomas J. Elder High and Industrial School in Sandersville. Thomas served as principal from 1889 to 1942.

After graduating from his father's school, Elder attended the historically Black Atlanta University, where he graduated magna cum laude in 1921. The same year, the Georgia native made his way to North Carolina for his first teaching job at the historically Black, all-women's Bennett College in Greensboro, where he taught mathematics for one year. The next year, he taught mathematics at the historically Black Elizabeth City State Teachers College (now Elizabeth City State University) in North Carolina. Shortly after, Elder went north to earn his Master of Arts in 1924 from Columbia University's Teachers College in New York.[29]

Of course, Elder, who graduated with honors from Atlanta University, had to leave the segregated South for graduate school since most HBCUs at the time suffered from lack of financial support for graduate-level programs and southern states' White colleges did not accept non-Whites. Perhaps the best compromise between the state and Black students concerning graduate and professional education opportunities was in Kentucky. In the 1930s, Charles W. Anderson became the first Black legislator in Kentucky since Reconstruction. Marion Brunson Lucas and George C. Wright wrote of Anderson's first month in office:

> He [Anderson] introduced a bill to appropriate state funds to 'pay the tuition of qualified students who desire courses at the University of Kentucky or other state-supported institutions which are denied to Negro students on account of the provisions of the Kentucky Constitution governing separate education.' The bill, known as the Anderson-Mayer State Aid Act, passed both the house and senate without a negative vote.[30]

This state policy was indicative of the South. Each of Anderson's fellow state legislators was White. To successfully support the educational efforts of other Blacks, Anderson secured, with no resistance, a policy that would fund Black education. The truth was that White legislators preferred financing a Black citizen's out-of-state education during the Great Depression instead of better financing their state-supported Black colleges or admitting Black students to its all-White colleges during that time.

Because of this policy, Elder traveled back and forth between his academic jobs at southern HBCUs and educational advancement opportunities outside of the South from 1924 to 1938. Starting in 1924, he served as the dean of college and teacher of mathematics for North Carolina College. During his nearly two decades in this position, Elder completed summer training at the University of Cambridge in England and the University of Chicago before earning a doctorate of education in 1938 from Columbia's Teachers College. Now, with a doctorate and extensive professional experience, Elder returned to Georgia in 1943, when he was named director of graduate school education at his alma mater, Atlanta University. After five years in Atlanta, Elder started his second stay in North Carolina—this time to become president of North Carolina College in 1948.[31]

As Elder steadily progressed through the academic ranks of Black colleges in the 1930s and 1940s, some of the Black presidents of HBCUs and other Black educators became critical of Black students' lack of consciousness of racial struggles facing the majority of the race. In 1930, during a commencement speech at historically Black Howard University, W. E. B. DuBois said, "Our college man today is, on the average, a man untouched by real culture.... The greatest meetings of the Negro college year, like those of the White college year, have been vulgar exhibitions of liquor, extravagance, and fur coats."[32] In 1933, noted historian and scholar Carter G. Woodson's *The Mis-Education of the Negro* blamed White-educated Black teachers of teaching the same inferior ideology that White teachers had taught them, and therefore, "the Negroes, thus mis-educated, are of no service to themselves."[33] In 1937, Lafayette Harris, president of historically Black Philander Smith College in Arkansas, spoke of Black students: "Probably nothing gives one more concern than the frequently apparent fatalistic and nonchalant attitude of many a Negro college student and educated Negro." And in 1938, Randolph Edmonds, a professor at historically Black Dillard University, echoed Woodson's ethos that, "The Negro youth is being educated to regard race with contempt, not only by White teachers in mixed schools, but by Negro instructors in Negro colleges."[34]

The "talented tenth"[35] had distanced itself from the struggles facing the majority of Black people; those Blacks struggling without formal education were fighting for their survival. As many of Elder's academic contemporaries saw it, it was time for Black college students to act.

A PROTEST TRADITION BEGINS

Despite the persistent critique of Black college students' apathy, mass protests were slowly establishing its place in America. Previous Black protests included Marcus Garvey's Back-to-Africa Movement of the 1920s and A. Phillip Randolph's proposed March on Washington in 1941;[36] however, these protests were sporadic. It was the 1950s that started the organized and widespread protest tradition that we now refer to as the modern Civil Rights Movement. Historians noted that this signified "[t]he persistent struggle had given rise to a protest tradition."[37] The first of many city-wide bus boycotts would occur in Baton Rouge, Louisiana. In 1953, weeks of protest of the city's public transportation stifled the Baton Rouge's local economy at a loss of $1,600 per day to the city. The local officials soon changed its bus seating policy to a first come, first serve basis, which did not restrict Blacks to having to defer their seats to Whites.[38] The next year, 1954, the landmark

Supreme Court *Brown v. Board of Education* decision declared "separate but equal" in American schools unconstitutional. In 1955, the historic Montgomery Bus Boycott occurred after Rosa Parks was arrested for refusing to give up her seat to a White patron. By the late 1950s, students started to lead demonstrations. One example, in 1959, two Florida A&M University students, sisters Patricia and Priscilla Stephens, joined Daisy Young, another Black woman, along with a few others, and planned a bus boycott and the city's bus system was desegregated with relative ease.[39] This is just one example that the protest tradition—sit-ins, boycotts, and other moments of activism—was active in dozens of southern states, including North Carolina, and students had taken ownership as being activists in America.

Activism in North Carolina

In Durham, during Elder's fifteen-year presidency at North Carolina Central, numerous sit-ins occurred between 1957 and 1960. Floyd McKissick, a young attorney who had led the NAACP Youth Division, Reverend Douglas Moore, and a group of young people, including a few White students at the predominately White Duke University, led Durham sit-ins of the local bus station waiting rooms, parks, hotels and other public places. In fact, in 1957, Moore and a few others were arrested for a sit-in demonstration at a Durham ice cream parlor, as the NAACP Youth Council coordinated these sit-ins.[40]

The Durham exhibition of the protest tradition was no different than the dozens of other demonstrations occurring in other southern cities. Leaders of churches and social justice organizations had organized people, many of which still teenagers, for this movement. In fact, each of the four North Carolina A&T students, at some point, had a connection with Black churches or equity organizations. The four students knew McKissick and George Simkins, Jr., who headed the NAACP chapter in Greensboro, as each of the North Carolina A&T students had been members of the NAACP Youth Council. Therefore, the four students knew about the Durham sit-ins, as well as other sit-ins across the South, prior to their demonstration at the local F. W. Woolworth lunch counter. Although "Greensboro Four" acted separately from the NAACP, McKissick became their legal counsel.[41] McKissick, on the relationship between the Durham and Greensboro demonstrations, said: "The two towns in North Carolina to really emphasize the movement and to push it were Durham and Greensboro, where there was the leadership and financial ability to support a youth movement."[42] For the youth, the scene had been set for February 1, 1960.

February One

Following the first day of the February 1960 lunch counter sit-ins, the tension grew between Black and White residents of Greensboro. The next day, February 2, more students joined the four to occupy the lunch counters; by day three, more than a hundred students were sitting at the Woolworth lunch counters waiting until Black customers could be served.[43]

By then, racial tensions heightened as White men staged a response to the sit-ins by attempting to occupy the lunch counter seats prior to the student activists.

On February 3, a *Greensboro Record* editorial stated "there is a dangerous vacuum in the relations between the races in Greensboro we fear."[44] The editorial noted that the "Negroes" are anything but passive and that "the White leadership of the community can ill afford to be passive and indifferent under the circumstances." The next day, sixty-three of the sixty-six lunch counter seats had been filled by Black students.[45] Tensions grew.

By February 6, a White teenager and twenty-two-year-old Black man were both arrested and charged for disorderly conduct at a downtown store. It was reported that officers said the two were pushing and shoving in the aisle next to the lunch counter of the store that had been occupied by about fifty to sixty Black students.[46] Another incident involved the arrests of three Whites for "assault with a deadly weapon—a burning piece of paper."[47] It was reported that the men set paper on fire beneath a Black man sitting at the lunch counter. The Woolworth's store was eventually closed during the melee after a bomb threat was called into the store.

Despite the tensions at the lunch counters, it was not as simple as Blacks versus Whites. Following the leadership of students from Greensboro's historically Black North Carolina A&T and Bennett College, White students from local predominately White colleges also protested to desegregate the lunch counters. By February 8, 1960, just one week after the first sit-in, national attention focused on North Carolina. That day the *Greensboro Record* editorial board reported that the city's interracial commission had decided to reorganize its membership "in order that it might better serve the community."[48] As a result, a nation of onlookers focused on the student movement in North Carolina and its colleges.

ELDER: A VOCAL LEADER

Elder focused a number of his speeches over the coming years on issues associated with the accompanying student sit-ins and racial inequality. One of these issues was the responsibility of the college. Alumni, legislators, and other campus constituents demanded college presidents either reprimand or demonstrate support of student protests. In response, Elder explained the duty of the college in relation to social action. The next issue he addressed Blacks' cultural and the societal status. Lastly, Elder offered suggestions for youth protestors and informed them of the leverage Blacks had in dictating social change.

The Responsibility of the College

In year fourteen of a fifteen-year presidency of North Carolina College, Elder delivered a speech at the predominately White Duke University in Durham on February 25, 1962. Titled "The Responsibility of the University to Society," his talk addressed college administrators' ongoing debate about the responsibility of the college when it came to student protests against segregation. Before attendees of a regional meeting for the National Student Association, Elder placed emphasis on student involvement in out-of-class affairs. In 1962, the student demonstrations were larger than those initial protests in the 1960s with crowds now inching towards 1,000 college students assembling for demonstrations at any given moment in any major city in North Carolina. As a result, Elder shared his views on the principles and generalizations that he believed should govern issues related to students. Although Elder did not directly speak about racial equality, which was the premise of the North Carolina student movement, he used this speech on Duke's campus to argue that students, just like faculty and staff, cannot separate their personal lives from their campus lives, and people should react to the part of their identity that is most salient to them.[49]

Elder said, "Persons do not always distinguish in their thinking between what the school actually is and what they think that the school ought to be." He added, "The assumption is conflicts and confusion arise regarding the responsibility of the university or college to individuals and individuals to the school from a misunderstanding or disagreement regarding the purposes of the institution, that is, what the school is designed to do." He challenged the audience that disagreement between and among groups, whether students, faculty, alumni or members of governing bodies, will occur.[50]

The notion of constant internal conflict on campuses is important because further examination of historical context shows the same spring as this speech, leaders of the predominately White Guilford College in Greensboro announced plans to enroll two Kenyan students for the upcoming fall of 1962.[51] By this time, Duke, where Elder was speaking, had only desegregated its graduate student population but had not yet enrolled Black undergraduates. The first Black undergraduate students would not enroll at Duke until 1963.[52] In fact, historian R. Scott Baker's work on the complexities of desegregation in the South detailed a 1953 study by sociologist

Guy B. Johnson, who found that administrators at southern predominately White colleges "had an interest in holding down the number of Negro enrollees."[53]

As Elder continued his speech at Duke, he said the college is responsible for the acquisition of knowledge and must have faith that its students will proceed with the application of that knowledge in a manner that best serves society. Therefore, without mention of race or racism, Elder said he will not dictate how students apply what they have learned. "When social action is taken, the school can only hope that a good job of teaching has been done. If the action taken reflects the use of a high level of intelligence and the use of a value system which has been refined through reflection and study of man's noblest aspirations, then the school can take a measure of pride in action," Elder added.[54] This stance suggests Elder had established himself as an educational leader in North Carolina who would not reprimand students for participating in the sit-ins.

This response stands out among how Black presidents of HBCUs responded to the student activism of the early 1960s. The October 1960 issue of *Ebony* magazine profiled Black college presidents and their responses to the student sit-ins. A distinct pattern emerged—many presidents of state-supported Black colleges suspended students and many private Black colleges, such as Fisk University, supported the students' efforts to desegregate public spaces. By the fall of 1960, more than 100 students at Black colleges had been expelled or placed on probation. Felton Clark suspended eighteen students at Southern University, Rufus B. Atwood expelled twelve students at Kentucky State College, and H. Councill Trenholm promised the governor and the all-White board that he would stop student demonstrators at Alabama State College.[55] The next year, in 1961, fourteen students were expelled from Tennessee A&I University during the Walter S. Davis administration for "misconduct" after being arrested during the Freedom Rides to desegregation public facilities along southern highways.[56] On the other hand, in North Carolina, Black presidents of both private and state-supported HBCUs were more aligned than different.

Among the private Black colleges in the state, Willa Player, president of the all-women's Bennett College in Greensboro, is noted by historian William H. Chafe as a president who supported students' cause by action. "Player offered firm support to her students. In addition, she was the first Black to turn in her charge card when Meyer's Department Store, a prestigious downtown establishment, refused to desegregate its dining room."[57] Among the state-supported Black colleges in the state, and as many presidents of similar institutions across the South reprimanded student demonstrators, Elder frequently spoke about issues of race and Blacks in the South. This is a likely explanation how and why Elder was invited to speak at Duke in 1962 before the National Student Association, an organization that supported the student sit-ins.[58] Yet, with an ongoing attempt to keep college desegregation to a minimum, even at places like Duke, it is unsurprising Elder used such crafty, and arguably safe, language before an audience on a predominately White campus.

His approach mirrored those of Black educators for nearly a century by the time of this speech. Black teachers were intricately tied to the community both in and out of the classroom throughout the Jim Crow era.[59] The strategic actions of Elder speaking before Whites were similar to the tradition of Black southern educators. In fact, it is possible that Elder saw similar actions when growing up in rural Georgia, where his father, Thomas J. Elder, was principal of the local industrial school for Blacks. At Black schools in the South, "the principal was the liaison with the White community. In this capacity, he advocated for the needs of the school—though always having to be politically astute if he wished to preserve his job—and reported back to the [Black] community the disposition of the board."[60] Most pertinent to understanding Elder's speeches are the similar expectations that were placed upon Black college presidents.

As historian Joy Ann Williamson-Lott's articulated in her study of college presidents in Mississippi during the student sit-ins of the 1960s, these leaders' duty was to "follow the directions of the [White] board of trustees and the [state] legislature" or be fired.[61] In North Carolina, historian Sarah Caroline Thuesen noted that the state was more favorable of Black colleges than other southern states but Black college presidents still "had to be exceptionally resourceful to survive."[62] As a result of these circumstances, the Black educational leaders knew that speaking to Whites about Black students' interests "would require a skillful negotiation of external constraints."[63] Understanding this context, Elder had more freedom when speaking before a predominately or all-Black audiences, and he willingly called out Black students that were not upholding the traditions of proud Black schools. One speech in particular is an exceptional example of this.

Straight Talk: A 'Cultural' Assessment

In 1960, Elder addressed students at Durham's Hillside High School. The exact date or the occasion of the speech is unknown, but Hillside is a public high school founded in 1923 for Blacks. By the 1930, Hillside had a positive academic reputation in North Carolina due to its multiple course offerings and its teachers, many of whom held four-year degrees from Black colleges.[64] Now thirty years later, Elder spoke frankly during his Hillside High address before a Black audience. This speech was organized into two distinctively different parts. Part two of this speech when Elder discussed the "powers"—buying power, the power of the ballot, power of religion and, power of the cultivation of the human mind—being acquired and used by Black people to fight segregation will be discussed later in this chapter. In part one, Elder juxtaposed the importance of mind cultivation with what he noted as a key factor in keeping the South's system of oppression alive and well.

Sharing stiff criticism, Elder used this speech to assess the academic prowess of Black students: "A mother in our community recently asked her child one day why he was not studying his school lessons. The child replied: 'I know enough. If I answer too many questions in class, my friends won't like me.'" Responses like this in the Black community, he said, exhibited a "pattern of mediocrity established by a group. Here we see a resistance to learning in these times when excellence in performance is required in modern life." [65] Elder elaborated:

> We are seeking a new order of things. We are seeking respect as competent human beings in every walk of life. The concept of mediocrity has no place in this new order. The Negro must, by his own efforts develop and maintain in his mind, as well as in the minds of others, new standards of performance, new attitudes regarding his ability to do a job as well as any other person and a new sense of his responsibility as a worker. [66]

Yet, Elder felt as many Black students were satisfied with their standings in society. "Strangely enough, in this modern age in which excellence in performance is becoming increasingly necessary, too many of our people, I fear, are indifferent toward this need for excellence."[67]

As evidence to support this statement, he said, on average per year, students enrolled at the University of North Carolina-Chapel Hill and Duke University used sixty-nine and thirty-eight library books, respectively. At North Carolina Central, students used twenty-one library books per year.[68]

Elder's critique fits the narrative historian Vanessa Siddle Walker uncovered in her work on segregated schools in the South. In summary, in spite of Black schools having inferior physical tools compared to White schools, these schools had "exemplary teachers" that demanded excellence. "Consistently remembered for their high expectations for student success, for their dedication, and for their demanding teaching style, these teachers appear to have worked with the assumption that their job was to be certain that children learned the material presented."[69] This was accomplished during an era when the average expenditure for school libraries in North Carolina per White student, for example in 1957–58, was $1.84 compared to $1.28 per Black student.[70] As a result of limited support from the state, scholars have noted that thousands of dollars were raised by Black residents in support of their local schools in North Carolina. This included funds for equipment, stage curtains, and public address systems, among other amenities, all "contributed by students, parents, and other community supporters."[71] It was common for Black parents during segregation to aid in their children's pursuit of education. "Their contributions during this period are most often linked with the philosophy of self-help, which had motivated their parents, and are driven by the financial needs of the schools."[72]

Therefore, Elder's criticism of Black students was his approach to racial uplift, the idea of lifting the youth of the race to endeavors previous generations could not attain. He took on a tone of collective support, one for both students and parents, because Black educators regularly used gatherings to inform Black parents of what they could do to help their children succeed.[73] Hillside High, despite its poor facilities and low-paid faculty, "produced more than its share of race leaders."[74] The school had a positive reputation for its productivity, and Elder knew this. Therefore, his criticism before the Hillside audience was one that served more as reminder that Elder knew more was expected of Blacks in order to earn equality, and therefore, Blacks had to be twice as good academically compared to Whites.

A Culture of "Quality Education"

Similarly, Elder's speech on September 10, 1962, before the North Carolina College faculty and staff echoed Black educators' belief in Black schools. At a heightened moment in the student protests, Elder used this speech to first tout the validity of North Carolina College as an institution to all of higher education, not just among historically Black institutions. This was his plea as hundreds of demonstrators protested just to the west in Greensboro in September 1962. This time Blacks targeted large cafeteria-style restaurants. Following the sit-ins from two years prior, Blacks expected other public places to follow in the path of local lunch counters that desegregated under pressure; however, the gradual desegregation of public spaces, such as theaters, ice cream parlors, and department stores, had stalled and protests picked up in 1962.[75]

With so much attention on segregation across the South, Elder used this speech to share the news that North Carolina College was as strong academically as some of the state's predominately White colleges, according to a state higher education official who had recently visited the campus. Elder saw this statement as "landmark in our history" and cause for faculty and staff to be motivated in the onward push toward helping the institution's students achieve academic success. Just five years prior, the college earned membership into the Southern Association of Colleges and Secondary Schools in 1957.[76] Not to suggest that Elder needed the state's opinion as validation because at Black schools during segregation, "[t]he belief that their school provided a good environment for learning was shared by its graduates, parents, and teachers."[77] Also, "...many [Blacks] valued the cultural form of teaching and learning that developed in the segregated schools."[78] But as stated earlier, Elder used this speech to motivate and validate the work of the faculty and staff on his campus. He said: "First, we must refuse to believe, and we must get our students to refuse to believe, that low academic achievement is inevitable ... The second imperative, which you may have doubtless guessed is hard work. It is a willingness and a determination to endure weariness of mind and body in order to attain the desired goal in achievement."[79] In the same manner as Black educators had long rallied the entire community, Elder, too, charged everyone to do their part in supporting the youth in its responsibility to chart its own course through academic excellence. As previously explained, it was common for a Black educational leader to call on the entire Black community to take part in the success of Black students. Elder had continued this tradition. Yet, while making the call for community-wide support in a March 1962 speech titled "Quality Education," Elder focused on what he called the "cultural poverty" of Black students' households.

This address, appropriately titled "Quality Education," was his delivered at historically Black North Carolina College. Elder placed emphasis on the oppressiveness of the state's White authorities and higher education governing bodies. This speech was only a month after his address at Duke University, where he did not mention race or socioeconomic disparities. Now, standing before his own campus, he spoke directly of racial and socioeconomic issues and the impact of these issues on the North Carolina College students' academic success. "There are many causes for this relatively poor showing. Some of these causes go back to the poor elementary and high school training; some are attributable to the cultural poverty of many of the homes from which students come; some are attributable simply to a relatively low level of aspiration on the part of some of the students." He continued: "The rapid expansion of knowledge, the increase in technical competence required for high level jobs, and the struggle to avert national annihilation calls for a tremendous surge forward in both the quality and quantity of education provided ... The high school graduates, for the most part, who enter North Carolina College, and indeed who enter all similar institutions, are found to be deficient in competences normally expected of college freshmen."[80]

Yet, were Blacks actually impoverished of a culture of learning? No, this was not the case because North Carolina, and the South at large, had practices that stifled, if not outright suffocated, Blacks' educational attainment.[81] In many cases, it was not the students' fault for Black schools' underperformance. Instead, the socioeconomic profile of Black communities had suffered tremendously in many American cities since World War II. For example, the same suffering occurred at Durham's Hillside High School, which excelled in the 1920s and 1930s and saw its graduation rates plummet by the 1950s and 1960s.[82] In his work on the city of Philadelphia shortly after the war, historian John P. Spencer argued "social decline went hand in hand with poverty and physical dilapidation."[83]

It is worth noting that some Whites felt equality in funding Blacks, particularly for education, was a waste of resources. This is important to note because Elder's emphasis on cultural poverty must be set within the context of others' social thought about Blacks' educational attainment, which many of the nation's prominent White researchers at large universities said was impossible. Historian Harry Morgan, in his 1995 work on Black children's education in America, wrote: "There were those who suggested that the educational expenditures of public funds to remove academic deficits of poor and Black children would yield few benefits because Black children were genetically fixed at a lower I.Q. level than that their White age-mates."[84] However, liberal advocates of many races argued the opposite and discredited the more conservative-minded racist assumptions with numerous programs and initiatives that proved inferiority wrong.

For instance, in larger American cities, the Ford Foundation financed the Great Cities School Improvement Program throughout the middle of the twentieth century. This program was targeted at increasing the cultural capital of students enrolled in America's struggling inner city schools. This capital was found as the primary cause, not mental inferiority, of why Black students were underperforming academically. Spencer wrote, "The Great Cities program added a new focus on how the economic and cultural background of many urban students supposedly affected their cognitive development. Recent research into environmental effects on cognitive development had suggested intelligence (IQ) was not fixed and, therefore, all children could learn, if properly prepared."[85] Inadequate funding was rampant. Black schools rarely received equal funding, and had little chance to achieve equal success.[86]

A Culture of Inequality

By September 1960, there were forty-three of the 100 counties in North Carolina where there was no student, regardless of race, enrolled in a school accredited by the Southern Association.[87] Although Black educators felt their schools were providing stellar education, Elder's assessment of cultural poverty of students attending North Carolina College or similar institutions was situated within a larger practice of educational inequality across the state. This is unsurprising when examining the historical context proceeding this moment. In North Carolina, the first public school law was enacted in 1839 with school districts being established with "having regard to the number of [White] children in each."[88] There was no mention of non-Whites' education. It was not until 1910 that the state allocated funds for Black public elementary schools, and by the 1931–32 academic year, only thirteen of 100 counties had any school with terms of eight months of longer for Black children.[89] The slow progress was not by happenstance. In 1937, a study suggested that "discipline" was needed to ensure an "orderly society," which simply meant that the South no longer feared Black people taking over, as they did during Reconstruction. "White leaders intent on creating the 'New South' saw Black schooling as a way to ensure 'permanent White supremacy' through teaching habits of obedience and deference,"[90] which would keep Blacks from returning to their "savage" ways. Therefore, it should be no surprise that southern leaders eventually placed some focus on Black education. In fact, Greensboro appointed its first supervisor of Black education near about the same time as the 1937 study was released. What may have reflected progress at the time actually looks more like the strategic placement of an overseer of Black schools. By 1937, there were seventy-five Black teachers in the city, and 68% of them had no college degree.[91] This aligns with the fact that in 1933–1934 the average Black teacher had two years of college compared to four years of college for a White teacher.[92] Also, about the time, Elder delivered this 1962 "Quality Education" speech, the appraised value of school property per pupil was $709.54 for Whites and $487.10 for Blacks. The dropout rate was roughly the same for Black and White students. North Carolina ranked seventh among eleven southern states for the percentage of Black students enrolled in approved and/or accredited schools at 32%. This means that in 1960, roughly seven out of every ten Black students in the state were enrolled in primary or secondary schools not accredited, or at the bare minimum approved, by the Southern Association.[93]

With such evidence of inequality, what would cause the president of a historically Black college, during the initial surge of student unrest against segregation, to speak this way before Black audiences about their "cultural poverty?" The timing of these critiques reeked of behavior detrimental to the student movement, especially at the onset of what would become years of student demonstrations. On one hand, to publicly suggest that Blacks' inferior academic performance as compared to White students, such as Elder did, may have motivated Hillside High students to work harder in the classroom. On the other hand, his speech likely catered significantly to what White authorities wanted to hear. Was Elder an "Uncle Tom?"[94] His leadership record over his fifteen-year presidency of North Carolina College suggests no. Yet, his speeches at North Carolina College and Hillside High School, both Black audiences, exemplify the safe game many leaders of Black colleges, especially those state-funded schools, had to play in an effort to temper Whites from actively removing what little support they gave to Black schools. This is what some historians that study the Jim Crow era have considered Black educators a "double agent."[95] Messages were conveyed to please Whites in hopes of long-term benefits to the Black community.

The "Powers" of Blacks

Revisiting Elder's speech at Hillside High, Elder also explained to the predominately Black high school audience about the "powers" being used by Blacks to fight segregation. This included buying power, which was indicative of the lunch counter sit-ins that strangled the profits of many local businesses. Also, he discussed the power of the ballot. This was a notable tool against segregation because of Black North Carolinian's access to the vote and the election Black officials prior to 1960. What he considered most important was the power to cultivate the human mind. In this part of his speech, when speaking of the numerous "powers," Elder instilled confidence in the young Black audience.

Speaking to this audience with a significant number of high school students, Elder explained how the recent boycotts and sit-in demonstrations show that buying power is a tremendous source of power. "How does the possession of tremendous power and its accompanying responsibilities affect the Negro? The answer is obvious. The Negro is a human being and whatever affects other human beings affect him," he said.[96] Simply put, local economies throughout the South were dependent upon Black buying power. As referenced previously in this chapter, the Baton Rouge bus boycott of 1954 stifled that city's economy in a matter of days. With nearly empty buses operating on bus routes, the city would lose $1,600 per day. This served as the blueprint for several other bus boycotts throughout the South.[97]

Elder was well aware of the power that comes with boycotting, and as a result, he commended "the youth of our race for the quality of maturity which they are exhibiting in seeking respect as human beings" and believed that "history will record to the credit of the Negro that this tremendous force was used in the early stages of its recognition as a means of correcting the evils of segregation."[98] Elder reminded Blacks that despite whatever ills or personal failures they have been taught were theirs, the future was in their control if they persevere.

At Hillside, Elder discussed the brutal reality that students faced during demonstrations against the Jim Crow South and its segregation. By the time he delivered this speech, individuals in the audience had seen people involved in civil rights initiatives suffer violence at the hands of those in favor of White supremacy during the 1950s. As the 1960s started, the threat of violence continued. Elder advised how a young person participating in the sit-ins is subject to the all types of "indignities," which they must endure without retaliation.[99] Not retaliating was to Blacks' long-term advantage.

This sort of discipline, the type of discipline that exuded perseverance despite difficulties, would be beneficial not only for successful sit-ins but also in other aspects of life. Elder added: "The Negro must by his own effort develop and maintain in his mind, as well as in the minds of others, new standards of performance, new attitudes regarding his ability to do a job as well as any other person, and a new sense of his responsibility as a worker."[100]

Earlier in the same speech, Elder criticized Blacks in depth for their inability to meet White academic standards. By the end, he set a new tone. This moment of racial uplift encouraged the audience to move beyond the past and start anew. In the future, it would no longer be acceptable to measure one's worth based on the standard set by traditional southern ways. For Blacks, the best weapons in the immediate fight against segregation were to use the many powers they possessed.[101]

CONCLUSION

It is true that "college presidents face a somewhat precarious task whenever they speak in public given that they have to address a multitude of audiences."[102] Elder was no different. This chapter demonstrates how Elder negotiated the complexities of society, time, region, and space in their public speeches between 1960 and 1964. The possibility of violence was an unfortunate reality in the South when it came to the clash between segregationist and desegregationist. Each day a student stepped off campus to participate in a demonstration, their life was at risk. Yet, if the same students did not commit themselves to the long-term fight for Blacks' equal access to rights, the pressure on federal legislators to pass what would become the Civil Rights Act would not exist.[103] In fact, Warmoth T. Gibbs, who served as president of the historically Black North Carolina A&T from 1956 to 1960, wrote in 1966: "Among the many causes that led to the passage of the Civil Rights Law by Congress in 1964, the movement that was initiated by A&T students on February 1, 1960, and the unfavorable conditions which it highlighted, is one of the first magnitude."[104]

This chapter concludes that Elder believed the students had the right to protest segregated public spaces. Students and others were private citizens and Elder felt it was not the responsibility of the college to impede upon citizens' rights. If students did not violate campus policies, the protests were acceptable. Elder demanded Black students accept academic responsibility and excel in the classroom as he was more critical of Black people in front of his own campus. Yet, as displayed in his 1962 speech at Duke, Elder was much more careful when speaking before White or mixed audiences. The manner in which college presidents offered advice on how students can navigate broader social issues lends the most insight into racial differences.

This chapter not only examines Elder's perspectives on this but it situates his views in a discussion about responsibility of the college and students, particularly in a moment of social unrest regarding issues of racial equality.

It cannot be understated how deplorable social conditions were for Blacks in America, especially those living under the rule of Jim Crow laws. For generations, Blacks had been segregated in nearly every aspect of life. This included education, employment and wages, health care, and a host of other public services. By 1960, many college students in the South, regardless of their race, had had enough. The focus of this chapter is not meant to only feature Elder and his leadership during moments of student unrest, but to also explore the complexities in how Black leaders negotiated their words. Words have meaning and this was understood by liberal supporters of students' demands for desegregation and the conservative antagonists of the 1960s. Elder and other Black educational leaders of this time held the hopes of many constituents before them each time they stood before an audience. The self-directed, student-initiated protests further complicated Black academic leadership. In fact, on March 3, 1960, Governor Luther Hodges mailed each president of a state-supported college a copy of Chancellor Gordon W. Blackwell's speech, which directed his students at the Women's College in Greensboro to cease student demonstrations. Hodges felt this approach should be adopted by each president.[105] Yet, many of the state's Black college presidents responded with a simple acknowledgement of receipt of the letter but no promise to adhere to the governor's suggestion.[106] The case of Elder explores how a Black leader strategically negotiated the complexities of time, society, region, and space in his public speeches that both advised Black youth protestors on how to improve their social standing and calmed White leaders who governed North Carolina College. The prominent themes—carefully speaking before non-Black audiences, community-wide support of Black students, and Blacks' powers—demonstrate how Elder negotiated these complexities with words of action in addressing issues of racial segregation.

NOTES

1. Eugene E. Pfaff, Jr., *Keep on Walkin', Keep on Talkin': An Oral History of the Greensboro Civil Rights Movement* (Greensboro, NC: Tudor Publishers, 2011), 85.
2. Ibid., 85.
3. University of North Carolina-Greensboro, "Oral History Interview with Warmoth T. Gibbs by Eugene Pfaff," May 17, 1977, Greensboro VOICES Collection, item 1.10.513.
4. Aldon D. Morris, *The Origins of the Civil Rights Movement: Black Communities Organizing for Change* (New York, NY: Free Press, 1984), 197.

5. "Letter correspondence between retired Professor W. P. Speas, Sr. and Wake Forest University President Harold W. Tribble," February 25, 1960, RG1.10, President's Office, Harold Wayland Tribble Papers, Z. Smith Reynolds Library Special Collections and Archives, Wake Forest University, Winston-Salem, North Carolina, USA; "Letter from Doug Holt, a Duke University alumnus, to the university," March 13, 1961, in the J. Deryl Hart papers, David M. Rubenstein Rare Book & Manuscript Library, Duke University Archives.

6. Vanessa Siddle Walker, *Their Highest Potential: An African American School Community in the Segregated South* (Chapel Hill: University of North Carolina Press, 1996), 1.

7. Joy Ann Williamson, *Radicalizing the Ebony Tower: Black Colleges and the Black Freedom Struggle in Mississippi* (New York, NY: Teachers College Press, 2008), 10; Sarah Caroline Thuesen, *Greater Than Equal: African American Struggles for Schools and Citizenship in North Carolina, 1919–1965* (Chapel Hill: University of North Carolina Press), 143; R. Scott Baker, *Paradoxes of Desegregation: African American Struggles for Educational Equity in Charleston, South Carolina, 1926–1972* (Columbia: University of South Carolina Press, 2006), 118.

8. C. Eric Lincoln, "The Black Heritage in Religion in the South," in *Religion in the South*, ed. Charles Reagan Wilson (Jackson: University Press of Mississippi, 1985), 35.

9. Herbert Baxter Adams (1887). The College of William and Mary: A contribution to the history of higher education. Washington, D.C.: U.S. Government Printing Office, 11.

10. Ibid.

11. Beverly McAnear, "College Founding in the American Colonies, 1745–1775," *Mississippi Valley Historical Review* 42 (1954): 25; John R. Thelin, *A History of American Higher Education* (Baltimore, MD: The Johns Hopkins University Press, 2011), 29–30.

12. Thelin, *A History of American Higher Education*, 29–30.

13. Lerone Bennett, *Before the Mayflower: A History of Black America* (New York, NY: Penguin, 1988), 172; Shaun R. Harper, Lori D. Patton and Ontario S. Wooden, "Access and Equity for African America Students in Higher Education: A Critical Race Historical Analysis of Policy Efforts," *The Journal of Higher Education,* 80 (2009), 393.

14. M. Christopher Brown II, "Good Intentions: Collegiate Desegregation and Transdemographic Enrollments," *The Review of Higher Education* 25 (2002), 264; Harper, Patton and Wooden, "Access and Equity for African America Students in Higher Education," 393.

15. Harper, Patton and Wooden, "Access and Equity for African America Students in Higher Education," 395.

16. James D. Anderson, *The Education of Blacks in the South, 1860–1935* (Chapel Hill: The University of North Carolina Press, 1988), 7.

17. Ibid., 240.

18. Antoine M. Garibaldi, *Black Colleges and Universities: Challenges for the Future* (Westport, CT: Greenwood, 1984), 233.

19. Harper, Patton and Wooden, "Access and Equity for African America Students in Higher Education," 395.

20. Anderson, *The Education of Blacks in the South*, 239.
21. Stephanie Y. Evans, *Black Women in the Ivory Tower, 1850–1954* (Gainesville: University of Florida Press, 2007), 109.
22. Anderson, *The Education of Blacks in the South*, 238.
23. Julian B. Roebuck & Komanduri S. Murty, *Historically Black Colleges and Universities: Their Place in American Higher Education* (Santa Barbara, CA: Praeger Publishers, 1993), 25.
24. Harper, Patton and Wooden, "Access and Equity for African America Students in Higher Education," 394; Anderson, *The Education of Blacks in the South*, 238.
25. Thelin, *A History of American Higher Education*, 138.
26. Michael Sugrue, "We Desired Our Future Rulers to be Educated," in *The American College in the Nineteenth Century*, ed. Roger L. Geiger. (Nashville: Vanderbilt University Press, 2000), 96.
27. History, North Carolina Central University, http://www.nccu.edu/aboutnccu/history.cfm (accessed 27 Jan. 2013).
28. Thuesen, *Greater Than Equal*, 90, 96.
29. Biographical Data Concerning Alfonso Elder, in the Alfonso Elder Papers, #50002. University Archives, Records and History Center in the James E. Shepard Memorial Library, North Carolina Central University.
30. Marion Brunson Lucas and George C. Wright, *A History of Blacks in Kentucky: In Pursuit of Equality, 1890-1980* (Lexington: University of Kentucky Press, 1992), 160.
31. Biographical Data Concerning Alfonso Elder.
32. Anderson, *The Education of Blacks in the South*, 276, 278.
33. Carter G. Woodson, *The Mis-Education of the Negro* (Washington D.C.: Associated Publishers, 1933), 24.
34. Anderson, *The Education of Blacks in the South*, 277.
35. The talented tenth is a term for the upper 10% Blacks as of the early 1900s. This group represented the most educated and financially stable of Blacks in America. Scholar W. E. B. Du Bois is credited with publicizing this term in his essay of the same name published in 1903. The talented tenth were expected to help the other 90% of the Black race by becoming leaders in education and social justice.
36. Morris, *The Origins of the Civil Rights Movement*, x.
37. Ibid., x.
38. Ibid., 24.
39. Frederic O. Sargent and Bill Maxwell, *The Civil Rights Revolution: Events and Leaders, 1955–1968.* (Jefferson, N.C.: McFarland & Company, 2004), 43.
40. Morris, *The Origins of the Civil Rights Movement*, 198.
41. Ibid., 198.
42. Pfaff, *Keep on Walkin', Keep on Talkin'*, 157.
43. William H. Chafe, *Civilities and Civil Rights: Greensboro, North Carolina, and the Black Struggle for Freedom* (New York, NY: Oxford University Press, 1981), 117–118.
44. "Editorial: Into Sharp Focus," *Greensboro Record*, February 3, 1960.
45. "Movement by Negros Growing," *Greensboro Daily News*, February 4, 1960.
46. "More Arrests Made in Store Agitation Here," *Greensboro Record*, February 6, 1960.

47. Ibid.

48. "Stronger Interracial Unit Requested," *Greensboro Record,* February 8, 1960.

49. Alfonso Elder, "The Responsibility of the University to Society with Special Emphasis on Student Involvement in Extra-Class Affairs," February 25, 1962, in the Alfonso Elder Papers, #50002. University Archives, Records and History Center in the James E. Shepard Memorial Library, North Carolina Central University.

50. Ibid.

51. "Race Relations at Guilford College," Civil Rights Greensboro http://library.uncg.edu/dp/crg/topicalessays/RaceRelGC.aspx (accessed 16 Feb. 2013).

52. "Introduction," *The Road to Desegregation at Duke,* http://exhibits.library.duke.edu/exhibits/show/desegregation (accessed 9 Dec. 2012).

53. Baker, *Paradoxes of Desegregation,* 134.

54. Elder, "The Responsibility of the University to Society with Special Emphasis on Student Involvement in Extra-Class Affairs."

55. Lerone Bennett, "The Plight of Negro College Presidents: Sit-In Demonstrations and Direct Attacks on Segregation Raise Crucial Problems for Educators," *Ebony,* October 1960, 138.

56. Reginald Stuart, "Tennessee State Freedom Riders Get Overdue Recognition," *Diverse: Issues in Higher Education,* September 8, 2008, accessed September 8, 2014, http://diverseeducation.com/article/11651/

57. Chafe, *Civilities and Civil Rights,* 135.

58. Angus Johnston, "A Brief History of NSA and USSA, http://www.usstudents.org/about/history/ (accessed 20 April 2014).

59. Vanessa Siddle Walker, "Caswell County Training School, 1933–1969: Relationships between Community and School," *Harvard Educational Review,* 63 (1993): 164; Adam Fairclough, *Teaching Equality: Black Schools in the Age of Jim Crow* (Athens, GA: University of Georgia Press, 2001), 16.

60. Vanessa Siddle Walker, "Valued Segregated Schools for African Americans Children in the South, 1935-1969: A Review of Common Themes and Characteristics," *Review of Educational Research,* 70 (2000): 275.

61. Williamson, *Radicalizing the Ebony Tower,* 118.

62. Thuesen, *Greater Than Equal,* 108.

63. Vanessa Siddle Walker, *Hello Professor: A Black Principal and Professional Leadership in the Segregated South* (Chapel Hill: University of North Carolina Press, 19.

64. Thuesen, *Greater Than Equal,* 61.

65. Alfonso Elder, "Address to Hillside High School Students," 1960, in the Alfonso Elder Papers, #50002. University Archives, Records and History Center in the James E. Shepard Memorial Library, North Carolina Central University.

66. Ibid.

67. Ibid.

68. Ibid.

69. Siddle Walker, "Valued Segregated Schools for African Americans Children in the South, 264–265.

70. *Equal Protection of the Laws in North Carolina,* Reports by the North Carolina Advisory Committee, 105.

71. Siddle Walker, "Caswell County Training School, 1933-1969," 166.

72. Siddle Walker, "Valued Segregated Schools for African Americans Children in the South," 271.

73. Siddle Walker, "Caswell County Training School, 1933–1969," 168.

74. Thuesen, *Greater Than Equal*, 63, 65.

75. Chafe, *Civilities and Civil Rights*, 154–155.

76. History, North Carolina Central University, http://www.nccu.edu/aboutnccu/history.cfm (accessed 27 Jan. 2013).

77. Siddle Walker, "Caswell County Training School, 1933–1969," 164.

78. Siddle Walker, "Valued Segregated Schools for African Americans Children in the South," 254.

79. Alfonso Elder, "The President's Address to the Faculty and Staff," September 10, 1962, in the Alfonso Elder Papers, #50002. University Archives, Records and History Center in the James E. Shepard Memorial Library, North Carolina Central University.

80. Alfonso Elder, "Quality Education at North Carolina College at Durham," March 1962, in the Alfonso Elder Papers, #50002. University Archives, Records and History Center in the James E. Shepard Memorial Library, North Carolina Central University.

81. *Equal Protection of the Laws*, 99, 104, 109 [which cited Laws of North Carolina, 1838–39; ch. VIII, sec. 3, 13.]; Sherick A. Hughes, *Black Hands in the Biscuits, Not in the Classrooms: Unveiling Hope in a Struggle for Brown's Promise* (New York, NY: Peter Lang Publishing, 2006), 21; Charles L. Glenn, *African-American/Afro-Canadian Schooling: From the Colonial Period to the Present* (New York: Palgrave Macmillan, 2011), 81, 100 [which cited Paul H. Buck, *The Road to Reunion, 1865–1900* (New York: Random House Vintage Books, 1959), 301]; Buck, *The Road to Reunion*, 301; Chafe, *Civilities and Civil Rights*, 23.

82. Thuesen, *Greater Than Equal*, 86.

83. John P. Spencer, *In the Crossfire: Marcus Foster and the Troubled History of American School Reform* (Philadelphia: University of Pennsylvania Press, 2012), 58, 59.

84. Harry Morgan, *Historical Perspectives on the Education of Black Children* (Westport, CT: Praeger Publishers, 1995), 144–145.

85. Spencer, *In the Crossfire*, 70, 76 [which cited Ellen Condliffe Lagemann, *The Politics of Knowledge: The Carnegie Corporation, Philanthropy, and Public Policy* (Chicago: University of Chicago Press, 1989), 211–12.].

86. William H. Watkins, *Black Protest Thought and Education* (New York, NY: Peter Lang Publishing, 2005), 38, 81.

87. *Equal Protection of the Laws*, 100.

88. Ibid., 99.

89. *Equal Protection of the Laws*, 99, 104, 109 [which cited Laws of North Carolina, 1838–39; ch. VIII, sec. 3, 13.].

90. Glenn, *African-American/Afro-Canadian Schooling*, 81, 100.

91. Chafe, *Civilities and Civil Rights*, 23.

92. Vanessa Siddle Walker, "African American Teaching in the South: 1940–1960," *African American Educational Research Journal*, 38 (2001): 763.

93. *Equal Protection of the Laws*, 104, 105, 109.

94. "Uncle Tom" is a derogatory term toward a Black man that is considered to be more concerned with the well-being of, and obedience to, White authorities than to himself or other Black people.

95. Adam Fairclough, *Teaching Equality: Black Schools in the Age of Jim Crow* (Athens, GA: University of Georgia Press, 2001), 16 [which cited Glenda Elizabeth Gilmore, *Gender and Jim Crow: Women and the Politics of White Supremacy in North Carolina, 1896–1920* (Chapel Hill: University of North Carolina Press, 1996), 186.].

96. Elder, "Address to Hillside High School Students."

97. Morris, *The Origins of the Civil Rights Movement*, 24.

98. Elder, "Address to Hillside High School Students."

99. Ibid.

100. Ibid.

101. Watkins, *Black Protest Thought and Education*, 38, 81.

102. This quote is from John Louis Lucaites, PhD, a professor of Communication and Culture at Indiana University. Lucaites' research concerns the relationship between rhetoric and social theory in the context of the relationship between race and identity. This quote was to the author in support of the study of college presidents' speeches during the North Carolina Student Movement for Civil Rights during the 1960s.

103. Warmoth T. Gibbs, *The History of North Carolina Agricultural and Technical College* (Dubuque, Iowa: W. C. Brown Book Company, 1966), 125.

104. Ibid., 125.

105. "Letter correspondence from Governor Luther Hodges to North Carolina A&T Trustee Robert H. Frazier and President Warmoth T. Gibbs," March 3, 1960, Luther Hodges Papers, North Carolina State Archives, Raleigh, North Carolina, USA.

106. "Letter correspondence from Winston-Salem State President Francis Loguen Atkins to Governor Luther Hodges," March 7, 1960, Luther Hodges Papers, North Carolina State Archives, Raleigh, North Carolina, USA.

CHAPTER 7

"WE DECLARE INDEPENDENCE FROM THE UNJUST LAWS OF MISSISSIPPI"

The Freedom Schools, Head Start and the Reconstruction of Education during the Civil Rights Movement

Jon N. Hale
College of Charleston

In this course of human events, it has become necessary for the Negro people to break away from the customs which have made it very difficult for the Negro to get his God-given rights. We, as citizens of Mississippi, do hereby state that all people should have the right to petition, to assemble, and to use public places. The government has no right to make or to change laws without the consent of the people. We, therefore, the Negroes of Mississippi assembled, appeal to the government of the state, that no man is free until all men are free. We do hereby declare independence from the unjust laws of Mississippi which conflict with the United States Constitution.

—The Freedom School students of St. John's Methodist Church
Hattiesburg, Mississippi, 1964[1]

Using Past as Prologue, pages 167–199
Copyright © 2015 by Information Age Publishing
All rights of reproduction in any form reserved.

Roscoe Jones and Joyce Brown led the Freedom School students that penned the declaration of independence noted above at a student-led conference in Meridian, Mississippi, during the Freedom Summer campaign of 1964. The timing of the declaration coincided with the historic desegregation of public schools in Mississippi. Beginning with a handful of schools in August of 1964, grassroots civil rights activists and the judiciary and executive branch ordered the reconstruction of the public school system by dismantling the dual and segregated school system in the Magnolia State. At the same time, the grassroots movement exemplified through the Freedom School model proffered a different vision of what education should look like as it was being reconstructed. Moreover, within one year of desegregation, local and federal organizers developed Head Start programs across the state of Mississippi to provide an early childhood education and to employ local people as part of the "War on Poverty." Local and young people like Jones and Brown, and the thousands of families connected to Head Start, shaped and were shaped by a movement that reflected a long struggle for quality education. The shift at the federal level to desegregate schools, coupled with the ongoing and decentralized push for a quality education through the Civil Rights Movement from the 1940s through the middle of the 1960s, constituted a fundamental reconstruction of public education in Mississippi that continues to frame the provision of education today.

The *Brown v. Board of Education* (1954) decision set the parameters for a reconstruction of public education that changed the entire public education system in the United States.[2] The *Brown* decision called for the political rebuilding of a public education system that served over eleven million schoolchildren across the South, which was nearly forty percent of public school students nationwide, in over 11,000 school districts.[3] The magnitude of the decision called for a massive overhaul of the education system and by 1971 a "unitary" system of public education emerged, replacing the system of segregated educational that operated since Reconstruction. This move constitutes a constitutional reconstruction of public education because the fundamental law of segregation that governed all schools in the South for the past century was constitutionally destroyed and replaced by a new set of laws that attempted to create for all students equal access to a quality education. Local and grassroots movements supported by federal policy determined that no student could be denied equal access to a public education by race. This policy is radical in a long view of history because it provided a constitutional and federal protection of the right to an equal education. But ten years after the *Brown* (1954) decision, schools were not living up to the ideals established in *Brown*. By 1964, only three school districts across Mississippi desegregated, and then only at the first grade level. The civil rights community radicalized this reconstruction of education as it proffered civil-rights based educational programs as an alternative to desegregation as proposed by the *Brown* decision. Though never fully embraced in the reconstructed and refashioned system of education, the Freedom School and Head Start program put forth a different lens by which to evaluate the history of school desegregation and the contemporary struggle to provide a quality education.

This chapter examines the history of the Freedom Schools and the Head Start program in Mississippi during the Civil Rights Movement to illustrate how local programs shaped local movements for quality education through goals of student activism and community control, among other objectives, as the public schools in the South were reconstructed through desegregation. Civil rights educational projects were grounded in the values that originated in the Black community as early as the eighteenth century.[4] The movement for a quality education continued through the early twentieth century. But the values central to this movement, such as self-determination and community control, ultimately challenged the NAACP's legal strategy that focused solely on desegregation of the public school system. By the middle of the 1960s, civil rights-based programs moved beyond viewing desegregation as the primary means to achieve a quality education. Programs like the Freedom Schools and Head Start were marginal when compared to the entire student population in Mississippi, but within the context of desegregation, these programs put forth powerful notions of educational reform. The Freedom Schools embraced alternative institution building that taught a politicized curriculum and facilitated radical and, at times, militant student activism grounded in Civil Rights Movement traditions. At the same time, Lyndon B. Johnson's domestic legislation reflected a radical federal expansion in education through the Elementary and Secondary Education Act and programs like Head Start, the early childhood education initiative that was part of his strategy to alleviate poverty. Head Start embraced community control, distributed financial support to local community members who worked in the schools, and fashioned a progressive curriculum that focused on the unique backgrounds of the students. As federal policymakers attempted to eliminate racial segregation in public education, the Freedom Schools and Head Start put forth notions of education that moved beyond desegregation to suggest that students should be a major part of the changing educational context of the 1960s and join the frontlines of the Civil Rights Movement through desegregating schools, protesting unequal conditions, boycotting schools that did not provide a quality education, and participating in building educational programs alternative and parallel to the public system provided by the state.

Civil rights education programs in Mississippi, as observed in the Freedom Schools and Head Start, are particularly significant in the context of desegregation and changing federal educational policy. The dynamic contextual interplay between the local and federal level framed the nature of public education of the Civil Rights Movement since the 1960s. It illustrates how the ideals of quality education embedded in the Civil Rights Movement and the legal challenges to segregation were not fulfilled. The rise of conservative politics that stymied the gains of the movement ultimately tempered educational and transformative gains made at the local level. As organizers and young people like Roscoe Jones organized civil rights projects, congressional leaders also mobilized around themes that stymied the influence of the Civil Rights Movement on the reconstruction of education.

THE ORIGINS AND CONTEXT OF A SECOND RECONSTRUCTION

Simply providing an education was an act of defiance due to fierce White resistance to the prospect of educating African Americans for equality. Local activists in Mississippi wanted to shape the institution of public education to be more inclusive, which eventually led to the movement to reconstruct this system, beginning in the 1940s. During the Second World War and the postwar period, legal avenues became available to equalize the public system of education. In June of 1940, the Supreme Court refused to review a teacher salary equalization case, *Alston v. City School Board of City of Norfolk,* thereby affirming a lower court's ruling that the salaries of Black and White teachers must be the same for equally qualified teachers.[5] By 1948, teachers in Mississippi joined the national struggle to equalize salaries and other resources appropriated for public education. A. L. Johnson, president of the Mississippi Association of Teachers in Colored Schools, wrote in January of 1948 that "now is the time for us to begin immediate aggressive action." He later penned in a letter to James A. Burns, the lawyer who represented the association in coordination with the NAACP, "The Negro children in this district have three inequalities: shorter school terms, no transportation, practically no equipment and poor building facilities. They need to file to equalize all of these in one bill. If you will do this at once, we will make an effort to get something started in this direction."[6]

In a clandestine meeting held at the Masonic Lodge in the capital city of Jackson, Mississippi, educators and other NAACP members met and invited Thurgood Marshall to discuss the possibility of filing an equalization suit. Gladys Noel Bates, a science teacher at Smith Robertson Junior High School and a card-carrying member of the NAACP, stepped forward to initiate the lawsuit that prodded the Mississippi state legislature to at least marginally address the growing need for reform through the equalization campaigns.[7] The community raised the funds to hire the lawyers necessary to follow through. The city and state made no gestures to begin to comply and, in fact, school district officials did not renew Bates' contract in response to her participation in the lawsuit.[8] Her fate was similar to other Black educators who stepped forward to challenge the unequal distribution of educational resources.[9]

Yet, Mississippi legislators eventually acquiesced to demands for equality, especially once the prospect of desegregation became apparent after the *Sweatt v. Painter* (1950) and *McLaurin v. Oklahoma* (1950) decisions. State policymakers ultimately chose to implement a $45 million program that moved toward equalizing school resources. Mississippi legislators never fully funded the equalization plan, however, and waited until the Supreme Court decision to desegregate was handed down until they actually began to implement the equalization plan.[10] But it was largely an empty rhetorical gesture. Educational funding followed the patterns of discrimination demonstrated in the political and economic conditions of Mississippi Blacks. Existing state law dictated that public schools' funds were to be distributed equally "in proportion to the number of educable children in each."[11] But local White officials were free to divert tax money legally designated to Black schools and openly spend it on White schools. Just like the registrars, local officials in charge of local funds were free to spend as they wished.

The attempts toward equalization generated a deleterious effect on African American education in Mississippi. Black students attending segregated schools between 1954 and 1965 comprised fifty-seven percent of school-aged students throughout the state of Mississippi. These students, however, received only thirteen percent of state funds.[12] By 1955, educational funding had continued to increase, but was far from equal to White funding. Local officials in Hattiesburg, for instance, appropriated $536,341, yet distributed $157,632 or approximately twenty-nine percent of the total fund for Black education.[13] Per-county spending on a dual system of education was similarly disparaging. North Pike County spent $30.89 for each white student and $.79 for each Black student. In South Pike County, White students were appropriated $59.55, whereas Black students were appropriated on average $1.35. In the city of Hattiesburg, the $61.69 spent for each Black student surpassed those of White rural students, yet paled in comparison to the $115.96 city White children were receiving.[14] Black teachers similarly suffered in terms of state funding. The average salary of a White teacher the year of the *Brown* decision was $2,177, while the average salary for a Black teacher was $1,244. Ten years later, in 1964, when state legislators were "equalizing" education to avoid integration, White teachers averaged $4,321, while Black educators only earned $3,566.[15]

After *Brown*, local Mississippians utilized the opportunity to pursue equality by way of desegregation. In August of 1954, a delegation from the Walthall County NAACP branch filed the first desegregation suits in the state. The petitioners quickly faced grand jury subpoenas on trumped-up charges. Though the charges were dropped, no desegregation suits were filed until after the 1955 "*Brown II*" implementation decision.[16] Within weeks of that decision, which ordered districts to integrate "with all deliberate speed," the NAACP instructed its branches throughout Mississippi to take immediate steps to integrate. Black parents filed desegregation petitions in Clarksdale, Jackson, Natchez, Vicksburg, and Yazoo City, only to be countered with fierce Citizens' Council resistance. In Yazoo City, the Citizens' Council published the names and addresses of the petitioners. Whites fired the petitioners who worked for them and independent businessmen lost business to boycotts. More than a dozen were forced to leave the area in order to find work. The council also published the names of petitioners in Vicksburg and Jackson, which was enough to end desegregation suits there.[17] The Citizens' Council went further than intimidating the parents who filed desegregation suits. When Mississippi was ordered to begin token integration in 1964, the Citizens' Council members sponsored the first private academy in Jackson.[18]

By the summer of 1964 when civil rights activists organized the Freedom Summer campaign, the largest organized voter registration project in the Civil Rights Movement that also spawned the Freedom Schools, Mississippi was the last state to begin the process of desegregating public schools. The reconstruction of public education therefore began slowly in the Magnolia State. Federal action to desegregate finally took place in 1964, when US District Judge Sidney Mize ordered school officials in Jackson, Biloxi, and Leake County to submit desegregation plans that would desegregate the public schools by July 15, 1964.[19] The requirements were that public schools would desegregate at least one grade per year, a strategy known as a "stair-step" plan, through which full desegregation was avoided. Jackson and Biloxi immediately appealed the decision but the order to desegregate was upheld, reluctantly, in early July 1964.[20] It was clear to school administrators that the equalization program would not deter desegregation.

Facilitated at the federal level but implemented on the local level, the historic reconstruction of public education developed unequally and along racial lines in Mississippi. Public Black educators were still the recipients of vastly different and unequal distribution of resources ten years after the *Brown* (1954) decision. One obvious result of *de jure* segregation policy and an underfunded dual system of education was a lack of educational attainment. Between 1954 and 1965, sixty-six percent of White students entering first grade completed high school. Only thirty-one percent of Black students entering the first grade would actually complete high school.[21] But the intersection of educational attainment, race, and economic standing throughout Mississippi is especially devastating, particularly in predominantly Black counties. In Belzoni, Humphreys County, which was seventy percent Black, thirty-two percent of the population completed four years of high school or more; there was a ten percent unemployment rate, and sixty-two percent of the population earned under $3,000 per year. In Hollandale, Washington County, which was fifty-five percent Black, twenty-six percent of the population completed four years or more of high school; there was a six percent unemployment rate, and sixty-one percent of the population earned under $3,000 per year. In Leland County, thirty percent of the population completed four years of high school or more, there was a nine percent unemployment rate, and forty-nine percent earned under $3,000 per year. When these rates are compared to the wealthiest counties in the state, the differences are drastic. In Clinton, one of the wealthiest counties in the state and only forty percent Black, seventy-four percent of the residents completed four years of high school or more, there was a three percent unemployment rate, and only thirty percent earned under $3,000 per year.[22]

The push for quality education and the legislative reaction to this organization established the parameters between which the struggle of the latter twentieth century would occur. The reconstruction of education during the Civil Rights Movement embodied the progressive push to become more inclusive, but which was tempered by recalcitrant politics that precluded the full realization of the ideals.

THE FREEDOM SCHOOLS AND THE RECONSTRUCTION OF EDUCATION

Ten years after the historic *Brown* decision and in the midst of the transformative reconstruction of public education, civil rights organizers established an alternative and grassroots network of Freedom Schools throughout the state of Mississippi. Organizers established over forty schools as part of the larger voter registration project that brought over 1000 White volunteers to the state during the summer of 1964. After the conclusion of the summer campaign and throughout the next year, young people envisioned a new society and understood the fall of 1964 as an historic moment in the movement that they formally declared "independence from the unjust laws of Mississippi." In this historic moment, Mississippi students applied the skills they cultivated, refined, and practiced during the Freedom Summer under the tutelage of a corps of freedom fighters and volunteers. Students desegregated public schools for the first time in the history of Mississippi, but, significantly, they also organized school boycotts and demanded a quality education within their own schools. Young people's level of political engagement, consciousness, and commitment while still in middle and high school constituted nothing less than an educational revolution in a state notoriously regarded for its poor quality of public education. More importantly, young people and the forms of activism they pursued put forth notions that schools should be desegregated, but that desegregation was but one means to achieve a quality education. Student activism suggested that education should include participatory notions of citizenship that valued the vantage point of students. Moreover, their conceptions of quality education included fair discipline, the right to free speech, and the notion that parallel and separate institutions can provide a quality education rather than public schools controlled by the state.

Civil rights organizers implemented a statewide Freedom School program as part of the Mississippi Freedom Summer project in 1964. The Freedom Schools taught a politicized curriculum that focused on American citizenship, government, and African American history and culture. The curriculum also included traditional academic subjects in math and English to combat the negative effects of a segregated education. Additionally, Freedom School teachers, mostly drawn from a large corps of northern (and White) volunteers, embraced a flexible and progressive pedagogy that focused on the students in order to meet their needs. The interracial interactions between White volunteer teachers and Black students and the political experiences of community organizing became noteworthy hallmarks of the Freedom Schools.[23] The Freedom Schools were an entrée for thousands of young people into the Civil Rights Movement and middle and high school students served as both the leaders and foot soldiers of the movement at the local level.

Student activists articulated their own agenda during a student-led convention in Meridian, which concluded the Freedom School program of the 1964 summer campaign. The first presumption of the convention was that students' collective political voices were an integral part of reconstructing society. The student delegates at the convention discussed issues related to jobs, schools, foreign affairs, and public accommodations in workshops, and they created demands for access to public accommodations, building codes for each home, integrated schools, a public works program, and the appointment of qualified Blacks to state positions.[24]

Collectively, the students drafted a list of demands to present to the state legislature, which read:

> In an age where machines are rapidly replacing manual labor, job opportunities and economic security increasingly require higher levels of education. We therefore demand:
>
> 1. Better facilities in all schools. These would include textbooks, laboratories, air conditioning, heating, recreation, and lunchrooms
> 2. A broader curriculum including vocational subjects and foreign languages
> 3. Low-fee adult classes for better jobs
> 4. That the school year consists of nine (9) consecutive months
> 5. Exchange programs and public kindergartens

6. Better-qualified teachers with salaries according to qualification
7. Forced retirement (women at 62, men at 65)
8. Special schools for mentally retarded and treatment and care of cerebral palsy victims
9. That taxpayers' money not be used to provide private schools
10. That all schools be integrated and equal throughout the country
11. Academic freedom for teachers and students
12. That teachers be able to join any political organization to fight for Civil Rights without fear of being fired
13. That teacher brutality be eliminated[25]

More importantly, the collective voice of students who had gone through a Freedom School education represents the notion that quality education includes an element of student activism and that trained young activists should determine the quality of their own education.

The Freedom School students and their peers began the 1964-1965 school year with a demonstrated public resolve to eradicate forms of discrimination found in their own schools. These demands backed up their declaration of rights and framed how the young activists were going to apply the political skills they acquired through a Freedom School education. The Freedom School students decided to use the public schools they attended as a base of operations. As Liz Fusco, the Freedom School coordinator after the summer campaign of 1964 until 1965, wrote of the young activists, "[students] began to become articulate about what was wrong, and the way things should be instead: why don't they do this at our school? was the first question asked, and then there began to be answers, which led to further questions."[26] Fusco captured the very essence of student activism after Freedom Summer. As young people recently educated in the principles, strategies, and methods of the movement, the former Freedom School students employed a broad concept of student activism that suggested that students should also be at frontlines of the Civil Rights Movement.

One of the first components of Freedom School activism consisted of participating in the historic desegregation of Mississippi by organizing the first wave of students to enter previously all-White schools. Though desegregation was not the primary aim of the students, it did constitute the first form of student activism during the 1964–1965 school year. Freedom School teachers and students were well trained in the organizational strategies of the movement and they had been fully exposed to the intimidation tactics used by segregationists. The Freedom School teachers in Jackson worked closely with the registration process occurring that fall. During the registration for first graders, Freedom School teacher Florence Howe and her student-volunteers canvassed the neighborhood to encourage parents to register their children. They talked to more than seventy families in August. The Freedom School teachers and their students could boast that they assisted eleven of the forty-three students to register in the previously all-White Jackson schools.[27] This larger campaign occurred as other groups like the Delta Ministry, the Mississippi Freedom Democratic Party (MFDP), the Mississippi Council on Human Relations, and the Student Nonviolent Coordinating Committee (SNCC) joined in the effort to desegregate the public schools throughout the state. This was not an effort spearheaded solely by Freedom School teachers and students; rather, it was a collective statewide effort that demonstrates how the Freedom Schools joined, led, and participated in the larger movement once the summer campaign concluded.

The Freedom School students did, however, emerge as young leaders in the effort to desegregate *all* levels of public education. Though the federal court issued strict guidelines that only elementary grades were to be desegregated, young activists attempted to enroll in all White high schools. Ben Chaney (a Freedom School student in Meridian whose brother was one of the three activists murdered at the beginning of the summer campaign) and twenty-one other students attempted to desegregate Meridian's high schools in early September. Nineteen other Black students attempted to register at high schools in Canton. Over twenty high school students attempted to desegregate schools in Jackson.[28] Segregationists effectively blocked the attempts and denied students the right to register at most high schools not yet under court order to do so. These early attempts at desegregation are significant because these were the first efforts to desegregate White schools beyond federal court order. In this way, student activists raised public awareness of the desire to desegregate at a much faster pace than the judicial branches intended.

It would not be long until Freedom School students joined the first waves of Black students to enroll in all-White schools as a result of freedom of choice plans.[29] During this phase, White school boards remained lukewarm, at best, to the idea of desegregation. During the 1964–1965 academic year, Jackson civil rights workers organized a series of workshops that discussed desegregation and generating support for the movement. It was out of these meetings that Hymethia Washington, a Freedom School student in Jackson, made the decision to desegregate the previously all-White Murrah High School.[30] She was one of twelve students to do so. African American families like Washington's family had to take the responsibility to enroll their children in White public schools. While Washington's parents were not dependent upon White income for a living and did not have to worry about losing their jobs when their daughter enrolled at Murrah High School, others were not so fortunate. The parents of the first Black students to desegregate the public schools could lose their jobs, and oftentimes did.[31] Like all students of color who desegregated schools for the first time, Washington and the other Freedom School students paid a heavy economic, social, political, and spiritual cost.[32]

Grassroots civil rights-based educational reform forced a strong White reaction that activists did not envision during the organization for desegregation. State lawmakers reacted to the push to desegregate by abandoning the public schools. The Mississippi state legislature established the foundation for a private system of education—one open only to Whites but which was legally justifiable. As plans slowly moved toward token desegregation, the Mississippi legislature passed a series of bills that authorized state-supported private schools. The state provided tuition in the form of tuition grants paid to individual families choosing to enroll in a private school, in addition to providing free textbooks to private schools.[33] The private academy system supported by the state was relatively small. In the fall of 1964, less than ten private schools opened. Tuition was expensive, and the schools were organized quickly. By 1968, there were forty-three state-supported private academies. They were overwhelmingly located in Mississippi's urban areas and the Delta (the northwest corner of the state that was overwhelmingly Black).[34] Though small in number, the system of private schools supported by the state was dwarfed by the number of private schools supported by private means. White segregationists ensured that privatization would be a viable option during the reconstruction of the school system during desegregation.

Young people were mindful of the stern resistance to desegregation both at the state level and within the schools they were expected to desegregate and embraced alternative means to quality education during the reconstruction of public education. The Freedom School students in Meridian at the end of Freedom Summer suggested multiple forms of activism beyond desegregating schools in their list of demands. As Roscoe Jones, one of the student leaders at the convention, recalled about the student demands:

> We never asked to be integrated, we only asked for equality. I never entered the civil rights movement for integration. I entered the civil rights movement to be equal. Integration is a byproduct of equality and we ended up getting the byproduct. We never wanted integration. We wanted to be equal.[35]

The student-led conference in Meridian articulated the local and grassroots desire to reconstruct education around principles of quality, not solely desegregation. The students demanded integration but, unlike the legal organization to achieve this end, they included many aspects of reform that addressed the totality of quality education. As a result, young people did not necessarily view desegregation as the only avenue of protest. After all, desegregating White schools was only one of the thirteen demands students articulated during the Freedom School convention and enrolling in all-White schools was ranked toward the bottom of the list.

Homer Hill, a Freedom School student in Clarksdale, was one of many student activists that chose not to desegregate all White schools. Hill was a peer to Elnora Fondren, a member of the NAACP Youth Council who desegregated the all-White Clarksdale High School by herself in September 1965. Vera Mae Pigee, the local leader from Clarksdale, escorted Fondren daily and organized funds to pay for safe transportation. Hill, a contemporary of Fondren's from the all-Black Higgins High School, recalled hearing the reports from his friend. "Elnora [Fondren] told me about the teachers forcing them to sit in the back of the classroom...and they told us about being harassed," Hill recalled. "They would block seats and desks around them so they would be sort of isolated...I didn't want to leave my high school; I didn't see the advantage of going to the white high school."[36] Cognizant of the exacting cost of desegregating White schools, Hill chose not to desegregate the all White schools in the Mississippi Delta.

Hill's reaction to desegregating an all-White high school illustrates the critical thinking Freedom School students (among other young people exposed to the harsh realities of desegregating White schools) exercised during the first years of desegregation in Mississippi. The first wave of students to desegregate public schools experienced enormous emotional and psychological tolls. The vast majority of students like Hill and their families chose not to pay an ultimate price for token desegregation and instead committed themselves to other forms of protest and discrimination. Interpreted another way, students like Hill remained committed to securing a quality education in ways that did not always translate into desegregating White schools and attending classes with White students.

Students shaped a political agenda based on these assumptions. The second component of student activism included the protests, demonstrations, and boycotts that emanated from segregated African American schools. This brand of politics constituted the most visible forms of protest among the young activists during the 1964–1965 school year. Freedom School activists possessed the commitment and political efficacy to systematically address issues, policies, and other events in ways that moved beyond desegregation, but in ways that still built upon their critical thinking, analysis, and examination of the conditions that surrounded them. The students made a very important decision at the student convention in Meridian. They entered the new school year acting of their own accord and worked *within* the schools, as opposed to abandoning the schools and enrolling full time in a local Freedom School. Therefore, Mississippi students actively boycotted their own schools, protested discriminatory treatment, and demanded a quality education by making explicit demands of the state of Mississippi. Built upon the networks and collective knowledge established and refined during the Freedom Summer campaign, protesting and boycotting segregated schools emerged as the most common form of student protest during the fall of 1964. Student protest suggested that student activism was an important component of educational reform.

To achieve their demands, the Freedom School delegation at the student convention in Meridian suggested that "a committee be set up to make recommendations for school walkouts to be carried out through the Jackson school system should any student be suspended for civil rights work, the committee may recommend the student body to walk out for the length of the suspension." Moreover, the students noted, "all walk-outs or demonstrations should be non-violent."[37] The Mississippi Student Union (MSU) was the primary organization that guided the student-led protests after the summer of 1964. Student activists organized the MSU during the previous year when high school students in Hattiesburg wanted to participate in the Freedom Day Voter Registration drive sponsored by civil rights organizers, but they were soon organizing and meeting on their own. According to the Freedom School convention program that was held in Jackson just days after the Meridian convention in August of 1964, "The latter part of the program will be devoted to the organization of the Mississippi Student Union. This will be the focal point of the convention. It is hoped a strong union will be the result of the Freedom Schools."[38] The union, in the Freedom School coordinator's words, was a student-led program whose aim was to apply "direct action to alleviate serious grievances."[39] The grievances were largely defined as issues that impeded the realization of a quality education. Students thus looked toward the MSU to respond to discriminatory policy at the local level with direct-action protest and organize for other changes within the schools. The Natchez chapter of the MSU is indicative of how plans unfolded after the Freedom Summer campaign. Students organized the Natchez chapter in early September of 1964 and the student union made plans to test public accommodations that were legally integrated by the Civil Rights Act, to picket local stores, to boycott schools, to protest inadequate and/or non-existent equipment, and to publish a student paper, among other considerations.[40]

At the beginning of the 1964 academic school year, therefore, a cadre of student activists across the state of Mississippi were committed to working on their own to secure a quality education. In the process, they acted upon the firm conviction that students should, and must, be at the center of the movement. Students questioned the conditions within their schools and adopted modes of critical inquiry. Students observed and took critical notice of the tangible aspects of unfulfilled promises in education and articulated a bold response. In Liberty (Amite County), students at Central High School petitioned the all-White school board for a quality education and better school facilities.[41] The grievances from Central High School addressed the quality of the curriculum used in the school, the library, the principal, teachers, courses, and physical facilities. Far from a place of complacency or passive acceptance of the remnants of Jim Crow that continued to endemically plague the public school system, students critically observed the schools the state provided, named the glaring shortcomings, and demanded change. At the same time, students also began to take greater action. "We believe, however," the petitioners, continued, "there are several things which would help solve these problems." To address the issues they identified, local activists called for Black citizens to be on the school boards and an increased representation of students and parents in school governance.[42]

As the students in Liberty suggest, there was no shortage of issues to protest after the Freedom Summer of 1964. One major point of contention was the treatment of and disciplinary measures taken against Black students in schools that were still segregated. A principal in Jackson, for instance, expelled a student for singing a Freedom song while school was in session. In Holmes County, a principal expelled two students for singing freedom songs during the lunch period. Another principal in Starkville expelled a student for distributing a MSU petition.[43] The disciplinary tactics experienced by student activists indicated that school administrators would punish any and all civil rights activity in the schools.[44] Moreover, protesting unfair treatment pointed to a larger issue that many of the principals, who were Black, were at the mercy of a White school board that dictated their actions. Across the state of Mississippi, students organized in response to disciplinary action that students deemed unfair and the structural discrimination that supported it. As their protests grew in scope, students demanded better resources and treatment, and forced school authorities to listen to their requests.

A burgeoning political voice among young student activists that spoke out against unfair treatment and distribution of resources persisted during the 1964–1965 school year and led to long-term protest that directly challenged the governance of schools. As students openly questioned issues that denied a quality education, they organized boycotts and sustained protests of the schools they attended. One of the first boycotts occurred in early August 1964, which set the tone for student activity during the upcoming year. The MSU created a partnership with community adults to form the Bolivar (County) Improvement Association. When students asked White volunteers to attend a meeting at McEvans High School, the African American principal asked them to leave if they did not have permission from the White superintendent. Students began a boycott as a result and demanded better resources for their school. The boycott was seventy-five percent effective, and the boycotting students attended the Shaw Freedom School instead of McEvans High School, which local authorities closed and placed armed deputies to quell what they saw as a dangerous situation. The boycott lasted for nearly two months until the students decided to return to school.[45]

The next major boycott occurred in Sharkey and Issaquena Counties and began in January 1965 when four hundred students wore pins to promote participation in the movement. Students refused to take off the pins, and the principal, who similarly had to follow the instructions of an all-White school board, subsequently expelled them. Over three hundred students decided to boycott.[46] Several hundred students stayed out of school for weeks. A small handful remained out of school until the beginning of the next school year. Similarly, thirty to forty students in Philadelphia carried the push for political equality when they fashioned SNCC, "One Man, One Vote" buttons. Wearing political pins and the school expulsions that often resulted were introduced into the courts as issues violating the rights to free speech granted to the students by the Constitution. The students who were suspended in Philadelphia for wearing buttons filed suit against the school board. In the case *Burnside v. Byars* (1966), the court determined that students had the right to wear the buttons in the interest of free speech. This case became the precedent that the Supreme Court cited in *Tinker v. Des Moines* (1969), which stated that young people in Iowa had the First Amendment right to wear a black armband to school in protest of the Vietnam War.[47]

The Issaquena-Sharkey boycott inspired further action across the state. Students attending the Indianola public schools boycotted in support of the Sharkey and Issaquena County students and events occurring in their own community. An unprecedented two thousand students stayed home in Indianola. Students were committed to MSU's statement that, "Negroes are fed up with inferior schools, extreme brutality by the police, and similar discrimination. We're doing something about it." The police brutality referred to the arrest of fifty-three protestors in Indianola and the police force's use of billy clubs and cattle prods to break up the demonstration.[48] Students in Indianola generated a reactionary response from local authorities who formally investigated the boycott and eventually blamed outside "agitators."[49] Like other students across the state who walked out of their own schools, the Issaquena-Sharkey County students remained committed to receiving an education and they provoked the local authorities to take their situation more seriously.

Student boycotts led to other instances of school walkouts across the state and, in some cases, radicalized older adults to boycott the schools their children attended. In Mississippi, the Benton County Citizens Club, a coalition of activists and local community members interested in enacting positive social change, wrote, "at least five counties are having school boycotts," which inspired them to organize.[50] The Citizens Club referred to the aforementioned boycotts and their statement indicates that the student-led movement increased awareness of a statewide struggle for quality education. The students drafted a petition, which over 300 community members signed. The petitioners demanded the termination of the principal and four teachers of Old Salem Attendance Center, the local segregated school that primarily served Black students. After the Board of Education in Benton County agreed to only meet their demands if the petitioners decided *not* to desegregate White schools and businesses, the Citizens Club decided to boycott the school.[51] Students and community adults who organized around this issue wrote that:

> We Negroes in Benton County have nothing EXCEPT our organized strength. With this strength we must stand together and show the nation that we refuse to cooperate with the Southern way of life, to be lied to, to be tricked, to be cheated, and to be told that we have no voice in our children's education... The only thing left for us is to keep our children out of school as a way of protesting their inferior education.[52]

Local high school students established Freedom Schools during the school boycott, much like other boycotters in Mississippi. In this case, the Freedom School students worked in conjunction with Rust College students.[53] Within two months, the Benton County workers reported that the boycott was ninety percent effective and achieved a degree of success in that the segregated Black school hired a "new principal who is favorable to civil rights."[54]

During the Bolivar, Issaquena, Sharkey and Benton County boycotts, students who walked out of the public schools attended Freedom Schools. Students led discussions about county politics, strategies for their respective boycotts, and the conditions of Blacks in Mississippi. Students who attended a Freedom School rather than the boycotted public school essentially engaged in another form of protest by creating an alternative system of education. The Freedom School classes organized by and for the boycotting students were, according to Freedom Summer volunteer Mary Aicken Rothschild, "chaos, but they represented the free expression of students that the staff had only theorized could be possible in November."[55] For many in the civil rights movement, the purpose of the Freedom Schools was to fill the void caused by school boycotts. This role restored an original vision as conceived in Boston, where organizers established Freedom Schools across the city during the citywide school boycott in 1963.[56] The idea that Freedom Schools would educate boycotting students also met the ideals expressed in Cobb's proposal. The students were questioning the political institutions of the state, they were organizing their own education, and they were committing themselves to the frontlines for civil rights in Mississippi.

The extended boycotts are exceptional considering that students decided at the student-led convention in Meridian that they would return to the public schools provided by the state of Mississippi. This did not preclude, however, the opportunity to attend a Freedom School as an extracurricular activity outside of school, after school hours or during the weekend. Nor did it prevent developing a parallel institution, as exemplified by the boycotts. The former was the most common form of student enrollment in the program and students were most active in shaping the Freedom Schools as a program supplemental to the public school education they received. Toward the end of the Freedom Summer campaign in early August, Staughton Lynd, director of the Freedom School project, announced that plans were being made for the continuation of Freedom Schools, as some volunteer teachers had already agreed to remain in the state. The Council of Federated Organizations (COFO) made a similar announcement in the winter of 1964 and stated that "the Freedom Schools will be continued in all areas where possible, but their scope will be somewhat limited as the majority of students will be in regular school full time."[57] Liz Fusco volunteered to continue to coordinate the Freedom Schools during the upcoming year. The schools functioned as a political supplement to the students' regular public school education. Freedom School courses were offered at night, during the weekends, and in the summer.[58] In the instances of student strikers boycotting the schools, the Freedom Schools served as the primary mode of education in instances where students refused to attend the public schools provided by the state of Mississippi.

The Freedom School model proffers a potent example of alternative institution building and an early form of community control during the reconstruction of public education. During a SNCC-sponsored conference in California in the fall of 1964, Bob Moses began to articulate a separate and alternative agenda later adopted and associated with the "Black Power" movement and the community control that emerged from this. Moses spoke directly about a potentially expanded role of the Freedom Schools. He asked: "Why can't we set up our own schools? Because when you come right down to it, why integrate their schools? What is it that you will learn in their schools? Many of the Negroes can learn it, but what can they do with it? What they really need to learn is how to be organized to work on the society to change it."[59] Moses' statement captures local activists' critique of desegregation long embodied in the Black freedom struggles "integrating" White schools translating into a horrific and compromising experience for a handful of children. The alternative to desegregating schools, or in Moses' words "to be organized to work on the society to change it," was captured within the Freedom School model.

The Freedom School model facilitated the historic desegregation and transformation of public education in Mississippi. More notably, however, it educated a cadre of students to articulate their own visions of quality education and to make their voices heard. Embodied within this notion was the idea that student participation was critical to the implementation of a quality education. The existence and governance of these alternative schools also put forth early notions of community control. As politics at the grassroots level put forth competing and normative notions of what quality education should be, the federal government also put forth conceptions of quality education that moved beyond the desegregation of schools.

HEAD START AND THE RECONSTRUCTION OF EDUCATION

As organizers worked at the local level around the Freedom School idea, the federal context had changed significantly to facilitate the reconstruction of public education. Not only did the federal courts begin to strike down "freedom of choice" plans that evaded desegregation, but legislative acts began to enforce the civil rights of disenfranchised people of color. Congress already passed the Civil Rights Act during the summer of 1964 and, after the Selma to Montgomery march that illustrated the need for tougher voter registration protection, Congress introduced legislation that led to the Voting Rights Act of 1965. The federal government became involved in other ways that shaped the contours of the local civil rights movement in Mississippi, specifically in regards to education. By the spring of 1965, President Lyndon B. Johnson signed the Elementary and Secondary Education Act (ESEA) into law, the most comprehensive and far-reaching educational policy passed in the history of American education.[60] Lyndon B. Johnson championed education as the means to alleviating poverty once and for all in the United States, which became an important piece of the "War on Poverty." As part of this campaign, the Johnson administration orchestrated the largest early childhood educational program in the history of the United States: Head Start, a federally funded program to provide education, nourishing meals, medical services and a positive social environment for children about to enter the first grade.

As the Freedom School idea was already mobilized in Mississippi, an early childhood program like Head Start that sought to educate disenfranchised youth gained the immediate support at the local grassroots level. "[The Freedom Schools] brought about Head Start for black children," Ida Ruth Griffen, a Freedom School student from Carthage, Mississippi, recalled. "Most of the people that were Freedom Riders," she remembered. "They are the ones who originated Head Start."[61] Others in the movement articulated similar connections between the Freedom Schools and President Lyndon B. Johnson's anti-poverty educational program. "They [Head Start and the Freedom Movement] had to come together at some point in time," Owen Brooks, a Delta Ministry activist enmeshed in Mississippi politics, including Head Start, remembered, "because they were the same people ... the same people were involved in the counties and communities so what was in place for political action also was in place to assist Head Start."[62] Mr. Brooks, active in the Mississippi Freedom Movement since 1965, and Freedom School student Ida Ruth Griffen clearly noted the connection between Head Start and the Civil Rights Movement. Upon first glance, the connection between the Freedom Schools, a grassroots and radical educational project, and Head Start, a massive federally funded early childhood education project, is unlikely. Yet, for Griffen, Brooks and others closely involved in the Mississippi movement, Head Start was a natural extension of the Civil Rights Movement.[63]

The scale of the Head Start program in Mississippi alone dwarfed the Freedom Schools, which placed the program in a stronger position to articulate notions of quality education during the reconstruction of public education. Less than one year after public schools first desegregated, over 25,000 young children enrolled in Head Start centers across Mississippi. Head Start was not founded with the objective to desegregate schools. The very existence of the program was based upon the assumption that educational intervention early in a child's life had important and lifelong repercussions. Head Start was not as much an alternative institution such as the Freedom Schools. Rather, it was the very first institutionalization of kindergarten and early childhood education in most of the Mississippi communities it served. By 1965, only sixteen states had statewide public kindergarten programs, though private, tuition-based kindergarten and nurseries existed in almost every state. In many of the Mississippi communities where early childhood education did not exist, some children had delayed enrollment in the school system until their seventh or eighth year.[64] The multitude of children and families the program served was nationally significant as well. The idea was immensely popular and within a two-month period during the summer of 1965, over 21,000 students received some form of kindergarten education where none existed before. According to one volunteer, "the word has spread and just the attempt to meet the current demands, without any recruiting for new centers, has stretched [our] resources to the limit." One of the immediate issues faced by programs that summer was what the Child Development Group of Mississippi referred to as "The Problem of Too Many Children."[65]

Federal funding provided new opportunities that the financially strapped Civil Rights Movement could not, which translated into committing resources to conceptions of quality education. In addition to the educational component, Head Start provided physical, health, and medical attention for every child enrolled in the program, which included delivering hot meals to children twice a day and arranging medical examinations and follow-up treatment to those who needed it.[66] "We went out in the schools of rural areas of Hinds County and examined the children at the school, and there was hearing and vision screening done by other groups during the day; but most of the examinations were at night or on Saturdays or Sundays," Dr. Jim Hendrick remembered about working with the program in Jackson. "It was a big affair. Everybody came, they was all dressed up . . . it was fun."[67] For those involved with the program, Head Start provided services to communities impoverished by the morally bankrupt system of Jim Crow. As the Reverend James F. McRee of the Delta remembered, "Head Start had something that we needed. Because what you had here were malnourished kids. Some kids were eating but one meal per day, and some were getting a meal whenever they could."[68] This component of the Head Start program developed the notion that a quality education provided more than an academic education and that the development of the "whole child" should also be addressed.

The federal government offered something else to the Black staff that ran Head Start centers that grassroots organizations running the Freedom Schools could not: gainful employment and substantial wages. Since Head Start was a significant component of the larger "War on Poverty," it sought to provide jobs to the unemployed. As such, federal paychecks amounted to a massive economic stimulus package to the state of Mississippi. At a time when farm labor paid fifteen dollars per week, Head Start employees were paid fifty to sixty dollars per week and the coveted teachers' positions paid seventy-five dollars per week.[69] In this way, federal intervention incorporated the economic wellbeing of educators in the conceptions of quality education that they put forth during the era of reconstructing public education. The education of the student was of the utmost importance, but the wellbeing of the educators, ideally selected from and for the community, was an important factor to consider in the provision of quality education.

The federal government endorsed a notion of "maximum feasible participation" as a way to govern Head Start and other programs part of the "War on Poverty." The idea privileged the employment of local people and parent and/or the local poor into the decision-making and practical implementation of the program.[70] Maximum feasible participation guided the decision-making process at the local level as Head Start programs incorporated people from the communities they served into governing boards. Local Head Start volunteers often implemented maximum-feasible participation by visiting their students' homes to work with the parents in ensuring the best development of children. Parent involvement, long recognized as an instrumental component in any child's education, was a very important part of Head Start from its inception and the program continues to value its importance today.[71] The notion of maximum participation also dovetails with elements of community control later associated with the Black Power movement, which sought to keep the control of institutions in the hands of those they served.[72]

The curriculum put forth by local people in Head Start also put forth civil rights based content during the reconstruction of public education. The Friends of Children of Mississippi (FCM), a community program that organized various Head Start centers throughout the state, was indicative of developing curriculum that centralized the importance of Black history and culture.[73] FCM, for instance, hosted a Black History and Consciousness Workshop in the summer of 1968. "It is hoped that the teachers will develop a more positive feeling about blackness," FCM organizers wrote, "and that they will in turn help develop such a feeling in the children they teach."[74] The federal government did not necessarily endorse a multicultural curriculum that programs like the FCM created. The governing principles they endorsed such as "maximum feasible participation" facilitated the development of curricula that local people aligned with their own aspirations.

THE NEW RIGHT AND THE CONSERVATIVE INFLUENCE

Civil rights-based educational programs proffered conceptions of quality education that coincided with the reconstruction of public education. The initial stages of Head Start were a phenomenal success for the Civil Rights Movement. The fact that over 21,000 children received an education, medical and health services, volunteers were reimbursed for their services, and participants were able to foster the goals of the Civil Rights Movement illustrate the ongoing work for ensuring a quality education. The gains made by the Freedom School students, too, suggested that the Civil Rights Movement was successful in educating young people in middle and high school to articulate and act upon their own demands. Perceived educational gains from the perspective of movement participants were short lived, however. As powerful Southern segregationists like John Stennis of Mississippi were forced to accept the desegregation of schools and the marginal protections the Civil Rights Act afforded to people of color, elected representatives committed to segregation focused on marginalizing the impact of civil rights educational programs. Since Head Start was tantamount to civil rights organization and it gained national notoriety in a short period of time, staunch opposition from White segregationists like Stennis soon followed federal investment in civil rights education.

The politics of Head Start is instructive because it illustrates the dynamic between local and federal levels in shaping the gains made by the educational programs of the Civil Rights Movement. As significant federal funding was attached to Head Start, the program in Mississippi inspired a national controversy that framed the rhetoric of the New Right. As historian Joseph Crespino has suggested, "Whites in Mississippi rearticulated their resentment of the liberal social policies that allowed for Black advancement in ways that would come to resonate with White Americans far outside of the Deep South. They conceived of their struggle against civil rights activists and federal officials not merely as a regional fight to preserve White supremacy but as a national battle to preserve fundamental American freedoms."[75] Thus, when local civil rights activists organized for federal funding for their Head Start programs, they entered a larger national context and on this stage they were opposed by grassroots organizers at the other end of the political spectrum, "cold warriors concerned about an expansive federal state ... and with parents opposed to federal school desegregations efforts, who wanted to determine where and with whom their children would attend."[76]

Mississippi legislators, elected officials and other conservative politicians critiqued Head Start in such a way as to connect it to the growing conservative movement at the national level. Less than one year prior to the implementation of Head Start, Barry Goldwater, a staunchly conservative Republican, decisively carried the state of Mississippi with eighty-seven percent of the vote. Goldwater also won other majorities in Alabama, Georgia, Louisiana, and South Carolina, the first time since Reconstruction the Deep South voted for a Republican candidate.[77] As Sunbelt scholars have noted, this political swing was the beginning of a movement that housed much of the race-neutral rhetoric and the defense of individual values, exemplified in the later battle over busing legislation in the early 1970s.[78] Mississippi Senator John Stennis, a vocal segregationist, although adopting on a national stage race-neutral rhetoric, attacked the Head Start program in his home state and charged the program with mismanaging funds and using federal money to subsidize civil rights demonstrations, including payment of fines and bail.[79] Congressional politicians like Stennis served as the national conduit by which to express growing disdain for Head Start and, by extension, other civil rights educational initiatives.

Stennis' stern resistance and objection to "welfare" did not deter the Office of Economic Opportunity, which renewed Head Start funding through 1966 and 1967. But the office steered federal funding away from civil rights organizations, namely the Children's Development Group of Mississippi (CDGM), which was by this time chastised as a radical civil rights program.[80] The government responded by sending auditors and investigators to formally evaluate the Head Start headquarters at Mt. Beulah.[81] Moreover, the federal government encouraged Mississippians to run Head Start programs through alternative Community Action Programs such as the Mississippi Action for Progress (MAP), which was governed by biracial and politically moderate boards.[82] Anti-Head Start sentiment was reinforced by national evaluations (conducted by outsiders and social scientific "experts"), such as the influential Westinghouse Report, which found no substantial gains in the cognitive or affective gains of Head Start students.[83] Under the guise of mismanagement of funds was a forceful rejection at the federal level, articulated through Stennis's objections from Capitol Hill, of the empowerment of thousands of Black women, children, and civil rights activists associated with the Head Start program.[84] Though the federal government did not abandon the project, federal guidelines dictated how the program should be run and by whom in ways that were antithetical to the movement.

Federal oversight ensured that the federal government and the American public would not support the civil rights framework of Head Start and, by extension, conceptions of quality education embedded within the Freedom School model.

To SNCC, the Congress of Racial Equality (CORE), and the more radical elements of the movement including Freedom School organizers, especially after the Atlantic City Convention of 1964, Head Start was doomed to fail solely because of its association with the federal government. SNCC and other movement leaders loudly criticized federal intervention through Head Start at the state and local level as well. Stakeholders in the movement were highly skeptical of federal money, paternalistic sentiments, and the prevalence of middle-class values associated with Head Start. The money invested in the program was interpreted as "buying out" activists who would otherwise be committed to the more radical elements of the civil rights movement. For those who orchestrated the Freedom Summer campaign, joining the program was tantamount to selling out, as Fannie Lou Hamer suggested, "by a few middle-class bourgeoisie and some of the Uncle Toms who couldn't care less."[85] Already skeptical of federal intervention after losing their challenge to seat the civil rights-based MFDP in Atlantic City, SNCC was "too politicized and too committed to alternative institutions to support" organizations funded by the federal government.[86] Discriminatory oversight and the federal push toward bi-racial moderate Head Start governing boards validated their suspicions.

Moreover, federal intervention carried with it paternalistic and problematic assumptions. At the federal level, Head Start was very much comprised of federal policy makers and "experts" in the field of education who held racist assumptions of the Black family, which was evident in their analysis of poverty. In light of the Moynihan Report, which was released to the Johnson Administration during the summer of 1965, an influential faction of federal policymakers traced the origins of poverty to the "pathology" of Black homes, which, according to experts, needed to be corrected by middle class and/or White values.[87] The African American home, they concluded, was culturally deprived of values that led to educationally, socially, and economically successful lives. While parent and home involvement is an innovative component of Head Start pedagogy, it does signify the problematic relationship between federal and local educational policy. SNCC and other activists who opposed Head Start and federal intervention were correct in that the government pacified or mitigated the direct-action component of the movement. Head Start did not train students or its teachers to protest and become key stakeholders in the ongoing struggle like the Freedom Schools had encouraged. Segregationist policy makers influenced the direction of Head Start by implementing moderate biracial governing boards that explicitly denounced full-time activity in the civil rights movement and the burgeoning influence of Black Power.

* * *

The educational initiatives of the Mississippi Freedom Schools and Head Start during the 1960s occured at the historic moment of desegregation. A network of young people transformed the idea of education for social change. They boycotted and even shut down the segregated schools they attended. In some instances they formed their own schools at the moment they were expected to desegregate the public schools. Though different in scope, the Head Start program embodied ideas of community control, teacher organization, and progressive curriculum at the same moment, too. Both ideas developed programs that embodied ideas that intersected with the federal context in ways that significantly limited their influence.

The grassroots organization that defined the Freedom Schools and Head Start would not incorporate itself into the mainstream discourse of educational reform as the public education system was reconstructed during the 1960s and 1970s. The architects of desegregation in Mississippi—the White governor, White school boards, and the White state legislature—organized to quell any progressive education movements from local communities. The national context buttressed ongoing hostility toward Head Start and continued discrimination at the state and local level. Federal guidelines established the parameters of desegregation through busing and unitary district development, among other plans, that overlooked a proven need and a solution to a broken school system. The struggle to provide a quality education through programs like the Freedom Schools and Head Start foreshadowed the civil rights generation's ongoing struggle to provide a quality education. This ensured the marginalization of conceptions of quality education that emerged from the Civil Rights Movement and relegated their ideas to alternative educational programs and local organization.

The tenacity of local organization around the Freedom Schools and Head Start illustrates a rich ideological context that surrounded the historic reconstruction of the public school system in the middle of the twentieth century. Local organizers, educators, and activists put forth effective models of quality education that called for student engagement, teacher organization, and community involvement. This discourse illustrates a brief moment where the federal government and local organizers put forth different though interconnected notions of reform. This history provides a framework through which to better understand the underlying tensions inherent in the contemporary push to restructure public education around the objectives of quality education as a constitutional right.

NOTES

1. "Declaration of Independence," in the MFDP papers, box 14, folder 4 "Freedom School: Background Data," the Martin Luther King, Jr. Center Library and Archives.
2. The history of desegregation and the *Brown v. Board of Education* (1954) decision and the place it holds in the historiography of American history is indicative of the importance of the decision. For an introductory overview, see: Richard Kluger, *Simple Justice: The History of* Brown v. Board of Education *and Black American's Struggle for Equality* (New York, NY: Vintage Books, 2004); James Patterson, *Brown v. Board of Education: A Civil Rights Milestone and Its Troubled Legacy* (Oxford: Oxford University Press, 2001); Michael J. Klarman, *Brown v. Board of Education and the Civil Rights Movement* (Oxford: Oxford University Press, 2007); Mark Tushnet, *Making Civil Rights Law: Thurgood Marshall and the Supreme Court, 1936–1961* (New York, NY: Oxford University Press, 1994); Lucas A. Power Jr., *The Warren Court and American Politics* (Cambridge: Belknap Press of Harvard University Press, 2000); Jack M. Balkin, ed., *What* Brown v. Board of Education *Should Have Said: The Nation's Top Legal Experts Rewrite America's Landmark Civil Rights Decision* (New York, NY: New York University Press, 2001); Alfred Kelly, "The School Desegregation Case," in Alfred Kelley, ed, *Quarrels That Have Shaped the Constitution* (New York, NY: Harper & Row, 1987).
3. Patterson, *Brown v. Board of Education*, xvi.
4. The history of self-determination and agency in nineteenth-century Black education is well known and has been explored in great detail. See: James Anderson, *Education of Blacks in the South, 1860–1935* (Chapel Hill: University of North Caroline Press, 1988); Christopher M. Span, *From Cotton Field to Schoolhouse: African American Education in Mississippi, 1862–1875* (Chapel Hill: University of North Carolina Press, 2009); V. P. Franklin, Black Self-Determination: A Cultural History of African-American Resistance (Brooklyn: Lawrence Hill Books, 1002); Heather Williams, "The Men Are Actually Clamoring for Books" and "We Must Get Education for Ourselves and Our Children" in *Self-Taught: African American Education in Slavery and Freedom* (Chapel Hill: University of North Carolina Press, 2005), 45–79.
5. For a history of equalization and the NAACP legal strategy that led to *Brown*, see: Mark V. Tushnet, *The NAACP's Legal Strategy Against Segregated Education, 1925–1950* (Chapel Hill: The University of North Carolina Press, 1987).
6. A. L. Johnson to Mr. A. J. Noel, January 14, 1948 and A. L. Johnson to James A. Burns, 23 February 1948, in Gladys Noel Bates Papers, Box 2, "Scrapbook, 1948–1960," MDAH. Similarly, organized educators in South Carolina within the Palmetto Education Association adopted aggressive stances on equalizing salaries and resources., see: John F. Potts, *A History of the Palmetto Education Association* (Washington, D.C.: National Education Association, 1978), 61–68.
7. Gladys Noel Bates, interview with Catherine Jannik, 23 December 1996, The University of Southern Mississippi Center for Oral History and Cultural Heritage; Charles Bolton, *The Hardest Deal of All: The Battle Over School Integration in Mississippi, 1870–1980* (Jackson, MS: University Press of Mississippi,

2005), 45–60; Edward S. Bishop Sr., interview with Charles Bolton, February 27. 1991; "Community in Which I live" (Gladys Noel Bates Papers, Box 3, "Speeches and Papers, 1948, 1968, 1991–1992."

8. "Address Delivered at the Black Women's Political Action Forum, 1 February 1991, Jackson, MS" in Gladys Noel Bates Papers, Box 3, "Speeches and Papers, 1948, 1968, 1991–1992"; Gladys Noel Bates, "The Gladys Noel Bates Teacher-Equalization Pay Suit, 16 May 1992," in Box 3, "Speeches and Papers, 1948, 1968, 1991–1992," MDAH.; Robert L. Carter to A. L. Johnson, 19 April 1949, in Gladys Noel Bates Papers, Box 2, "Scrapbook, 1948–1960," MDAH; Bolton, *Hardest Deal of All*, 46–49.

9. The Charleston County School District in South Carolina did not renew the contract of Septima Clark for her involvement with the NAACP, see: Charron, *Freedom's Teacher*, 242–247. Other educators who lost their jobs in South Carolina due to their work with the NAACP and equalization include J. T. W. Mims, principal of Bell Street High School and president of the Palmetto State Teachers Association from 1942 to 1944 and J. R. McCain, PSTA president between 1946 and 1948, Potts, *A History of the Palmetto Education Association*, 66–67. The reaction of White educational policymakers contributes to the prevailing thesis that Black teachers were not active in the Civil Rights Movement.

10. Bolton, *The Hardest Deal of All*, 33–60; Neil R. McMillen, "Development of Civil Rights, 1956–1970," in *A History of Mississippi*, ed. Richard Aubrey McClemore (Hattiesburg: University of Southern Mississippi, 1973), vol. 2, 154–157; "Amendment Gains Nod of Approval in Tuesday's Vote; Pearl Rive County Votes Against Proposal," *Weekly Democrat*, 23 December 1954; "Private School System Setup is Considered" *Vicksburg Evening Post,* 9 December 1953, in "Education 1950–1956" subject file, Mississippi Department of Archives and History (hereafter referred to as MDAH).

11. Bolton, *Hardest Deal of All*, 76.

12. Ibid., 73.

13. Division of Administration and Finance, *Biennial Report and Recommendations of the State Superintendent of Public Education, Scholastic Years 1953–1954 and 1954–1955,* 130.

14. Len Holt, *The Summer That Didn't End* (New York, NY: Marrow, 1965), 102.

15. Division of Research, College of Business and Industry, *Mississippi Statistical Abstract 1971*, (Meridian: Mississippi State University, 1971) 184–185.

16. John Dittmer, *Local People: The Struggle for Civil Rights in Mississippi* (Urbana: University of Illinois Press, 1994), 46.

17. Ibid., 49–51.

18. Michael W. Fuquay, "Civil Rights and the Private School Movement in Mississippi, 1964–1971," *History of Education Quarterly* 42, no. 2 (Summer, 2002): 159–180.

19. "Johnson May Speak Today." *The Clarion-Ledger*, 6 June 1964; "Legislature Coming Back," *The Clarion-Ledger*, 7 June 1964; "Lawmakers Head Home; Will Return on June 17," *The Clarion Ledger*, 8 June 1964. For a thorough and complete history of the desegregation of Mississippi public school system, see: Bolton, *Hardest Deal of All.*

20. "Appeal In School Case Won't Stop Integration," *The Clarion Ledger*, 8 July 1964; "Biloxi to Join Court Appeal," *The Clarion-Ledger*, 9 July 1964.
21. *Mississippi Statistical Abstract 1971*, 171.
22. *Mississippi Statistical Abstract 1970*, 80.
23. The history of the Freedom Schools has been well documented. See: Jon Hale, "'The Student as a Force for Social Change': The Mississippi Freedom Schools and Student Engagement," *The Journal of African American History* 96, No. 3 (Summer 2011), 325–347; Jon Hale, *The Freedom Schools: A History of Students at the Front Lines of the Mississippi Freedom Movement* (New York: Columbia University Press, forthcoming 2016); William Sturkey, "'I Want to Become a Part of History': Freedom Summer, Freedom Schools, and the Freedom News," *The Journal of African American History* 95 (Summer–Fall 2010): 348–368; Daniel Perlstein, "Teaching Freedom: SNCC and the Creation of the Mississippi Freedom Schools," *History of Education Quarterly* 30 (Autumn 1990): 297–324; William Sturkey and Jon Hale (eds.), *To Write in the Light of Freedom: The Freedom School Newspapers: Writings, Essays and Reports from Student Activists During the Civil Rights Movement* (Jackson: University Press of Mississippi, 2015).
24. "1964 Platform of the Mississippi Freedom School Convention," in MFDP papers, box 14, folder 16, "F. S. Convention," The King Center Library and Archives; Sandra Adickes, *Legacy of a Freedom School* (New York, NY: Palgrave Macmillan, 2005), 86–87; Sally Belfrage, *Freedom Summer* (New York, NY: Viking Press, 1965), 91–92.
25. "Public Accommodations," SNCC papers, Subgroup A, Series 15, box 101, folder, "MSP—Freedom Schools, Curriculum Materials."
26. Liz Fusco, "Freedom Schools in Mississippi, 1964," SNCC Papers, subgroup A, Series 15, box 101, folder "MSP—Freedom Schools, Curriculum Materials," the King Center Library and Archives.
27. Florence Howe, "Mississippi's Freedom Schools: The Politics of Education," *Harvard Educational Review* 35 (1965), 155–156; Bolton, *Hardest Deal of All*, 110–114.
28. "19 Negroes Apply at Canton High," *The Clarion-Ledger*, 4 September 1964; "18 Negroes Seeding Transfer to Canton," *Hattiesburg American*, 3 September 1964; "Meridian Leaders Take Legal Action," *Hattiesburg American*, 4 September 1964; "Integration Sought By Meridian Group," *The Clarion-Ledger*, 5 September 1964; "Canton, Summit Integration Attempts Are Turned Back," *The Clarion-Ledger*, 9 September 1964; "Canton School Turns Back Negro Pupils," *Clarksdale Press Register*, 8 September 1964; "High Schools in Jackson Bar Negroes," *Clarksdale Press Register*, 10 September 1964; Bolton, *Hardest Deal of All*, 111–112.
29. Bolton, "Freedom of Choice for Whites: Massive Resistance by Another Name," in *The Hardest Deal of All*, 117–140.
30. Bolton, *The Hardest Deal of All*, 149; Hymethia Washington Thompson, interview with the author, 4 July 2012.
31. Ibid., 141–142. For extensive oral histories of the desegregation of Murrah High School in 1969–1970 school year, see "Murrah High School Oral History Project," (MDAH).

32. For historical documentation of students' experiences in desegregating all-White school, see Millicent Brown's "Somebody Had to Do It" oral history project http://somebody.claflin.edu/ Te project is a multi-disciplinary study to identify, locate, and acknowledge African American "First Children" who desegregated America's schools. The Project seeks to create a database of those "First Children" whose narratives are needed to adequately and accurately interpret the issues and results associated with the *Brown vs. Board of Education* (1954) Supreme Court decision, and Title VI of the 1964 Civil Rights Act.

33. State plans endorsed a scholarship grant at $165 per year that limited aid to those attending nonsectarian schools, and it also required that local districts provide a supplemental thirty-five-dollar stipend. U.S. District Judge Oren R. Lewis refused to stop grant payment for private schools, despite NAACP challenges. *Laws of the State of Mississippi, 1964*, 5; "Committee to Request State Scholarship Plan" *The Clarion-Ledger*, 18 June 1964; "Tuition Grant approved by Senate," *The Clarion-Ledger*, 7 July 1964. "Judge refuses to Break Up Alleged Segregation Plans" *The Clarion-Ledger*, 10 July 1964.

34. Fuquay, "Civil Rights and the Private School Movement in Mississippi," 168–172.

35. Roscoe Jones, interview with the author, March 18, 2014.

36. Hamlin, *Crossroads at Clarksdale*, 169–171; Hill, interview with the author, 25 September 2011.

37. "Freedom Schools, Jackson," SNCC papers, Subgroup D, Appendix A, Reel 68.355, 344–445. University of Illinois; MFDP papers, box 17, folder 8, "Freedom Schools, Jackson," the King Center Library and Archives.

38. "Freedom Schools, Jackson," SNCC papers, Subgroup D, Appendix A, Reel 68.355, 344–445. University of Illinois; MFDP papers, box 17, folder 8, "Freedom Schools, Jackson," the King Center Library and Archives.

39. Liz Fusco, "Freedom Schools in Mississippi, 1964," SNCC papers, Subgroup A, Series 15, box 101, folder, "MSP—Freedom Schools, Curriculum Materials."

40. "Freedom Schools, Natchez," SNCC papers, Subgroup D, Appendix A, Reel 68.361.541; "Freedom Schools, reports, July 10-Dec. 27, 1964," SNCC papers, Subgroup D, Appendix A, Reel 68.366,566–567.366, University of Illinois; "The Mississippi Student Union Convention—December 1964, MSU folder, Freedom Information Service Library, Jackson, Mississippi.

41. "Amite County List of Grievances: Introduction," SNCC Papers, subgroup A, series 15, box 101, folder "MSP—Freedom Schools, Curriculum Materials," the King Center Library and Archives. The document produced by students does not include a date, but it can be inferred the protest occurred in the fall of 1964.

42. Ibid., "Amite County List of Grievances: Introduction," SNCC Papers, subgroup A, series 15, box 101, folder "MSP—Freedom Schools, Curriculum Materials," the King Center Library and Archives.

43. "Massive School Boycott in Indianola, Press Release 22 February 1965," FIS; "Freedom Fighter: Issaquena MSU," Mississippi Student Union folder, FIS.

44. Gael Graham, *Young Activists: American High School Students in the Age of Protest* (DeKalb, IL: Northern Illinois University Press, 2006), 45–63.

45. Rothschild, *A Case of Black and White*, 110–115; "Issaquena M.S.U. Freedom Fighter, August, 1965," Mississippi Student Union folder, FIS; Bolton, *The Hardest Deal of All*, 111.

46. Mary Aicken Rothschild, *A Case of Black and White: Northern Volunteers and the Southern Freedom Summers, 1964–1965* (Westport, CT: Greenwood Press, 1982), 110–115; "Issaquena M.S.U. Freedom Fighter, August, 1965," Mississippi Student Union folder, FIS.

47. Burnside v. Byars, 363 F.2d n. 22681 (5th Cir. 1966); Tinker v. Des Moines, 393 U.S. 503; 89 S. Ct (1969); Staughton Lynd, interview with the author, August 28, 2006.

48. "Massive School Boycott in Indianola, COFO news release, Freedom Schools," miscellaneous folder, FIS.

49. "Youth Court Eyeing School Attendance," *Enterprise-Tocsin*, 25 February 1965. Ironically enough, the town of Indianola required Black students to attend public schools, though six months earlier the town provided a charter for a private White segregationist academy, see "Local Group Given Charter to Operate Private School," *Enterprise-Tocsin*, 13 August 1964. Some of the leaders in the boycott movement did not return to school. The leaders of the Issaquena boycott took paying jobs with the Delta Ministry, a civil rights organization based in the Mississippi Delta, and one of the leaders became the first to integrate the all-White Issaquena-Sharkey public school, Rothschild, *A Case of Black and White*, 115.

50. "Let's Keep Our Children Out of School," 2, in Aviva Futorian Papers, Folder 1, Wisconsin State Historical Society archives, Madison WI.

51. Ibid., 1.

52. Ibid., 2.

53. "Dear Fellow Members of the Great Society," 15 March 1965, in Aviva Futorian Papers, Folder 1, Wisconsin State Historical Society archives, Madison WI.

54. "Dear_____" 7 May 1965, in Aviva Futorian Papers, Folder 1, Wisconsin State Historical Society archives, Madison WI.

55. Rothschild, *A Case of Black and White*, 115.

56. The Boston Freedom Schools, organized during the winter of 1963 after local activists boycotted public schools in the city, were a significant model of civil rights education that helped lay the curricular foundation of the Mississippi Freedom Schools, MFDP Papers, box 14, folder 6, "Boston Freedom Schools," The King Center Library and Archives; James and Jeanne Breeden, interview with Tess Bundy, October 22, 2012, Leyden, MA (transcript in possession of author and interviewer). For excellent analysis of the Boston movement, see Tess Bundy, "Chapter 2: I realized it was more than myself: "The Birth of a Mass Movement for Educational Liberation, 1959–1965" (PhD diss., University of Maryland, 2014).

57. "COFO Program," in Robert Reingrass Papers, Folder 1, Wisconsin State Historical Society Archives, Madison WI.

58. "Freedom Schools, correspondence," SNCC papers, Subgroup D, Appendix A, Reel 67.335,540. University of Illinois.

59. Bob Moses, quoted in Dittmer, *Local People*, 326. Moses's statements on the value of maintaining segregated schools, like Stokely's Black Power proclama-

tion, was not necessarily new. W. E. B. Du Bois in 1935 asked, "Does the Negro need separate schools"? The answer suggested no, but in the racialized climate of Jim Crow, desegregated schools would only hurt the students who had to attend. Du Bois wrote, among other things, about the emotional and physical toll taken by Black students integrating all White schools. W. E. B. Du Bois, "Does the Negro Need Separate Schools?" *The Journal of Negro Education* vol. 4, no. 3 (July 1935): 328–335; Moses's statement in many ways anticipated the development of the latter Black Panther Liberation Schools of the late 1960s, see Daniel Perlstein, "Minds Stayed on Freedom: Politics and Pedagogy in the African-American Freedom Struggle," *American Educational Research Journal* 39, 2 (Summer 2002): 249–277.

60. Hugh Davis Graham, *The Uncertain Triumph: Federal Education Policy in the Kennedy and Johnson Years* (Chapel Hill: University of North Carolina Press, 1984); Adam R. Nelson, "The Federal Role in American Education," in William J. Reese and John L. Rury, eds., *Rethinking the History of American Education* (New York, NY: Palgrave MacMillan, 2008); Stephen Bailey and Edith Mosler, *ESEA: The Office of Education Administers at Law* (Syracuse: Syracuse University Press, 1968); Julie Roy Jeffrey, *Education for Children of the Poor: A Study of the Origins and Implementation of the Elementary and Secondary Education Act of 1964* (Columbus: Ohio State University Press, 1978). More nuanced and comprehensive policy analysis places the origins of Head Start in and the "rediscovery" of poverty during the Kennedy administration, which was in part triggered by mainstream accounts of poverty, such as Michael Harrington's *The Other America: Poverty in the United States*, that conveyed to the American public the existence of poverty in the land of prosperity, see: Maris Vinovskis, The Birth of Head Start (Chicago: University of Chicago Press, 2005), 2–34; Philip Meranto, *The Politics of Federal Aid to Education in 1965: A Study in Political Innovation* (Syracuse: Syracuse University Press, 1967), 16–20; Michael Harrington, *The Other American: Poverty in the United States* (New York, NY: Macmillan, 1962).

61. Ida Ruth Griffin O'Leary, interview with the author, 4 September 2008.

62. Owen Brooks, interview with the author, 1 July 2010.

63. For an eloquent and comprehensive historical account of Head Start, see: Crystal Sanders, "To Be Free of Fear: Black Women's Fight for Freedom Through the Child Development Group of Mississippi" (PhD diss, Northwestern University, 2011).

64. Tom Levin Papers, Series I, Box 3, "West Point Evaluation—District 4—R. Myers, Employees," The King Center Archives; Tom Levin Papers, Series I, Box 3, "Grant Applications," "Application for Project Head Start," The King Center Archives; Zigler and Muenchow, Head Start, 30; Polly Greenberg, "Three Core Concepts of the War on Poverty: Their Origins and Significance in Head Start," in *The Head Start Debates*, eds., Edward Zigler and Sally J. Styfco (Baltimore: Brookes Publishing Company, 2004), 62–63.

65. Child Development Group of Mississippi Papers, Box 1, Folder 1, "Training Proposals, 1965," "Proposal for a Summer Program," Schomburg Center for Research in Black Culture (hereafter referred to as the Schomburg Center).

66. Laura Johnson, interview with the author, 25 June 2010; Floree Smith, interview with the author, 24 June 2010; Edward Zigler, Sally Styfco and Bonnie Gordic, "What is the Goal of Head Start?: Four Decades of Confusion and Debate," *NHSA Dialog* 10, no. 2 (2007): 85–86; Polly Greenberg, *The Devil Has Slippery Shoes: A Biased Biography of the Child Development Group of Mississippi* (New York, NY: Macmillan Publishing, 1969), 181–208; For a full description of CDGM goals, see "Proposal for Structure of Child Development Project for Mississippi Communities—Summer 1965," in Tom Levin Papers, Series 1, Box 3, "Grant Applications," The King Center.

67. Dr. Jim Hendrick, interviewed by Lavaree Jones, 10 May 1989, Head Start Oral History Interviews, MWANRC.

68. Rev. James F. McRee interview transcript, Head Start Oral History Interviews, 44–45, MWANRC.

69. Dittmer, *Local People*, 368–373; Payne, *I've Got the Light of Freedom*, 329; Rothschild, *A Case of Black and White*, 117; James McRee Papers, Volume II, Box 3, "Teacher Development and Program for Children," MDAH; Laura Johnson, interview with the author, 25 June 2010; Floree Smith, interview with the author, 24 June 2010; Joe Morse, interview with the author, 10 June 2010.

70. Lillian B. Rubin, "Maximum Feasible Participation: The Origins, Implications, and Present Status," Annals of the American Academy of Political and Social Science 385, no. 1 (September 1969): 14–29; on this phrase as the challenging question central to CDGM and Head Start, see Greenberg, The Devil Has Slippery Shoes, 3–17.

71. Hilda Wilson Papers, Box 4, Folder 30 "Press Releases," (MDAH).

72. For further discussion of education and education during the Black Power era, see: Dionne Danns, *Something Better for Our Children: Black Organizing in Chicago Public Schools, 1963–1971* (New York, NY: Routledge, 2003); Dionne Danns, "Chicago High School Students' Movement for Quality Public Education, 1966–1971," *The Journal of African American History* 88, no 2 (Spring, 2003): 138–150; Jerald E. Podair, *The Strike that Changed New York, NY: Blacks, Whites, and the Ocean Hill-Brownsville* (New Haven: Yale University Press, 2002), 32–42; Mario Fantini, Marilyn Gittell, and Richard Magat, *Community Control and the Urban School* (New York, NY: Praeger Publishers, 1970).

73. Hilda Wilson Papers, Box 4, Folder 12, "History of FCM," MDAH

74. Hilda Wilson Papers, Box 4, Folder 33, "Workshops—Black history consciousness," MDAH. The goals of FCM in adopting a Black curriculum focused on several guiding principles, including: "To assist pupils in gaining information that will enable them to respect the African heritage; to develop within the pupils an appreciation of the fact that great civilization existed in ancient Africa; to give pupils information that will enable them to understand the variety of African cultures and to eliminate stereotypes in their thinking; to develop an understanding and appreciation of the importance of African nations in the UN; to give the children information about African heroes of the past and the leaders of the present; to develop an appreciation of Africa's cultural and creative contribution to art, literature, and science; to develop an improved self-image on the part of Afro-American pupils as a result of the knowledge

of the contributions of the African peoples," see: Hilda Wilson Papers, Box 4, Folder 20, "notes by Hilda Wilson," MDAH.

75. Joseph Crespino, *In Search of Another Country: Mississippi and the Conservative Counterrevolution* (Princeton: Princeton University Press, 2007), 4.

76. Crespino, *In Search of Another Country*, 4. For a larger discussion of the rise of the "New Right," see: Matthew D. Lassiter and Joseph Crespino, *The Myth of Southern Exceptionalism* (Oxford: Oxford University Press, 2010); Kevin Kruse, *White Flight: Atlanta and the Making of Modern Conservatism* (Princeton: Princeton University Press, 2005); Lisa McGirr, *Suburban Warriors: The Origins of the New American Right* (Princeton: Princeton University Press, 2001); Matthew D. Lassiter, *The Silent Majority: Suburban Politics in the Sunbelt South* (Princeton: Princeton University Press, 2006); Bruce J. Schulman, *The Seventies: The Great Shift in American Culture, Society, and Politics* (New York, NY: The Free Press, 2001). See also: Sanders, "To Be Free of Fear."

77. Crespino, *In Search of Another Country*, 1; James C. Cobb, *The South and America since World War II* (Oxford: Oxford University Press, 2011), 121–122.

78. Kruse, *Silent Majority*, 132–147; McGirr, *Suburban Warriors*, 239–240; Schulman, *The Seventies*, 56–58.

79. "OEO is Readying Head Start Report," *The Clarion-Ledger*, 3 August 1965; "Head Start Payment for Fines Revealed," *The Clarion-Ledger*, 14 September 1965; "Stennis Asks Probe of Report," *The Clarion-Ledger*, 14 August 1965.

80. Hilda Wilson papers, Box 4, Folder 12 "History of FCM," MDAH; Dittmer, *Local People*, 373–384; 635–656; see also: Sanders, "To Be Free of Fear."

81. Though mismanagement and less-than-perfect budgetary restraint were found, it was not to the degree that Stennis charged. Moreover, the OEO forced the resignation of Tom Levin, the founder of CDGM, and pressured CDGM to move its headquarters from Mt. Beulah, which had become known as a civil rights headquarters. "Shriver Denies U.S. Funds Used to Bail CR Agitators," *The Clarion-Ledger*, 22 August 1965; Greenberg, *The Devil Has Slippery Shoes*, 259–279.

82. Dittmer, *Local People*, 375–383; Payne, *I've Got the Light of Freedom*, 329, 343; "Well, Mt. Beulah is Closed," *Jackson Daily News*, 15 October 1965; "12 Man Board Replaces CDGM," *Jackson Daily News*, 30 September 1966; "Bi-Racial Group is Reported Slated For CDGM Takeover," *The Clarion-Ledger*, 1 October 1966.

83. Victor Cicirelli, "The Impact of Head Start: An Evaluation of the Effects of Head Start on Children's Cognitive and Affective Development." Report presented to the Office of Economic Opportunity (Report No. PB 184 328), Washington, D.C., Westinghouse Learning Corporation (1969), 9–11.

84. For a full discussion of the politics of early childhood education, see: Sanders, "To Be Free of Fear."

85. Fannie Lou Hamer, quoted in Dittmer, *Local People*, 378.

86. Rothschild, *A Case of Black and White*, 118. For the radicalization of SNCC, see also Carson, *In Struggle*, 133–211; Hogan, *Many Minds One Heart*, 197–225.

87. For a discussion of the Moynihan Report and its origins, influence and implications within the Johnson administration, see David Carter, *The Music Has Gone Out of the Movement: Civil Rights and the Johnson Administration 1965–1968*

(Chapel Hill: University of North Carolina Press, 2009); 51–74. For a large discussion on the culture of poverty, see Oscar Lewis, *La Vida: A Puerto Rican Family in the Culture of Poverty* (New York, NY: Random House, 1966) and Oscar Lewis, *Five Families: Mexican Case Studies in the Culture of Poverty* (New York, NY: Random House, 1959).

CHAPTER 8

THE RISE AND FALL OF A BLACK PRIVATE SCHOOL

Holy Name of Mary and the Golden Age of Black Private Education in Chicago, 1940–1990

Worth Kamili Hayes
Tuskegee University

The decades following World War II will inexorably be marked by African Americans' struggle for public school integration. This watershed period witnessed the culmination of their protracted struggle against unequal education with the signature *Brown v. the Board of Education* victory. Though many racialized inequities stubbornly persist, countless activists, attorneys, and parents have used *Brown* to make great strides in desegregating American society.

Ironically, this era of *Brown*, with its ostensible focus on integration, was also a golden age of Black private education. A short list of scholars such as Lisa M. Stulberg have chronicled how African Americans reconciled their faith in racially mixed schools while also championing separate Black

Using Past as Prologue, pages 201–220
Copyright © 2015 by Information Age Publishing
All rights of reproduction in any form reserved.

institutions. This fidelity to Black schools had many sources and range from racial pride and trust in Black teachers to anxiety over the process and slow pace of desegregation (especially in northern cities).[1] This essay builds on this often neglected history and attempts to show the depth, rich history, and conflicted politics of Black educational institutions which emerge from a variety of forces. Though the stakes and political terrain has changed, this tradition of seeking alternatives to traditional public education continues in the Black community and animates the highly contentious debate over school choice.[2]

This chapter examines the expansion and eventual decline of Black private education in Chicago by detailing the history of Holy Name of Mary School (HNM). Established in 1940, HNM bears the distinction of being Chicago's first Catholic school founded for Black students and primarily staffed by African American teachers. Most other schools were taught by members of predominantly White religious orders and were opened to Blacks only after their parishes experienced racial transition.[3] Nonetheless, HNM shared much in common with other Black private schools of the era. Its initial rise was fueled by the growth of the city's Black population and this community's frustrations with the failures of the city's racially discriminatory public school system. HNM's popularity continued even as attacks on the city's segregated public and private school systems intensified. Ironically, these protests would prove to be a mixed blessing for HNM and other Black private schools. Though supportive of Civil Rights Era desegregation efforts, HNM saw its enrollment decline as Black Chicagoans' housing and educational opportunities gradually expanded. Thus, like many other public schools, particularly those in the South, HNM's history reflects the hope generated and pain caused by the era of *Brown*.[4] For all that was gained, much was lost.

BLACK PUBLIC AND PRIVATE EDUCATION IN TWENTIETH CENTURY CHICAGO

Like many other Northern cities, Chicago's public school system experienced great strains in race relations following the mass migration of African Americans from the South. From 1910 to 1960, Chicago's Black population grew from 44,103 to approximately 813,000 residents. Although African Americans experienced racism prior to this population influx, the mass migration exacerbated the staunch discrimination that would characterize the experiences of Black students for much of the twentieth century.[5] By 1930, eighty-two percent of all African American children in Chicago's public educational system attended schools that were at least ninety percent Black. In the 1950s and 1960s, studies by the NAACP and Urban League revealed that ninety-one percent of Chicago's elementary schools were de facto segregated and that Black public schools were disproportionately overcrowded, received less money than White public schools, and were more likely to be staffed by less-experienced teachers.[6]

Black Chicagoans opposed these oppressive conditions in a myriad of ways. In the 1940s, local community groups and larger organizations such as the Chicago and Northern District Association of Colored Women (CNDA), the Citizens Schools Committee (CSC), and the Chicago Urban League (CUL) lobbied the Chicago school board, publicized the poor state of Black schools through public tours, and initiated petition drives to transfer Black students from overcrowded schools.[7] Nonetheless, African American educational activism in Chicago seemingly tempered in the 1950s while it accelerated on the national scene with the *Brown* victory. Not until the 1960s did Black Chicagoans protest educational discrimination by employing widespread direct action demonstrations. Beginning in October 1963, the Coordinating Council of Community Organizations (CCCO), Chicago's preeminent Civil Rights organization, led citywide protests involving more than 200,000 students. This was followed nearly three years later when the Southern Christian Leadership Conference and Rev. Martin Luther King Jr unsuccessfully attempted to desegregate Chicago's racially stratified housing market and school system. Shortly after, many Chicago activists grew disenchanted with earlier struggles for integration and launched a local community control movement. At its height in 1968, this youth-led struggle included more than 20,000 students who sought greater autonomy and a curriculum centered on Black history and culture.[8]

Given the apparent difficulty of achieving meaningful public school reform, African American parents increasingly sought redress in Chicago's private educational sector. In the Archdiocese of Chicago, the world's largest private school system, the number of schools that accepted Black students grew from six in 1939 to twenty-three in 1960.[9] Chicago also became a major center for the Black nationalist independent school movement. By the early 1980s, the Chicago metropolitan area had the largest number of such institutions throughout the country.[10] The city is also home to other notable Black private schools such as the Marva Collins Preparatory School, New Concept Development Center, and one of the leading branches of the Nation of Islam's Sister Clara Muhammad national school system. This local pattern reflected broader national trends. By 1981, approximately 270,000 Black elementary school children attended private schools in the United States.[11]

Though private schools may have provided a preferable learning environment, it was no safe haven from racism. In 1917 Archbishop George Mundelein issued the Archdiocese of Chicago's version of "separate but equal," and prevented Blacks from attending the same schools as Whites. African American parents could only send their children to St. Monica's, a

South Side Catholic elementary school reserved for Blacks. Despite this racial affront, African Americans continued to agitate for Catholic education. This coupled with an out-migration of White families from older Catholic parishes forced Mundelein to expand the number of schools for Blacks to six by 1935. On Chicago's South Side, St. Anselm's and Corpus Christi's parish schools were opened to African Americans in 1932 and 1933, respectively. On the West Side, Black students began attending Holy Family School in 1933 and St. Malachy's in 1935. St. Dominic's on the Near North Side also ended its Whites-only policy in 1935.[12]

A HARD FOUGHT VICTORY

This push for educational alternatives soon reached Chicago's far South Side Morgan Park community. Although several Black parents in Morgan Park sent their children to these newly opened Catholic schools, a growing number desired a parochial school that was closer to their homes. Consequently, Morgan Park's African American community, particularly the St. Martin de Porres Guild, a local group of Black Catholic women, organized fundraisers to open a church and school in the area.[13] Their advocacy attracted the support of a local White minister, Father John F. Ryan, who helped them successfully petition the archdiocese to establish a new parish for African Americans in Morgan Park. Archbishop Samuel Stritch, who replaced George Mundelein in 1940, named the parish Holy Name of Mary and appointed Ryan its pastor.[14]

The grassroots movement to establish HNM and other Black private schools rivals that of the city's anti-racist struggle for public school reform. Actually, engagement in the private school sector was more sustained than its public counterpart. After the aforementioned protests against public school segregation and overcrowding in the 1940s, the 1950s were relatively quiet. Nonetheless, African Americans' vigilance for access to Catholic schools remained consistent well past the 1970s. Their steadfast position on private schools may have been due to an intuitive sense that the fight for meaningful public school reform would not bear immediate results. Other strategies would have to be simultaneously employed.

This bottom-up struggle to establish Black schools was not without precedent. James Anderson reminds us that the local communities were primarily responsible for the establishment of Black schools, both public and private, throughout the post-Civil War South.[15] Obviously, the development of Black private schools in Chicago and other Northern urban areas occurred within a different historical context. Nonetheless, it can be argued that this mode of educational engagement, and perhaps activism, was much broader in terms of time and space, than is often acknowledged.

Although seeing the need for educational alternatives, African Americans did not overlook the racial affronts of the Catholic Church. The *Chicago Defender* lambasted the archdiocese's segregationist policies with the same disdain as it did racism in public schools. The newspaper called for the termination of St. Monica's school if it remained segregated and even compared Archbishop Mundelien to infamous Southern racists James Vardaman and Ben Tillman.[16] Morgan Park's Black community also drew the ire of the *Defender*. Arguing that the neighborhood's African American community lent its "support for segregation," the newspaper opined that a better strategy would be to demand access to nearby White parishes. [17] It is plausible that most Black Chicagoans shared the *Defender's* indignation. However, the newspaper's position of foregoing Catholic education because of the archdiocese's segregation policy was disputed by many families as evinced by Black Catholic schools' rapid expansion.

After gaining permission to open HNM, Ryan subsequently secured the commitment of the Oblate Sisters of Providence (Oblates or OSP) to staff the school, making Holy Name of Mary the first school in the archdiocese to be primarily operated and staffed by African Americans. Established in 1829, the Oblates are the first permanent African American order of nuns. Initially guided by the mission of providing for the "Christian education of young girls of color," the OSP opened schools for young men and women within and outside of the United States by the mid-twentieth century.[18]

Holy Name of Mary's Golden Age

Holy Name of Mary became the religious order's nineteenth school when it opened its doors in September 1941. The enthusiasm demonstrated to establish the school was continued after it began. The school's initial enrollment of 110 students exceeded its modest accommodations. After securing a permanent location, its student body continuously grew and peaked at more than 450 pupils in the mid-1960s.[19] The school was supported by an active Parent Teacher's Association, which among other functions, raised money for the school. This financial support was critical because tuition, HNM's primary source of income, did not cover all of the school's operating expenses. Also, like several other predominantly African American schools in the Archdiocese of Chicago, the school's parents were required to attend Mass once a month and attend a series of theological classes.[20] These requirements were designed to ensure that parents were familiar with lessons learned at Holy Name of Mary with the hope of reinforcement at home.

Additional sources of support came from the school's local community. The St. Martin de Porres Guild (which later changed its name to the Holy

Name of Mary Ladies Guild) continued to hold fundraising activities for the school. Neighborhood residents also lent material aid and volunteered in the school.[21] Even the *Chicago Defender,* which continued to admonish discrimination and segregation in the Archdiocese of Chicago, declined to criticize HNM's racial composition. By the middle 1950s and into the 1960s, the newspaper even began to feature Holy Name of Mary's school and parish events.[22]

Several factors account for the advocacy and support HNM received from Chicago's Black community. HNM's racial exclusivity notwithstanding, private education indicated a particular cultural capital for Black families and communities. This desire for private education was accompanied by a disdain for the racial discrimination in Chicago's public schools. In *Black Metropolis,* St. Clair Drake and Horace Cayton's canonical study of Black Chicago, the sociologists noted that African American parents sent their children to Catholic schools to avoid the problems found in public schools, particularly overcrowding. Drake and Cayton also uncovered that many African American parents believed that parochial schools offered more rigorous academic training and a stronger emphasis on discipline and character development.[23]

Ironically, certain conditions in HNM were similar to those found in Chicago's Black public schools. Though overcrowding was possibly Black Chicagoans' greatest grievance against the public schools, HNM also had extremely large class sizes. In the early 1950s, some HNM classes had one to thirty-nine teacher-to-student ratios. By 1964, some classes had enrollments as high as fifty-nine students.[24] Nonetheless, HNM parents obviously preferred the school's educational program over public institutions despite these classroom conditions. It is likely that parents distinguished the reasons why HNM and Black public schools had high student-to-teacher ratios. HNM's class sizes were large because of the school's high demand. Chicago's public schools, on the other hand, had disproportionately large enrollments because administrators' commitment to segregation left Black parents with few options.[25]

The families who sent their children to HNM tended to be socioeconomically diverse, yet many were remembered to be economically secure. Sister Clementina Givens, who taught at Holy Name of Mary from 1950 to 1955, recalls that though students from working class families attended, most HNM parents owned their own homes.[26] Cumulative records, which were much like student transcripts, show that many parents held professional positions such as teachers, engineers, and electricians. Nonetheless, many other parents worked in working class occupations such as barbers, repairmen, and janitors.[27]

The class diversity of Holy Name of Mary students resembled the mixed socioeconomic character of the predominantly Black, eastern Morgan Park area, where many of the students resided. Through much of the 1940s to 1960s, Morgan Park's African American family income and median school years completed was higher than most other predominantly Black neighborhoods in Chicago. However, the relative affluence of Morgan Park's Blacks should not be overstated. The income and educational levels of Blacks in Morgan Park consistently trailed Whites who lived in the neighborhood.[28]

Though a private education was held in high esteem by many African American parents, Black schools also held a special meaning to them. Even as racially separate schools were increasingly seen as problematic by *Brown* supporters, many African Americans differentiated their disdain for the power structure that produced segregated schools, from these schools themselves. This position was famously argued by W. E. B. Du Bois, who posited that Black separate schools could shield African American students from unsympathetic White teachers. Moreover, Black teachers' racial identity made them best suited to understand the experiences of Black students as well as prepare them for what they could expect in a White-dominated world after they graduated.[29] Historians, particularly Vanessa Siddle Walker, have similarly argued that Southern Black public schools institutionalized an educational culture of care that sustained Black students and the communities they came from.[30]

Advocacy for Black schools was shared by members of the Oblate Sisters of Providence. Perhaps the most clearly articulated position regarding the efficacy of Black schools was written by Sister Mary of Good Counsel Baptiste. Baptiste would eventually go on to hold influential positions in the religious order such as superior general and assistant dean of the Oblates' only school of higher education, Mount Providence College.[31] In her master's thesis, she argued that the common racial identity of Black teachers and students allowed for an effective classroom intimacy that was absent among White instructors and Black pupils. She went on to posit that societal racism and stereotypes made Black students hesitant in expressing themselves in front of White teachers for fear of not positively representing their race. On the other hand, Black students did not fear that Black teachers would see their shortcomings as indicative of all African Americans. Baptiste further argued that Black teachers' experiences with racism in the United States mandated that they see education as a tool of ridding society of discrimination and to instill in students racial pride through the study of Black history and culture.[32]

Fighting on Two Fronts: Patriarchy and Racism

Although Black schools could potentially provide a safe haven for African American students, Oblate teachers were less secure. Women in general and nuns in particular, have played a critical role in the development of the Catholic Church in the United States. Nonetheless, their voices have often been marginalized by the institution's male dominated leadership. [33]

Nuns working with African American communities have faced unique challenges to their autonomy. Sisters involved in this sphere often struggled with conservative Catholics who wanted to maintain the racial status quo and liberals who supported their mission, yet felt men should dictate how they participated in anti-racist work. These clashes became heightened in the 1960s as more nuns joined the ranks of civil rights activists. Their engagement with this struggle was bolstered by the Second Vatican Council (1962–1965), where Church officials eased restrictions placed on nuns and encouraged them to work with marginalized groups. Many nuns came to Chicago and joined sisters already actively working with the local Black community. Their efforts included providing enrichment and vocational education for children and adults, fighting to keep Catholic schools in Black neighborhoods open, and fostering interracial understanding by setting up gatherings between Black and White Chicagoans. Though forging new, fruitful relationships with African Americans, nuns consistently encountered Catholic officials who were uncomfortable with their new assertiveness.[34]

The Morgan Park Oblates' early experiences with Father Ryan and other diocesan authorities foreshadowed the struggles that many nuns would face in the 1960s. Initially, it would seem that the sisters would get along fine with Ryan as he petitioned the archdiocese to establish HNM and specifically requested the Oblates. The priest was also among a growing number of post-World War II Catholic liberals who sought to use Church doctrine as a means to ameliorate racial discrimination.[35] However, Ryan's professed commitment to liberalism did not stem his sexism or tyranny. HNM teachers wrote several letters to their headquarters in Baltimore about Ryan's overbearing leadership style. They complained that he unilaterally placed students in inappropriate grades, cancelled student activities, and temporarily placed a layperson in an administrative role in the school without OSP permission.[36] Furthermore, he consistently asserted that he was the sole authority of the school and the sisters had a secondary role.[37]

These examples of patriarchy could be found in the interactions between priests and nuns, regardless of race. Nonetheless, evidence shows that the race of the Oblates and the Morgan Park student body colored Ryan's authoritarianism. In one of his rants, Ryan exclaimed that the Oblates were better suited for "scrubbing, cooking or doing laundry work" rather than educating children.[38] The Oblates also noted that although Ryan was among Chicago's White liberals, he maintained a paternalistic attitude towards Blacks. They noted that "Father does not want to work <u>with</u> our people but he wishes to work <u>for</u> them and this is what he is doing at the present time. Just working for our people giving us only what he judges best." (emphasis in original quote).[39] The sisters believed that Ryan expected to work among impoverished and downtrodden African Americans, but was surprised and disappointed upon finding out that Morgan Park's Black community included several middle class residents who were "cultured" and "well mannered."[40] In this way, the Oblates' experience at HNM resembled the history of Blacks in the post-Civil War South who resisted the efforts of Northern missionaries who sought to direct the education of freedmen and women without the approval of African Americans themselves.[41]

The sisters' attempts to seek redress for Ryan's excesses were largely unsuccessful. They reported Ryan to archdiocesan authorities who overlooked Ryan's behavior. The OSP headquarters responded to their appeal by encouraging patience. Ryan's behavior caused such unrest among parents that the Oblates feared that the conflict "might end in a riot."[42] Nonetheless, Ryan's tenure at the school was short-lived. Beset by health problems, the priest left the school in 1949 and was replaced by clergy who were more respectful of the Oblates and largely granted them autonomy in school matters.[43]

Though choosing not to challenge the racist and patriarchal hierarchy of the Catholic Church, the Oblates were far from apolitical. As R. Scott Baker notes, schools were important sites of Black activism where "African Americans created an evasive and oppositional culture…in spite of white opposition."[44] Cognizant of the foundational work of the St. Martin de Porres Guild, the Oblates recognized that Holy Name of Mary was part of a larger antiracist movement to provide African Americans with a greater array of educational opportunities. However, the Oblates' efforts against White supremacy involved more than just creating new school buildings for Black students to enter. The sisters believed that the HNM's curriculum should be tailored to the students' specific needs and used more broadly for racial uplift. In talking to a group of antiracist Black Catholics, Sister Mary Laurentia Shortt, HNM's second principal, expressed this perspective by noting that it was the charge of Oblate teachers "to bring to fruition the highest potentialities of our race."[45] Similarly, former teacher Sister Clementina noted that the Oblates aimed "to bring our little Black children up to par, and to get them into being in leadership roles as adults."[46]

One of the most prominent ways the Oblates demonstrated the race's potential was through teaching Black history and culture. As early as 1946, HNM developed programs and activities for Negro History Week. The sisters had to be quite resourceful to teach the subject because Black history was not a major feature in the Archdiocese of Chicago's curriculum until the 1960s. Former HNM teacher, Sister Mary Reginald Gerdes recalls that she had to develop reading lists and bring her own materials because of the dearth of materials provided by the archdiocese. [47] The Civil Rights Movement in particular provided the Oblates with a prime opportunity to explore Black history and social justice with students. Sister Mary Clementina remembered that she and other HNM teachers kept students abreast of the rapidly changing developments of the movement. She, however, explains that these lessons weren't purely intellectual exercises, but "were necessary because we wanted to move up. We didn't want to stay doormats."[48]

The Oblates' lessons on the Civil Rights Movement coincided with the Catholic Church's protracted engagement in the Black freedom struggle. Catholic religious and laypeople were visible participants in major civil rights demonstrations such as Albany, Selma, and Washington D.C. during the March on Washington.[49] Developments in Chicago reflected this national trend. Albert Meyer and John Cody, who succeeded Samuel Stritch as archbishop in 1958 and 1965, respectively, more forcefully expressed their identification with antiracism. Cody, in particular, was heralded for excommunincating racist Catholics in his previous post as Archbishop of New Orleans. In Chicago, he promoted liberal policies such as residential integration and African American membership in predominantly White unions.[50] Under the two archbishops' leadership, Catholic priests, nuns, and laypersons increasingly used direct action techniques to attack residential segregation and racial discrimination in (public and private) schools and various Chicago Catholic institutions. In addition, Chicago's primary antiracist organization, the Chicago Catholic Interracial Council, was an important coalition member of the city's most prominent civil rights organization, the Coordinating Council of Community Organizations.[51]

Like their Catholic counterparts, the Oblates engaged the Civil Rights Movement outside of the school walls. Particularly, the parish became a site where community members demonstrated their support of the antiracist struggle. Throughout the 1960s, the parish held community-wide programs that celebrated Black history and culture. And like the Oblates' classroom activities, these parish programs were not only held to memorialize Black leaders of the past, but to inspire the present and future leaders to develop a commitment to social justice. The parish also hosted local civil rights activists such as Chicago Urban League Executive Director Edwin Berry and organized programs to demonstrate their support of Southern protests.[52] Through these activities, the Oblates and the HNM parish demonstrated their support of the integrationist aims of the Civil Rights Movement. Nonetheless, the maintenance and development of Black institutions created in part by segregation, such as HNM, were seen as complementary to this strategy, rather than contradictory.

Along with the Civil Rights Movement, HNM was deeply affected by Black Power activism. From the late 1960s through much of the 1970s, the school demonstrated a greater racial consciousness which reflected trends in the broader movement. White images of Jesus and Mary on school architecture and literature were replaced with Black ones. Courses on "Afro-American studies" were provided for students and adults in the parish. This racial consciousness was clearly demonstrated in 1978 when the *Chicago Sun-Times* published HNM student Sheryl Walkup's essay which protested the Rolling Stones' objectification of Black women in the song "Some Girls." Walkup specifically credited her school and parish for encouraging her to take the stand.[53]

HNM's distinction as the city's first Black school staffed by Black teachers also became a new selling point in an era of community control protests and the burgeoning independent school movement. However, unlike these Black Power educational initiatives, the HNM community saw racially separate schools as one of many strategies to ensure Black children received a quality education. Despite its exceedingly slow pace in Chicago, many still believed in the promise of integration.

Facing a New Terrain

HNM's advocacy of integration and racially separate Black private schools grew increasingly difficult to sustain after the 1960s and 1970s. Progress in desegregation, albeit gradual, made HNM and similar institutions increasingly vulnerable as more schools opened their doors to African Americans. As early as 1945, Archbishop Stritch overturned his predecessor's segregation policy and proclaimed that all Catholic schools would be open to Black students. Though many recalcitrant Catholics initially ignored his proclamation, the number of African Americans in Chicago's Catholic schools steadily increased in the following decades. Less than 5,000 African Americans attended Catholic schools in Chicago at the time of Holy Name of Mary's founding. By the 1983–1984 school year, more than 29,000 Black children were enrolled in archdiocesan schools.[54]

While some schools remained predominantly White or even achieved a degree of racial parity during this period, many other Black students entered schools that were largely abandoned. As Chicago's Black population grew, many White residents fled to the metropolis's outer environs. The city's White population decreased from seventy percent in 1960 to forty percent in 1990. Catholics were definitely part of this mass exodus. During Archbishop Meyer's tenure, all but three of the thirty newly established parishes in the Archdiocese of Chicago were created in suburban areas. Subsequent archbishops were also forced to contend with this problem.[55] Schools that remained in the city were faced with teaching students who were less tied to the parish, more economically vulnerable, and in most cases less interested in Catholic theology as they were its educational system.

While some parishes kept their schools open and considered the new circumstances as an opportunity for outreach, others saw the situation as too daunting. In 1964, nearly 366,000 students attended approximately 500 schools in the archdiocese. By 2007, only 98,225 students were enrolled in the parochial school system's 257 schools. Between 1990 and 2003 alone, eighty Catholic schools were closed in Cook and Lake Counties.[56]

As they had in the past, African Americans continued to seek educational alternatives. Some took advantage of opportunities in the center city. For example, St. Margaret's of Scotland, also located in Morgan Park, which had previously excluded Black students, became a predominantly Black parish in the 1970s.[57] Other Black families, however, joined the citywide exodus to the suburbs. Metropolitan Chicago's Black suburban residents grew from only 25,000 in 1940 to more than 230,000 in 1980.[58] Undoubtedly, the public and private educational options in Chicago's suburban outer ring helped fuel this migration.

The mobility of Chicago's Black middle class hit Morgan Park especially hard. As had been the case in many other urban communities, Black neighborhoods in Morgan Park become more racially concentrated and poorer. The population of Morgan Park declined by nearly 5,000 residents from 1970 to 1990 and the proportion of African Americans increased from forty-eight percent to sixty-five percent during this period. All three of the predominantly Black census tracts in Morgan Park experienced rises in poverty and unemployment. One tract saw its poverty rate more than double.[59] The population decline and rise in poverty suggest that middle class families, those that could afford a private school education, were moving away from Holy Name of Mary and were being replaced by poorer families who may have desired a private school education yet whose circumstances made it an unaffordable luxury.

This was compounded by steady increases in tuition. After World War II, the operating costs for American schools skyrocketed. While taxes could cover the rise in public school expenditures, private schools relied on tuition increases. Spikes in tuition became more routine and burdensome by the 1960s as both Holy Name of Mary and the archdiocese raised school fees.[60] It is no coincidence that the Oblates also increasingly commented on parents' inability to pay school expenses starting in the 1960s. This led the school to develop new policies for collecting tuition such as withholding report cards and diplomas from students who were not current. These measures, however, were unsuccessful for by 1976 the Oblates considered closing Holy Name of Mary as a result of the hardships caused by "increased tuition rates."[61]

Staffing problems added to HNM's difficulties. Like many other religious societies, the Oblates often accepted less money than lay teachers. These "contributed services" kept many parishes financially solvent. However, after reaching its zenith in the 1960s, the number of American nuns consistently declined. Many of the progressive movements that nuns participated in such as civil rights, women's liberation, and the Second Vatican Council led them to critique their own subordination within the Catholic Church. These movements also gradually opened more societal opportunities for women, making life as a nun less attractive.

The Oblates were also affected by this trend and experienced great difficulty recruiting new members. By 1977, fifty percent of the Oblates' total membership was sixty years or older.[62] These difficulties inevitably affected the number of nuns the Oblates could send to HNM. In 1969, superior general Sister Mary of Good Counsel Baptiste, whose master's thesis championed Black schools, informed HNM pastor, Father Vader that the Oblates lost twenty-four members the previous two years and therefore would have to reduce the number of sisters sent to the school from eight to six. Four years later, the superior general wrote Vader to tell him that additional reductions in the religious order's membership prevented her from promising a specified number of nuns to the school. Furthermore, she was unable to replace an Oblate teacher at Holy Name of Mary if a sister left for any reason.[63] This decline in Oblate teachers would have been easier to bear if HNM would have been able to maintain the enrollment figures it enjoyed in its earlier years. However, to the school's dismay, greater competition and demographic trends caused the school's student population to drop. The school admitted 356 students in 1970. By 1975, 312 students attended and ten years later HNM's enrollment dropped to 247 students. By 1995, only 195 students were enrolled.[64]

These developments took their toll on Holy Name of Mary. As early as 1976, the Oblates reviewed the feasibility of continuing their work in Chicago. A report conducted by several of the sisters acknowledged the lack of Oblate teachers, enrollment declines, and the financial difficulties that these circumstances caused. Resolute in their mission, the sisters determined that HNM remain open.[65] Nonetheless, HNM's problems continued and eventually forced the school to close in 2002.

Challenges at Holy Name of Mary reflected much broader trends. In 1964, nearly 366,000 students attended approximately 500 schools in the Archdiocese of Chicago. By 2007, only 98,225 students were enrolled in the parochial school system's 257 schools. While some new schools opened in the city's suburbs, many of the shuttered schools were located in neighborhoods such as Morgan Park that had seen the worst of the city's urban crisis. The golden age of Black private education was over.[66]

CONCLUSION

Several historians of Southern public school desegregation have uncovered the "unintended consequences," and even as one argued, the "burden" of *Brown*.[67] Not only did "massive resistance" persistently delay its implementation, but when carried out, the decree negatively impacted many previously segregated Black schools and the communities that sustained them. The impact of desegregation on Chicago's Black private schools was surprisingly similar. This seminal victory, fought so hard for by countless African Americans, simultaneously dismantled many of the institutions that nurtured, educated, and employed them for so long. The Southern example demonstrates the marginal role Blacks played within the governmental structures that administered desegregation. The decline of Holy Name of Mary, however, was largely due to the decisions made by African Americans themselves within the context of urban decline. Their desire for educational alternatives persisted after the founding of HNM and culminated in a widespread exodus to schools that had previously excluded Black students.

Although this essay focuses on the decline of Black schools within the Archdiocese of Chicago, these troubles were not limited to Catholic schools. Founded by three Black female educators five years after HNM, Howalton Day School eventually became one of Chicago's highest achieving schools as evidenced by a 1971 *New York Times* article which reported that its first graders attained the highest reading averages among all public and private first grade students in the greater Chicago area.[68] Despite this success, Howalton closed its doors in 1986 as a result of many of the same problems that plagued HNM. Even schools that opened and made names for themselves in the 1970s and 1980s did not go unscathed by this period of decline. New Concept Development Center, the leading Black nationalist private school in the city, transitioned to a charter school in 1998. Marva Collins Preparatory School, which received national acclaim, was forced to close in 2008. Like HNM, the school experienced major financial difficulties long before it decided to shut its doors. Though HNM is featured in this study, the 1970s onward can definitely be classified as the nadir of Black private schools in Chicago, sectarian and non-sectarian.

Unfortunately, the school conditions that sparked the initial growth of Black private education still persist today. Schools in Chicago's inner-city and other Northern urban areas are largely segregated and underperforming. Consequently, African Americans have figured prominently in current debates over school choice. Some pundits accuse Blacks who support school choice as unwittingly siding with conservative reformers who are more interested in serving their corporate backers rather than the marginalized students impacted by their policy directives.[69] The history of HNM and other Black private schools suggests that this perspective gives conservatives too much credit. African Americans who pursue school choice are not necessarily duped by the right but rather are following in the footsteps of their predecessors who actively sought and created alternatives in the best interests of their children. As long as inequality continues it would be foolish to think that African Americans would circumscribe their strategies for pursuing a quality education. It seems likely that African Americans' array of tactics will only expand, possibly restoring another golden age of educational alternatives.

NOTES

1. Lisa M. Stulberg, *Race, Schools, and Hope: African Americans and School Choice after Brown* (New York, NY: Teachers College Press, 2008); Mwalimu J. Shujaa, ed., *Beyond Desegregation: The Politics of Quality in African-American Schooling* (Thousand Oaks, CA, Corwin Press: 1996).
2. For works that have tackled the history of Black private education see Diana T. Slaughter and Deborah J. Johnson, eds. *Visible Now: Blacks in Private Schools* (New York, NY: Greenwood Press, 1988); Jacqueline Jordan Irvine and Michèle Foster, eds. *Growing Up African-American in Catholic Schools* (New York, NY: Teachers College Press, 1996); James G. Cibulka, Thomas J. O'Brien, and Donald Zewe, *Inner-City Private Elementary Schools* (Milwaukee: Marquette University Press, 1982).
3. A Catholic parish is a defined space that functions to serve the religious, educational, and social needs of the Catholic community that resides in it. Therefore, a parish usually has associated institutions such as a church and parochial school for its parishioners.
4. See especially, David S. Cecelski, *Along Freedom Road: Hyde County, North Carolina and the Fate of Black Schools in the South* (Chapel Hill: University of North Carolina Press, 1994) and Vanessa Siddle Walker, *Their Highest Potential: An African American School Community in the Segregated South* (Chapel Hill: University of North Carolina Press, 1996).
5. Michael Homel, *Down From Equality: Black Chicagoans and the Public Schools: 1920–1941* (Urbana: University of Illinois Press, 1984).
6. Homel, *Down from Equality;* Mary Herrick, *The Chicago Schools: A Social and Political History* (Beverly Hills: Sage, 1971); "De Facto Segregation in the Chicago Public Schools," *The Crisis,* February 1958, 88–92.
7. Homel, *Down From Equality.*
8. Alan B. Anderson and George W. Pickering, *Confronting the Color Line: The Broken Promise of the Civil Rights Movement in Chicago* (Athens: The University of Georgia Press, 1986); Dionne Danns, *Something Better for Our Children: Black Organizing in Chicago Public Schools, 1963–1971* (New York, NY: Routledge, 2003).
9. James Sanders, *Education of an Urban Minority: Catholics in Chicago, 1833–1965* (New York, NY: Oxford University Press, 1977), 214.
10. *Fundisha!—Teach!,* 5, no. 3 (1981) in CIBI Folder, from the private collection of Soyini Rochelle Walton.
11. Sanders, *Education of an Urban Minority,* 219; Diana T. Slaughter and Deborah J. Johnson, eds. "Introduction and Overview," in *Visible Now,* 2; James G. Cibulka, "Catholic School Closings: Efficiency, Responsiveness, and Equality of Access for Blacks," in *Visible Now,* 146.

12. Harry C. Koenig, S.T.D., *A History of the Parishes of the Archdiocese of Chicago Published in Observance of Centenary of the Archdiocese, 1980* (Chicago: Catholic Bishop of Chicago, 1980), 378; Joseph J. McCarthy, "History of Black Catholic Education in Chicago, 1871–1971" (PhD diss., Loyola University of Chicago, 1973).

13. Holy Name of Mary Parish 60th Diamond Jubilee, September 17, 2000, Collection Pertaining to the Historically Black Neighborhood of Morgan Park, Ridge Historical Society, Chicago, Illinois. Hereafter known as RHS.

14. Holy Name of Mary Parish 50th Golden Anniversary Program, 1990, Vertical File 150, Archives of the Oblate Sisters of Providence, Baltimore, Maryland. Hereafter known as AOSP; "Catholic Pastor Heads Negro Welfare Group," *Chicago Defender,* November 9, 1946, 7.

15. James D. Anderson, *The Education of Blacks in the South* (Chapel Hill: University of North Carolina Press, 1988).

16. "Jim Crow School," *Chicago Defender,* 29 March 1913, p.4; "Big Step Backward," *Chicago Defender* 17 November 1917, p. 8.

17. "Local Catholics Seen as Lending Support to Segregation Program," *Chicago Defender,* August 11, 1934. The Holy Name of Mary parish's official history, written during its fifty year anniversary, recalled that prior to its establishment "Black Catholics preferred to worship with other Black Catholics" and Blacks in Morgan Park were "desirous of having their own church." See Holy Name of Mary Parish 50th Golden Anniversary Program, 1990, Vertical File 150, AOSP.

18. Diane Batts Morrow, *Persons of Color and Religious at the Same Time: The Oblate Sisters of Providence, 1828–1860* (Chapel Hill: University of North Carolina Press, 2002); Sharon C. Knecht, *Oblate Sisters of Providence: A Pictorial History* (Virginia Beach, VA: Donning Company Publishers, 2007).

19. Annals, September 8, 1941, Box 15, Folder 7, AOSP; Annals, September 7, 1966, Box 17, Folder 3, AOSP.

20. Annals, May 14, 1954, Box 16, Folder 2, AOSP; Estella Anderson Faulk, "A Study of Catholic Education for Negroes in the Archdiocese of Chicago," 32; John C. Owczarek to Parents, September 1955, Missions, Illinois: Holy Name of Mary: Correspondence (1968–1975), Box 14, Folder 7, AOSP.

21. Annals, February 15, 1942, February 24, 1942, November 26, 1942, Box 15, Folder 7, AOSP.

22. For examples of the *Chicago Defender's* coverage of Holy Name of Mary events see Marion B. Campfield, "Mostly About Women," *Chicago Defender,* August 20, 1955, 14; Ethel L. Payne, "E. African Bishop Visits White Fathers of Africa," *Chicago Defender,* November 13, 1956, 3; "Edwin Berry to Talk in Morgan Park, *Chicago Defender,* January 25, 1962, 2; "Holy Name of Mary Celebrates Silver Jubilee," *Chicago Defender,* September 11, 1965, 12.

23. St. Clair Drake and Horace Cayton, *Black Metropolis: A Study of Negro Life in a Northern City,* Revised and Enlarged Edition (New York, NY: Harper and Row, 1962), 413–414.

24. Missions: IL: Chicago Holy name of Mary School and Students: Class Groups, Box 6, Folder 12; AOSP.

25. Homel, *Down From Equality.*

26. Sister M. Clementina Givens, O.S.P., interview by author, July 26, 2008.

27. Holy Name of Mary Pupil Record Cards, Joseph Cardinal Bernardin Archives and Records Center of the Archdiocese of Chicago, Chicago, IL. Hereafter known as Bernardin Archives.; Holy Name of Mary Student Cumulative Folders, Bernardin Archives.

28. Philip M. Hauser and Evelyn M. Kitagawa, eds. *Local Community Fact Book for Chicago, 1950* (Chicago: Chicago Community Inventory, University of Chicago, 1953), 7, 308; Evelyn M. Kitagawa and Karl E. Taeuber, eds. *Local Community Fact Book for Chicago, 1960* (Chicago: Chicago Community Inventory, University of Chicago, 1963), 165.

29. W. E. B. Du Bois, "Does the Negro Need Separate Schools," *Journal of Negro Education* 4 (July 1935): 328–335; Derrick Aldridge, *The Educational thought of W. E. B. DuBois: An Intellectual History* (New York, NY: Teachers College Press, 2008), 82–85.

30. Vanessa Siddle Walker, *Hello Professor: A Black Principal and Professional Leadership in the Segregated South* (Chapel Hill: University of North Carolina Press, 2009); Walker, *Their Highest Potential;* Cecelski, *Along Freedom Road.*

31. Knecht, *Oblate Sisters of Providence,* 111. A superior general is the head of a religious society.

32. Mary of Good Counsel Baptiste, O.S.P., "A Study of the Foundation and Educational Objectives of the Congregation of the Oblate Sisters of Providence and of the Achievement of These Objectives as Seen in Their Schools," (MA thesis, Villanova College, 1939).

33. For the experiences of women in the Catholic Church see Mary Jo Weaver, *New Catholic Women: A Contemporary Challenge to Traditional Religious Authority* (San Francisco, CA: Harper and Row, 1985); James Kennally, *The History of American Catholic Women* (New York, NY: Crossroad, 1990); Carol K. Coburn and Martha Smith, *Spirited Lives: How Nuns Shaped Catholic Culture and American Life, 1836–1920* (Chapel Hill: University of North Carolina Press, 1999).

34. Amy L. Koehlinger, *The New Nuns: Racial Justice and Religious Reform in the 1960s* (Cambridge, MA: Harvard University Press, 2007); Suellen Hoy, *Good Hearts: Catholic Sisters in Chicago's Past* (Urbana: University of Illinois Press, 2006).

35. John T. McGreevy, *Parish Boundaries: The Catholic Encounter With Race in the Twentieth-Century Urban North* (Chicago: University of Chicago Press, 1996); Holy Name of Mary Parish, 50th Golden Anniversary Program, 1990, Vertical File 150, AOSP; Irene Steyskal, "5 Race Nuns Placed in a Parish Here," *Chicago Tribune,* October 19, 1941, SW1.

36. A layperson is a worshipper who is not a member of a clergy or a religious order. Sister M. Laurentia, O.S.P., to Mother Teresa Shockley, O.S.P., February 23, 1946, Box 18, AOSP; "Issues transfers without letting the sisters know the reason", Box 18, AOSP; Father Ryan to Mother Laurentia, O.S.P., February 21, 1946, Box 18, AOSP; Annals, February 16, 1944, Box 15, Folder 7, AOSP. Sister Mother Teresa Shockley, O.S.P., to Sister M. Claude, O.S.P., April 1, 1943, Box 18, AOSP; Notes on Holy Name of Mary School, Box 18, AOSP; Notes on the Holy Name of Mary School Term 1946–1947, Box 18, AOSP.

37. Sister Jean Marie, O.S.P. to Mother Teresa Shockley, O.S.P., Undated, Box 18, AOSP; "Issues transfers without letting the sisters know the reason", Box 18,

AOSP; Sister M. Laurentia, O.S.P., to Mother Teresa Shockley, O.S.P., February 23, 1946, Box 18, AOSP.

38. "Issues transfers without letting the sisters know the reason", Box 18, AOSP; Sister M. Laurentia, O.S.P., to Mother Teresa Shockley, O.S.P., February 23, 1946, Box 18, AOSP.

39. Sister Jean Marie, O.S.P. to Mother Teresa Shockley, O.S.P., Undated, Box 18, AOSP.

40. Ibid.

41. See Anderson, *Education of Blacks in the South*; Heather Andrea Williams, *Self-Taught: African American Education in Slavery and Freedom* (Chapel Hill: University of North Carolina Press, 2005), 80–95.

42. Sister Jean Marie, O.S.P. to Mother Teresa Shockley, O.S.P., Undated, Box 18, AOSP.

43. Givens, O.S.P. Holy Name of Mary parish was presided over by archdiocesan priests, who were under the governance of the archdiocese of Chicago. Other parishes were headed by archdiocesan priests or priests who belonged to religious orders that were not under the governance of the Archdiocese of Chicago.

44. R. Scott Baker, *Paradoxes of Desegregation: African American Struggles for Educational Equity in Charleston, South Carolina, 1926–1972* (Columbia: University of South Carolina Press, 2006), 39.

45. Sister M. Laurentia, O.S.P. "The Oblate Sisters of Providence and Higher Education," *The Chronicle* 5, no.1 (January 1932), 8–9 in Congregation: Sisters-Deceased Shortt, Sr. M. Laurentia, Box 72, Folder 13, AOSP.

46. Sister M. Clementina Givens, O.S.P., interview by author, July 26, 2008.

47. Sister M. Reginald Gerdes, O.S.P., interview by author, August 8, 2008.

48. Sister M. Clementina Givens, O.S.P., interview by author.

49. See John T. McGreevy, *Parish Boundaries,* 133–173.

50. John T. McGreevy, *Parish Boundaries,* 186–187, 221; Steven M. Avella, *This Confident Church: Catholic Leadership and Life in Chicago, 1940–1965* (Notre Dame: University of Notre Dame Press, 1992), 306–308, 344–346.

51. Steven M. Avella, *This Confident Church,* 295–297, 309–311. Nonetheless, the Catholic Church's support of the Civil Rights Movement should not be overstated. Catholic bishop Joseph Durick, along with other Alabama Clergymen famously penned "A Call for Unity" which expressed their opposition to the movement, which inspired Rev. Martin Luther King Jr.'s iconic "Letter from Birmingham Jail." Martin Luther King would be met with even more virulent opposition in 1966 when he traveled to Chicago's heavily Catholic neighborhoods in an effort to desegregate the city's neighborhoods and schools.

52. Holy Name of Mary 12th Annual Homecoming and Tea, August 28, 1960, Vertical File 150, AOSP; "Edwin Berry to Talk in Morgan Park, *Chicago Defender,* January 25, 1962, 2; Annals, March 13, 1965, Box 17, Folder 3, AOSP.

53. Holy Name of Mary Church Program in Annals, Box 18, Folder 2, AOSP; Holy Name of Mary Parish 60th Diamond Jubilee, September 17, 2000, RHS.; Sheryl Walkup, "Mick Jagger Owes Black Women an Apology!" *Chicago Sun-Times,* October 12, 1978 in Vertical File 150, AOSP.

54. Sanders, *The Education of an Urban Minority,* 215–219; Cibulka, "Catholic School Closings" in *Visible Now,* 146.

55. Harry Koenig, S.T.D., *A History of the Parishes of the Archdiocese of Chicago,* xviii–xxi; John L. Rury, "Race, Space, and the Politics of Chicago's Public Schools," *History of Education Quarterly* 39, no.2 (Summer 1999: 121–123. Also see William Julius Wilson, *The Truly Disadvantaged: The Inner City, The Underclass, and Public Policy* (Chicago: University of Chicago Press, 1987).

56. Diane Rado, "Catholics Fight for Their Schools" *Chicago* Tribune, February 27, 2007, 1; Lori Olszewski, "Church Showing Faith in Schools" *Chicago Tribune,* May 23, 2007, 1; Tracy Dell'Angela and Manya A. Brachear, "Up to 40 Catholic Schools May Close" *Chicago Tribune,* November 13, 2004, 1.

57. Harry Koenig, S.T.D., *A History of the Parishes of the Archdiocese of Chicago,* 563.

58. Andrew Wiese, *Places of Their Own: African American Suburbanization in the Twentieth Century* (Chicago: University of Chicago Press, 2004), 116, 212.

59. The Chicago Fact Book Consortium, *Local Community Fact Book, Chicago Metropolitan Area, 1990* (Chicago: Academy Chicago Publishers, 1995). 211.

60. Archbishop Cody to Mother Mary of Good Counsel, (n.d.), Administration: Sup. Gen/Baptiste,. Correspondence: Holy Name of Mary (Chicago) 1955–1977, Box 17, Folder 4, AOSP; Annals, September 7, 1966, Box 17, Folder 3, AOSP.

61. Proposal for Re-evaluating Plans to Withdraw the Oblate Sisters of Providence from Immaculate Conception School, Three Rivers, Michigan, (undated, 1976), Box 15, Folder 3.

62. James Sanders, *Education of an Urban Minority,* 204; Statistics on Current Status of Membership, Congregation: Education: Oblate Education Board, Box 19, Folder 8, AOSP.

63. Mother Mary of Good Counsel Baptiste, O.S.P. to Anthony J. Vader, March 31, 1969, Administration: Sup. Gen/Baptiste. Correspondence: Holy Name of Mary (Chicago) 1955–1977, Box 17, Folder 4, AOSP; Mother Mary of Good Counsel Baptiste, O.S.P. to Anthony J. Vader, October 26, 1973, Administration: Sup. Gen/Baptiste. Correspondence: Holy Name of Mary (Chicago) 1955–1977, Box 17, Folder 4, AOSP.

64. Annals, September 8, 1970, Box 18, Folder 3, AOSP; Holy Name of Mary Faculty, 1974–1975, Holy Name of Mary School Administrative Files, Bernardin Archives; Holy Name of Mary School Survey, 1984–1985, Holy Name of Mary School Administrative Files, Bernardin Archives; Holy Name of Mary School Survey, 1994–1995, Holy Name of Mary School Administrative Files, Bernardin Archives.

65. Proposal for Re-evaluating Plans to Withdraw the Oblate Sisters of Providence from Immaculate Conception School, Three Rivers, Michigan, (undated, 1976), Box 15, Folder 3.

66. Diane Rado, "Catholics Fight for Their Schools" *Chicago* Tribune, February 27, 2007, 1 Tracy Dell'Angela and Manya A. Brachear, "Up to 40 Catholic Schools May Close" *Chicago Tribune,* November 13, 2004, 1.

67. Raymond Wolters, *The Burden of Brown: Thirty Years of School Desegregation* (Knoxville: The University of Tennessee Press, 1984).

68. John M. Culkin, "40 Characters 40," *New York Times,* July 20, 1977, 14. Howalton also received national press in the article, "Linda Knows Trick from Joke," *Christian Science Monitor,* May 1, 1971, 11.

69. Lisa M. Stulberg, *Race, Schools, and Hope,* Eric Rofes and Lisa M. Stulberg, *The Emancipatory Promise of Charter Schools: Toward a Progressive Politics of School Choice* (Albany: State University of New York Press, 2005).

CHAPTER 9

"WHY ARE YOU GOING ALL THE WAY UP THERE TO THAT WHITE SCHOOL?"

Oral History, Desegregation, and Chicago Experiences

Dionne Danns
Indiana University

Oral history has played a significant role in researching and understanding the history of Black education in the post World War II era. Because many potential participants are still alive, those who study the postwar era have an added advantage of hearing the voices of ordinary people, discovering new meaning and interpretations for their research, and creating a conversation between written documents and the expertise of study participants. Though oral history certainly comes with its limitations, like any other types of sources researchers may use, interrogating oral history adds richness to studies that often could not be captured with written archival documents alone. This chapter will examine both the increasing and var-

Using Past as Prologue, pages 221–250
Copyright © 2015 by Information Age Publishing

ied use of oral history methodology in school desegregation research as well as provide an example from a Chicago desegregation research study I have conducted that gives us a glimpse of what Black school desegregation participants experienced—attending segregated elementary schools, choosing desegregated high schools instead of segregated neighborhood high schools, and how community members responded to their choices. Attending desegregated schools was mainly a choice for a better education than neighborhood high schools could provide. This chapter highlights the various ways scholars have utilized oral history to enrich their research and our understanding of school desegregation.

According to Barbara W. Sommer and Mary Kay Quinlan, "Oral history is primary-source material created in an interview setting with a witness to or a participant in an event or a way of life for the purpose of preserving the information and making it available to others. The term refers both to the process and the interview itself."[1] Ken Howarth states, "Oral history is both a subject and a methodology, a way of finding out more by careful, thoughtful interviewing and listening."[2] Historians can use oral history as a methodology to supplement their studies by conducting a few interviews as part of their sources, or as a project where groups of people are interviewed to understand events or history of a community.

For a long time, mainstream historians were skeptical about the use of oral history as a source of evidence. Some of the major concerns have been the reliance on memory and the tailoring of participants' experiences based on perception and emotions.[3] Additionally, some historians worried that people's viewpoints and versions of the story may be inconsistent when interviewed again.[4] However, Paul Thompson acknowledged the potentially transformative power of oral history as it can provide a central place to the "people who made and experienced history." It can change the content, purpose, and focus of history.[5] Though William W. Cutler III viewed it as supplemental to research, he saw oral history as a source for filling the gaps of written records and providing historians with perspective for understanding the past.[6] Exploring his mother's memories, historian Richard White eloquently stated that history and memory are sometimes enemies, though both are necessary for understanding the past. He underscored that memory is an important guide, "but memory, like history, is better thought of as plural rather than singular." Comparing historians use of memories to a detective's use of sources, White wrote, "They compare them, interrogate them and match them one against the other. Memory can mislead as well as lead."[7]

Oral history, like other tools of history, does not stand alone. Nonetheless, it provides a way for the stories of ordinary people—whose voices are not typically captured in existing records—to be heard. Participants' stories and their interpretations of those stories, provide an avenue for creating meaning for both the participant and the historian. Using oral history as an important support or as the central basis for a historical study significantly alters how we understand and interpret the past. Without oral history, so much of history and as well as additional written sources (which remain in the hands of individuals) would be lost.

The process of oral history at times becomes as important as the stories themselves. Finding people to interview, knowing the direction of a study, completing IRBs (Institutional Review Board) for the university, asking the right questions, re-interviewing participants, gaining the trust of participants, actively involving them in the process, rewarding their time, determining what will be used and left out, and reconciling potentially inaccurate information are all part of the process. Scholars have to also contemplate face-to-face interviews verses phone or video interviews.[8] New technologies for recording interviews when distance is a challenge may help expand the number of participants but may also lead to the loss of personal connection and trust among interviewer and participant. In addition, interviews are more accessible to other scholars and the public through digital technology.[9] These all become important aspects of the process. Much of it is trial and error. Even the best training will not cover discrepancies that arise when dealing with human beings. Many historians are used to dealing with archival documents and their human interactions are limited to the archivists to make sure they get access to the right papers. The interaction with interview participants whose lives one may want to explore is often a delicate balance. In spite of its intricacies, limitations, and obstacles, oral history is truly an enriching element for historians to pursue.

Scholars use a variety of disciplines to inform historical research and therefore discuss their interviewing methods differently depending on the disciplinary lens they have chosen to use. Some call their oral interviews oral history, while others call it oral testimony, qualitative interviews, or ethnographic interviews. For the sake of simplicity, I will discuss these works under the umbrella of oral history, while using the terminology individual scholars have chosen for their work.

An important, and at times contested, aspect of oral history is the challenge to long held historical narratives. Over the last four decades, a number of studies have emerged which paint far more positive experiences of some segregated southern schools than exists in the collective memory.[10] Two studies on segregated Black schooling experiences in North Carolina provide a great example of what can be uncovered with oral history. Vanessa Siddle Walker's book, *Their Highest Potential*, relies on ethnographic interviews to gain a fuller understanding of the strengths of one segregated school, including the elements of caring for students, the professionalism the school's teachers and principal displayed, and the meaning of such a school to its community. Seeing her work as both ethnographic and historical, Walker seeks to understand the culture of a group from the group's perspective while also recreating a culture that is no longer in existence.[11] Like Walker, Hilton Kelly's *Race, Remembering, and Jim Crow's Teachers* deals directly with the conflicting collective memory around Black schools in the Jim Crow era. He used oral history to demonstrate that "African Americans benefit from segregated schooling. The idea that there could have been no benefits in the all-black public school illustrates the limits of the dominant collective memory of these schools." [12] Both authors provide a counternarrative to the belief that somehow all segregated Black southern schools were inferior and, therefore, had no redeeming qualities. Their studies show evidence of excellent schools and educators in segregated, southern schooling environments. Oral history and ethnographic interviews disrupt the typical narratives about Black schools and educators and provide voices to those overlooked in the past.

Oral history has also been an integral part of desegregation research. Scholars have interviewed judges, lawyers, government officials, teachers, students, parents, and community activists in pursuit of desegregation in a variety of locations. While there are numerous books on desegregation, a few are highlighted here for the authors' various uses of oral history and their focus on Black education. Richard Kluger's monumental work, *Simple Justice*, David S. Cecelski's *Along Freedom Road*, R. Scott Baker's *Paradoxes of Desegregation*, and Jack Dougherty's *More than One Struggle*, are examples of scholars utilizing oral history to provide a rich and intricate first hand analysis of how desegregation took shape, the movements organized for and against it, and the overwhelming sacrifices of participants.[13]

Kluger examines the history that led to the *Brown v. Board of Education* decision and interviewed or corresponded with over 100 people who played a role in the case. As he discussed his sources, Kluger noted that two of the Supreme Court justices wanted their interviews to be limited to their views and not the discussion among justices, and he wrestled with whether those deliberations should remain a secret from the public. In unearthing a rich history he had to make decisions based on how much information the justices were willing to give.[14] This speaks to the ways that historians collaborate and negotiate with participants in ways they may not have to do with public records. Beyond the justices, Kluger highlights a variety of participants to unfold a complex and watershed moment in American history.

Cecelski, Baker, and Dougherty skillfully use oral history as they investigate local responses and experiences with desegregation. Cecelski's research focused on Blacks who struggled to hold on to their historic schools in the face of one-sided desegregation in Hyde County, North Carolina. He notes that "oral testimony has been indispensible."[15] Interviewing parents, students, teachers, government officials, and civil rights activists helped Cecelski uncover an often glossed over Black response to desegregation. Baker highlights the important struggles Blacks in South Carolina waged to gain access to quality schooling and the additional barriers of standardized testing. His use of oral history unveils the desire of teachers to provide students with high quality education, the challenges teachers made to unequal teacher salaries, and student and teacher experiences in the fight for desegregation and the aftermath.[16] Dougherty illuminates the generational civil rights struggles for quality education that occurred in Milwaukee and the "contested nature of historical memory in Black school reform movements."[17] He investigates how the numerous perspectives of activists from different generations enrich our understanding of the rise and fall of school reform movements in the 1960s. Each of these important studies effectively incorporated oral histories in their narratives and analyses.

While the use of oral history in desegregation studies has persisted, a new set of studies privileging and centralizing oral histories, has emerged. Two recent books on Louisville desegregation, Sarah Garland's *Divided We Fall* and Tracy E. K'Meyer's *From* Brown *to* Meredith, provide examples of the different ways oral history can be central to a study. Both authors thoroughly contextualize and analyze the interviews, but each uses the interviews in different ways. Garland and K'Meyer focus on the process of desegregation and participant experiences while providing the history of how desegregation unraveled in Louisville and Jefferson County, Kentucky.[18]

K'Meyer's *From* Brown *to* Meredith moves away from traditional studies of desegregation and uses oral histories as standalone entities. She contextualizes the interviews at the beginning and end of each chapter, but uses groups of interview transcripts in the middle of the chapter. According to K'Meyer, "This approach tightens the focus on local people by using their words, takes advantage of the richness of the available oral sources, and reveals additional layers of information and interpretation." Additionally, K'Meyer attempts to use oral history as a "shared public memory." Through interviews she and others conducted in several oral history projects, K'Meyer attempts to unveil the complicated perspectives of participants of various Louisville school desegregation policies.[19] This approach to oral history is certainly more cautioned against, though she does a fine job of organizing and evaluating the meaning of the brief vignettes.

Garland's *Divided We Fall* also examines Louisville school desegregation and centers on oral history. Unlike K'Meyer, Garland focuses on the Black community and their beloved Central High School. Various reforms to school desegregation limited the access of Central to Black students who wanted to attend the magnet school there. A heavily enforced quota system meant few Black students would have access. Garland chronicles the story of parents, teachers, students, and activists who opened access to Central through a court case, but the case eventually led to the dismantlement of school desegregation in Jefferson County in the *Meredith v. Jefferson County* (2007) case.[20] The use of oral history in this project helps us understand the motives of Black community members in their desire for access to a cherished school. Like Cecelski's *Along Freedom Road,* Garland's book shows us the desire of Black communities to maintain control and access to their own schools.

Another type of oral history desegregation studies exist that is organized with the intent to understand what school desegregation meant to those students who participated. Because many desegregation studies focus on the fight for desegregation, court cases, reactions, and implementation, the collective schooling experience of students attending desegregated schools is often untold. Many desegregation books, including those listed above, relay the experiences of some students and teachers because of the use of oral history. Yet, these newer desegregation studies focus on group experiences within desegregated schools. Through the examination of one school in a less studied area or of many schools throughout the country, Caroline Eick's *Race-Class Relations and Integration in Secondary Education* and Amy Stuart Wells et al.'s *Both Sides Now* give an in depth look at desegregated schooling experiences from students' perspectives.

Eick's *Race-Class Relations and Integration in Secondary Education* uses oral history to chronicle three generations of high school students' experiences from the period right before desegregation until the year 2000 in a Baltimore County suburban high school. The students' experiences are central to understanding how one school can be transformed over three generations from divided to integrated to re-divided. Additionally, race, class, gender, and ethnicity impacted whether meaningful integration occurred. In the close of her book, Eick grapples with the methodological boundaries of oral history in educational history. She indicates that her archival research was used to contextualize the interviews rather than to serve as a contradiction. Her emphasis was on meaning making and the perceptions of the participants rather than "truth" finding.[21]

In Wells et al.'s groundbreaking study, oral history is used to gain a collective understanding of the experiences of students at six different high schools around the country in order to connect "personal perspectives about school desegregation...in a systematic way."[22] In *Both Sides Now,* Wells et al. interviewed over 242 mostly Black, White, and Latino graduates from the class of 1980 and found that the largely positive experiences students gained from schools did not impact the larger society.[23] A subset of the graduates were interviewed a second time to capture a more in depth snapshot of their experiences. These graduates were featured prominently in the book. This study examined schools that have the traditional Black/White desegregation, but also at those schools where desegregation affected Blacks, Whites, Latinos, and Asians. Because a variety of schools were examined, region, demographics, and policy implementation all played a role in the students' experiences. The authors argued that the students found their interracial interactions valuable, but once leaving school most were back in segregated worlds. The students were transformed, but society had not changed to support their high school experiences.

Each of the examples above provides a snapshot of how scholars focused on school desegregation and have used oral history to gain insight into their studies. Whether oral history was infused throughout the study or was central to the study, each book shows the various ways scholars approached oral history and their understanding of its importance to their research. Each of these scholars would not have been able to reveal the histories they captured without the use of oral history.

CHICAGO STUDY

While I have provided samples of the use of oral history methodology in the previous section, this section will look closely at my work on Chicago. Following in the footsteps of the Wells et al. study, I developed an oral history project to learn about the experiences of graduates from desegregated Chicago public high schools. Many students had limited opportunities for desegregated elementary school experiences, chose desegregated high schools rather than attend neighborhood high schools when given an opportunity, and had to address the responses to community members who either criticized or encouraged their high school choices. The choice students made to attend a desegregated high school was an educational choice based on the negative perceptions of neighborhood high schools.

Brief Historical Background of Chicago

There is a well documented history of school segregation in Chicago.[24] As Blacks came north to Chicago during the Great Migration, they were contained to certain neighborhoods as a result of racist real estate policies.[25] The school system operated in such a way as to assign students to their neighborhood schools. As a result, segregated neighborhoods led to segregated schools. Beginning in the late 1950s and early 1960s, Black Chicagoans began to demand desegregation of schools. Some Chicagoans displayed their displeasure with inequities associated with school segregation through court action, sit-ins, school boycotts, and a Title VI (1964 Civil Rights Act) complaint to the federal government.[26] These efforts were largely ignored during Superintendent Benjamin C. Willis's administration. In 1968, under the guidance of a different superintendent, James Redmond, Chicago schools created a limited desegregation plan that was heavily protested by Whites in the neighborhoods affected. In spite of all the protests, about 500 Black students were eventually bused annually from two overcrowded schools in a predominantly Black neighborhood to eight underutilized White schools.[27] The school system at the time had well over 500,000 students. The outrage over such a small plan was evidence of the concern some Whites had about school desegregation.

In the 1970s, Chicago schools faced pressure from the State of Illinois to desegregate its students. The Chicago Board of Education formed a City-Wide Advisory Committee (CWAC) which created a school desegregation plan with community input. Most aspects of the CWAC's plan became a part of Access to Excellence which Superintendent Joseph P. Hannon and his staff created in 1978. Access to Excellence left out CWAC's calls for mandatory back up policies in case voluntary desegregation did not work. Illinois State Board of Education did not fully accept the plan, because it had no mandatory provisions. The State Board was certain that voluntary desegregation measures alone would not result in substantial desegregation. The federal government became involved with student desegregation in 1979 as the Office of Civil Rights in the Department of Health, Education and Welfare stated that Access to Excellence was not legally acceptable.[28] They turned the case over to the Justice Department for litigation in 1980. The case led to a consent decree which was most effective in desegregating Chicago's predominantly White schools and provided compensatory funding for the rest of the schools which remained highly segregated.[29]

Chicago's storied desegregation history provides a great backdrop for this study. Graduates from three desegregated public high schools (Von Steuben, Bogan, and Whitney Young) were interviewed. Each of these schools was desegregated at different times. Von Steuben already had a good mix of students but greatly increased the numbers of Black students and decreased the numbers of White students as a result of the consent decree. Although Von Steuben had over 10 percent Blacks attending the school since 1966 and a growing number of Latinos and Asians in the 1970s, it was clearly desegregated by the time of Access to Excellence.[30] It became a metropolitan school under the consent decree in the early 1980s further decreasing the number of White students. In 1987, the last time a racial head count was taken before study participants graduated, Von Steuben was 33.3 percent White, 32.3 percent Black, 18.2 percent Hispanic, and 16.4 percent other. The demographic data indicate that Bogan was most impacted by school desegregation efforts, particularly as it relates to plans created after the consent decree. Although Black students had transferred to Bogan prior to the consent decree, it had minimal impact on the school. By 1987, Bogan was 42.1 percent White, 28.7 percent Black, 19 percent Hispanic, and 10.1 percent other. Whitney Young was created as a magnet school with a desegregation focus as part of its design, although the school had been predominantly Black. It was the only school in this study that had Blacks as the majority of the school population in 1977. The school increased the percentage of Blacks and lost more than half the White student population between 1977 and 1991 because of the consent decree. Black Chicago Board of Education members wanted to make sure Whites would not dominate the best schools since they accounted for less than 20 percent of the school population.[31] Although the school was predominantly Black, the high quality of the school and its magnet school status helped to keep the school desegregated. In 1987, Whitney Young was 15 percent White, 63.9% Black, 13.4 percent Hispanic, and 7.8 percent other. The three schools provide a good mix of four racial/ethnic categories and also represent three different parts of the city of Chicago. Von Steuben is on the North Side of the city, Whitney Young is on West Side of the city, and Bogan is on the city's South Side.

Methodology/ Construction of the Oral History Project

As I conceptualized this study, the work of Wells et al., "How Desegregation Changed Us," influenced my methodology. Based on information from that article, I used class reunions as the basis for recruitment for my study.[32] Reunions served as an important source for recruiting large numbers of potential participants. I received a New Frontiers in the Arts and Humanities grant (funded by the Lilly Foundation) from Indiana University in 2008 to conduct the research. The grant provided funding to hire four graduate students to help conduct interviews. In the spring and summer of 2008, I searched for class of 1988 reunions for most of the city's desegregated high schools.[33] The profile of the schools desired were those that had a sizable representation of Whites, Blacks, Hispanics, and Asians.[34] Of the ten desegregated schools that fit the profile, only half were having reunions that year. The determining factor for gaining access to a class reunion was whether a school committee or professional business organized the reunion. If a business was organizing the reunion, as two schools had, there was very little chance of accessing the reunion. The businesses would not return phone calls or pass information on to the school committee. If there was contact information for one of the committee members, usually the website coordinator, then there was a stronger possibility of gaining entry. Von Steuben was the first reunion I was able to attend. Von Steuben's website coordinator also e-mailed information about the study to school alumni through their website after the first round of interviews and that gave us additional participants. Once I gained access to the second reunion, Bogan reunion organizers posted the information about the study on the reunion website so alumni had prior knowledge of our coming.

Whitney Young did not have a class of 1988 reunion. During the process of our interviews, a sibling of a person interviewed attended Whitney Young High School and wanted to be interviewed. As a result of conducting the first Whitney Young interview, I contacted a sibling of another interviewee who had also attended Whitney Young. I also contacted two friends who had attended Whitney Young. I attempted to gain access to the Whitney Young Class of 1989 reunion and was unable although I had a lot of communication with a committee member and could name a classmate who had already been interviewed. I was told, "The committee agrees that we will be available for you but that we will not use the reunion as a platform to get interview subjects."[35] While there are other ways to gather names of alumni for interviews, the reunions serve as a place to ensure that participants gathered attended those schools. It was also a far easier way to gather participants. I tried to get messages on the school's alumni website to no avail, and while I had access to other potential participants, I did not have access to graduates from the class of 1988. Although there are only four participants from Whitney Young and none of them were from the class of 1988, it is important to leave the school in the study because of the socioeconomic class dynamics among the African Americans that seemed a unique dimension to the students at this school.

At the two class reunions graduate students and I attended, a large number of participants signed up for interviews. Of those participants, we conducted seventy-two interviews, sixty-eight of whom were students and four were teachers. Of the sixty-eight student participants interviewed, thirty were Black, eighteen were White, fourteen were Latino, and six were of mixed race/ethnicity (five of whom were Latino and White, one Asian and White). While the focus was on students from the class of 1988, participants from other classes were also suggested by interviewees. Sixty of the sixty-eight alumni graduated in 1988. Other participants graduated in 1986, 1987, 1989, 1990, and 1991.

After conducting seventy-two interviews between June and August 2008, the interviews were transcribed. I created themes as I edited the transcriptions to make sure they were consistent with the recordings. Because this study used oral history methodology and I wanted to understand the experiences of participants as a group based on themes that were salient across interviews, the software Atlas served as an organizing essential tool for this study and to code data thematically across interviews.

STUDENT EXPERIENCES

Though this is a multi-ethnic study which tracks students experiences in elementary school, high school, college and beyond, this section will focus on Black participants' experiences in segregated elementary schools, how they chose to attend desegregated schools, their views of the neighborhood high schools they did not attend, and perceptions of community members about the choices they made to attend schools outside the neighborhood. This snapshot of the larger study helps us understand how Black students in a largely segregated, northern city like Chicago, experienced successful all-black elementary schools but made decisions to attend desegregated high schools in part based on their negative perceptions of largely segregated neighborhood high schools.

Much of the literature on the impact of school desegregation notes the sacrifices Black students made in order to attend desegregated schools. Black students often had to travel farther, were bused to White schools as their schools were closed, or had former Black schools reshaped to make them more attractive to White students.[36] Opponents and critics of desegregation point to these sacrifices, especially because unless there was two-way busing, Whites maintained much of their privilege as desegregation was implemented. On the other side, proponents of desegregation focus on the gains Black students made as a result of desegregation. This includes access to more resources, closing of the achievement gap, positive interaction with White students, etc.[37] What scholars of school desegregation are highlighting more in recent studies are the complex interactions and interpretations of students who attend desegregated schools. Through the use of oral history methods, this portion of the larger study, will demonstrate how individuals made decisions about leaving their neighborhoods to go to high school once the choices were made available to them as a result of school desegregation policies.

Many Black Chicago school desegregation participants for this study enjoyed their segregated elementary schools and felt that they received a great education from caring teachers. Though some Black participants attended desegregated elementary schools, the experiences of Black participants in segregated Chicago elementary schools in some ways mirror the caring environments of segregated Black schools in the South.[38] Chicago Public Schools, in spite of numerous efforts to desegregate, remained highly segregated. The long history of segregation and ineffective desegregation plans did little to alter the segregated conditions of many public schools.[39] As a result, a number of participants spent their elementary years in highly segregated schools and some noted that their schools were all Black. Ten of the schools where participants mentioned they attended were more than 90% black (nine over 95 percent, with three at 100 percent in the 1978–79 school year). In the 1983–84 school year, eleven schools were over 90 percent Black (six were 100 percent black, another three over 99 percent Black).[40]

Participants recalled positive experiences in these highly segregated elementary school environments. One participant, Josephine, said that she enjoyed elementary school because the school had predominantly Black teachers who "really cared about us. There was a really strong knit community and school system, and I felt like my best teachers were in grammar school. . . . The teachers, I think [knew] you better and [cared] more about you." [41] Charlotte, another participant thought that Black teachers "would embrace you a little bit more like family." Comparing her segregated, neighborhood elementary school to high school, Charlotte noted, "So going to school in the neighborhood, most of us, teachers were African American descent, you feel closer. I mean it is different." According to Charlotte, her desegregated high school had a different feel: "when you go to high school, that's in a different neighborhood. . . . You are in a school that is more diverse. So you have different ethnicities and then you're dealing with teachers of different ethnicities too. It's just, overall, integrated. And so initially when you get there it's not as warm."

Other participants spoke to the excellent training they received from elementary teachers. Angela stated that, "I had excellent teachers in my grammar school, so I had a strong foundation to continue." Similarly, Kelly noted that her teachers were really caring. "Well I went to a wonderful elementary school because the teachers really cared. My seventh and eighth grade teachers in particular made a huge difference in my life because I graduated valedictorian from my eighth grade class. . . . Two teachers really kind of pushed me and showed me that I could set a goal and work towards it and actually obtain it. And so that was wonderful for me." Both Angela and Kelly believed that the strong foundation they received from caring elementary school teachers prepared them for high school.

The caring environment that the elementary schools students describe is similar to segregated schools in the South. [42] Yet, unlike southern schools where it was likely that all the teachers and principals are Black, many segregated northern schools also had White teachers and principals. Although Black teachers had historically been assigned to Black schools in Chicago, their predominance at most of those schools peaked in the mid-1970s until faculty desegregation policies prevented all Black staffs in the late 1970s.[43] Along with a caring environment, participants also recognized that Black history and culture was stressed far more in elementary school than in their desegregated high schools. Despite the positive experiences some Black participants had in segregated elementary schools, they and their families made a conscious decision to attend desegregated high schools. Black students who attended desegregated elementary schools also saw a benefit of continuing at desegregated high schools.

Attending desegregated schools in Chicago was no easy task for Black students who were largely segregated on the West and South Sides of the city. Most of the desegregated schools were located on the Southwest Side, near the loop, or on the North Side. The city initiated open enrollment in its high schools as a way to help school desegregation occur.[44] Students could apply to a number of schools and chose a school that selected them. Test scores became an important determinant for some of the more highly selective schools like Whitney Young and Von Steuben. Participants were asked, "Why did you decide to participate in school desegregation?" This question gave them an opportunity to talk about why they chose to attend a particular high school. Some of the participants did not really view high school choices as a choice for desegregation, but rather a process for choosing a high school or making the best educational choice they could based on the options they had.

Von Steuben was very far north and some distance from where most Blacks in the city lived. As a result, the school's staff had to make a targeted effort to recruit Black students from the West and South Sides. Black participants who were not from the North Side did not know Von Steuben was an option unless they were recruited, advised by counselors, or attended school recruiting fairs. Schools that were readily known to participants were in the neighborhood, highly selective, or had great sports reputations (and were therefore on the news).

Ed, like other Black participants, remembered a recruiter coming to his elementary school to publicize Von Steuben. He and another person from his elementary school were recruited. "If I remember it was one of the school counselors who came to our school to recruit both of us, to get us there because we had good grades. . . . I guess they were wowing us about Von Steuben . . . . And they're the only ones who, I think, reached out and said 'look we want you to come to this school up here.' And I think that was one of the biggest factors." This helped him make a decision about Von Steuben.

Anthony was also recruited. He remembered a factor for his attending Von Steuben was the possibility to go to a school with people who did not look like him. Because he lived in a segregated Black world on the West Side of Chicago, he viewed White recruiters as a sign of importance.

> I remember recruiters coming to our school when I was in elementary school in '84. . . . You know, I guess to sell their high school. . . . And I remember . . . being raised in . . . inner city over there on the West Side where I've never really been exposed to non-Black Americans. Everybody was Black. So here are these White people, as we call it, in our school . . . . We figured they were important, you know, for something. But they were talking about high school. I didn't know what school I wanted to go to. I was valedictorian. So I could have went to pretty much any school I wanted to go to. I'd never heard of no Von Steuben. Not on Pulaski and Polk Street in Chicago.

Anthony stressed how Whites, in what seemed like a position of authority to a young child, were viewed as important in an all Black school. However, there were two dynamics at work. First, the fact that he was being recruited at all, when this was not happening for other students already lent prestige to the recruiters. Second, being recruited by Whites, when he was not used to seeing many Whites gave their visit an added sense of importance.

Teresa was also recruited to Von Steuben. The recruitment, mixed with the fact that she wanted to go where her mother could not easily visit, helped her to make a decision. Recalling her choice, Teresa stated,

> It was a fluke! I wanted to go to Whitney Young, but they turned me down.... I didn't want to go to Lindblom. Although I heard Lindblom was a good school, it was too close to my house and I didn't want my mother just showing up! 'Cause she had a habit [of doing so]. I promise that was the reason! She had a way of just showing up at school, to check and see if you were doing what you were supposed to be doing. And so I said, "Well I'm gonna fix her!" I said, "I'm not going to Lindblom, no matter where I go, I'm not going to Lindblom." And she said I couldn't go to Bogan. She said I couldn't go to Julian. And these were all schools my friends were going to. I really didn't know any other schools; and then Von sent a recruiter to my elementary school. And I said, "Okay, well I'll go here." I didn't know where it was! I didn't know how to get there! I just knew that it sounded far and that Mom, if she was gonna show up, she would have to... sneak up and plan her sneak attack! It was a fluke.... I had never even heard about Von Steuben.

Teresa's recollection while funny, speaks to the recruiter being important aspect for Black students choosing Von Steuben.

For other Black students, counselors played an important role in their choosing Von Steuben. Melissa says she "dropped the ball on applying to school." Her mother did not want her to go to the schools her family members attended. She wanted to go to Hyde Park High School, but her father thought it was too far. Melissa recalled her counselor's role in the process. "So the counselor was like, 'Well let me see. I'm going to call Von and see if they have some spots. I know someone there.' So she called up there, and she faxed over my report card... and my test scores and all that. She said, 'Yeah, they accepted you.' And so then my mom took me up there to register for my classes. So that's how I ended up at Von!" The counselor having an associate at Von, and Melissa having the necessary qualifications helped her get into Von Steuben.

Jaquese had the assistance of a Von Steuben counselor her family liked. Her parents told her she could not go to Marshall, the neighborhood school. As they were visiting schools to make a decision, Von stood out. Jaquese chose Von after she and her parents went to visit the school and spoke with a counselor there. Because her parents liked the counselor, and they were given a tour of the school and felt comfortable, it made their decision easier. Though her family had visited other schools, they did not have the same level of comfort they had at Von. Another appealing factor was the academic recognition Von had. Jaquese stated that "Von is one of the top schools. At the time, it was Lane, Whitney, and Von. They were always the top three. . . . That helped solidify the decision for her parents."

A number of other students had their parents help them with their decision to choose Von Steuben. Charman said, "My mother made me go." Part of the reason she said it with a sense of regret was that she had to miss a school event to attend Von Steuben's orientation; but she also wanted to go to school with her friends. She stated, "I do remember going to orientation though because my mother made me miss my eighth grade picnic. And I just remember some of the seniors taking us around. And I was still kinda upset about going there because I wanted to go where my friends were going." Terrace, another student, also remembered her parents "felt that the education was better [at Von] as opposed to being in our neighborhood school."

Elizabeth used high school fairs to help her choose her Von Steuben. "I used to go to those high school fairs . . . so I must have gotten something in the mail from them. . . . I thought that I wanted to be a doctor as many kids did. I heard that Von Steuben was a math and science school, so I thought I should go to a math and science school." The high school fairs exposed Elizabeth to Von Steuben, Von matched her career aspirations, and she was also aware that it was a top school. "I knew that I was going to go to one of the better public schools. So, back then, it was usually in the top five, ten Chicago public high schools. I was going to go to one of those." Her parents also influenced her decision. "They did not want me to go to the neighborhood high school for sure. But they were not that interested in the too well rated high schools on the South Side that I could have gone to. I was going to go to Lindblom and I thought Lindblom and Hyde Park, I might have even registered at those schools. At least one of them I did. But when I found out about Von Steuben and that it was a math and science school, we switched." While the South Side also had good schools, some parents were concerned about the neighborhoods around the schools. Yet others wanted to expose their children to a desegregated world, different from the segregated worlds in which they lived.

Other participants' families were influential as well. Maleta wanted to go to a school outside of her neighborhood, but she also had siblings who had gone to Von. "I knew I wanted to go outside of the box, out of my community to go to school. I knew that that was my goal." She wanted to go to Lane Tech, but her mother believed that it was too far. Von was actually further than Lane, but her mother most likely felt comfortable with her attending a school her siblings had attended.

A number of participants had a love or interest in science and math or liked the academic focus of Von. Trénace recalled, "You had to be of certain caliber to get into Von Steuben or Lane Tech or any of them." For Cornelius and Octavia, science and math were the selling points. Cornelius had initially attended Curie High School. Curie had a performing arts focus. He transferred to Von Steuben in his second year. "I always wanted to go into the sciences, and I didn't get accepted to Whitney Young. I went to Curie for a year then I transferred to Von Steuben because I knew I wanted to do the science and math... I knew I needed the foundation in science and math as opposed to performing arts for a career in science." Octavia simply recalled, "It was a science and metropolitan [school], it was a math and science center, and I loved math. And I wanted to get out of my neighborhood... to meet other people. So, I wound up at Von Steuben." When asked how she heard about Von, "I think maybe one of my grammar school teachers had mentioned it. She knew I loved math and it was a math and science academy. I think that's how."

School counselors, recruitment, parents, school fairs, and academics all played an important part to why these students chose to go to Von Steuben, which was on the North Side of Chicago. These students were coming from the West and South Sides. Their pursuit of a better education than their neighborhood schools offered, combined with the options provided as a result of desegregation, gave them the chance to pursue enhanced academic opportunities.

Black students made their decision to attend Bogan High School because of the influence of family and friends and the school's reputation. Angela had other family members who had gone to Bogan, while Kenneth had friends from the neighborhood who were going to Bogan. Like Angela, Charlotte had a cousin who had attended Bogan. Charlotte said her cousin had spoken highly of Bogan, and her mother also wanted her to attend the school. LaDonna remembered it mostly being her parent's decision. Bogan was much closer than Whitney Young or Lindblom, the two other schools to which she had been accepted. She was "all geared up" to go to Whitney Young, but her parents wanted her to go to Bogan.

Kelly's situation was a little different. Her mother's friend suggested that she attend Bogan. Kelly recalled, "I went to a school that was out of my district.... I was valedictorian so I had great grades and everything and that's how I could get out of my district. 'Cause my district school was Calumet; I was not going to Calumet. My mother wanted me to go to Simeon. I was not going to Simeon. So a friend of my mother's suggested to her that I go to Bogan. And would you know I got accepted. They let me in." Kelly could not decide on a school, nor did she want to go the school her mother suggested. Her mother's friend helped her to expand her options and to pick a school she wanted to attend. Like Kelly, Rayshawn did not want to go to Calumet. She said, "the school that was in my neighborhood was Calumet, and there was no way in God's green earth we were going to Calumet [laughter]. It was the pits then, and it remained the pits until they shut it down a few years ago. That was a challenging, gang infested school."

Stanford noted the lottery system for getting into a Chicago high school. He could have gone to his neighborhood high school, but his mother did not want him to attend that school. "I took a test for Lindblom, Whitney Young... didn't exactly get in at those two—test scores weren't high enough. But I did fill the form out for Bogan. I went to Bogan." Rayshawn could have gone to a Catholic school, but her family could no longer afford private school. She had been also accepted to Lindblom. Her parents influenced her decision to go to Bogan. The influence of family members and friends help make Bogan a viable option for participants of this study.

Whitney Young was one of the elite schools in the city. It was created as a magnet school and was highly selective. A number of participants from Von Steuben and Bogan mentioned applying to Whitney Young. While a few were accepted and chose other schools, others were unable to gain access. This demonstrates the reputation of Whitney Young and how making the cut was seen as prestigious. For Eve, getting into Whitney Young was a relief. She described the process: "We had to take a test to get in. Once you got a certain score on the test, then you were eligible to be in a lottery to get into Whitney Young... Once I took the test and it was like, 'okay I think I did well.' When I got the letter, I remember it was like, 'Okay I was accepted. Woo!' I called my girlfriend and we both actually got in." Eve was fortunate to have gotten into Whitney Young when so many other participants did not or did not attend because of the distance.

Josephine had attended Whitney Young as a seventh grader in 1984. She had to test to get into the academic center. Since she had been a junior high student there, the transition to high school was easier. Her older sister had also attended Whitney Young and was part of the first graduating class, and her brother went to Von Steuben. In discussing her choice to attend the academic center she recalled,

[My sister] had attended and so she knew about the academic center. My teachers had always encouraged me in school, and I'd always done well in school. I think they thought this was a great opportunity for me to continue nurturing my love of learning. I applied to the academic center and there were actually a couple of girls on my block who had gone to like a really good elementary school. Like everybody knew about B. F. Skinner. Skinner was like "Woo!" That was like the fantastic, special school. They were all transferring to Whitney Young. That also added a little more cache to Whitney Young for me. I just thought it would be fun. My sister kind of helped guide me through and that's how I wound up there. But I didn't think of it as desegregation. They called it a magnet school. So in my mind, what that meant was that you had to test to get in, that it was a public school that got extra finances from the city and the state, that kids would be coming from all over the city to come there, and that they had cool programs and cool facilities.

The perception of the school appealed to her, and her sister's assistance helped make it a reality. Like Eve and Josephine, Cassandra went there because she thought it was the best school in the city and her brother had attended there.

Students who were fortunate enough to get into Whitney Young viewed it as a top school and did not view desegregated as the primary factor for their choice their decision as a choice for desegregation. After all, Whitney Young was predominantly Black (63 percent in 1987). Each of these participants was made aware of the opportunity at Whitney Young from family members. The magnet program and the high ranking was the reason they chose the school over other highly ranked schools or neighborhood schools that did not provide the same academic rigor.

Comparison to Neighborhood Schools

Leaving neighborhood high schools also came with social and academic consequences. Students seized the opportunity to attend desegregated schools because of the academic enhancement these schools provided. Whitney Young began as a magnet school and was a top city school. Von Steuben had a science focus and was also seen as an excellent school. Likewise, Bogan was far better than some of the surrounding neighborhood schools participants would have attended. The general feeling among study participants was that they were fortunate to attend one of these three schools and not their neighborhood schools. A host of issues associated with inner city schools were mentioned as for the reasons neighborhood schools were not as good as the schools participants attended including issues of safety, gangs, low expectations, negative peer pressure, and the poor reputations of these schools. Going to the three desegregated schools meant participants would more likely avoid the pitfalls of urban life including gang affiliation. Some of ways the participants discussed the schools they avoided was at times based on their perceptions of these schools. Other times they witnessed the differences in friends and siblings who had not attended desegregated schools.

Chicago schools were famously called the worst in the nation in 1987 by the Secretary of Education William Bennett. His observations were based on the high dropout rates (43 percent) and dismal ACT test scores (bottom 1 percent in the nation).[45] In spite of the Bennett's bleak assessment of the schools, the city had its share of great schools, good schools, and struggling schools. Many predominantly Black high schools on the city's West and South Sides were viewed as poor academic institutions because the curriculum was not necessarily focused on college preparation. The Urban League conducted a study in 1979 which critiqued the Access to Excellence school desegregation plan for the continued systemic failure to provide quality education to most of the city's Black and Latino students. In an analysis of Advance Placement (AP) courses, the report found that all predominantly White schools had at least one AP course, while fifteen predominantly Black and Latino high schools had no AP courses.[46] The Board of Education did not provide the opportunity for students attending these schools to be adequately prepared for college.

Predominantly Black schools like Lindblom, Kenwood, and Hyde Park had good reputations and sent many of their graduates on to college. The leadership at these schools created an atmosphere where students were expected to excel. Yet, these schools were not highly desegregated. Additionally, as gang activity increased around some of the predominantly Black schools, some parents were afraid to send their children in that atmosphere regardless of high quality education some Black schools could offer. As mentioned above, some participants ended up going to other schools since their parents did not want them to travel to these schools.

Participants were asked "how different were your experiences at school from schools in your neighborhood?" While this question led to participant conjecture, as many had never visited the schools they readily denigrated, their perceptions of some of the city's schools supports their beliefs that they chose the correct schools. Additionally, their perceptions give us further evidence about the views, right or wrong, about the schools they would have had no choice but to attend just a few years earlier before desegregation made school choice possible. In the 1970s, the Urban League often railed against the limited opportunities students confined to segregated schools would continue to have as the Chicago Board of Education put most of the academic enhancement programs at predominantly White schools.[47] In the board's Comprehensive Student Assignment Plan, created as a result of the consent decree, there was a concerted effort to put a number of enhancement programs at various schools. Hence, Von Steuben became a Metropolitan School of Sciences. Bogan was paired with Calumet High School and the feeder pattern for the high school increased. Additional magnet schools and programs were created and joined Whitney Young (already a magnet). Other high schools, including segregated schools were given specialty programs. Marshall High School was given a medical and health services program to try to attract White students.[48] The enhancement program failed to attract White students or Black participants in this study. While these programs at segregated schools may have helped to develop some schools better academically, it was not enough to change the negative reputations many Chicago high schools had as not being the place to go if one had college aspirations.

As noted earlier, in choosing to attend desegregated schools, some participants wanted to be challenged academically. Tracy who attended Von Steuben commented,

> Well I really don't see a whole lot of people that are graduating from Marshall at that given time [or] had a lot of college opportunities... I wanted to excel, and so I wanted to go somewhere where it was more of a challenge.

Jacquese, who also attend Von Steuben, noticed the difference in what students were focused on in the neighborhood.

> A lot of them ended up gang banging, a lot of them ended up getting pregnant. So it was like, I don't know, it seemed like by me going to Von and everybody at Von, it seemed like the kids we more geared... towards finishing. Like, you know, 'I can't wait 'til prom, I can't wait 'til graduation, I can't wait 'til college.' There was more of that aura going around.

She saw more students dropping out of her neighborhood school. Her parents also told her she would not attend Marshall when she was making her high school choice. Marc also focused on academics and believed that his neighborhood school "wasn't touted to me as a school known for its academics. So again, that was what was important to me was trying to do well academically and for what I perceived my goals were for myself. So, whenever I had options to try to capitalize on reaching those goals, then that's what I did." A school with positive academic environment meant that the expectations for success permeated throughout the school. Tracy, Jacquese, and Marc had certain academic aspirations that they did not believe neighborhood schools offered based on what they witnessed from siblings or neighbors.

The biggest deterrent for many participants was the belief that their neighborhood high schools were gang infested. Cassandra attended Whitney Young and she also viewed all the schools near to her South Side home negatively. "I mean the image, I never went up to them, but the image was a lot of fighting, basically going on. And we working class, middle class, and so it was more, so you wanted to go to the good school, the magnet school." Cassandra was eligible to go to Whitney Young and her brother had attended the school before her. This likely meant that she would not have found neighborhood schools without the same type of academic rigor as an option. It was not simply a fact that the schools in her neighborhood were Black, because she attended the predominantly Black Whitney Young.

SieraMedora, who attended Von Steuben, thought there was more of a focus on fashion or sports and less on academics at the school in her neighborhood.

Well, the schools in my neighborhood were actually all Black. The teachers had been there like forever...I think [the students] did more fighting than they did anything else. I think the schools in the area, all my friends, most of them, everything was more of a fashion thing for them...A lot of the friends in my neighborhood ended up getting pregnant, and dropping out, stuff like that. I was never exposed to any of that, 'cause of where I went I guess...I mean education wise I would say I got a better education there than most friends at home.

Again, schools that had limited academic rigor were more likely viewed negatively particularly if it was perceived that gang activity surrounded the school. Violence or fighting was a fact of life in some of the city's predominantly Black schools. Whether or not this fighting was gang related did not lessen the negative image fights could give a school. Those with options to go elsewhere typically chose to do so.

Angela was from the West Side and her neighborhood was mostly Blacks and Hispanics. Her neighborhood school was Farragut. Farragut was by far the most negatively viewed by both Black and Hispanic participants in this study. Angela's perception of Farragut was, "That's not one of the best schools to attend." While she believes she had a strong elementary education in her neighborhood, she knew she would not go to her neighborhood high school. "You know, there'd be too many issues with the gangs and what not. And who has the best this and the best that. It was too much stress. So I knew I was gonna have to go to another school outside of my neighborhood.... My neighborhood high school was very gang-oriented. Just to be able to walk through the door, you were taking a chance. You would have been going to that school taking a chance every single day."

Farragut High School once had a history of activism in the late 1960s and early 1970s as teachers were organizing with students for community control and quality education.[49] Even in the midst of organizing, there was a shooting in the lunch room. The dropout rates were fairly high for students, though some came back to school while it was run by the community. The school was located in one of the poorest communities in the city. Many participants viewed Farragut with disgust. Josephine's perception of Farragut and other schools in her community really illustrate the negative view. "I just heard so many awful things about Farragut. And the perception of Farragut was...it was just a wasteland. You know, it was just, kind of where you went just to pass the time. I just imagine that it was just this really miserable place, with low expectations and just kind of like a bunch of sweat hogs. I mean I don't even know, because I don't think I've ever been to Farragut. But it wasn't even in the cards for me." Josephine further commented about other West Side schools. "I just remember having this perception that all those schools on the West Side were just 'Blah!'...I'd never even set foot in most of them to really even know that. But it was just, that was the perception, like 'Yuck!' You don't want to go to those schools. So I never really even thought about those schools as an option."

The neighborhood schools were probably not as bad as these participants recalled, particularly since many never even set foot in the schools. Yet, one cannot ignore the perceptions of these schools, some of which had negative reputations for a long time. As students, teachers, and community members organized for community control and quality education in the 1960s, they noted that school resources including textbooks and curriculum were outdated, schools were overcrowded, and there was more focus on discipline than education.[50] In 1965, Clarence James recounted the vast overcrowding of Marshall High School and the lack of stimulating curriculum.[51] There were not enough seats if everyone showed up. Students organized protests at individual schools on the South and West Sides. They eventually conducted citywide boycotts of schools. One of the most intriguing demands they gave to the Board of Education was the call for "more homework." The rest of their demands dealt with more Black history courses and other academic improvements. At Harrison High School, student activists demanded an end to academic tracking. Beyond an increase in Black history courses, their demands for more academic rigor were largely ignored. Opportunities for desegregation and open enrollment gave academically gifted students options for a better education that students in the 1960s did not get despite demands.[52]

The recognition by participants that there were indeed great Black schools in the city lends credence to their recognition that race alone did not determine the worth of a school. Other negative factors including poor academics, higher dropout rates, gang activity, and other perceived negative peer pressure impacted their perceptions of these high schools. Those who thrived in all Black elementary schools recognized the excellent education they could receive in a Black school. However, many of the high schools nearby did not have similar reputations for students with college aspirations. This made academically enhanced desegregated high schools all the more attractive to Black participants of this study. Though this chapter does not indicate it, Latino and Whites participants also thought their attendance at Von, Whitney Young, and Bogan were the better options than other nearby schools.

Neighbor Reactions

In spite of the negative views of neighborhood high schools, some of the participants' neighbors could not understand why they would want to attend a school far from home. Attendance at schools outside one's neighborhood was viewed differently by community members. Because of desegregation policies, students had access to open enrollment and could go to school where they were accepted. Those who took advantage of these policies transferred for sports or academics. For some Black participants who attended schools outside of their neighborhoods, they were viewed as uppity. Some community members thought leaving the neighborhood was an act of betrayal. This was certainly not what all Black participants experienced. Some neighbors had pride in or curiosity about the participants' ability to go to better or different schools.

Participants were asked "How did your community respond to your attendance at a desegregated school?" Black participants who went to Von Steuben were more likely to face ridicule because people in the neighborhood had never heard of the school, and it was so far on the North Side. Many did not recognize the school as academically enhanced, but just as a White school. Terrace's comments explain how her neighbors' viewed her going to Von: "They didn't take it too well. They looked at that as almost like a betrayal." She further stated, "Well first of all when they found out what high school you go to, they're like 'you go all the way up north' and then they look at you as being White or a snob." For Sonji, people questioned her for attending a White school. "A lot of them was [sic] like, 'Why are you going all the way up there to that White school?'" She typically responded, "That's where I wanted to go. That's where I chose to go." Others were viewed as nerds or stuck up for not attending the neighborhood high school. SieraMedora recalled people thought that she believed she was better than they were for attending a White school. She often heard comments like "Why you got to get out the neighborhood? Why you think you better than us? Why you want to act like a White girl? . . . Why you got to go so far? Why can't you go to school with us? . . . Your school ain't no better than ours." Jacquese's neighbors also viewed her as stuck up. She noted, "They thought of me as being stuck up, a smarty. I just didn't fit in at all." These participants' memories of neighbors' responses should not be associated with "acting white" popularized by Signitha Fordam and John Ogbu.[53] The neighbors' perceptions discussed above were largely in response to them attending White schools far away from home, not a response to them taking advantage of academic opportunities. The same responses were not given to students who attended Whitney Young.

For other Von Steuben graduates, people in their neighborhoods simply had not heard of Von because it was not nearby or a sports powerhouse. For Marc and Ed, people wondered why they would travel so far to go to school. Marc said, "I think people were surprised. It's like, 'Wow, that's quite a trip, isn't it?' 'Oh yeah,' I said, 'it takes about an hour to get there on a good day.' Beside that sort of incredulity regarding the travel time, I don't think anyone mentioned to me personally, say, 'Oh, what are you doing that for?' or 'Why?' I never got those sort of questions." Ed had the similar sense about the neighborhood response. "I don't think it was negative. . . . I believe that they felt it was positive that I was going to school 'up north.' . . . They thought it was kind of odd." Marc and Ed further support the view that leaving the neighborhood was the bigger factor in why neighbors responded the way they did.

Participants who attended Whitney Young faced mixed reactions with people questioning how they spoke, being seen as odd, or neighbors recognizing a good opportunity. Josephine was told that she spoke "proper" which was just another way of saying she sounded White.

> I think my community always saw me as different. The predominantly Black neighborhood—I lived in K-Town . . . I think I was seen as really studious. And for some reason . . . I don't know how I wound up talking the way I talk. Some people would say, "Oh you talk so proper," or "Oh you talk so white." And what's interesting is that my parents are from the South and they have a southern accent, which I conjure up on a dime. Then I had some White teachers and then some Black teachers. All my friends all the way through sixth grade were either Latino of black. But I always quote, 'talked proper.' And so, I would get a little bit of grief.

Talking "proper" was the way Blacks often referred to other Blacks who did not speak Black Vernacular English or sounded more like Whites. For some Black Chicagoans, authenticity came with how one sounded rather than what one said, especially if one grew up in segregated Black neighborhoods.

Like Josephine, Eve thought people viewed her family as odd because she did not go to the neighborhood schools.

> My parents really wanted to push us to excel. So the kids already thought, kind of, 'Okay, she not going to grade school with us, you know middle school with us.' . . . And so they're like, "okay what's up with her?" . . . The friends who were close to me, they understood and knew what I was doing and why I was doing it. But other people were kind of like, what's up with that. They go, that's . . . kind of the goody, goody family, you know. So, to a degree I just took it in stride.

The reactions Josephine and Eve received were more about how they spoke and the fact that they left the neighborhood for schooling differing slightly from comments Von Steuben students received.

Unlike Josephine and Eve, Cassandra received positive feedback. She said, "They were happy because at the time, [Whitney Young] was number one. . . . People weren't like, you think you better than anybody else. They'd say, 'Oh you're going to Whitney Young, that's good!'" Although Eve and Josephine caught some grief, Whitney Young was more popular than Von Steuben and therefore, more people had heard of it as a top academic school. The school was also located on the West Side and not the predominantly White North Side. Still Eve and Josephine could not escape being viewed as strange either for the way they spoke or for going to schools outside the community.

Black participants who attended Bogan were less likely to experience negative comments. For the most part, since many Bogan participants came from the South Side and went to school on the Southwest Side, they were more likely to have friends who attended Bogan and more people in their neighborhoods who had heard of the school. Most said there was no issue with members of the community or people viewed their attendance at Bogan as positive. Only a few black students experienced some teasing from family and friends. Darlisa faced questions from her brothers about her choice to attend a White school. "Oh, my brothers used to always talk about me [saying you're] 'going over to that White school, thinking you all of that.' But, you know how brothers are! But as far as everybody in the community, they never knew what school I went to, because I never talked about it, you know? I didn't really hang outside?" Aside from Darlisa, a few other people mentioned some teasing. Rayshawn recalled Bogan being called "weak" because there were White students who attended. Though she knew people nearby who also attended the school, people still made fun of Bogan.

> There were a lot of people that stayed around Damon Avenue, so maybe about half a mile away, all in that vicinity, they went to Bogan. So, all of us were fine with it. The rest of the city, at least in our culture that went to the other high schools, when we said we went to Bogan: "Ew! You go to Bogan?" I said, "No, Bogan is a good school." "Bogan is weak!" So we had that kind of competition, and I think it was because it was so mixed. . . . I looked at it as that was their lack of knowledge. They didn't understand it, and they were missing out in the long run. So I didn't take it to be anything personal.

Neighbors or family members making fun of Bogan students for attending a White school, viewed association with Whites as a weakness or lame. In this sense, neighbors found pride in attending Black schools.

Of the three schools, participants from Von Steuben remembered more negative comments from neighborhood peers than the other schools. Again, this was likely due to the fact that they attended a little known school that was far away from their neighborhoods. Two Whitney Young participants sometimes experienced people viewing them as outsiders either for the way they spoke or because they attended schools outside the neighborhood. For Bogan graduates, the ridicule seemed more like harmless competition among friends and family members who viewed Bogan as "weak" because it was a not a Black school.

CONCLUSION

Chicago graduates of desegregated high schools offer interesting information about their segregated and desegregated experiences. Many coming from segregated neighborhoods attended segregated elementary schools where they thrived in caring environments. They were usually among the best at their elementary schools. As a result of the limited desegregation Chicago offered, participants were given an opportunity to escape neighborhood high schools they viewed as gang infested and difficult learning environments. While their perception of the neighborhood high schools may have been exaggerated, it speaks to the unfairness of desegregation as most students are unable to participate and were therefore not given the same opportunities.

Though this is a brief look at experiences of Black Chicago participants' in segregated elementary schools, how they chose their schools, their perceptions of neighborhood schools, and neighbor reactions to their attendance at desegregated schools, oral history methodology helps to highlight both the differences and similarities of student experiences in different schools, neighborhoods, cities, and regions around the country. Participants attending segregated elementary schools chose desegregated high schools largely as an academic choice since the formally White schools had garnered the academic enhancement opportunities the Board of Education consistently failed to give most predominantly Black schools despite protests in the 1960s and 1970s. As a part of the consent decree, schools that were not desegregated were supposed to receive compensatory funding for school improvement. A study, "Who Benefits from Desegregation," found that only 5.9 percent of minority students benefited from desegregation efforts and those who attended desegregated schools also received the same or more funding for academically enhanced programs than peers in segregated schools.[54] The academic choice participants and their families made meant they benefited in ways that their peers attending neighborhood high schools could not.

In closing, oral history has fundamentally changed historical research on Black education with the addition of participant voices. Furthermore, it has helped historians of school desegregation gain valuable insight from school desegregation participants. The inclusion of these voices in historical studies transforms what we know about history. It brings a bottom up view to history and provides historians and readers with new information and meaning making that often cannot be found in archival documents alone. Despite the potential limitations of participants' memories and perceptions of the past, oral history methodology when interrogated and corroborated with other sources, brings an important aspect to historical research. This methodology, used in various forms of Black educational history, is essential to gaining an understanding of what occurred in schools, caused protests, sparked reforms, motivated behavior, and helped students, teachers, community activists, school officials, judges, and politicians make important decisions about the education of Black youth.

NOTES

1. Barbara W. Sommer and Mary Kay Quinlan, *The Oral History Manual*, second edition (Lanham, MD: AltaMira Press, 2009), 1.
2. Ken Howarth, *Oral History: A Handbook* (Phoenix Mill, UK: Sutton Publishing, 1998), 4.
3. Jan Vansina, *Oral Tradition as History* (Madison: University of Wisconsin Press, 1985), 4–5;
4. Donald A. Ritchie, *Doing Oral History: A Practical Guide*, second edition (Oxford: Oxford University Press, 2003), 27.
5. Paul Thompson, *The Voice of the Past: Oral History* (Oxford: Oxford University Press, 1988), 2.
6. William W. Cutler III, "Oral History: Its Nature and Uses for Educational History," *History of Education Quarterly* 11 (Summer 1971): 184–194.
7. Richard White, *Remembering Ahanagran: Story Telling in a Family's Past* (New York, NY: Hill and Wang, 1998), 4.
8. Video interviews include the use of technology that allows the researcher and participant to see each other though they are not in the same place. Skype is an example.
9. Jack Dougherty and Candace Simpson, "Oral History Interviews: Who Own Oral History, A Creative Common Solution." http://ontheline.trincoll.edu/oral-history/creative-commons/ retrieved September 2, 2014.
10. See Thomas Sowell, "Black Excellence: The Case of Dunbar High School." *Public Interest* 35 (Spring 1974): 1–21; Thomas Sowell, "Patterns of Black Excellence." *Public Interest* 43 (1976): 26–58; Faustine Jones, *A Traditional Model of Educational Excellence: Dunbar High School of Little Rock, Arkansas* (Washington, D.C.: Howard University Press, 1981); David S. Cecelski, *Along Freedom Road: Hyde County, North Carolina, and the Fate of Black Schools in the South* (Chapel Hill: University of North Carolina Press, 1994); Vanessa Siddle Walker, *Their Highest Potential: An African American School Community in the Segregated South* (Chapel Hill: University of North Carolina Press, 1996); Vivian Gunn and Curtis L. Morris, *Creating Caring and Nurturing Educational Environments for African American Children* (Westport, Conn.: Bergin and Garvey, 2000); Vivian Gunn Morris and Curtis L. Morris, *The Price They Paid: Desegregation in an African American Community* (New York, NY: Teachers College Press, 2002); Sonya Ramsey, *Reading, Writing, and Segregation: A Century of Black Women Teachers in Nashville* (Urbana: University of Illinois, 2008); Hilton Kelly, *Race, Remembering, and Jim Crow's Teachers* (New York, NY: Routledge, 2010); Vanessa Siddle Walker, *Hello Professor: A Black Principal and Professional Leadership in the Segregated South* (Chapel Hill: University of North Carolina Press, 2009); Alison Stewart, *First Class: The Legacy of Dunbar, America's First Black Public High School* (Chicago: Lawrence Hill Books, 2013); Sharon Gay Pierson, *Laboratory of Learning: HBCU Laboratory Schools and Alabama State College Lab High in the Era of Jim Crow* (New York, NY: Peter Lang, 2014).
11. Though Walker calls her interviews of parents, students, teachers and administrators ethnographic interviews, they are still discussed here for the similar-

ity to oral history. Other disciplines use interviews as a form of qualitative methodology to gain access to historical events. Walker, *Their Highest Potential.*

12. Hilton Kelly, *Race, Remembering, and Jim Crow's Teachers*, 10–11.

13. Richard Kluger, *Simple Justice* (New York, NY: Vintage Books, 1975); David S. Cecelski, *Along Freedom Road: Hyde County, North Carolina, and the Fate of Black Schools in the South* (Chapel Hill: University of North Carolina Press, 1994); R. Scott Baker, *Paradoxes of Desegregation: African American Struggles for Educational Equity in Charleston, South Carolina, 1926–1972* (Columbia: University of South Carolina Press, 2006); Jack Dougherty, *More than One Struggle: The Evolution of Black School Reform in Milwaukee* (Chapel Hill: University of North Carolina Press, 2004).

14. Kluger, *Simple Justice*, 789.

15. Cecelski, *Along Freedom Road*, 14.

16. Baker, *Paradoxes of Desegregation.*

17. Dougherty, *More than One Struggle*, 4.

18. Sarah Garland, *Divided We Fail: The Story of an African American Community That Ended the Era of School Desegregation* (Boston, MA: Beacon Press, 2013); Tracy E. K'Meyer, *From* Brown *to* Meredith: *The Long Struggle for School Desegregation in Louisville, Kentucky, 1954–2007* (Chapel Hill: University of North Carolina Press, 2013).

19. K'Meyer, *From* Brown *to* Meredith.

20. Garland, *Divided We Fail.*

21. Caroline Eick, *Race-Class Relations and Integration in Secondary Education: The Case of Miller High* (New York, NY: Palgrave Macmillan, 2010), 1–2, 160.

22. Amy Stuart Wells, Jennifer Jellison Holme, Anita Tijerina Revilla, Awo Korantemaa Atanda, "How Desegregation Changed Us: The Effects of Racially Mixed Schools on Students and Society," 5. http://cms.tc.columbia.edu/i/a/782_ASWells041504.pdf (accessed January 18, 2008.)

23. Amy Stuart Wells, Jennifer Jellison Holme, Anita Tijerina Revilla, Awo Korantemaa Atanda, *Both Sides Now: The Story of School Desegregation's Graduates* (Berkeley: University of California Press, 2009), 5–7, 44.

24. See Michael W. Homel, *Down From Equality: Black Chicagoans and the Public Schools, 1920–41* (Urbana: University of Illinois Press, 1984); James R. Grossman, *Land of Hope: Chicago, Black Southerners, and the Great Migration* (Chicago: The University of Chicago Press, 1989); Alan B. Anderson and George W. Pickering, *Confronting the Color Line: The Broken Promise of the Civil Rights Movement in Chicago* (Athens: The University of Georgia Press 1986); James R. Ralph, Jr., *Northern Protest: Martin Luther King, Jr., Chicago, and the Civil Rights Movement* (Cambridge, MA: Harvard University Press, 1993); Dionne Danns, *Something Better for Our Children: Black Organizing in Chicago Public Schools, 1963–1971* (New York, NY: Routledge, 2003).

25. See Allan H. Spear, *Black Chicago: The Making of a Negro Ghetto, 1890–1920* (Chicago: The University of Chicago Press, 1967); Chicago Commission on Race Relations, *The Negro in Chicago: A Study of Race Relations and a Race Riot* (Chicago: University of Chicago Press, 1922).

26. Anderson and Pickering, *Confronting the Color Line*; Ralph, *Northern Protest*; Danns, *Something Better for Our Children.*

27. Dionne Danns, *Desegregating Chicago's Public Schools: Policy Implementation, Politics, and Protests, 1965–1985* (New York, NY: Palgrave Macmillan, 2014); William Anton Vrame, "A History of School Desegregation in Chicago Since 1954" (PhD Dissertation, University of Wisconsin, 1970); Paul E. Peterson, School Politics Chicago Style (Chicago: University of Chicago Press, 1976), 143–185; Dionne Danns, "Racial Ideology and the Sanctity of the Neighborhood School Policy in Chicago," Urban Review 40 (Spring 2008): 64–75.

28. Danns, *Desegregating Chicago's Public Schools*; Connie Lauerman, "State Board Charges City Schools with Bias," *Chicago Tribune*, February 27, 1976, 1, 19; Geof Dubson, "State Prods Chicago on School Desegregation," *Chicago Sun-Times*, December 10, 1976, 5; Linda Wertsch, "Desegregation Go-Ahead for City," *Chicago Sun-Times*, May 12, 1978, 3; Meg O'Connor, "Chicago's School Plan gets State OK, with Reservations," *Chicago Tribune*, May 12, 1978, 5; Joseph P. Hannon, "Statement" in *Chicago Board of Education Proceedings*, October 17, 1979, 504.

29. *United States of America v. Board of Education City of Chicago*, "Consent Decree," 1–8.

30. Casey Banas, "City's Public Schools Now 52 Pct. Negro: Whites Drop to 41.5 percent," *Chicago Tribune*, October 25, 1967, 10.

31. Danns, *Desegregating Chicago's Public Schools*.

32. Wells et al., "How Desegregation Changed Us."

33. It is important to note that much of the protests over school desegregation had subsided by the time students from Class of 1988 entered high school.

34. American Indians were less than a percent of the population at most schools.

35. Dionne Danns e-mail communication with Whitney Young reunion organizer July 22, 2009.

36. Derrick Bell, *Silent Covenants:* Brown v. Board of Education *and the Unfulfilled Hopes for Racial Reform* (New York, NY: Oxford University Press, 2004); Wells et al., *Both Sides Now*; Cecelski, *Along Freedom Road*; Garland, *Divided We Fail.*

37. Wells et al., *Both Sides Now*; James T. Patterson, Brown v. Board of Education: *A Civil Rights milestone and Its Troubled Legacy* (Oxford: Oxford University Press, 2001).

38. Walker, *Their Highest Potential.*

39. See Danns, *Desegregating Chicago's Public Schools*.

40. The increase from 10 to 11 percent was because one of the schools did not have data for the 1978–79 school year. Chicago Board of Education, "Racial Ethnic Survey, 1979," Chicago Board of Education Archives; G. Alfred Hess Jr., Christina A. Warden, Lisa Korte, and Linda Loukidis, "Who Benefits from Desegregation: A Review of the Chicago Desegregation Program 1980 to 1986," (Chicago: Panel on Public School Policy and Finance, December 1987), I–VIII.

41. I have chosen to only use the first name or a pseudonym for each participant. Therefore, there will be no citations for the quotes.

42. Vanessa Siddle Walker, *Their Highest Potential.*

43. Danns, *Desegregating Chicago's Public Schools*.

44. Board of Education, "Comprehensive Student Assignment Plan," vol. I, January 22, 1982.

45. Casey Banas and Devonda Byers, "Education Chief: City Schools Worst," November 8, 1987. Retrieved September 30, 2014. http://articles.chicago-tribune.com/1987-11-08/news/8703230953_1_dropout-rate-public-schools-mayor-harold-washington

46. Chicago Urban League, "Access to Excellence: An Analysis and Commentary on the 1978–79 Program Proposals," 1, 1979, ERIC ED 187 780.

47. Chicago Urban League, "Access to Excellence."

48. Board of Education, "Comprehensive Student Assignment Plan," 240, 256.

49. Danns, *Something Better for Our Children,* 99–106; Dionne Danns, "Chicago Teacher Reform Efforts and the Politics of Educational Change," in *Black Protest Thought and Education,* ed. William Watkins (New York, NY: Peter Lang, 2005), 179–196.

50. Danns, *Something Better for Our Children,* 70–71.

51. Danns, "Chicago High School Students' Movement for Quality Education, 1966–1971," *Journal of African American History* 88 (Spring 2003): 138–150.

52. Danns, *Something Better for Our Children,* 75–88.

53. Signitha Fordam and John Ogbu, "Black Students' Success: Coping with the Burden of 'Acting White,'" *Urban Review* (Fall 1996): 176–206.

54. G. Alfred Hess, Jr., Christina A. Warden, Lisa Korte, Linda Loukidis, "Who Benefits from Desegregation: A Review of the Chicago Desegregation Program 1980 to 1986," (Chicago: Panel on Public School Policy and Finance, December 1987), ii–iii.

PART III

CONTEMPORARY HISTORY AND FUTURE DIRECTIONS

CHAPTER 10

CONTROL AND INDEPENDENCE

Black Alternatives for Urban Education

Elizabeth S. Todd-Breland
University of Illinois at Chicago

The struggle for school desegregation was prevalent in Black education re-form efforts during the Civil Rights Era. By the late 1960s, however, support for the utility of school desegregation began to wane within many Black urban communities outside of the South. Black parents and community members in rural, urban, and suburban communities across the country wanted high quality education. However, struggles for better educational opportunities for Black children also varied by place and political context. Education struggles in the North and West were waged in political land-scapes that were initially positioned outside the purview of the Supreme Court's *Brown v. Board of Education* decision. Deindustrialization of the former core in the Northeast and Midwest, and White flight from cities and urban public schools, produced an increasing number of city school systems with Black majorities. These conditions generated a particular set of ideological and tactical responses. In cities outside of the South, where

Using Past as Prologue, pages 253–274
Copyright © 2015 by Information Age Publishing
All rights of reproduction in any form reserved.

attempts to desegregate schools were rarely implemented on any significant scale, Black education reformers often found desegregation an impractical and undesirable solution to remedy educational inequality.[1]

Black education reformers increasingly turned their attention to pursuing alternative strategies to achieve "quality education," rather than desegregation. Plans to achieve quality schooling came in many forms, but generally emanated from the position that past desegregation efforts failed to create equitable educational opportunities for Black students or increase Black academic achievement in a meaningful way. After enduring years of White backlash and hostility in response to attempts to desegregate, many African American parents and educators still did not see marked improvements in the quality of schooling available for their children. As Black communities became increasingly disappointed and disillusioned with the prospect of desegregation, it seemed more important and effective to focus on increasing the quality of the schools that Black students actually attended, rather than continue to pursue desegregation strategies. For many Black students, particularly those in urban schools, the schools that they actually attended were highly segregated and predominantly Black. New struggles emerged against racialized educational inequities that proposed alternative visions of the best way to achieve quality education for Black youth.[2] These Black educational alternatives included approaches with self-determinist objectives created by and for African Americans—including community control and the creation of independent Black institutions. This chapter analyzes the development of African Americans' frustration with the enactment and discourse of desegregation and the alternative strategies put forth by Black educators, parents, students, and community members to reform urban public schools outside of the South beyond struggles for school desegregation.

BLACK AMBIVALENCE ABOUT DESEGREGATION

Mid-twentieth century civil rights protests for school desegregation did not emerge from a singular tradition of Black education reform. Within African American communities, education has occupied a place of heightened importance because of linkages between education and freedom: from struggles for literacy under slavery, to challenges in finding schooling to meet the needs of freed people, to civil rights era linkages between literacy, education, and liberation.[3] Historically, desegregation has not been the only, or even the most dominant, strategy that Black people have pursued to achieve equity or liberation. During Reconstruction former slaves welcomed support from Northern benevolent and missionary societies, Republican officials, and the Freedmen's bureau in fighting for universal public education. However, as historian James Anderson explained, based on an ethic of self-reliance and self-determination, Black Southerners also established their own schools across the South in the years after emancipation.[4] African Americans' focus on education and building schools to serve Black children continued into the twentieth century.[5] William Watkins noted that during the nineteenth and early-twentieth century, efforts to reform African American education generated a variety of Black ideological approaches to education reform: Black nationalist and Pan-Africanist appeals to racial unity, separatism, and a non-Eurocentric curriculum; democratic-socialists' positioning of schools as sites to challenge an unjust U.S. social-political order; Christian humanists' support for a classical liberal education; and progressive-liberalism in the tradition or Carter G. Woodson.[6] Thus, mid-twentieth century civil rights protests for school desegregation emerged as part of a longer history of diverse educational struggles for freedom and justice. By the mid-twentieth century, desegregation was perceived by some in Black freedom struggles as the most appropriate tool to attack inequality.

However, even at the height of mid-twentieth century civil rights protests to desegregate public accommodations, many African Americans expressed ambivalence about integration. African Americans across the country were overwhelmingly opposed to the way that segregation was used as a tool to constrain their liberties and deny access to opportunities. They also vehemently objected to the way that segregation was used as a tool to stigmatize Black people.[7] In response, some came to support integration, believing that Black children would never be granted an equal public education until White children were forced to learn and go to school under the same conditions as Black children. However, as Charles Payne documented, opposition to the ills of segregation did not always map onto an ideological commitment to integration. In the period leading up to the *Brown* case, the NAACP had to work very hard to convince Black parents that integration would be a better route to achieving quality education for their children than educational equalization.[8] Many Black parents wanted equal school resources and facilities, but were not necessarily ideologically wedded to a philosophy of integration. Furthermore, much in the way that W. E. B. Du Bois argued in the 1930s, some African Americans doubted that a struggle solely against segregation could eliminate the structural political, economic, and social constraints on their lives. Instead, many argued that any push for desegregation must also be coupled with the strengthening of Black institutions.[9]

Across the country, Black education reformers soured on plans to desegregate schools. Massive resistance by Whites and slow progress in improving the quality of Black education tempered the promises of equality hoped for with the *Brown* decision and subsequent desegregation protests. While certain civil rights groups remained ideologically wedded to school integration, over the course of the 1960s, support declined for efforts to desegregate the increasingly segregated schools in many Black urban neighborhoods. Well before the courts stepped in to constrain the ability of urban school districts to pursue metropolitan solutions to the problem of school segregation in the 1970s, Black parents and community members complained that proposed desegregation plans placed the burden of desegregation disproportionally on the backs of Black families.

Busing plans designed to desegregate schools often required that far more Black students board buses to get to school than White students, in what came to be characterized as "one-way" busing. In Milwaukee Public Schools an elaborate busing plan was put in place. By the 1979–80 school year, 79 percent of students attended "racially balanced" schools.[10] The plan included busing to schools within the city and some suburban schools as well. However, the burden of busing was placed squarely on African American students and families. As the proportion of White students in the schools declined and the proportion of Black students in the system increased, new schools were built in White neighborhoods at the same time that schools in Black neighborhoods were closed or turned into city-wide magnet or specialty schools. This resulted in 80 percent of Black students being bused to school, while 80 percent of White students were not bused to attend school.[11] While the implementation of busing in Milwaukee was largely a peaceful process, in other cities busing plans elicited violent responses. Most notably, the virulent and at-times violent protests by White groups opposing busing in cities like Boston and Chicago, made it clear that White massive resistance was not exclusively a Southern phenomenon.[12]

While some Black parents supported busing plans, many others opposed them. Black parents feared for the safety and wellbeing of their children if placed in hostile all-White schools. In districts with limited busing plans, they also questioned the logic of busing a few students to under-enrolled schools without any plan for improving the deteriorating schools in African American neighborhoods for those students left behind.[13] Before becoming the first African American woman to head a major urban school system as the Superintendent of Washington, D.C. Public Schools, Barbara Sizemore expressed her ambivalence about integration as a strategy to improve Black academic achievement. In response to a proposed one-way busing plan for children in Chicago she stated: "To bus only the Negro children into White schools would be just another way of saying that Black is bad or inferior. We have already had too much of that. If Black children are to be bused, then White children should also be bused. I don't believe in segregation, but neither do I believe in teaching inferiority."[14] By making the case that it was demeaning to suggest that Black students could only achieve academically if they went to school with White children, Sizemore connected arguments for desegregation with arguments that supported notions of Black inferiority. Like Sizemore, in response to one-way busing plans and other schemes for desegregation, many Black parents and educators started to find integration politically inexpedient and offensive. Consequently, a growing contingent of Black education reformers during the late 1960s abandoned integration as a viable solution for improving Black student achievement in public schools.

Bolstered by Black Power politics, community-based groups sought to achieve control of the public institutions serving their neighborhoods, rather than fighting for the desegregation of schools. The new strategies for improving Black academic achievement that emerged from this period were concerned with improving the quality of education that Black children received in urban schools—whether segregated schools or not—rather than pursuing the goal of achieving racially integrated schools. In these cities, attempts at integration had failed, or when a degree of desegregation had been achieved it still failed to create equitable educational opportunities for the majority of Black students. Moving forward, many Black education reformers pursued strategies that sought to improve Black academic achievement and obtain quality education within Black communities in predominantly Black schools.[15]

QUALITY EDUCATION: BLACK ALTERNATIVES FOR URBAN EDUCATION

In reflecting back on struggles for desegregation, activists and scholars have questioned whether they were fighting for the right thing. Beginning in the 1970s, Derrick Bell, the civil rights lawyer and scholar who litigated many desegregation cases, wondered whether desegregation alone could deliver quality education for Black students and questioned the ability of court orders to remedy inequality more broadly.[16] Bell was not alone in this critique. As support for desegregation efforts declined, Black education reformers developed a number of strategies, legal and extra-legal, that can be categorized broadly under the umbrella of *quality education*.[17] Quality education strategies were based on the premise that past desegregation efforts failed to create equitable educational opportunities for Black students. This failure required a renewed focus on increasing Black students' educational achievement levels by improving the *quality* of the predominantly Black schools that Black students actually attend.[18] Amongst other strategies, Black education reformers worked in this manner to improve the quality of Black education through attempts to establish community control of schools and build independent Black educational institutions.

Community Control

In the 1950s and 1960s school districts made efforts to decentralize the administration of large urban school systems. Researchers and policymakers supported decentralization as an administrative intervention that would enhance innovation, accountability, and efficiency in large centralized urban school systems bogged down by bureaucracy. In cities—including, New York, Detroit, Philadelphia, Boston, Baltimore, and St. Louis—administrative decentralization created new district, area, and regional-level administrators. These administrators varied in their level of actual power and often operated as buffers between central administration and dissatisfied parents and community members. Thus, administrative decentralization did not necessitate an increase in community participation or control of schools. However, in cities where decentralization plans were underway, local Black civil rights groups and leaders of War on Poverty programs often led the push for decentralization in hopes of achieving greater parental and community control over school decisions. Unfortunately, the creation of new administrative positions through decentralization rarely met activists' expectations for inclusion, and often explicitly avoided the label of "community control." Political theorist Jane Anna Gordon, distinguishes between the aims of decentralization and community control, with the former being primarily concerned with administrative restructuring of public school systems, and the latter being primarily concerned with which members of society are placed in decision-making positions within these administrative structures. Scholars have demonstrated that Black parents and community organizations seized upon the decentralization efforts already underway in many large urban school systems, to demand community control of schools.[19]

Community control proponents asserted a political agenda that linked Black liberation with Black educational achievement. Joy Williamson-Lott argued that the Black nationalist and radical proposals of community control advocates prompted fear and apprehension in conservatives and liberals because community control challenged traditional structures of authority and arguments for desegregation. Community control was at once both a specific alternative to school desegregation and part of a broader Black political project for liberation, of which education was just one—albeit a very important—piece.[20] Thus, desegregation and community control challenged structures of power in different ways.

The ideological distinction between a politics of desegregation and a politics of community control centered on differing views of who wielded the power to create change in schools. Proponents of desegregation argued that as long as Black and White children attended separate segregated schools, Black children would never be granted educational opportunities equal to their White counterparts. They sought changes from boards of education and other government officials, the bodies that they saw wielding the power to transform the material conditions and allocation of resources to schools. In order to create change in schools then, it was necessary to court the allegiance, and/or force the hand, of the school board and local

officials to look out for the interests of Black students; or replace government officials resistant to change with officials who supported school desegregation. Alternatively, proponents of community control argued that the
power to improve Black educational achievement already existed within
Black communities in the collective energies of community members, administrators, teachers, parents, and students who believed that Black students could succeed academically in predominantly Black schools located
within their own communities.

For community control advocates, it was not necessary to desegregate a
school in order to pursue Black student achievement. During the 1960s and
1970s, Black activists and educators pursued alternative educational models for Black students that emerged from struggles for community control;
including Howard Fuller in Milwaukee, Barbara Sizemore in Chicago and
Washington, D.C., and Jitu Weusi (Leslie Campbell) in Brooklyn.[21] While
community control advocates acknowledged the structural critique of the
racialized inequitable distribution of resources put forth by desegregation
advocates, they argued that the proposition that Black student achievement
was linked to the proximity to White children implied Black inferiority.
Community control advocates wanted more resources for schools serving
Black children, but they also wanted the Black community to control the
resources, policies, curriculum, and staffing of these predominantly Black
schools. The goals of community control were educational and political:
to improve educational achievement by securing political power for the
community to participate in school affairs and determine school policies.[22]

Community control efforts were implemented in communities across
the country, but one of the most intense struggles over community control
of schools that reverberated on the national stage took place in the Ocean
Hill-Brownsville community in Brooklyn, New York. In 1968, the Ocean
Hill-Brownsville experiment with community control of schools descended
into a power struggle between the largely White and Jewish leadership of
the New York City teachers union and Black teachers, administrators, and
community members. Scholars have used the Ocean Hill-Brownsville crisis
to make broader claims about the political impact of community control
efforts; in particular, emphasizing the ways that community control challenged the tenuous interracial alliances of postwar racial liberalism that
supported movements for desegregation.[23] In cities across the country,
community control efforts illuminated racial conflicts between former
allies in the push for school desegregation. However, foregrounding the
implications of Black–White conflict between communities and teachers
unions and focusing on New York City alone can obscure the unique local
dynamics that shaped struggles for community control.

While common ideological threads and activist networks united disparate
community control efforts across the country, community control strategies

also developed in response to specific local political conditions as a product of local histories. Community control in Chicago developed out of the local history of previous Black struggles for racial justice against the Chicago Democratic machine. In the late 1960s, Black Chicagoans who had lived through earlier movements for desegregation in the city, like Rev. Arthur Brazier in the Woodlawn neighborhood, came to embrace community control.[24]

In the postwar years, Woodlawn had rapidly transitioned from a predominantly White neighborhood to a predominantly Black neighborhood. The Hyde Park community, including the University of Chicago, borders Woodlawn to the North. Between 1950 and 1960 the residential population of the Woodlawn neighborhood transformed from 86 percent White to nearly 90 percent non-White.[25] Initially, a relatively small group of economically stable middle-class African Americans settled in Woodlawn to escape the overcrowded neighborhoods of the historic Black Belt, further north of Woodlawn. Throughout the 1950s, lower income African Americans also settled in Woodlawn. A segment of these newer Black residents had relocated to Woodlawn after being displaced by slum clearance-urban renewal projects in the Hyde Park neighborhood. Woodlawn also increasingly became a final destination for thousands of Black migrants from the South who arrived at the 63rd Street stop of the Illinois Central Railroad, located in the heart of the Woodlawn community.[26] In a neighborhood of just over one square mile, the residential population ballooned to more than 70,000 residents by 1960.[27] As was the pattern in many overcrowded Black neighborhoods in the city, to accommodate this population growth single-family homes and large apartments were converted into efficiency and kitchenette apartments and hotels. The number of bars, gambling venues, and other "vice" industries expanded to serve more transient populations.[28] Local clergy organized in response to the deteriorating social and material conditions in Woodlawn, eventually creating The Woodlawn Organization (TWO). Rev. Arthur Brazier emerged early on as a strong local leader capable of identifying community concerns and organizing to address these concerns. As TWO's President, Brazier organized the local community to fight against encroachment by the University of Chicago, exploitative business practices by White merchants, and overcrowding in Black neighborhood schools.[29]

By 1967, like others during the time, Brazier had tired of integration as a means to increase the quality of education for Black children in the neighborhood. A former supporter of school desegregation, Brazier had become more ambivalent about desegregation: "We aren't forgetting about integration but we aren't waiting for it either . . . It is an insult to tell me that there have to be White kids in my school before it can be a good school. We want good Black schools now."[30] By 1969, Brazier and TWO had more fully rejected integration as a practical solution to the problem of poor schooling in Black neighborhoods:

The integrated community is, for the most part, a myth, an act of wishful thinking. The idea of group integration is still promoted by well-intentioned efforts of groups and interracial committees who involve themselves in promoting brotherhood weeks, writing resolutions, and passing out testimonials and awards—all of which have no meaning or effect upon the masses of black people who are struggling for survival.... Black people must build up their own communities and make them desirable places to live, work, play, and send their children to school. This means encouraging people to remain in their community and helping them to improve the quality of living in it.... To build up their own communities black Americans must acquire power. The need is not for slogans or rhetoric, but for mass-based organizations that can develop the kind of power necessary within the black community to change the domination of white power structures that continue to exploit black people.[31]

Brazier argued that integration was important insofar as it was necessary to bring down the barriers and discrimination that limited opportunities for African Americans to live and work wherever they chose. However, in terms of education, he came to argue that it was more important for African Americans to become empowered to develop and improve the quality of life within their own communities and schools. He would come to articulate these ideas further as a leader of the push for community control of schools in Chicago through the Woodlawn Experimental Schools Project (WESP).

The development and implementation of WESP provided the vehicle for a group of Black Chicagoans to work within the public school system to develop, articulate, and work to enact community control as a political alternative to integration/desegregation strategies that dominated the previous era of protest politics. WESP operated from 1968 to 1971 with federal funding under Title III of the Elementary and Secondary Education Act. WESP implemented community control in several Woodlawn public schools by bringing together historically hostile partners: the Chicago Board of Education, the University of Chicago, and TWO. This tenuous alliance was forged only after Brazier sent a complaint to the U.S. Office of Education that required that the University include TWO in their proposal for an educational research and development center in Woodlawn.[32] Brazier was the face of WESP in the community, but a White man from the University of Chicago, Dr. Willard Congreve, served as the director of WESP during its initial start up phase. When Congreve stepped down in 1969, Brazier and TWO selected Barbara Sizemore, a community control advocate and highly respected Black educator in the city to serve as the new WESP director.[33]

As leaders of WESP, Brazier and Sizemore employed a notion of community control that advocated collaborative community decision-making, while working with government and private institutions to improve educational opportunities for Black children in the Woodlawn neighborhood. A Woodlawn Community Board was created as a quasi board of education for the experimental district.[34] WESP staff and volunteers organized more than 500 parents from the community into parent councils, developed school-based enrichment and training programs, employed community members as teachers' aids in classrooms, and created new decision-making structures in the participating schools that increased the decision-making power of parents, teachers, students, and community members in the day-to-day operations and curriculum of the schools. During her tenure as director, Sizemore theorized a model of collective decision-making forged on the ground in WESP as the CAPTS aggregate decision-making model. CAPTS referred to bringing *c*ommunity representatives, *a*dministrators, *p*arents, *t*eachers, and *s*tudents to the table as decision-makers in schools.[35] The alternative political and ideological vision of WESP promoted Black self-determination and community control as the most appropriate means to provide quality education for Black students.[36]

Under Sizemore's leadership, WESP became more representative of the racial make-up of the community, but WESP's bargaining power with respect to the University and the Chicago Board of Education decreased. The twenty-one-member Woodlawn Community Board that governed WESP initially had a White majority. However, during Sizemore's tenure the board had been reorganized to include eighteen Black board members and more board members who actually lived in Woodlawn.[37] Chicago Public Schools leaders were less willing to negotiate, compromise, and cede control of their schools to WESP when it was led by Sizemore, a Black woman, and the reconstructed Black-majority Board, than when WESP was led by Dr. Willard Congreve, a White man from the University of Chicago. The White men from the University and the Board of Education who collaborated with Brazier and TWO to found WESP had access to powerful business and political interests in the city in ways that Sizemore did not. They were able to negotiate, navigate, and garner special favors from the Chicago Public Schools, Chicago Board of Education, and local and federal government agencies.[38] Ultimately, Sizemore's limited power vis-à-vis these traditional sites of power made true community control of schools in Woodlawn illusory.

WESP ended before Brazier and Sizemore's vision of community control was ever completely realized. By attempting to flatten hierarchies and increase the range of people making decisions within schools, WESP challenged many existing political and school-based norms and practices. The politics on the ground within the schools were messy and rife with conflicts over programmatic content and questions of authority, expertise, and inclusion. The Chicago Board of Education, backed by Chicago's powerful Mayor Richard J. Daley, ultimately rebuffed WESP's ability to implement significant changes in the schools and Sizemore's authority to control teacher hiring, firing, and evaluation. Local and federal funding for the project was terminated by the summer of 1971. As the University of Chicago retreated and WESP's authority was diminished, the relationship between WESP staff, TWO, parents, teachers, and the Board also crumbled.[39] As an experiment in community control, WESP exposed the limits to which the Chicago Board of Education and the University of Chicago were willing to cede their control to the community. The administrators of WESP explicitly worked to avoid the types of conflicts with the teachers union that had escalated in New York. Rather than primarily characterized by conflict with the teachers union, community control in Woodlawn faced challenges precipitated by the University of Chicago and Chicago's particular brand of machine politics.

While decentralized experimental districts were created by administrative reorganization in communities like Woodlawn and Ocean Hill-Brownsville, other community control efforts were implemented from the bottom up. For example, led by science teacher Hannibal Afrik (Harold Charles), Black teachers protested and organized to gain control of the curriculum, oust a racist principal, and hire more Black administrators at Farragut High School on the West Side of Chicago.[40] The twin goals of many Black education reformers like Afrik—to realize high levels of Black educational achievement and pursue Black liberation more broadly—were central to a range of efforts to improve the quality of Black education during this period, of which community control was but one strategy. Afrik went on to become a national leader of another alternative approach to achieving quality schooling for Black children, through the creation of Black independent schools.

Independent Black Institutions

The politics of Black education during the late 1960s and 1970s took on many different forms, including the creation of a small, but ideologically significant, group of Black independent schools and institutions focusing on educating Black youth and families using culturally relevant and Pan-African-centered curricula. While many community control advocates tried to provide Black students with a quality education by changing the organizational and power structure within public schools, others questioned the capacity of state-run public schools to appropriately educate Black children all together. Rather than attempting to improve educational opportunities Black students within public schools, the founders of independent Black schools felt it was necessary to pursue quality education strategies that circumvented the state-run education system completely. The opening of independent Black schools was not primarily a response to the failures of desegregation, but a specific educational alternative created by and for African Americans.[41]

Independent Black schools were not a new construct of the civil rights era. African American churches and communities had established schools since before emancipation. Beginning in the late eighteenth century Black religious denominations and benevolent societies established schools for African Americans.[42] In addition to Black colleges and universities established during the late nineteenth century, a system of Black private primary and secondary schools operated during the twentieth century; schools like Piney Woods in Mississippi, Howalton Day School in Chicago, and dozens of Nation of Islam schools across the country. Independent predominantly Black private and parochial schools provided an alternative for parents who did not feel that public schools could address the academic, social, and cultural needs of Black students.[43] Inspired by Black freedom struggles of the mid-twentieth century, movements for alternative schooling for African Americans during the late1960s and 1970s offered a particular vision of society and pedagogy that rejected ideologies of White supremacy and the economic oppression perceived to permeate traditional public schooling.[44] As movement schools, Student Nonviolent Coordinating Committee freedom schools and Black Panther schools fostered a new political consciousness among students by implementing curricula and pedagogy that challenged racism and inequality in society. These schools positioned education as a central site for generating societal change by acknowledging, and building on, the struggles experienced by Black students and their families.[45] Additionally, the number of African-centered schools also grew during this period influenced by political and cultural nationalist movements that similarly valued education.

The Council of Independent Black Institutions (CIBI) was founded in 1972 as an umbrella organization for Black independent schools across the country that shared a common interest in having Black people control and organize educational institutions serving Black children.[46] CIBI was established as a national network that included independent African-centered schools in New York, Washington, D.C., Los Angeles, Chicago, the San Francisco Bay Area, New Orleans and other locations around the country. CIBI held annual conferences, workshops, and gatherings for its members and served as a hub where representatives from independent Black schools across the country shared best-practices, collaborated to produce curricula, and facilitated a national science fair with students from member schools.[47] Leaders argued that the existing U.S. educational order asserted the superiority of political and cultural elites in U.S. society. They saw a need for new forms of education and schooling that promoted an alternative worldview with Black people and Black culture at its center. CIBI institutions incorporated this context and political education into all aspects of the schools' curriculum, administration, teaching, and work with parents and families.[48]

Many Independent Black Institutions during this period developed out of struggles for community control of public schools and sought to challenge the existing U.S. racial and social order. In New York, Uhuru Sasa Shule, led by Jitu Weusi, emerged in response to the struggles for community control of schools waged by community members and Black teachers in Oceanhill-Brownsville.[49] Hannibal Afrik, a Chicago leader of Black teachers' struggles for community control of public schools, founded Shule Ya Watoto, an independent Black educational institution that promoted African-centered education on the West Side of Chicago. These schools rejected desegregation as a means of challenging the existing social and racial order in the United States. The founders of CIBI, including Afrik, argued that: "School desegregation as a strategy does not challenge in any fundamental way the cultural and political authority of the ruling elite in the United States over the schooling and education of people of African descent. The African-centered institution-building model that has evolved in CIBI clearly does so by seeking power over education and schooling."[50] Through education, CIBI schools sought to fundamentally challenge the existing racialized social order by generating a new vision for a social order centered on the histories and experiences of Black people.

Like many community control advocates of the era, CIBI's Pan-Africanist and Black Nationalist member schools were not invested in desegregation. CIBI was founded during the Black Power era and emphasized the importance of Black institution-building and African-centered education. The language and symbols of Black Power, emphasizing racial pride, Black empowerment, and self-determination resonated with many African Americans. While integrationist groups asked how education could be made better for Black students through protest against, and negotiations with, White business and political elites, CIBI schools were asking a different kind of question: How do you change the consciousness of a people? CIBI schools sought to empower African Americans to achieve quality education and change the social, political, and economic conditions within their own communities through a transformation of the consciousness of Black people. Integrationists and proponents of independent Black institutions both looked to education as a site to achieve significant positive change in the lives of African Americans. However, their solutions were drastically different.

Carol Lee and Haki Madhubuti (Don L. Lee), founders of independent Black educational institutions in Chicago and founding members of CIBI, were insistent that establishing independent Black institutions was key to the liberation of Black people. They argued that the problem for Black people was not the existence of racially isolated African American communities and schools that needed to be integrated, but the racist under-resourcing and systemic neglect of Black communities by the traditional White power structure. Along with others, they founded the Institute of Positive

Education in 1969 and the New Concept Development Center—the school affiliated with the Institute of Positive Education—in 1972.[51] They defined Independent Black Institutions as: "*Independent*—void of outside control and influence; *Black*—in color, culture and consciousness; *Institution*—a structured program aimed at correcting a deficiency, giving concrete alternatives for our people."[52] Establishing an African-centered curriculum and value system was central to the mission of these independent schools.

CIBI schools maintained that an important purpose of education was to transmit from one generation to the next knowledge, values, and spiritual and cultural beliefs. Given this, it was important to CIBI member schools that Black students participate in a form of education that explicitly reinforced the history of their identity as African peoples within and beyond the U.S. context. African-centered independent Black schools embraced a distinction between schooling and education. As explained by Mwalimu J. Shujaa, traditional White-led public schooling served as a mechanism to tie students to "the social order framed by the nation state," while education located "thinking within an African historical-cultural context." CIBI schools nurtured Black self-determination and worked to provide an Afrocentric alternative to the Eurocentric pedagogy and practices of traditional urban public schools.[53]

Like many CIBI institutions, the Institute of Positive Education, was grounded in the directives and philosophies of a Black value system called *Kawaida*, developed by Maulana Ron Karenga, the Black cultural nationalist leader of the Los Angeles-based U.S. Organization. Kawaida incorporated beliefs and principles from multiple African civilizations. It evolved from a quasi-religious philosophy with political undertones into an ideology and way of life aimed at creating fundamental societal change.[54] The ideology and program of Kawaida merged African American oratorical, cultural, and political traditions with cultural, religious, and communal values from a number of African countries—particularly incorporating many Kiswahili and Zulu words and concepts.[55] The *Nguzo Saba* (The Seven Principles) constituted a key component of Kawaida philosophy. The Nguzo Saba outlined the seven guiding principles that should guide Black people's lives. They included: UMOJA (Unity), KUJICHAGULIA (Self-Determination), UJIMA (Collective Work and Responsibility), UJAMAA (Cooperative Economics), NIA (Purpose), KUUMBA (Creativity), and IMANI (Faith).[56]

The seven principles of the Nguzo Saba served as a type of civic code and blueprint for how Black people should live and interact with each other and the broader world on a daily basis. Today, millions celebrate these core values in the annual celebration of Kwanzaa. Kwanzaa was one of many holidays and practices promoted by Karenga, the US Organization, and other Black cultural nationalist groups in the 1960s and 1970s to provide a shared recognition of African Americans' African cultural roots.[57] For CIBI institutions that made the Nguzo Saba a central part of their curriculum and school culture, the seven principles were more than just a set of precepts to be acknowledged at celebrations and holidays. This value system was a fundamental element of what quality education meant in these schools and a focal point of the schools' ideological framework and curriculum.[58] In CIBI schools, transforming Black students' consciousness was central to the project of providing quality education.

CIBI schools' independent status provided a means to work within a set of political possibilities and constraints unlike those of other quality education advocates who sought engagement with the state or operated within traditional public schools. As independent institutions, CIBI schools had the freedom and flexibility to operate autonomously to create and teach an alternative African-centered curriculum that cultivated a unique African Diasporic subjectivity amongst staff members and students in their schools. However, at times the doctrine and ideology of these schools also limited the ability of the institutions to expand further within broader Black communities that did not necessarily share the same worldview. As independently funded and operated schools, CIBI member schools also struggled financially. While some of the original CIBI institutions eventually closed, others, like the New Concept Development Center, are still in operation today.[59] A number of African-centered schools have also transitioned in more recent years into charter schools. CIBI's insistence on the importance of, what today would be called culturally relevant education, has become central to discussions of pedagogy and practice in the broader professional education community.[60]

In debates about urban education today, race and culture loom large as issues to be addressed in the classroom, at the administrative level, and in research. While Kawaida adherents may still be limited in number, the currency of culturally relevant education proposed by CIBI and other independent Black educational institutions has endured within the education community at-large. Furthermore, building curriculum based on culturally relevant pedagogy is an enduring feature of diverse attempts to achieve quality education for Black children.[61]

CONCLUSION

While decades have passed, the nation's urban public schools remain unequal and largely segregated by race. Despite the concerted efforts of students, parents, educators, and activists fighting for quality education, many of the programs, institutions, and advocacy groups that embraced community control and independent Black institutions were short-lived or not able to deliver on the promises of creating meaningful educational change.

This is in part due to internal challenges and conflicts, but also a result of the strident opposition faced by these efforts. Black educational alternatives that emphasized control and independence have collided in recent decades with the proprietary decentralization plans of neoliberal public and private entities that have come to see urban education as a new frontier for capital investment. Recent court decisions have also paved the way for policies that favor corporations and roll back Civil Rights Era gains.[62]

In this context, efforts to pursue alternative strategies to achieve quality education in still-segregated urban schools have also persisted. The impact of independent Black institutions and the community control movement can also be seen in contemporary education reform debates. Independent Black educational institutions' emphases on culturally relevant curriculum have become an enduring part of the discourse among education researchers and practitioners. Additionally, like the quality education efforts documented in this chapter, urban education debates today tend to center on competing visions of how to best improve the quality of urban schools, which predominantly serve students of color.

Although the actors in contemporary education debates are not necessarily the same education reformers from the decades immediately following *Brown*, the lines of contention in present-day debates remain stark. Contemporary proponents of "school choice" policies and defenders of traditional public schools have both used language reminiscent of the community control advocates of the past in framing the importance of their arguments. Urban education has become a new frontier for capital investment by hedge funds, philanthropic interests, and non-profits. Increasingly, these interests have helped to fund moves toward the privatization of urban public schooling with the support of municipal governments. As a collaborative project between a school system and a private university, WESP served as an early forerunner to the public-private partnerships that characterize many contemporary urban education reforms. The expansion of private interests in public schools through voucher programs and the expansion of charter schools have challenged the role of public entities in the future of urban education altogether.[63]

School choice advocates have repurposed the Black self-determinist language of community control in a proprietary assertion of parents' and communities' right to choose between public, private, and public–private hybrid forms of schooling. However, the supposedly "free" market where these decisions are being made is often highly segmented, unequal, and marred by a lack of actual choices. On the national stage, the Obama administration has furthered the Bush administration's corporate-style education reform policies that encourage market-based principles of competition, privatization, charter school expansion, and a reliance on standardized testing. As during the 1960s and 1970s, there have been multiple Black political responses to these policies. In pursuit of quality education, many Black parents have sought out charter schools and taken advantage of school choice programs. However, just as Black support for desegregation strategies did not signify a whole-hearted belief in the necessity of racial integration, Black families who utilize school choice programs or send their children to charter schools, do not necessarily embrace the broader politics of school choice policies. Additionally, it is rare that Black poor and working-class parents in particular, ever fully realize the increased control and independence that they often seek out through "school choice" options.[64]

Parents, teachers unions, and community groups from Black and Latino urban neighborhoods who oppose the privatization of public education have also employed elements of community control philosophies. Advocates for school choice and the expansion of charter schools have faced opposition from parents, community groups, and teachers unions who have fought to preserve traditional public schools by increasing funding and resources for neighborhood public schools. These groups have drawn on the discourse and practices of the community control movement in their community organizing techniques and appeals to dismantle the structural and institutional racism and inequality that continues to support highly inequitable schooling for students of color and low-income students in urban public schools. Desegregation is still not part of the national discourse on education, making the history of past Black educational alternatives for urban education all the more relevant to contemporary education reform debates. It seems likely that seeking out alternative strategies for achieving quality education in racially segregated schools will remain salient in urban education for the foreseeable future. How might we further use the history of Black self-determinist alternatives for urban education reform to shape a more just educational system today?

NOTES

1. I am not suggesting that proponents of community control, funding equalization, or independent Black institutions did not also exist in Southern cities. Nor is this chapter a comparative study of cities in the South and those outside of the South. But, this chapter focuses specifically on Black education reformers' strategies to improve K–12 education in cities outside of the South. There is, in fact, also significant diversity amongst cities outside of the South by: size of city, region (Northeast, Midwest, and West), size of Black population within the cities, etc. However, I argue that considering the politics and strategies put forth by Black education organizers given the set of social, judicial, and political constraints and possibilities present in cities outside of the South remains an important pursuit that contributes to our broader understanding

of Black politics and education reform historically and in our contemporary moment.

2. Ronald D. Henderson, et al., "High-Quality Schooling for African American Students," in *Beyond Desegregation: The Politics of Quality in African American Schooling*, ed. Mwalimu J. Shujaa (Thousand Oaks, CA: Corwin Press, Inc., 1996), 181–82; Elizabeth S. Todd-Breland, "Barbara Sizemore and the Politics of Black Educational Achievement, 1963–1975," *Journal of African American History* (forthcoming).

3. Theresa Perry, "Up From the Parched Earth: Toward a Theory of African American Achievement," in *Young, Gifted, and Black: Promoting High Achievement among African-American Students*, eds. Theresa Perry, et.al. (Boston, MA: Beacon Press, 2003), 11–13, 19; James D. Anderson, *The Education of Blacks in the South, 1860–1935* (Chapel Hill, NC: University of North Carolina Press, 1988).

4. Anderson, *The Education of Blacks in the South*, 4–11. In addition to the widespread growth of Black schools during Reconstruction, a number of Southern Black schools were also established before emancipation.

5. Ibid., 156–162; 285. Between 1914 and 1927 Black Southerners raised over $3.5 million, to match philanthropist Julius Rosenwald's funds, and build 3,769 schools in Southern Black communities.

6. William H. Watkins, "Reclaiming Historical Visions of Quality Schooling: The Legacy of Early 20th Century Black Intellectuals" in *Beyond Desegregation: The Politics of Quality in African American Schooling*, ed. Mwalimu J. Shujaa (Thousand Oaks, CA: Corwin Press, Inc., 1996), 9–25.

7. Charles M. Payne, "'The Whole United States is Southern!': Brown v. Board and the Mystification of Race," *Journal of American History* 91, 1 (2004), 89.

8. Payne, "'The Whole United States is Southern!'," 90–91; Adam Fairclough, *Better Day Coming: Blacks and Equality, 1890–2000* (New York, NY: Penguin Books, 2000).

9. Payne, "'The Whole United States is Southern!'," 89–91. Payne notes, W. E. B. Du Bois's essays in in the 1930s advocating for the development of race-based institutions contributed to his ouster from the NAACP, which embraced the fight for integration as a core component to their legal strategy. William Edward Burghardt Du Bois, *The Autobiography of W. E. B. Du Bois: A Soliloquy on Viewing My Life From the Last Decade of Its First Century* (International Publishers: New York, NY: Oxford University Press, 2004), 291–308.

10. Christing J. Faltz and Donald O. Leake, "The All-Black School Inherently Unequal or a Culture-Based Alternative," in *Beyond Desegregation*, 235.

11. Faltz and Leake, "The All-Black School Inherently Unequal or a Culture-Based Alternative," 235–237.

12. Jeanne Theoharis, "'I'd Rather Go to School in the South': How Boston's School Desegregation Complicates the Civil Rights Paradigm," in *Freedom North: Black Freedom Struggles Outside the South, 1940–1980*, eds. Jeanne Theoharis and Komozi Woodard (New York, NY: Palgrave McMillan, 2003); Ronald Formisano, *Boston Against Busing: Race, Class, and Ethnicity in the 1960s and 1970s*, 2nd Edition (Chapel Hill, NC: University of North Carolina Press, 2003); Dionne Danns, *Desegregating Chicago's Public Schools: Policy Implementation, Politics, and Protests, 1965–1985* (New York, NY: Palgrave Macmillan, 2014).

13. Danns, *Something Better for Our Children: Black Organizing in Chicago Public Schools, 1963–1971* (New York, NY: Routledge, 2003), 66–71.

14. Betty Washington, "No Retreat: Dr. Redmond," *The Chicago Defender*, August 26, 1967, 1.

15. Joseph Cronin, *The Control of Urban Schools: Perspective on the Power of Educational Reformers* (New York, NY: The Free Press, 1973) 182–183.

16. Derrick Bell, *Silent Covenants:* Brown v. Board of Education *and the Unfulfilled Hopes for Racial Reform* (New York, NY: Oxford University Press, 2004). 4–10, 181–189.

17. Ronald D. Henderson, et al., "High-Quality Schooling for African American Students," 181–82.

18. Ibid.

19. Cronin, *The Control of Urban Schools,* 189–202; Marilyn Gittell and Alan Hevesi, eds. *The Politics of Urban Education* (New York, NY: Frederick A. Praeger, Inc., 1969), 305–307; Marilyn Gittell and T. Edward Hollander, *Six Urban School Districts: A Comparative Study of Institutional Response* (New York, NY: Praeger, 1968), 75–76; George R. La Noue and Bruce L.R. Smith, *The Politics of School Decentralization* (Lexington, MA: Lexington Books, 1973), 15–19; Mario Fantini, et al., *Community Control and the Urban School* (New York, NY: Praeger Publishers, 1970), 71–76, 97–99, 228–236; Allan C. Ornstein, *Metropolitan Schools: Administrative Decentralization vs. Community Control* (Metuchen, NJ: The Scarecrow Press, Inc., 1974), ix–xi; Dan A. Lewis and Kathryn Nakagawa, *Race and Education Reform in the American Metropolis: A Study of School Decentralization* (Albany, NY: State University of New York Press, 1995), 1–9; Jane Anna Gordon, *Why They Couldn't Wait: A Critique of the Black-Jewish Conflict over Community Control in Ocean Hill-Brownsville (1967–1971)* (New York, NY: Routledge Falmer, 2001), 8–24; Todd-Breland, *Barbara Sizemore and the Politics of Black Educational Achievement.*

20. Joy Williamson, "Community Control with a Black Nationalist Twist: The Black Panther Party's Educational Programs," in *Black Protest Thought and Education,* ed. William H. Watkins (New York, NY: Peter Lang, 2005), 138, 152.

21. Elizabeth Todd-Breland, "'To Reshape and Redefine Our World': African American Political Organizing for Education in Chicago, 1968–1988," (PhD diss., University of Chicago, 2010), 115–143; Williamson, "Community Control with a Black Nationalist Twist," 143–148; Jack Dougherty, *More Than One Struggle: The Evolution of Black School Reform in Milwaukee* (Chapel Hill, NC: University of North Carolina Press, 2004), 170-178; Mwalimu J. Shujaa and Hannibal T. Afrik, "School Desegregation, the Politics of Culture, and the Council of Independent Black Institutions," in *Beyond Desegregation*, 254–56.

22. Ibid., Gittell, et al. *Local Control in Education: Three Demonstration School Districts in New York City* (New York, NY: Praeger Publishers, 1972), 1, 64; Jerald Podair, *The Strike That Changed New York, NY: Blacks, Whites, and the Ocean Hill-Brownsville Crisis* (New Haven, CT: Yale University Press, 2002), 4–8; Daniel Perlstein, *Justice, Justice: School Politics and the Eclipse of Liberalism* (New York, NY: Peter Lang, 2004), 6–8.

23. Ibid., Todd-Breland, *Barbara Sizemore and the Politics of Black Educational Achievement,* (forthcoming).

24. Alan B. Anderson and George W. Pickering, *Confronting the Color Line: The Broken Promise of the Civil Rights Movement in Chicago* (Athens, GA: University of Georgia Press, 1986), 91–98; Arthur M. Brazier, *Black Self-Determination: The Story of The Woodlawn Organization* (Grand Rapids, MI: Eerdmans Publishing Company, 1969), 16–20.

25. Brazier, *Black Self-Determination:* 11; John Hall Fish, *Black Power/White Control: The Struggle of The Woodlawn Organization in Chicago* (Princeton, NJ: Princeton University Press, 1973), 12.

26. Arnold R. Hirsch, *Making the Second Ghetto: Race and Housing in Chicago, 1940–1960*, 1983, Reprint (Chicago: Univ of Chicago Press, 1998), 157–170; Brazier, *Black Self-Determination*, 25; Fish, *Black Power/White Control*, 12.

27. Brazier, *Black Self-Determination*, 10–11; "Woodlawn," Encyclopedia of Chicago <http://www.encyclopedia.chicagohistory.org/pages/1378.html> 1 May 2010.

28. Brazier, *Black Self-Determination, 24*–25.

29. Ibid; Fish, *Black Power/White Control*, 13.

30. Arthur Brazier as quoted in Fish, *Black Power/White Control*, 176.

31. Brazier, *Black Self-Determination*, 17–18.

32. Brazier, *Black Self-Determination*, 11, 17–18, 60–62; Barbara A. Sizemore, *Walking in Circles: The Black Struggle for School Reform* (Chicago: Third World Press, 2008), 57–58; Fish, *Black Power/White Control*, 179–180.

33. Fish, *Black Power/White Control*, 220–221.

34. Included on the initial 21-member board were seven representatives from TWO, seven representatives from the University of Chicago, and seven representatives from the School Board. Brazier, *Black Self-Determination*, 61; Sizemore, *Walking in* Circles, 57–64.

35. Fish, *Black Power/White Control*, 201–205; Woodlawn Experimental Schools Project End of Project Report, June 1972, Allison Davis Papers, University of Chicago Special Collections, Chicago, IL.; Todd-Breland, *Barbara Sizemore and the Politics of Black Educational Achievement*, (forthcoming).

36. Woodlawn Experimental Schools Project End of Project Report; "Making the Schools a Vehicle for Cultural Pluralism," [1971?] Sol Tax Papers, University of Chicago Special Collections; Memorandum to Woodlawn Community Board Members, 9 May 1969, Levi Administration Records, University of Chicago Special Collections; Fish, *Black Power/White Control*, 201–205, 218.

37. Fish, *Black Power/White Control*, 218–220.

38. Ibid., 230.

39. After conflict at Hyde Park High School among the school's principal, teachers, students, and WESP staff, school system administrators took the power away from WESP. Faith C. Christmas, "Blasts U.S. School Order," *Chicago Daily Defender*, September 29, 1970, 2; "Charge Board Killing Black School Project," *Chicago Daily Defender*, October 17, 1970; Toni Anthony, "Arrest Nine Waller Students," *Chicago Daily Defender*, April 8, 1971, 1; Fish, *Black Power/White Control*, 227–229; Sizemore, *Walking in Circles*, 59–61; Todd-Breland, *Barbara Sizemore and the Politics of Black Educational Achievement*, (forthcoming).

40. Dionne Danns, "Chicago Teacher Reform Efforts and the Politics of Educational Change," in *Black Protest Thought and Education*, ed. William Watkins (New York, NY: Peter Lang, 2005), 179–180, 188–194.

41. Soyini Walton, Interview with Author, Audio Recording, Chicago, IL, October 9, 2014; Carol Lee, Interview with Author, Audio Recording, Chicago, IL, March 11, 2009; Haki Madhubuti, Interview with Author, Audio Recording, Chicago, IL, November 23, 2010.

42. Gail Foster, "Historically Black Independent schools," in *City Schools*, Diane Ravich and Joseph Viteritti, eds. (Baltimore, MD: Johns Hopkins Press, 2000), 293; Joan Davis Ratteray, "The Search for Access and Content in the Education of African Americans," in *Too Much Schooling Too Little Education: A Paradox of Black Life in White Societies*, ed. Mwalimu J. Shujaa (Trenton, NJ: Africa World Press, Inc., 1994), 128–129, 131–133.

43. Anderson, James D. *The Education of Blacks in the South*, 2–3; Alferdteen B. Harrison, *Piney Woods School: An Oral History* (Jackson, MS: University Press of Mississippi, 1982); Kamili Worth Hayes, "The Very Meaning of Our Lives: Howalton Day School and Black Chicago's Changing Educational Agenda, 1946–1985," *American Educational History Journal* 37,1 (2010): 75–94; Diana Slaughter and Deborah Johnson, "Introduction and Overview," in *Visible Now: Blacks in Private Schools*, eds. Diana Slaughter and Deborah Johnson (New York, NY: Greenwood Press, 1988), 1–5; Haroon Kharem and Eileen M. Hayes, "Separation or Integration: Early Black Nationalism and the Education Critique," in *Black Protest Thought and Education*, 82; Joan Davis Ratteray and Mwalimu Shujaa, "Defining a Tradition: Parental Choice in Independent Neighborhood Schools," in *Visible Now: Blacks in Private Schools*, 184–187.

44. Perlstein, "Minds Stayed on Freedom: Politics and Pedagogy in the African American Freedom Struggle," in *Black Protest Thought and Education*, 55.

45. Williamson, "Community Control with a Black Nationalist Twist," 152–154; Jon Hale, "'The Student as a Force for Social Change': The Mississippi Freedom Schools and Student Engagement," *The Journal of African American History* 96, 3(2011): 325–347.

46. Mwalimu J. Shujaa and Hannibal T. Afrik, "School Desegregation, the Politics of Culture, and the Council of Independent Black Institutions,"254.

47. Carol D. Lee, Interview with author, 2009.

48. Science for Nation Building Science Fair, [1977], Folder Science Curr., Soyini Walton Personal Papers, Private Collection, Chicago, IL; Kofi Lomotey and Craig C. Brookins, "Independent Black Institutions: A Cultural Perspective," in *Visible Now: Blacks in Private Schools*, eds. Diana Slaughter and Deborah Johnson (New York, NY: Greenwood Press, 1988), 168–172; Carol D. Lee, Interview with author, 2009.

49. Lomotey and Brookins, "Independent Black Institutions: A Cultural Perspective," 166; Foster, "Historically Black Independent schools," 293–294.

50. Shujaa and Afrik, "School Desegregation, the Politics of Culture, and the Council of Independent Black Institutions," 265.

51. Carol D. Lee, Interview with author, 2009.

52. Don L. Lee, *From Plan to Planet, Life Studies: The Need for Afrikan Minds and Institutions* (Detroit: Broadside Press, Institute of Positive Education, 1973), 9.

53. Mwalimu J. Shujaa, "Education and Schooling: You Can Have One Without the Other," in *Too Much Schooling Too Little Education*, 28; Carol D. Lee, "African-Centered Pedagogy: Complexities and Possibilities" in *Too Much Schooling Too Little Education*, 295–297; Agyei Akoto, "Notes on an Afrikan-centered Pedagogy," in *Too Much Schooling Too Little Education*, 319–325; Shujaa and Afrik, "School Desegregation, the Politics of Culture, and the Council of Independent Black Institutions," 266–267.

54. Scot Brown, *Fighting for US: Maulana Karenga, the US Organization, and Black Cultural Nationalism* (New York, NY: New York University Press, 2003), 163.

55. Brown, *Fighting for US*, 34–36, 163.

56. Lee, *From Plan to Planet*, 80.

57. Brown, *Fighting for US*, 68–69.

58. New Concept Handbook, 1978, 6, Folder IPE, Soyini Walton Personal Papers, Private Collection, Chicago, IL.

59. Carol D. Lee, Interview with author, 2009.

60. Gloria Ladson-Billings, "But That's Just Good teaching! The Case for Culturally relevant Pedagogy," *Theory Into Practice* 34, 3 (1995): 159–165; Gloria Ladson-Billings, *The Dreamkeepers: Successful Teachers of African American Children* (San Francisco, CA: Jossey-Bass Publishers, 1994); Carol D. Lee, "Profile of an Independent Black Institution: African-Centered Education at Work," *The Journal of Negro Education* 61, 2 (1992): 160–177; Carol D. Lee, *Culture, Literacy, & Learning: Taking Bloom in the Midst of the Whirlwind* (New York, NY: Teachers College Press, 2007); Carol D. Lee, "The Centrality of Culture to the Scientific Study of Learning and Development: How an Ecological Framework in Education Research Facilitates Civic Responsibility," *Education Researcher* 37, 5 (2008): 267–279.

61. Ibid.

62. Robert Barnes, "Divided Court Limits Use of Race by School Districts," *Washington Post*, June 29, 2007, < http://www.washingtonpost.com/wp-dyn/content/article/2007/06/28/AR2007 062800896.html> 1 May 2014; Kocoras, C. P., Consent Decree memorandum opinion, *United States v. Board of Education of the City of Chicago*, 80 C 5124, 2009; Chicago Public Schools, Magnet schools, consent decree <http://www.cps.edu/Pages/ MagnetSchoolsConsentDecree. aspx> 30 April 2014.

63. Todd-Breland, "'To Reshape and Redefine Our World,'" 169–170, 235–242; Mary Pattillo, "Everyday Politics of School Choice in the Black Community," *Du Bois Review* (forthcoming); Lisa Stulberg, *Race, Schools, and Hope: African Americans and School Choice After Brown* (New York, NY: Teachers College Press, 2008); Diane Ravitch, *Reign of Error: The Hoax of the Privatization Movement and the Danger to America's Public Schools* (New York, NY: Alfred A. Knopf, 2013), 15; Pauline Lipman, *The New Political Economy of Urban Education: Neoliberalism, Race, and the Right to the City* (New York, NY: Routledge, 2011); Michael Fabricant and Michelle Fine, *Charter Schools and the Corporate Makeover of Public Education: What's at Stake?* (New York, NY: Teachers College, 2012).

64. Ibid.

CHAPTER 11

AFRICAN AMERICAN EDUCATION IN THE AGE OF ACCOUNTABILITY, 1975–2005

R. Scott Baker
Wake Forest University

During the long Civil Rights Movement, public schools were battlegrounds in the struggle for racial equality. Decades of grassroots activism, NAACP litigation, and federal intervention expanded opportunity and combined with civil rights measures and Great Society programs to fuel significant gains in African American achievement and attainment. As African American activists continued to challenge the racial discrimination that pervaded schools, generations of moderate southern politicians—Jimmy Carter, James B. Hunt, William J. Clinton, and George W. Bush built bi-partisan coalitions that turned educational policy away from a civil rights agenda of opportunity and sought to promote racial equality through accountability. Seeing testing as a way of improving education and promoting racial equality, New South moderates became architects of American educational policy during the last quarter of the twentieth century, and crafted a new,

Using Past as Prologue, pages 275–305
Copyright © 2015 by Information Age Publishing
All rights of reproduction in any form reserved.

durable, and increasingly national discourse in education that emphasized accountability and achievement rather than access and opportunity.[1]

The turn to accountability in education was part of a broader shift in American politics from liberal to conservative ideas. "Between Richard Nixon's departure from the White House in 1974 and the return of the Republican George W. Bush in 2001," Godfrey Hodgson argued, "a new conservative consensus was forged." While African Americans and their liberal political allies used federal power to eliminate state-sanctioned segregation and promote racial equality through the expansion of opportunity, the new bi-partisan conservative consensus emphasized individual responsibility rather than state intervention. Patrick J. McGuinn and Maris A. Vinovskis associated the turn to accountability with the publication of *A Nation at Risk* in 1983, but Paul Manna and Jesse H. Rhodes have shown that this report was significant because it resonated with and accelerated an accountability movement that was already underway especially in the South. As the courts forced school districts to eliminate the vestiges of state-sponsored discrimination, moderate southern governors turned to minimum competency tests, (MCTs), as a politically expedient alternative to the task of making educational opportunities available to all students on equal terms. When states began requiring all students to pass a competency test to receive a high school diploma in the late 1970s and early 1980s, critics charged that competency testing was a conservative reaction to efforts to equalize educational opportunity. Peter W. Airasian argued that MCTs were an "administrative device" that educational and political authorities used to regain "power and control" over education that the courts assumed during the process of school desegregation. In a prescient critique, David K. Cohen and Walt Haney wrote that MCTs changed "ideas about responsibility," for educational achievement, and seemed "to promise a contraction of social responsibility." African American activists contested this contraction through political and legal campaigns. Charging that MCTs required the demonstration of skills that schools had not provided African American students with an opportunity to develop, African Americans challenged MCTs in the courts, but federal judges upheld the constitutionality of these exams as a remedy for the legacies of state-sponsored segregation and discrimination. The 1983 and 1984 decisions in *Debra P. v. Turlington* sanctioned broader testing and shaped the future of test based accountability in the decades to come.[2]

During the second wave of test based accountability in the 1980s, states raised high school graduation requirements and aligned standards with new tests to determine if students were learning more. Scholars of the standards movement such as John F. Jennings and Diane Ravitch have shown that the southern governors who led this movement in the 1980s built support for accountability by arguing that more demanding academic course requirements and the alignment of standards with more rigorous tests would improve the performance of African American students. Seeing standards based reforms as a way of ensuring that African American students were taught a common curriculum, the NAACP and a new generation of advocates including The Education Trust and The Citizen's Commission on Civil Rights endorsed these reforms, and standards, testing, and accountability were increasingly seen as civil rights measures. The rhetoric of standards based testing was alluring, but the accountability reforms of the 1980s failed to address the ways in which the intensification of racialized tracking, inequitable funding, and the resegregation of schools limited African American students' opportunities to learn. Studies by Linda Darling-Hammond, Joy Williamson-Lott, Amy Stuart Wells, John L. Rury, and others have demonstrated that comprehensive desegregation, Great Society programs and civil rights measures expanded opportunity and contributed to significant increases in African American educational achievement and attainment. By the late 1980s, however, Black educational advancement stalled as accountability became an increasingly popular and expedient means of promoting racial equality in education.[3]

American politics continued to shift to the right in the years after 1990, and moderate southern governors and presidents ratcheted up the stakes attached to tests. More comprehensive and coercive forms of test based accountability were institutionalized in elementary and secondary schools as Supreme Court rulings in *Board of Education v. Dowell* and *Freeman v. Pitts* sanctioned the resegregation of schools, and state legislatures resisted judicial mandates to redistribute educational resources more equitably. Linda M. McNeil has shown how testing intensified as schools resegregated and racial inequities within and between schools widened. Drawing on his contested record of using testing to close achievement gaps in Texas, George W. Bush consolidated the bi-partisan and bi-racial consensus about accountability that emerged in the 1970s and gathered strength in the 1980s and 1990s. Arguing that test based accountability would challenge the "soft bigotry of low expectations," in 2001 President Bush convinced bi-partisan majorities in the United States Congress to support No Child Left Behind, (NCLB). Passed following the September 11 attacks, NCLB elided troubling questions about the efficacy of test based accountability raised by prominent scholars such as Robert L. Linn and Richard Elmore.[4]

By the beginning of the twenty-first century, I contend, test-based accountability had largely eclipsed the expansion of educational opportunity as a way of promoting equality in education. Comprehensive desegregation, civil rights measures, and Great Society programs expanded opportunity, but NCLB, like the accountability reforms it evolved out of and derived from, treated the symptom—racial differences in achievement and attainment—rather than the cause—racial disparities in opportunity. The long struggle to desegregate schools remains unfinished, but the expansion of educational opportunity did more to promote racial equality than test based accountability.

OPPORTUNITY

During the middle decades of the twentieth century, African American activists and attorneys waged legal campaigns that convinced the Supreme Court to invalidate state-sanctioned segregation and redefine the meaning of educational opportunity. These campaigns began in the 1930s when Charles Hamilton Houston and Thurgood Marshall harnessed Black demands for broader educational opportunities to the constitutional guarantee of equal protection. Legal victories in teacher salary and higher education cases forced southern authorities to increase, but not equalize, spending on African American education and laid the groundwork for *Brown v. Board of Education.* In 1954, the Supreme Court held that "segregation with the sanction of law deprive[s] Negro children of the benefits they would receive in a racially integrated school system." Even where separate schools were tangibly equal, the court held, state-sanctioned segregation prevented African American students from the opportunity to "discuss and exchange views," prepare for the exercise of "public responsibilities," serve in the armed forces and "learn his profession. Separate educational facilities are inherently unequal." While the Court ruled that education is "a right which must be made available to all on equal terms," a congressionally mandated survey by James S. Coleman and his colleagues, found that by 1965 Black students continued to attend schools where classes where larger, the number of textbooks was not sufficient, and science and language laboratories less available. Like the *Brown* court, Coleman's *Equality of Educational Opportunity* exhaustively analyzed tangible school characteristics, but emphasized the benefits of social class and racial diversity in schools. The report showed that student achievement is "strongly related to the educational backgrounds and aspirations of other students in the school." By bringing Black and White students of different social classes and different educational backgrounds together in the same schools, Coleman concluded, desegregation would "in the long run" have "positive effects" and "consequences" for African Americans.[5]

The Coleman report was published as a rising tide of African American protest, enforcement of the Civil Rights Act of 1964, and increasingly insistent court orders forced officials to dismantle dual school systems. The direct action demonstrations that began in Birmingham in the spring of 1963 and spread throughout the nation in the summer raised the political and economic costs of continued segregation, and led President Kennedy to send a civil rights bill to congress. These demonstrations, Kennedy's assassination, and President Johnson's legislative skill convinced an anxious congress to pass the Civil Rights Act of 1964. Title IV of the Act authorized the Attorney General to initiate school desegregation suits. Title VI granted the Department of Health, Education, and Welfare (HEW) the power to enforce a ban on racial discrimination in schools that received federal funds. In 1965, Johnson secured passage of The Elementary and Secondary Education Act (ESEA) which made one billion dollars of federal aid available to school districts for compensatory education programs. Under guidelines promulgated by HEW in 1965 and 1966, to receive ESEA funds, school districts were required to increase the number of Black students who attended desegregated schools. Federal officials used the carrot of ESEA funds with the stick provided by Title VI to increase the percentage of African American students who attended desegregated schools. Prodded by new conceptions of desegregation crafted by HEW, in 1968, the Supreme Court in *Green v. New Kent County* ordered school officials to "come forward with a plan that promises to realistically work now," and create "unitary school system[s] in which racial discrimination would be eliminated root and branch." Finding that segregation limited opportunity, in 1969 Judge James B. McMillan instructed officials in Charlotte to fashion "affirmatively a school system as free as possible from the lasting effects of historical apartheid." In 1971, the Supreme Court endorsed McMillan's sweeping decision in *Swann v. Charlotte Mecklenburg*, and sanctioned the use of busing to eradicate "the vestiges of state imposed segregation." African American leaders praised the decision. "Separate but equal schools have never been equal and are not now equal. The only way to make certain that Black Americans receive an equal educational opportunity is to put them in the same classrooms with Whites," the Leadership Conference on Civil Rights declared.[6]

Even as educational authorities resisted and retaliated, the *Swann* decisions and persistent pressure from the NAACP, local activists, the courts, and HEW comprehensively desegregated schools. Between 1968 and 1980, the percentage of African American students in the South who attended schools that were 90 percent minority fell from 64 percent to 33 percent as the percentage of African Americans who attended majority White schools rose from 23 percent to 37 percent. As comprehensive desegregation increased African American access, officials resisted and retaliated—closing rather desegregating historically Black schools, dismissing and demoting thousands of educators, and marginalizing Black students. Testing and tracking intensified as officials used legally defensible means to separate Whites and Blacks in schools, creating structural barriers in an effort to interrupt integration.[7]

Persistent legal and political pressure expanded educational opportunity for African Americans. During the 1970s, African Americans and their liberal allies challenged structural barriers. HEW officials used provisions of the Civil Rights Act of 1964 to reduce the number of single race classrooms and expand African American access to advanced classes in desegregated schools. In Charlotte, where pressure from attorneys, local activists, the courts, and HEW was particularly intense, desegregation "undoubtedly improved educational opportunities for many African American students," Davidson Douglas argued. Jacquelyn Dowd Hall noted that "as Black students escaped from schools of concentrated poverty," they gained access to "preschool and after school programs, smaller classes, and superior facilities." African American students who graduated from high school in 1980, Amy Stuart Wells and her colleagues have shown were "more likely to be in close proximity to the same curriculum, teachers, and school resources and status." John L. Rury and Shirley A. Hill contended that while Black students "endured attacks, harassment, and indifference and hostility from educators, African American students persevered, and many ultimately made desegregation work in their favor."[8]

In spite of the discrimination that pervaded the process of desegregation, African Americans realized significant educational gains. Comprehensive school desegregation broadened educational opportunity and combined with Great Society programs and civil rights measures to produce substantial increases in African American achievement and a significant narrowing of the gap between Black and White reading scores on the National Assessment of Education Progress (NAEP) as Figure 11.1 shows. Among

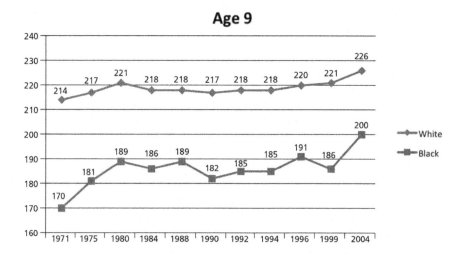

Figure 11.1 National Assessment of Educational Progress Reading Scores, 1971–2004. *Source:* National Center for Education Statistics, NAEP 2004 Trends in Academic Progress. Washington, DC: U.S. Department of Education, 2005. *(continued)*

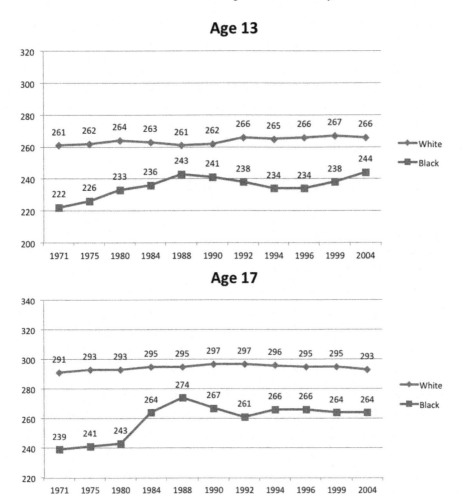

Figure 11.1 (continued) National Assessment of Educational Progress Reading Scores, 1971–2004. *Source:* National Center for Education Statistics, NAEP 2004 Trends in Academic Progress. Washington, DC: U.S. Department of Education, 2005.

seventeen year olds, for example, a fifty-two point gap in reading between Blacks and Whites in 1971 fell to thirty-one points by 1984. For all age groups, the greatest gains were achieved by students in the Southeast where schools were most comprehensively desegregated. African Americans also achieved striking gains in educational attainment. As James D. Anderson argued, "the inspiration and social climate," fostered by civil rights and desegregation movements accelerated African American educational advancement. Rury and Hill estimated that while 35 percent of African American nineteen year olds graduated from high school in 1960 compared to

65 percent of Whites, by 1980, 64 percent of African American nineteen year olds graduated from high school compared to 78 percent of Whites. Even as Blacks bore the burden of desegregation, schools provided African American students with access to networks that promoted social mobility. African American students who graduated from desegregated schools were more likely to graduate from college and secure higher paying jobs. Measures of achievement and attainment show that by the 1980s Blacks were closer to equality with Whites than at any time in the twentieth century.[9]

MINIMUM COMPENTENCY TESTING

It was in this context, a context defined by rising African American expectations and deepening economic anxieties that accountability began to eclipse opportunity as a way of promoting racial equality in education. As the courts continued to press authorities to dismantle the vestiges of segregation and discrimination, moderate New South politicians—Jimmy Carter of Georgia, Reuben Askew of Florida, James B. Hunt of North Carolina, Lamar Alexander of Tennessee, Richard Riley of South Carolina—turned to accountability as a politically expedient way of shifting the educational discourse away from concerns about opportunity and discrimination and forging a new, durable and increasingly national consensus about the need for greater student accountability in schools. While NAEP test results showed that students, especially African American students, were performing better than in the past, the malaise of the 1970s and sluggish economic growth, fueled the perception that the quality of schooling had deteriorated as schools desegregated. MCTs provided a way of talking about improving the quality of education and promoting economic growth without addressing the discrimination that persisted in desegregated schools.

The turn to accountability began during the minimum competency movement of the late 1970s and early 1980s. This movement was centered in the South, and MCTs were institutionalized as hundreds of school districts remained under court and HEW desegregation orders. The adoption of MCTs in the South illustrate how MCTs were intertwined with and helped displace desegregation as a remedy for the legacies of educational apartheid. In Florida, Sherman Dorn and Deanna Michael have shown, "once desegregation was underway the state began to develop and implement a state-wide testing program." In an address to the North Carolina Legislature in 1977, Governor James B. Hunt declared that "the trauma of desegregation was over," and convinced the legislature to begin requiring that all students pass a competency test to receive a high school diploma. Like MCTs established in Florida and North Carolina, Virginia's competency program required students to demonstrate mastery of the math and reading skills thought necessary to function in society, and explicitly held students responsible for passing the test. Moderate Black leaders in Florida, Virginia, North Carolina, and South Carolina tended to support competency testing. Dr. Prenzell Robinson, the president of historically African American St. Augustine College, endorsed MCTs because they would "help underachievers." Dudley Flood, the highest ranking African American official in the North Carolina State Department of Education, argued that MCTs would "provide relief for kids" who were neglected in desegregated schools. However, Gerda Steele, the Education Director in the NAACP's national office, charged that schools in North Carolina, Virginia, Florida, and other states "are not providing students with instruction on completing a tax form, balancing a checkbook, or understanding price differences in comparison shopping—areas measured by the test." Proponents of MCTs responded to African American opposition by arguing that Black students would "benefit most from competency testing," as one official in North Carolina noted. MCTs were adopted in every southern state by 1986 as Figure 11.2 shows.[10]

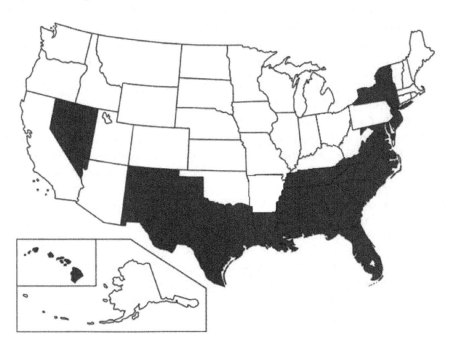

Figure 11.2   States that required State-Wide High School MCTs, 1976–1986. Florida, 1976, New Jersey, 1976, North Carolina, 1977, Maryland, 1977, Nevada, 1977, New York, 1977, Virginia, 1978, Hawaii, 1978, Alabama, 1981, Tennessee, 1981, Mississippi, 1982, South Carolina, 1984, Texas, 1984, Georgia, 1985, Louisiana, 1986, New Mexico, 1986. John Robert Warren and Rachael B. Kulick, "Modeling Enactment of High School Exit Exam Policies," *Social Forces 86,* (2007): 216–217.

By the fall of 1978, competency testing had become one of the most contested issues in American education. Support came not simply from statehouses, but also from the White House where Deanna Michael argued President Carter "continued his strong support for the use of testing to increase accountability" that he developed as governor of Georgia when the schools were desegregated. Like other southern moderates, Carter believed that testing would motivate students to learn more. After Ronald Mottl, a conservative Democrat from Ohio who shared Carter's opposition to busing, scheduled hearings on a bill to establish a national competency test, Carter told HEW secretary Joseph Califano to develop an administration proposal for a "mandatory" national achievement test. In the spring of 1978, Califano convened a conference where former HEW secretary Harold Howe raised "the difficult question of whether the national mood for improving basic skills performance has hidden within it overtones of racism." At another conference, scholars warned that "any setting of statewide minimum competency standards for the awarding of the high school diploma exceeds present measurement arts, and will create more social problems than they can conceivably solve." While attempts to establish a national test failed, the Carter administration supported the 1978 reauthorization of the ESEA that provided federal funding for state MCTs, and increased the capacity of state testing agencies to develop and administer these tests.[11]

As state officials proceeded with plans to implement competency programs, African Americans challenged the constitutionality of MCTs in Georgia, North Carolina, and Florida. African American plaintiffs charged that MCTs perpetuated the effects of past and present discrimination through tests that unconstitutionally denied disproportionate numbers of African Americans diplomas. Protracted litigation in Florida established precedents that shaped the future of test based accountability in the United States. Florida began administering a functional literacy test in 1977, but Judge George Carr found that African American students who were required to pass MCTs, began their schooling in separate and unequal institutions where disparities in physical facilities, course offerings, and instructional materials limited African American access to knowledge and skills that were tested. After the schools were formally desegregated, discrimination persisted through "disparate busing schedules, lingering racial stereotypes, disproportionate terminations of Black principals, and a high incidence of suspensions. At the eleventh hour and with virtually no warning," Carr held students were required to pass a hastily constructed test "covering content that may not have [been] taught" in the public schools. "Punishing the victims of past discrimination for deficits created by an inferior educational environment neither constitutes a remedy nor creates better educational opportunities," Carr ruled. School officials could continue to administer the test, but Carr's 1979 ruling in *Debra P. v. Turlington* enjoined officials from using test scores to deny diplomas until all students pursued their education in schools "without the taint of the dual system."[13]

Educational authorities removed the "taint of the dual system" by narrowing the curriculum, teaching to the test, and creating remedial programs that sharply increased African American pass rates on MCTs. W. James Popham who designed and defended Florida's program in court believed that MCTs "systematically isolated student deficits in fundamental skills" and allowed teachers to correct those deficits in remedial programs. During congressional hearings on MCTs in the South, one school official from Goldsboro, North Carolina noted that students who did not pass the test in the fall of their junior year were placed in remedial classes where "the entire curriculum is based on the competency tests and the teaching of basic skills." A 1984 survey by the Southern Regional Educational Board found that "teaching the material" and better "test taking skills," improved student performance. In Florida, African American pass rates rose from 22 percent in 1979 to 90 percent in 1983. Similar increases occurred in Georgia, Virginia, North Carolina, and Texas in the years after MCTs were introduced.[13]

Eager to end judicial involvement in the resolution of the complex educational problems brought to the surface by desegregation, in the early 1980s the courts lifted injunctions on diploma sanctions and upheld the constitutionality of MCTs. In 1983, Judge Carr ruled that "educational opportunity" in Florida "had been equalized in a constitutional sense." Finding that the state's MCT was a "fair" assessment of what was taught in the public schools, Carr held that "the test was necessary to overcome whatever effects of past purposeful segregation remain in schools." A year later the Eleventh Circuit Court of Appeals affirmed Carr's decision. The court acknowledged "discomfort over unfairness if discriminatory vestiges caused students to fail the test," but held that competency programs and the diploma sanction remedied these vestiges by creating "objective standards" and "a climate of order" that motivated students and produced "remarkable improvement" in the percentage of Black students who passed the MCTs. The *Debra P.* rulings established MCTs as a constitutional remedy for the vestiges of discrimination and an alternative to court ordered desegregation. As test based accountability began to eclipse the expansion of opportunity as a way of promoting racial equality in education, holding individual students responsible for outcomes became what Daniel Koretz called "a cornerstone of American educational policy."[14]

While the proponents of MCTs argued that accountability would benefit Blacks, diploma sanctions reduced African American educational attainment. Barbara Learner, who served as an expert witness for the state of Florida in *Debra P.*, asserted that the effects of minimum competency "were uniformly positive" for minority students. However, Robert C. Serow's analysis of diploma sanctions in Virginia, Maryland, North Carolina,

Florida, and other states showed that "while the diploma denial *rate* in most states tends to be small, the actual number of students so penalized is actually quite substantial." In 1980, for example, the state of North Carolina denied diplomas to 984 African Americans or 4.4 percent of the Black seniors compared to 288 Whites or 0.5 percent of White seniors. As states phased in competency requirements and enforced diploma sanctions in the 1980s, Serow warned that "that before too long there may be 100,000 or more students who have completed the required twelve years of school without receiving a diploma." Drawing on 1990 census data, Thomas S. Dee has shown that diploma sanctions reduced "the probability of completing high school" among African Americans. Rather than benefitting Blacks, as proponents claimed, MCTs exacted a significant and disproportionate toll on African American students. This result presaged the broader adverse effects of test based accountability policies on African American students in the decades to come.[15]

STANDARDS BASED ACCOUNTABILITY IN THE 1980s

During the 1980s, accountability continued to displace opportunity as a means of promoting racial equality in education as states stiffened high school course graduation requirements, developed standards about what all students should know, and began administering new more rigorous secondary tests. Scholars tend to attribute these reforms to the publication of *A Nation at Risk* (*ANAR*) in 1983, but as Jesse Rhodes argued, this report is "best seen in the context of a broader movement that both preceded and elaborated on it." *ANAR* is significant not because it set a new direction in American education, but because the report resonated with, and accelerated, the turn to accountability that was already well underway especially in the South. *ANAR* sharpened this turn by making Great Society programs and court ordered desegregation causes of purported declines in student achievement and slow economic growth. *ANAR* lent legitimacy to President Ronald Reagan's efforts to dismantle desegregation, and endorsed reforms that continued to shift educational policy and practice away from the expansion of opportunity and emphasize the need for higher standards and more testing. During the 1980s, the NAACP developed a "more realistic" position on testing, and along with a new generation of civil rights advocates, endorsed standards based accountability as a way of ensuring that all students were taught a common curriculum. But as states held all students to new higher standards of performance, growing racial segregation, within and between schools, and unequal and inadequate funding, limited African American opportunity. By the end of the 1980s, Black educational advancement stalled.[16]

President Reagan's Commission on Educational Excellence was charged with "assessing the degree to which major social and educational changes in the last quarter century have affected student achievement." The Commission argued that the achievement gains made after the Soviet Union launched Sputnik in 1957 had been "squandered." Emphasizing "an unbroken decline" in SAT scores between 1963 and 1980, the report claimed that "the educational skills" of the current generation of students "will not even approach those of their parents." A significant cause of the alleged collapse in achievement, were "multiple and conflicting demands" placed on schools by civil rights measures and court ordered desegregation. Using the schools to solve "social and political problems" the commissioner's argued "exacted an educational cost." University of Utah President, David P. Gardner, who chaired the commission, believed that "the most serious problems arose from the greater inclusion of economically and socially deprived and minority members that tend to lower demands on all students." Enough attention had been devoted to equality of opportunity, the report argued. Schools needed to focus on excellence in order to promote economic growth.[17]

To promote excellence, *ANAR* urged state and local officials to raise high school graduation requirements and increase testing. Attempts to advance racial equality through the schools, the report asserted, led educators to lose sight of the "basic purposes of schooling." During the 1960s and 1970s, educators created "a cafeteria style curriculum," and as a result, the percentage of students enrolled in the general track that was neither academic nor vocational grew from 12 percent in 1964 to 42 percent in 1979. Noting that "a significant movement" to raise high school graduation requirements "had already begun," the report recommended that states adopt what it called the New Basics: a high school curriculum that required all students to complete four years of English, three years of math, science and social studies and two years of foreign language for the college bound. While *ANAR* noted that "all regardless of race or class are entitled to a fair chance," the report did not question or challenge the structural barriers to equality within schools, arguing that "the grouping of students should be guided by the academic progress of students and their instructional needs." *ANAR* urged educators to create "new equally demanding" but tracked courses "for students who did not plan to continue their formal education immediately." The commission renewed calls for a nationwide (but not federal) system of state and local standardized tests administered "at major transition points from one level of schooling to another and particularly from high school to college." Explicitly criticizing MCTs as falling "far short of what was needed," the report recommended that all students be required to pass "rigorous exams before they received diplomas."[18]

When *ANAR* was released at a White House Ceremony in April of 1983, Reagan praised the commission's "call for an end to federal intrusion" in education. During the 1980 presidential campaign, Reagan pledged to "remove control of our schools from the courts and the federal government and return it to local school boards where it belongs." He believed that Great Society Programs "encroached on local prerogatives," "wasted money," and "made the schools worse." In 1981, Reagan persuaded Congress to cut funding for the ESEA by $1 billion or 15 percent, and devolve control over the allocation of ESEA funds to state and local authorities through block grants. As Adam Nelson noted, the 1981 reauthorization of the ESEA brought a "sudden retreat from federal efforts to promote compliance with civil rights statutes and desegregation guidelines and left it to states to address these problems." Reagan's 1981 budget also eliminated funding for innovative school desegregation programs.[19]

Reagan used *ANAR* to support his campaign to dismantle court ordered desegregation. Echoing the commission's contention that the schools had been asked to do too much, Reagan argued that the enforcement of civil rights laws and court ordered desegregation "compromised the quality of learning in our classrooms." Court orders requiring schools to "correct long standing injustices in our society" such as racial segregation were directly related, Reagan asserted, to declining student achievement. In a campaign stop in Charlotte on the eve of the 1984 election, Reagan denounced busing because it made "innocent children pawns in a social experiment. And we've found out that it failed." Gary Orfield and Susan Eaton have shown that Reagan's Justice Department "supported some of the school districts that the Justice Department had once sued for intentional segregation." In 1985, courts in Virginia sanctioned the return to segregated neighborhood schools in Norfolk. "After only two decades," Hall noted, "the courts effectively abandoned the effort to enforce desegregation," and schools began to gradually resegregate by race as well as class. The Reagan administration's retreat from federal efforts to promote equal educational opportunity continued to shift decision making to the states.[20]

Moderate southern governors anticipated and endorsed the commission's and Reagan's critique of desegregation and an accountability agenda of higher standards, more academic courses, and tougher graduation tests. In March of 1983, several weeks before *ANAR* was published, the *New York Times* reported that "sweeping changes in educational policy are being pursued throughout the South by a growing number of political leaders." Several governors including James B. Hunt, William J. Clinton, and Lamar Alexander served on education commissions that issued excellence reports foreshadowing the arguments in *ANAR*. Hunt, for example, convened and chaired the Education Commission of the States Task Force on Education for Economic Growth which published *Action for Excellence* in 1983. The *New*

York Times praised Hunt for "enacting sweeping education reforms without expanding the budget by using standardized tests as key measures." Hunt shared the commission's and Reagan's views on equity arguing that the discourse in education "has been too long dominated by fairness issues." Hunt believed that "the weight of multiple tasks led schools to struggle and sometimes stumble. It is time to put learning first."[21]

Putting learning first meant expecting more of students and increasing the number of academic courses that were required to graduate from high school. By the end of 1980s, forty-three states had raised high school graduation requirements from as few as sixteen courses to as many as twenty-four courses. Several states approved new requirements in math, science, and computer literacy, and Missouri, Oklahoma, Rhode Island, and Virginia established different requirements for standard and college preparatory diplomas. States also developed standards defining what all students should know and be able to do and thirty-seven states established statewide tests to measure what students were learning. Governors, led by New South moderates, argued that higher graduation requirements and the alignment of standards with new end of course tests would ensure that students were actually learning more. The National Governors Association declared that new course requirements and more rigorous tests would raise the performance of all children.[22]

By speaking to one of the central arguments in legal challenges to MCTs—that tests required Black students to demonstrate knowledge and skills that they did not necessarily have an opportunity to learn—the reforms of the 1980s increased African American support for accountability. While the NAACP was critical of *ANAR* for emphasizing excellence rather than equity, the association expressed support for additional high school graduation requirements and achievement tests as a way of ensuring that all students had an opportunity to study a common curriculum. The NAACP called for a moratorium on minimum competency testing in 1978 and challenged the constitutionality of MCTs in the courts, but during the 1980s, the association began to develop what NAACP Executive Secretary Benjamin Hooks called "a more realistic" attitude toward testing. At a conference on legal strategy, NAACP leaders declared that since tests are "here to stay, time and effort would be better used to find ways to [help] African Americans successfully pass these barriers to entry. Until the tests are changed, we must help our youth prepare for them." A 1987 report argued that all students should have "equal opportunities for developing test sophistication (coaching)," and recommended that test scores be "disaggregated" by race. The association also began to support efforts to raise African American SAT scores in test prep clinics in Atlanta, New York, and San Francisco.[23]

The NAACP's more realistic stance on testing was part of a bi-racial consensus about the need for higher standards and greater accountability that gathered strength during the 1980s. Facing financial shortfalls, The NAACP secured "more funding from corporations," and Timothy Minchin and John A. Salmond suggested that corporate funding "dented the NAACP's social activism." By the 1980s, Jack Greenberg, who had served as President of the NAACP Legal Defense and Education Fund, recalls that the NAACP "no longer had the primacy it held in years past," and a new generation of organizations including The Citizen's Commission on Civil Rights and The Education Trust emerged as important advocates for African American education.[24]

As desegregation efforts began to wane, William L. Taylor, a long time civil rights attorney, created The Citizen's Commission on Civil Rights in 1981. Taylor believed that "while bad testing should be challenged the major harm being done to children was not by testing." In political and policy debates, Taylor argued that "good assessments [were] the means for linking higher standards with determination of student progress for the purpose of accountability." Kati Haycock, who worked with the Children's Defense Fund, shared many of Taylor's views. In 1988, Haycock secured funding from the Ford Foundation, the Carnegie Corporation, and the Hewlett Foundation and established The Education Trust. The Education Trust produced critical reports documenting disparities in funding and achievement, but the organization proved willing to relax demands for opportunity to learn standards and greater spending in order to expand accountability, a position that endeared The Education Trust to conservatives. Crafted during the increasingly conservative 1980s, this new African American educational agenda defined standards, testing, and accountability as civil rights measures that would ensure that students had access to a rigorous curriculum.[25]

Rather than addressing what was perhaps that most significant unfinished business of the long struggle to desegregate schools, the standards based reforms of the 1980s reinforced racialized tracking, and, to a considerable extent, excellence came at the expense of equity. Black students remained underrepresented in advanced classes with the greatest resources and the highest quality instruction and overrepresented in lower level classes where curricula and instruction were generally weaker. During the early 1970s, the Department of Education's Office of Civil Rights (OCR) aggressively challenged tracking that produced racially identifiable and racially isolated classes, but Congress eliminated this enforcement authority during the Carter Administration. As a result, African American access to advanced classes declined. In 1978, OCR data showed that 2.1 percent of Whites in the United States were enrolled in gifted programs compared to 1.3 percent of Blacks. By the middle of the 1980s, Kenneth Meier's comprehensive study of 174 large school districts found that "a White student is 3.2 times more likely to be assigned to a gifted class than a Black student." In North Carolina, African American enrollment in gifted and talented programs declined. Between 1978 and 1986, African Americans comprised 30 percent of the students and Whites comprised 68 percent of the students in the North Carolina public schools. However, the percentage of gifted and talented students who were African American fell from 12 percent in 1978 to 6.9 percent by 1986 as the percentage of students in gifted and talented programs who were White rose from 87 percent to more than 90 percent.[26]

Racialized tracking systems limited African American access and achievement. As Roslyn Mickelson has shown: "the effects of ability grouping and tracking are cumulative: young students who possess similar social backgrounds and cognitive abilities but who learn in different tracks become more and more academically dissimilar." Racial disparities at the secondary level were compounded because White students received more information about and had greater access to advanced classes. As high school students were required to complete new graduation requirements, studies by the Education Trust showed that African Americans remained underrepresented in higher level courses and disproportionately represented in lower level courses and special education programs.[27]

As a result, most African American students did not necessarily have an opportunity to learn the more advanced course material or the higher level skills that the new end-of-course tests sought to measure. It was far easier to mandate additional coursework than ensure what was taught in new courses. New graduation requirements required students to complete more academic courses and as enrollment in these courses surged, Thomas Toch found that there was "a proliferation of courses that treated academic courses with extreme superficiality. The vast majority of students were getting little more exposure to rigorous course work than they did previously." William Clune and his colleagues argued that higher graduation requirements failed to get students into more "rigorous courses," produce a more "uniform curriculum," or convey "higher-order thinking skills." As officials in North Carolina administered new end of course algebra tests, they acknowledged that African Americans were "underrepresented in algebra classes across the state" and that not all students had "the opportunity," to prepare for the test. During the 1980s and early 1990s, advocates pressed for national opportunity to learn standards to ensure that all students were provided with the chance to learn what was tested, but attempts to enact these national standards floundered in the face of conservative opposition in congress and the Clinton administration's unwillingness to aggressively promote them.[28]

While raising graduation requirements did not increase most African American students' opportunities to learn, more demanding high school exams exacerbated the problem of teaching to the test that began to emerge during the minimum competency movement. By attaching tests to new ostensibly more demanding courses, politicians and policymakers limited the intended benefits of these reforms. As one study noted, end-of-course tests reinforced "rote instruction." During the 1980s, there was increasing evidence that test preparation practices were most commonly used in predominately minority schools. Linda M. McNeil has shown that accountability reforms established in Texas in 1984 created "a system of testing and test preparation" that increasingly came to "substitute in minority schools for the curriculum available to more privileged students." Commercial test-prep scripts began to take "the place of traditional curricula and instructional activities for students." In a report to the College Board in 1985, Linda Darling-Hammond argued, that "the effects of these practices are worst for those who most need improved educational programs. Those who start out 'behind' receive the most drill on skills, and the least exposure to real books, ideas, and writing that might ultimately close skills gaps."[29]

Unequal and inadequate funding exacerbated these problems. Critics charged that standards based tests of the 1980s held students to the same level of performance without providing equal educational opportunities. During the 1980s, advocates filed dozens of legal challenges that sought more equitable and adequate funding through court enforcement of state constitutional obligations that required, for example, a "thorough and efficient" a "general and uniform" "an adequate" or "a sound basic" education. School finance reformers in North Carolina argued that the state required "a uniform level of performance without providing a uniform level of resources. We think the issue of equality in resources should be addressed before the state demands equal performance." Plaintiffs in low wealth and predominately minority Robeson County, North Carolina sued the state arguing that it was not complying with the state's constitutional obligation to provide "equal opportunities for all students." A state court rejected this claim, ruling that while the constitution required equal access to schools, it did not require absolutely "equal educational opportunities" for all students. Courts in other states issued similar rulings. In Georgia, for example, the court held that "education is vital but not fundamental." Between 1983 and 1989, Margaret Rose Westbrook has shown, "no state invalidated its funding scheme." While students were responsible for performance, state court decisions held that educational authorities were not accountable for providing adequate funding and resources.[30]

By the end of the 1980s, African American educational advancement stalled. After more than a decade and a half of significant increases, the NAEP reading scores of African Americans began to decline and achievement gaps that had narrowed between 1971 and 1988 began to widen as Figure 11.1 shows. The confluence of policies and practices associated with the turning away from the expansion of educational opportunity—the resegregation of schools, the intensification of racialized tracking, and unequal and inadequate funding combined to limit African American opportunity and achievement. Recent research also shows that after increasing during the 1960s and 1970s, the African American graduation rate stopped rising in the 1980s when two of three African Americans and three of four Whites completed high school. Accountability policies, higher course graduation requirements, and high school tests contributed to this stagnation. Because African American students did not necessarily have the opportunity to learn what state's required for graduation, accountability policies did more to limit African American educational attainment than raise African American achievement. Thomas S. Dee estimates that "among Black students, higher curricular requirements reduced the probability of graduating from high school by roughly two percentage points." The stalling of African American educational advancement might have prompted a reconsideration of the turn to accountability and greater attention to the expansion of educational opportunity, but as the political and legal landscape continued to shift to the right, momentum for higher standards, more testing, and greater accountability continued to grow.[31]

A TIME FOR RESULTS, 1990–2005

By the 1990s, the bi-partisan and bi-racial consensus that emerged in the late 1970s and gathered strength in the decade that followed made test based accountability the central focus of educational reform. During the third phase in the evolution of test based accountability in the years after 1990, politicians and policymakers implemented more comprehensive and coercive forms of accountability and ratcheted up the stakes attached to test results. As states heightened pressure on students and teachers to raise scores and continued to resist the redistribution of educational resources, a series of Supreme Court decisions signaled the end of court supervised school desegregation. While a growing number of states, including ten states in the North and West, adopted more challenging high school graduation tests, the post 1990 reforms placed increased emphasis on testing students in elementary schools and using state test results to rank schools, sanction educators, and retain students. As in earlier phases, these reforms were promoted by moderate southern politicians and policymakers including Presidents William J. Clinton and George W. Bush. Civil Rights advocates such as The Education Trust and The Citizen's Commission endorsed more comprehensive forms of test based accountability and became part of a coalition of moderate politicians, federal judges, business leaders, and educational conservatives that built support for passage of NCLB.[32]

Dominated by Nixon, Reagan, and George H. W. Bush appointees, the Supreme Court continued to dismantle desegregation plans in the 1990s paving the way for the steady resegregation of schools. The Supreme

Court's decisions in *Board of Education v. Dowell* in 1991 and *Freeman v. Pitts* a year later placed clear limits on what educational authorities were required to do to address the vestiges of state-sanctioned segregation and discrimination. *Dowell* found that districts in which students were racially isolated could be declared unitary, and absolved of court oversight, if educational authorities had made "good faith efforts" to achieve unitary status. Although more than 50 percent of Black students in DeKalb County, a suburb of Atlanta, were attending schools that were more than 90 percent Black, Justice Kennedy writing for a conservative majority, held in *Pitts* that "where resegregation is a product not of state action but of private choices, it does not have constitutional implications." *Dowell* and *Pitts* declared that enough had been done to make educational opportunities available to African Americans on equal terms, and sanctioned the return to segregated schools. By the end of the 1990s, 200 school districts had been released from court oversight. While the percentage of Black students in majority White schools rose to 42 percent in 1986, by 2002, less than 30 percent of Black students were enrolled in majority White schools. Increasing segregation concentrated poverty in majority African American schools. In the region and the nation, African Americans were considerably more likely to attend schools where a majority of students were poor. By 2002, more than 60 percent of Black students in the United States attended high poverty schools compared to 18 percent of Whites. In the South, 62 percent of Black students and 7 percent of Whites were enrolled in schools where 90 to 100 percent of students were poor, and 82 percent of Whites and 5 percent of Blacks attended schools where less than 10 percent of students were poor. Students in high-poverty schools were taught by teachers with fewer formal credentials and offered fewer advanced courses.[33]

As the possibility of continuing comprehensive desegregation dimmed, school finance reformers used a newly developed adequacy theory to secure decisions in state courts requiring levels of funding that were necessary to bring students to acceptable levels of performance. But decisions in some states did as much to legitimize accountability systems as equalize or redistribute resources. The Education Trust argued that standards and testing created "a commitment that policymakers will provide oversight and *resources* to meet those standards." Adequacy advocates prevailed in Arizona, Kentucky, New Jersey, New York, North Carolina, and Texas, but as James E. Ryan has shown, governors and state legislatures "fiercely opposed the judicially mandated redistribution of educational resources to districts attended primarily by minority students," and opportunity continued to be "strongly influenced by different levels of property wealth." While adequacy arguments were designed to promote more equitable funding, rulings in North Carolina and Texas illustrate how state accountability systems were used to elide constitutional obligations. In North Carolina, the state court made the performance of students on state tests rather than "substantially equal funding," the standard for demonstrating compliance with the state constitutional guarantee of equal educational opportunity. In Texas, the court held that the state constitution required substantially equal resources for schools, and in 1989 ordered the legislature to take immediate action to address per pupil spending that ranged from as little as $2,112 per student to as much as $19,333 per student. In 2005, however, the Texas Court adopted a new "results oriented" standard of funding that established "no duty to fund public education at any level other than what is required to achieve [the constitutionally mandated] 'general diffusion of knowledge'" as measured by state test scores. The court rejected plaintiff's arguments because of "undisputed evidence that standardized test scores were rising." As adequacy advocates yoked school spending to state definitions of proficiency, test scores, not opportunity, became the arbiter of whether or not a state complied with constitutional requirements.[34]

Testing intensified as schools resegregated and funding disparities persisted. By the 1990s, a growing number of states required the annual administration of standardized tests. State accountability policies raised the stakes attached to test scores and used them to rate educational institutions in an effort to compel teachers to raise achievement. In Texas, test scores were disaggregated by race and ethnicity and school ratings based on test scores were published in local newspapers. Georgia Governor Roy Barnes established a test based accountability program where scores were used to identify failing schools, and shame educators who worked in them. While Florida's schools were plagued by textbook shortages and overcrowding, in 1995 the state commissioner of education publicized a list of the lowest performing schools in an effort to spur educators and students toward higher levels of performance. Schools that received A and B ratings were given higher funding in the form of teacher stipends while those with D and F ratings received no support. These incentives encouraged teachers to abandon low performing schools and transfer to higher performing schools. While ratings, sanctions, and incentives were politically popular, evidence suggests that they did little to increase the capacity of schools to improve African American students' opportunities to learn. "Without substantial investments in capacity," Richard Elmore argued, ratings, sanctions, and incentives tend to "aggravate the existing inequalities between low-performing and high-performing schools and students."[35]

As critics raised questions about the capacity of states and districts to turn-around low performing schools, President Bill Clinton and Texas Governor George W. Bush campaigned to end social promotion, the advancement of students to higher grades on the basis of age rather than performance on tests. In a 1998 memo to Secretary of Education Richard Riley, who served as governor in South Carolina during the 1980s, Clinton called for the "appropriate use of tests and other indicators" to determine if students "meet rigorous academic standards at key points in their schooling career. Students should not be promoted past fourth grade if they cannot read independently and should not enter high school without a solid foundation in math." In Texas, Bush endorsed the retention of third, fourth, and eighth graders who did not pass the Texas Assessment of Academic Skills (TASS) tests in math, reading, and writing. By 2001, seventeen states had enacted policies requiring students in elementary school to pass a standardized test to be promoted and thirteen enacted policies to use standardized test scores to make promotion decisions in middle schools. Although plaintiffs in several southern states challenged the use of test scores to retain students, the courts, citing *Debra P.*, upheld the practice because it benefitted "low achievers" and provided "a remedial year [to] "catch up on skills" and "perform better in the future."[36]

Yet, states did not have the capacity to end social promotion. When officials in North Carolina considered not promoting fifth graders who had not passed math tests, they confronted the problems posed by retaining 20 percent of all fifth graders and 38 percent of African American fifth graders an estimated 22,000 students. The chair of the state board of education, Phil Kirk complained that principals don't have "the backbone to enforce the policy," but many principals agreed with the conclusions of the National Research Council that "simply repeating a grade does not generally improve achievement; moreover, it increases the dropout rate." Without the funds or the facilities to retain so many students, North Carolina's attempt to end social promotion floundered in the face of the complex issues that were well beyond the capacity of tests to solve.[37]

Like other forms of test based accountability, the use of standardized tests to retain students had a racially disparate impact on African Americans. While states pledged "extra help," and "focused interventions" including tutoring and summer school, states did not necessarily provide funding. Moreover, as David K. Cohen argued, there was "an appreciable lack of professional capacity" about how to improve instruction in "the schools in which improvement is most needed many of which chiefly enroll disadvantaged students." A 1997 National Research Council report showed that by age eleven, "5 to 10 percent more Blacks than Whites are enrolled below grade level. By age seventeen, "rates of age-grade retardation range from 40 to 50 percent among Blacks compared to 25 to 35 percent among Whites." Although the American Psychological Association, the American Educational Research Association, and the National Council on Measurement guidelines stated that it was inappropriate to use standardized test scores by themselves to retain pupils, getting tough on students, teachers, and schools was more expedient than making the kinds of investment and capacity that might have improved instruction and opportunity.[38]

The combination of increased retention and new high school exit exams (HSEE) established in the 1990s limited African American educational advancement. By the end of the 1990s, more than 20 states and several large urban districts required students to pass high school exit exams (HSEE) and in some cases end-of-course tests in academic subjects. Politicians and policymakers argued that new more challenging tests would force teachers to align instruction with state standards and ensure that students were learning more challenging content. While African American and Latino plaintiffs in Louisiana, Kentucky, and Texas challenged the constitutionality of these exams, the courts, citing *Debra P.,* upheld their constitutionality. As with student retention, court decisions were at odds with the opinions of experts. Jennifer J. Holme and her colleagues' comprehensive review of the effects of HSEE concluded that "the most methodologically rigorous studies are nearly unanimous in the conclusion that 'more difficult' exit tests are associated with increases in dropout rates, delays in graduation, and increased rates of GED attainment." In Florida, the state with the best longitudinal evidence, racial disparities in pass rates widened after the *Debra P.* decisions of 1983 and 1984. By 2003, when students were required to pass the new Florida Comprehensive Assessment Test, 19 percent of African American students and 5 percent of Whites were denied diplomas on the basis of test scores. Racially disparate results were also evident in Texas, California, and other states.[39]

Although proponents of accountability asserted that testing would close achievement gaps and promote equality, critics questioned the validity of test results. In an influential report, David Grissmer and Ann Flanagan argued that accountability systems in Texas and North Carolina "produced evidence of disadvantaged student's scores rising more rapidly than those of advantaged students." As governor of Texas between 1994 and 2000, George W. Bush won acclaim for his reform efforts. Amy Wilkens of The Education Trust asserted that "the Texas model is one of the best hopes for introducing equity into American education." However, state NAEP test scores show that achievement gaps between White and Black students in Texas increased between 1994 and 1998 according to a study by Stephen P. Klein. This evidence Robert L. Linn argued "raises serious questions about the trustworthiness of TAAS results." In North Carolina, another state that was seen as a model for NCLB, Aubrey Amrein and David Berliner showed that a narrowing of racial achievement gaps on NAEP math tests during the 1990s was an "illusion" produced by a sharp increase in the "exclusion" of students with Individualized Education Plans who were disproportionately African American.[40]

The accountability reforms of the 1990s, like those of the 1980s, did not raise African American achievement relative to Whites. Longitudinal evidence on educational achievement and attainment provides limited support for the argument that test based accountability benefits African Americans. "We find little evidence that most forms of accountability have placed any downward pressure on the achievement gap," Douglas N. Harris and Carolyn D. Herrington noted in a recent review. As Figure 11.1 shows, the achievement gaps between African Americans on NAEP reading tests were wider in 1999 than they had been in 1988. By almost all accounts, test based policies did not close racial differences in graduation rates. By the beginning of the twenty-first century, scholars began to develop new ways of measuring high school graduation rates. Christopher Swanson's cumulative promotion index suggested that by 2001, 50 percent of African Americans completed high school in four years compared to 68 percent of Whites. As in the past, the inability of the 1990s reforms to achieve intended goals did not lead to a reconsideration of the assumptions behind test based accountability.[41]

By the beginning of the twenty-first century, accountability had largely displaced opportunity as the principal means of promoting racial equality in education. Drawing on his contested record of using accountability to close racial achievement gaps in education, George W. Bush convinced large bipartisan majorities in Congress that test based accountability would challenge the "soft bigotry of low expectations." Bush's language and the idea that accountability rather than opportunity would leave no child behind consolidated the bi-partisan conservative consensus about accountability that emerged in the late 1970s and gathered strength in the decades that followed. NCLB was crafted by a former moderate southern governor, but it was also shaped and endorsed by liberal stalwarts such as Representative George Miller and Senator Edward Kennedy. NCLB was also supported by the new generation of civil rights advocates. William Taylor of The Citizen's Commission on Civil Rights argued that "when schools and districts are held accountable for the achievement of all students, the means are at hand to force them to improve the quality of schooling provided for previously neglected students." Signed into law in 2002, NCLB required annual testing of students in the third through eighth grade, the administration of tests in high schools, progress in raising high school graduation rates, and sanctions against schools that did not make adequate progress in closing racial achievement gaps. NCLB, like the accountability measures it evolved out of and derived from treated the symptom—racial differences in achievement and attainment—rather than the cause—unequal educational opportunity. [42]

"When reforms aim at basic institutional changes or the eradication of deep social injustices," David B. Tyack and Larry Cuban argued, "the appropriate time period for evaluation may be a generation or more." The long intergenerational struggle to desegregate schools was interrupted, but comprehensive school desegregation, civil rights measures, and Great Society programs expanded educational opportunity. Broader opportunity fueled substantial gains in African American achievement and attainment, and, by the 1980s, brought African Americans closer to equality with Whites. African American educational advancement stalled as the southern moderate architects of American educational policy turned the nation away from a civil rights agenda of opportunity and institutionalized test based accountability as a way of promoting racial equality in education. The MCTs that were established in the late 1970s and early 1980s, the standards based reforms of the 1980s, the comprehensive forms of accountability of the 1990s, and NCLB were more expedient than effective. These reforms did not produce the expected results because they failed to address and tended to exacerbate pervasive and pernicious racial disparities in educational opportunity. By the beginning of the twenty-first century, however, the coalition of southern moderates, federal judges, and new civil rights advocates that emerged in the late 1970s and gathered influence in the years that followed had redefined the issue of racial inequality in education. The problem was no longer a lack of opportunity, but a lack of responsibility, effort, and motivation on the part of African Americans that could be addressed through testing. Test based accountability will almost certainly persist because the faulty assumptions underpinning accountability continue to command broad bi-partisan support in political and policy circles, and because reforms since the late 1970s wove testing into the fabric of schools in ways that will be difficult to unravel.[43]

NOTES

1. Numan V. Bartley, *The New South 1945–1980* (Baton Rouge, LA: Louisiana University Press, 1995). Several southerners also served as secretaries of education: Lamar Alexander of Tennessee under President George H. W. Bush, Richard Riley of South Carolina under William J. Clinton, and Rod Paige of Texas under George W. Bush.

2. Godfrey Hodgson, *More Equal Than Others: America from Nixon to the New Century* (Princeton, NJ: Princeton University Press, 2004), 24; Patrick J. McGuinn, *No Child Left Behind and the Transformation of Federal Education Policy* (Lawrence, KS: University of Kansas Press, 2006), vii, 45; Maris A. Vinovskis, *From A Nation at Risk to No Child Left Behind: National Goals and the Creation of Federal Education Policy* (New York, NY: Teachers College Press, 2009), 17; Paul Manna, *School's In: Federalism and the National Education Agenda* (Washington, DC: Georgetown University Press, 2006), 98; Jesse H. Rhodes, *An Education in Politics: The Origins and Evolution of No Child Left Behind* (Ithaca, NY: Cornell University Press, 2012), 44; Arthur E. Wise, *Legislated Learning: The Bureaucratization of the American Classroom* (Berkeley, CA: University of California Press, 1979); Peter W. Airasian, "State Mandated Testing and Educational Reform: Context and Consequences," *American Journal of Education,* 95 (1987): 405; David K. Cohen and Walter Haney, "Minimums, Competency Testing, and Social Policy," in *Minimum Competency Testing: Motives, Models, Measures and Consequences,* eds. Richard M.

Jaeger and Carol K. Tittle (Berkeley, CA: McCutchan Publishing Corporation, 1980), 12–13; *Debra P. v. Turlington,* 564 F. Supp. 177 (1983), 730 F. 2d 1405 (1984).

3. John F. Jennings, *Why National Standards? Politics and the Quest for Better Schools* (Thousand Oaks, CA: Sage Publications, 1998), 11; Diane Ravitch, *National Standards in American Education: A Citizen's Guide* (Washington, DC: Brookings Institution Press, 1995), 54; Linda Darling-Hammond, Maria E. Hyler, and Joy Williamson-Lott, "From Retrenchment to Renewal: African American Education, 1975–Present," in *The Oxford Handbook of African American Citizenship, 1865–Present,* eds. Henry Louis Gates, et al. (New York, NY: Oxford University Press, 2012), 641; Amy Stuart Wells, et al., *Both Sides Now: The Story of School Desegregation's Graduates* (Berkeley, CA: University of California Press, 2009), 19; John L. Rury and Shirley A. Hill, *The African American Struggle for Secondary Schooling, 1940–1980: Closing the Graduation Gap* (New York, NY: Teachers College Press, 2012), 175.

4. Lorraine M. McDonnell, *Politics, Persuasion, and Educational Testing* (Cambridge, MA: Harvard University Press, 2004); Linda M. McNeil, *Contradictions of School Reform: Educational Costs of Standardized Testing* (New York, NY: Routledge, 2000); Peter Sacks, *Standardized Minds: The High Price of America's Testing Culture and What We Can Do to Change It* (Cambridge, MA: Perseus Publishing, 2000); Stephen P. Klein, et al. "What Do Test Scores in Texas Tells Us?" Rand Issue Paper no. 202 (Santa Monica, CA: Rand Corporation, 2000); Robert L. Linn, *The Design and Evaluation of Educational Assessment and Accountability Systems* (Los Angeles, CA: National Center for Research and Evaluation, Standards and Student Testing, 2001); *Board of Education v. Dowell,* 498 U.S. 237 (1991); *Freeman v. Pitts,* 503 U.S. 467 (1992); James E. Ryan, *Five Miles Away, A World Apart: One City Two Schools and the Story of Equal Opportunity in Modern America* (New York, NY: Oxford University Press, 2010); Andrew Rudalevige, "No Child Left Behind: Forging a Congressional Compromise," in *No Child Left Behind? The Politics and Practice of School Accountability,* eds. Paul E. Peterson and Martin R. West (Washington, DC: Brookings Institution Press, 2003), 34; Richard Elmore, *Building a Strategy for School Leadership* (Washington, DC: Albert Shanker Institute, 2000).

5. *Brown v. Board of Education.* 347 U.S. 483 (1954), 493, 495; James S. Coleman, et al., *Equality of Educational Opportunity* (Washington, DC: Government Printing Office, 1965), 10, 311, 29.

6. Clay Risen, *The Bill of the Century: The Epic Battle for the Civil Rights Act* (New York, NY: Bloomsbury Press, 2014). Title IV of the Civil Rights Act of 1964 authorized the "Attorney General to initiate and maintain appropriate legal proceedings for relief and that the institution of an action will materially further the orderly achievement of desegregation in public education." Title VI states "no person in the United States shall on the ground of race, color or national origin, be excluded from participation in, be denied the benefits of, or be subjected to discrimination under any program or activity receiving Federal financial assistance." See Mark G. Yudoff, David L. Kirp, Betsy Levin, and Rachel F. Moran, *Educational Policy and the Law* (Belmont, CA: Wadsworth Group, 2002), 468–469; R. Scott Baker, *Paradoxes of Desegrega-*

tion: African American Struggles for Educational Equity and Access in Charleston, South Carolina, 1926–1972. (Columbia, SC: University of South Carolina Press, 2006), 157, 165; *Green v. New Kent County,* 391 U.S. 430 (1968), 437–8; *Swann v. Charlotte Mecklenburg Board of Education,* 300 F. Supp. 1358 (1969), 1363; 402 U.S. 1 (1971), 26; Leadership Conference on Civil Rights, "Statement," folder 21, box 15, Fred D. Alexander Papers, University of North Carolina Charlotte.

7. Gary Orfield and Nora Gordan, *Schools more Separate: Consequences of a Decade of School Resegregation* (Cambridge, MA: Harvard Civil Rights Project, 2001), 31, 33; Michael Fultz "The Displacement of Black Educators Post Brown: An Overview and Analysis," *History of Education Quarterly,* 44 (Spring 2004): 42; U.S. Senate Select Committee on Equal Educational Opportunity, *Hearings on the Status of School Desegregation* (Washington, DC: Government Printing Office, 1971); P. R. Morgan and James M. McPartland, "The Extent of Classroom Segregation Within Desegregated Schools," ERIC Document 210405.

8. Davison Douglass, *Reading, Writing, and Race: The Desegregation of the Charlotte Schools* (Chapel Hill, NC: University of North Carolina Press, 1995), 253; Jacquelyn Dowd Hall, "The Long Civil Rights Movement and the Political Uses of the Past," *Journal of American History,* 91 (2005): 1263; Wells, et al., 19; Rury and Hill, 175.

9. James D. Anderson, "The Schooling and Achievement of Black Children: Before and After *Brown v. Topeka,*" in *The Effects of School Desegregation on Motivation and Achievement,* eds. David E. Bartz and Martin L. Maehr (Greenwich, CT: JAI Press, 1984), 119; Linda Darling-Hammond, *Equality and Excellence: The Educational Status of Black Americans* (New York, NY: College Entrance Examination Board, 1985), 24; Rury and Hill, 5.

10. Deanna L. Michael and Sherman Dorn, "Accountability as a Means of Improvement: A Continuity of Themes," in *Education Reform in Florida: Diversity and Equity in Public Policy,* eds. Kathryn M. Borman and Sherman Dorn (Albany: State University of New York Press, 2007), 87; James B. Hunt, *Addresses and Public Papers of James Baxter Hunt Jr., Volume 1, 1977–1981* (Raleigh, NC: Division of Archives and History, 1982), 8; Graduation Competency Testing Program, Virginia, Fall 1978, NAACP Papers, Part 8, box 341, folder 2; Gerda Steele, "Competency Testing Problems Ahead," "Information Sheet" 19 October 1978, Kelly Alexander Papers, (KAP) box 8, folder 23; Ann Ramsbotham, *The Status of Minimum Competency Programs in Twelve Southern States* (Atlanta, GA: Southern Education Foundation, 1980), 3; *Raleigh News and Observer,* 4 August 1978; 20 August 1978; *Durham Morning Herald,* 4 August 1977; 11 September 1978.

11. Deanna Michael, *Jimmy Carter as Educational Policymaker: Equal Opportunity and Efficiency* (Albany, NY: State University of New York Press, 2008), 4, 18, 83, 92; Jimmy Carter, *White House Diary* (New York, NY: Farrar, Straus and Giroux, 2010), 145, 72, 75; Lawrence J. McAndrew, *The Era of Education: The Presidents and the Schools, 1965–2001* (Chicago: University of Illinois Press, 2006), 44, 46; Joseph A. Califano, Jr., *Governing America: An Insider's Report from the White House and the Cabinet* (New York, NY: Simon and Schuster, 1981), 296–297; Remarks of Harold Howe, KAP, box 8, folder 23; National Academy of Education, *Improving Educational Achievement: Report of the National Academy of Education* (Washington,

DC: Government Printing Office, 1978), iv, 9; Congressional Quarterly, *Almanac 1978* (Washington, DC: Congressional Quarterly, 1978), 557, 563.

12. Order, Green, v. Hunt, No. 78-539, 3 April 1979, National Archives, Ellenwood, GA; *Anderson v. Banks,* 520 F. Supp. 472 (1981); *Debra P. v. Turlington,* 474 F. Supp. 244 (1979), 249, 252, 257, 265, 269.

13. National Institute of Education, *Minimum Competency Clarification Hearing* (Washington, DC: The National Institute, 1981), 13, 646, 839; Southern Regional Education Board, *Measuring Educational Progress in the South: Student Achievement* (Atlanta, GA: Southern Regional Educational Board, 1984), 4; *Debra P.,* 1979, 248, 257; *Debra P. v. Turlington,* 730 F. 2d 1405 (1984), 1415.

14. *Debra P. v. Turlington,* 564 F. Supp. 177 (1983), 186, 188, 189; 730 F. 2d 1405 (1984), 1415–1416; Daniel Koretz, *Measuring Up: What Educational Testing Really Tells Us* (Cambridge, MA: Harvard University Press, 2008), 56–57.

15. Barbara Lerner, "Good News About American Education," *Commentary,* 91 (March 1991): 22; Robert C. Serow, "Effects of Minimum Competency Testing for Minority Students: A Review of Expectations and Outcomes," *Urban Review,* 16, (1984):72–73; Jay P. Heubert, "Minimum Competency Testing and Racial Discrimination: A Legal Analysis and Program Review for Lawyers" (EdD Dissertation, Harvard University, 1982), 133; Thomas S. Dee, "The First Wave of Accountability," in *No Child Left Behind? The Politics and Practice of School Accountability,* eds. Paul E. Peterson and Martin R. West (Washington, DC: Brookings Institution Press, 2003), 223, 225.

16. Rhodes, 44; Ravitch.

17. National Commission, 2, 5, 7, 9, 11; *New York Times,* March 29, 1983.

18. National Commission, 20, 22, 24, 30.

19. *Chicago Tribune,* May 1, 1983; McAndrews, 167, 122; Adam R. Nelson, *The Elusive Ideal: Equal Educational Opportunity and the Federal Role in Boston's Public Schools, 1950–1985* (Chicago, IL: University of Chicago Press, 2005), 226.

20. *New York Times,* June 30, 1983; *Washington Post,* June 30, 1983; *Charlotte Observer,* October 9, 1984; Gary Orfield and Susan Eaton, *Dismantling Desegregation: The Quiet Reversal of Brown v. Board of Education* (New York, NY: The New Press, 1996), 17; Hall, 1261.

21. *New York Times,* March 20, 1983; Task Force on Education for Economic Growth, *Action for Excellence* (Denver, CO: Education Commission of the States, 1983); *New York Times,* November 13, 1983; *Newsweek,* May 9, 1983; North Carolina Commission on Education and Economic Growth, *Education for Economic Growth* (Raleigh, NC: author, 1983).

22. National Center for Educational Statistics, *Digest of Educational Statistics, 1985–1986* (Washington, DC: Government Printing Office), 1986, 10–17. Table 65; Jennings; Thomas B. Timar and David L. Kirp, "Education Reform in the 1980s: Lessons from the States," *Phi Delta Kappan,* 70 (1989): 506; Thomas Toch, *In the Name of Excellence* (New York, NY: Oxford University Press, 1991).

23. Julius Chambers, interview with author, Charlotte, North Carolina, 16 December 2011; Legal Strategy Conference, NAACP Papers, part 7, box 81, folder 8; Benjamin Hooks to Dr. Bernard Chambers, 18 September 1986, NAACP Papers, part VII, box 81, folder 9; Standards and Assessment, 1987, NAACP Papers, Education, 1980–1988, series IX, box 452; Rhodes, 14.

24. Julius Chambers, interview with author; Jack Greenberg, *Crusaders in the Courts: How a Dedicated Band of Lawyers Fought for the Civil Rights Revolution* (New York, NY: Basic Books, 1994), 485; Timothy Minchin and John A. Salmond, *After the Dream: Black and White Southerners since 1965* (Lexington, KY: The University Press of Kentucky, 2011), 202.

25. William L. Taylor, *The Passion of My Times: An Advocates Fifty Year Journey in the Civil Rights Movement* (New York, NY: Carroll and Graff Publishers, 2004), 194, 198, 201; Rhodes, 141; *Education Week,* 8 June 1988; 21 September 1988.

26. See for example, William H. Thomas to Mr. Robert R. Servers, January 11, 1973, Department of Health Education and Welfare, Department of Education, Office of Civil Rights, National Archives, Ellenwood, Georgia; National Center for Educational Statistics, *Condition of Education, 1981* (Washington, DC: Government Printing Office, 1981) Table 2:13; Kenneth J. Meier, Joseph Stewart, Jr. and Robert E. England, *Race, Class and Education: The Politics of Second Generation Discrimination* (Madison, WI: University of Wisconsin Press, 1989), 5; Department of Education, "Elementary and Secondary Civil Rights Survey," 1978–1986, United States Department of Education, Washington, DC.

27. Rosalyn A. Mickelson, "When Are Racial Disparities in Education the Result of Racial Discrimination? A Social Science Perspective," *Teachers College Record.* Retrieved March 9, 2005 from www.tcrecord.org. 7; Jeanne Oakes, *Keeping Track: How Schools Structure Inequality* (New Haven, CT: Yale University Press, 1985), 206–207; Wells, et al., 99; Rosalyn A. Mickelson, "Subverting *Swann*: First and Second Generation Discrimination Segregation in the Charlotte-Mecklenburg Schools," *American Educational Research Journal,* 38, (2003): 232–233. The Education Trust, *Education Watch, 1994* (Washington, DC: Author, 1994).

28. Toch, 102; William H. Clune, Paul White, and James Patterson, *The Implementation and Effects of High School Graduation Requirements: First Steps Toward Curricular Reform* (New Brunswick, NJ: Center for Education Policy, 1989), 47; North Carolina Department of Public Instruction, *Report on Student Performance* (Raleigh, NC: Author, 1989), 1; Vinovskis, 70.

29. Consortium for Policy Research in Education, *Ten Years of State Education Reform, 1983–1993* (Philadelphia, PA: Author, 1994), 6; Linda M. McNeil, *Contradictions of School Reform: Educational Costs of Standardized Testing* (New York, NY: Routledge, 2000), 155, 3; Darling-Hammond, *Equality and Excellence,* 44.

30. Yudof, Kirp, Levin, and Moran, 800; Senate Minutes, 1985, North Carolina General Assembly, Raleigh, North Carolina; Margaret Rose Westbrook, "School Finance Litigation," *North Carolina Law Review,* 73 (2004–5): 2129; *Britt v. North Carolina State Board of Education,* 357 S.E. 2d 433, (1987), 436; *Hornbeck v. Somerset Board of Education* 295 MD 957 (1983); Ryan, 146; *McDaniel v. Thomas,* 285 S.E. 2d 156 (1981).

31. James J. Heckman and Paul A. LaFontaine, "American High School Graduation Rate: Trends and Levels," *The Review of Economics and Statistics,* 92 (May 2010): 245; Dee, 225.

32. John Robert Warren and Rachael B. Kulick, "Modeling Enactment of High School Exit Exam Policies," *Social Forces,* 86 (2007): 216–217.

33. *Board of Education v. Dowell*, 498 U.S. 237 (1991), 249–50; *Freeman v. Pitts*, 503 U.S. 467 (1992), 476–78; Gary Orfield and Chungmei Lee, "*Brown* at 50: King's Dream or *Plessy's* Nightmare?" (Cambridge, MA: Civil Rights Project at Harvard University, 2004), Retrieved, July 21, 2005; Gary Orfield and Chungmei Lee, "Why Segregation Matters: Poverty and Educational Inequality," (Cambridge MA: Civil Rights Project at Harvard University, 2005) 18, 22. Retrieved, December 10, 2013; Richard D. Kahlenberg, *All Together Now: Creating Middle Class Schools through Public School Choice* (Washington, DC: Brookings Institution Press, 2001), 67–76.

34. Ryan, 172, 153; *Hoke v. Board of Education,* No. 95 CVS 1158 (2002), 109–110; *Edgewood Independent School District v. Kirby*, 777 S.W. 2d 391 (1989), 396–98; Kevin Casey, "The Funding Gap 2004: Many States Still Shortchange: Low-Income and Minority Students," (Washington, DC: The Education Trust, 2004), 15; *Neely v. West Orange-Cove Consolidated Independent School District*, 176 S.W. 3d 746 (2005), 769–70, 788–90.

35. McNeil, 233; Wayne J. Urban and Jennings Waggoner, Jr., *American Education: A History* (New York, NY: Routledge, 2011), 419–420; Michael and Dorn, 102; Elmore; Lynn Olson, "The Great Divide," *Education Week,* January 9, 2003.

36. American Federation of Teachers, *Making Standards Matter 2000: A Fifty State Report on Efforts to Implement a Standards System* (Washington, DC: Author, 2001); Jay P. Heubert and Robert M. Hauser, *High Stakes: Testing for Tracking, Promotion, and Graduation* (Washington, DC: National Academy Press, 1999), 115; *Education Week*, February 11, 1998; *Bester v. Tuscaloosa Board of Education,* 722 F.2d 1514 (1984); *Erik v. Causby* 977 F. Supp 384 (1997), 388–389; *New Orleans Times-Picayune,* 18 September, 2001.

37. *Raleigh News and Observer,* October 4, 2001; Heubert and Hauser, 129; Department of Public Instruction, *North Carolina Public Schools: Statistical Profile, 2002* (Raleigh, NC: Author, 2002).

38. Linda A. Bond and Diane King, *State High School Graduation Testing: Status and Recommendations* (Oak Brook, IL: North Central Regional Educational Laboratory, 1995), 6; David K. Cohen, "Standards-Based Reform," in Ladd, ed., 124; Heubert and Hauser, 122; American Educational Research Association, American Psychological Association, and National Council on Measurement in Education, *Draft Standards for Educational and Psychological Testing* (Washington, DC: American Psychological Association, 1998).

39. Warren and Kulick, 217; *Rankins v. Louisiana Board of Education,* 635 So. 2d 250 (1994); *Williams v. Austin Independent School District,* 796 F. Supp. 251 (1992); Robert L. Linn, "Assessments and Accountability," *Educational Researcher,* 29 (March 2000): 8; Jennifer Jellison Holme, Meredith P. Richards, Jo Beth Jimerson, and Rebecca W. Cohen, "Assessing the Effects of High School Exit Examinations," *Review of Educational Research,* 80 (December 2010): 476–526; Brian Jacob, "Getting Tough? The Impact of High School Graduation Exams," *Educational Evaluation and Policy Analysis,* 23, (2001): 116; Florida Department of Education, *School Diploma, Certificate, and GED Report* (Tallahassee: Florida Department of Education, 2003).

40. David Grissmer and Ann Flanagan, *Exploring Rapid Achievement Gains in North Carolina and Texas* (Washington, DC: National Goals Panel, 1998), 1; *New York*

Times, October 30, 2000; Klein, et al.; Linn, 28; Aubrey L. Amrein and David C. Berliner, "High Stakes Testing, Uncertainty, and Student Learning," *Educational Policy Analysis Archives,* 10, 18 (2002): 36, Retrieved January 9, 2009, from www.epaa.asu.edu.

41. Douglas N. Harris and Carolyn D. Herrington, "Accountability, Standards, and the Growing Achievement Gap: Lessons from the Past Half-Century," *American Journal of Education,* 112 (February 2006): 209; Holme, Richards, Jimmerson, and Cohen; Jacob; Christopher Swanson, *Who Graduates? Who Doesn't? A Statistical Portrait of Public High School Graduation, Class of 2001* (Washington, DC: The Urban Institute, 2004).

42. *Education Week,* November 15, 2000; Rudalevige, 34; Manna, 118, 126; Rhodes, 150.

43. David B. Tyack and Larry Cuban, *Tinkering Toward Utopia: A Century of Public School Reform* (Cambridge, MA: Harvard University Press, 1995), 7.

CHAPTER 12

REASSESSING THE ACHIEVEMENT GAP

An Intergenerational Comparison of African American Student Achievement before and after Compensatory Education and the Elementary and Secondary Education Act (ESEA)

Christopher M. Span
University of Illinois at Urbana-Champaign

Ishwanzya D. Rivers
IDLR Educational Consulting

The "achievement gap," or the gap between the academic achievement of students from traditionally underrepresented or minority backgrounds and White students, has in recent years dominated contemporary considerations and conversations in the field of education, much as the concept of the "disadvantaged child" and cultural deficits dominated education

Using Past as Prologue, pages 307–324
Copyright © 2015 by Information Age Publishing

discourse in the 1960s. Closing the gap seems to be the focus of everyone interested in education from former President George W. Bush who instituted "No Child Left Behind" (NCLB), to the current President, Barack Hussein Obama, who supports much of the concept of NCLB, to television anchorwoman Soledad O'Brien, host of the CNN documentary, *Black in America,* to everyday educators, parents, and citizens who simply want to see schoolchildren perform at their highest level.[1]

Several methods have been employed to measure the achievement gap between White students and students from underrepresented or minority backgrounds, particularly African Americans, who until 2009 were the largest minority group in the United States. Comparing the academic performance of students on standardized tests—such as reading or doing mathematics at or above grade level—has been one of the most common assessments, as has it been to compare the highest level of educational attainment (such as obtaining a high school diploma or a college degree). More recently, some researchers have sought to shift or reframe conversations around the achievement gap to assessing the historical and sociopolitical conditions that established the gap in the first place. For instance, in her 2006 American Education Research Association (AERA) Presidential Address, Gloria Ladson-Billings in a deeply passionate and moving speech argued that the intense focus and scrutiny on the achievement gap between minority students and their White counterparts has been sorely misplaced. In her mind (and the authors of this article agree with her) the focus of the debate should not be simply on the obvious factors—such as the cultural mismatch of students and teachers, curricular policies and school resources, pedagogical practices, etc.—that exacerbate the gap. The debate should be redirected toward examining and articulating the "education debt" that has accumulated over time; this "debt" is intergenerational and, to Ladson-Billings, is the primary cause of the gap. To her, minority students and their school communities have been most impacted by education debt because of how their race or ethnicity, gender, socioeconomic status, heritage, and particular histories in the United States have directly influenced their access, preparation, and educational outcomes. In both a plea and a call to action, Ladson-Billings used her presidential address as a platform to challenge education researchers to rethink their strategies in examining the achievement gap and, in some ways, for these researchers to consider applying a historical lens to their analysis in order to best assess why students are achieving or underachieving.[2]

As historians, particularly historians of education who have studied the specifics of the African American past and the impact the vices of slavery and segregation have had on this group's lived experiences and outcomes, we encourage the challenge to rethink the achievement gap and compensatory education. The purpose of history is to study change over time and to offer the best assessment of *what happened* with the source material evidence available to us. For modern U.S. historians of education, who utilize their training to additionally explain *what is happening* in American schooling, if assessing the achievement gap is one area of inquiry, it should be no different. The achievement gap should not be simply a comparison of one racial or ethnic group to another. Instead it should be an intergenerational comparison of a group's academic performance over an extended period of time, independent of peer groups. It should assess the successes and limitations of a group from one generation to the next and seek to offer an interpretation of *what happened* or *what is happening* within this group and the historical context of the time.

We want to use the methodology of intergenerational comparison over seventy years, to place the concept of compensatory education into perspective, and link it to modern discourse about achievement gaps. Knowing that in a short article we cannot do justice to such a big sweep of history and to other scholarship, we want to point to some trends, in a relatively concise way, in a broad-brush approach to a complicated topic. Generally speaking, comparing the outcomes of one group to another makes very little sense; it personifies the household adage of comparing apples to oranges. This is particularly true when assessing achievement. Suppose, for example, someone compared the scholastic achievement scores and educational attainment of Native Americans to Asian Americans. One group's existence predates the founding of the colonies that formed this nation; the other group is comprised of more recent immigrants to the United States. Would this be a fair comparison? If so, why? If not, why? By this logic would it be fair to compare the educational experiences and outcomes of African Americans to Whites? Rarely do two groups—whether males to females, or African Americans to Whites, or native born persons to immigrants, or even parents to children— have the same historical experiences in the United States, so why should we presume that they would have comparable experiences in school?

This article seeks to provide a counter-assessment that shifts the discourse and analysis away from what African Americans have not achieved, to what they have accomplished independent of peer groups. Using data from the *Digest of Educational Statistics*, we argue that an intergenerational comparison is a more productive, progressive method to interpret data used to gauge the achievement gap. We apply this method by comparing the academic achievement scores and educational outcomes of African Americans from 1940 to 2008 and use the metrics of average reading scores in fourth and eighth grade and high school and college completion, those most often applied in assessing the achievement gap. When studied through the lens of history, this approach recognizes the achievements that African American students, historically disadvantaged because of their race, have made from one generation to the next, rather than simply offering an invidious evaluation of what they have not accomplished in comparison to a group who has, conversely, been historically advantaged because of their race.[3] We argue that since the inception of the Elementary and Secondary Education Act (1965), and the compensatory education programs—such as Head Start and Title I—that have grown out this Act, African Americans have made some of the greatest strides in improving their educational performance and outcomes in virtually every measureable category used to assess the achievement gap.

READING ASSESSMENTS

Examining reading assessments in historical perspective provides a useful example of the intergenerational approach to evaluating achievement. In 2009, using data from the National Assessment of Educational Progress (NAEP), the U.S. Department of Education's National Center for Education Statistics reported that based on a 500-point scale "the national reading average for African-American fourth-graders was 203 points, compared to 230 points for White students." For eighth-graders, the national reading average "was 259 points for African-Americans and 290 points for white students."[4] It is obvious that a gap exists between the two groups, but what is unclear is why or how the gap began, whether it has declined or increased, and if so, by how much, or for how long? Rarely is historical context or longitudinal data presented to best assess what these numbers mean. Data of this sort are usually presented as an end product, not as a longitudinal projection of the past, present, and future considerations of student achievement.

When NAEP data are studied more closely over an extended period of time (see Figure 12.1), one has an opportunity to gain a better appreciation of the progress African American students have made independent of their peer groups. In 1971, NAEP offered its first assessment on reading to the public. Figure 12.1 illustrates the NAEP average reading scores of nine-year old African American, White, and Latino/as children between 1971 and 2004. There is a "gap" between the groups when they are compared to one another, but what is more striking is the intergenerational progress these groups made, when studied independently of each other and over an extended period of time, although their gains were not monotonic. In 1971, White fourth graders averaged a reading score of 214 and by 2004 the average score was 226, an increase of twelve points. For African American fourth graders the average reading score was 170 in 1971, but by 2004, the score was 200; an increase of thirty points. For fourth grade Latinos/as, the average reading scores were unavailable for 1971, but between 1975 and 2004 the average reading scores steadily improved for the group by twenty-two points. Of the three groups assessed, it is clear that African Americans

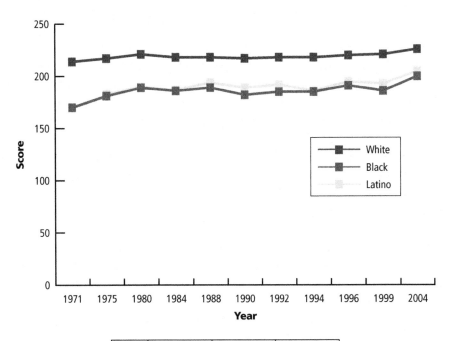

	White	Black	Latino
1971	214	170	N/A
1975	217	181	183
1980	221	189	190
1984	218	186	187
1988	218	189	194
1990	217	182	189
1992	218	185	192
1994	218	185	186
1996	220	191	195
1999	221	186	193
2004	226	200	205

Figure 12.1 NAEP averge student scale score in reading, age 9, 1971–2004. *Source:* Adapted from Table 110: Average Student Scale Score in Reading, by Age and Selected Student and School Characteristics: Selected Years, 1971 to 2004, http://nces.ed.gov/programs/digest/d04/tables/dt04_110.asp

had the most pronounced gains in this thirty-three year period. The progress is mentioned in the literature on the achievement gap, but rarely is it emphasized in a manner that stresses these gains independent of comparison and what this progress means in re-accessing or reframing African American achievement in school.[5]

Similar progress can be seen if one assesses NAEP data for eighth graders over an extended period of time (See Figure 12.2). In 1971, White thirteen year olds in the eighth grade had an average reading score of 261. By 2004, their average reading scores increased to 266, an increase of five points. African Americans eighth graders in 1971 had a mean reading score of 222,

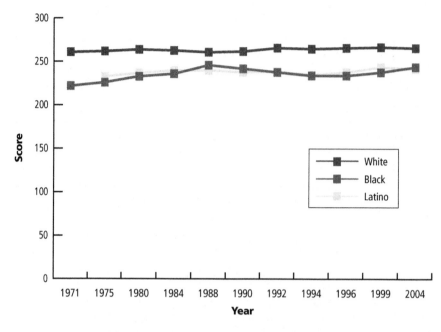

	White	Black	Latino
1971	261	222	N/A
1975	262	226	233
1980	264	233	237
1984	263	236	240
1988	261	243	240
1990	262	242	238
1992	266	238	239
1994	265	234	235
1996	266	234	238
1999	267	238	244
2004	266	244	242

Figure 12.2 NAEP averge student scale score in reading, age 13, 1971–2004. *Source:* Adapted from Table 110: Average Student Scale Score in Reading, by Age and Selected Student and School Characteristics: Selected Years, 1971 to 2004, http://nces.ed.gov/programs/digest/d04/tables/dt04_110.asp

and by 2004, the average reading score was 244; an increase of twenty-two points. For Latinos/as, the average reading score was 233 in 1975 and by 2004 it was 242, an increase of nine points. Again, African Americans had the most identifiable change of the three groups in this thirty-three year period. Why?

The answer requires historical context. Up until the passage of the 1964 Civil Rights Act, most African Americans lived under the oppressive system of segregation known as Jim Crow and African American children attended segregated schools. Jim Crow defined every aspect of Black life and consigned African Americans to a life of servitude and subordination. The education debt that African Americans accrued within this oppressive system is incalculable. Voting and other forms of civic engagement, landownership, economic self-sufficiency, freedom of choice, and access to quality public accommodations and schools were either severely circumscribed or simply denied to African Americans. Much of this would change after *Brown v. Board of Education* (1954), the Civil Rights Act of 1964, and the Elementary and Secondary Education Act (ESEA) 1965. As historian Michael J. Klarmen demonstrates, prior to the passage of "the 1964 Civil Rights Act, only one Black child in a hundred in the South attended a racially mixed school."[6] He further illustrates that *Brown* was virtually ineffective in achieving desegregation because of the massive resistance on the part of White southerners to the ruling and the fact that by 1964—a decade later—less than one percent of all desegregation suits had received a ruling from the courts.

Given the resistance and slow pace to comply with *Brown*, Attorney General Robert F. Kennedy removed desegregation complaints from the courts and placed them under the authority of the Department of Health, Education, and Welfare (HEW). In addition, he demanded that HEW threaten to "withhold federal education funds from districts that continued to segregate."[7] According to Klarmen, "the percentage of southern black children in desegregated schools shot up from 1.18 percent in 1964 to 6.1 percent in 1966, 16.9 percent in 1967, 32 percent in 1969, and roughly 90 percent in 1973."[8] Concomitantly, to receive any additional federal monies associated with Title I, Head Start, or any other compensatory education programs, schools that had purposefully segregated or denied African Americans equal access to a quality education under Jim Crow would now have to comply with the more stringent guidelines established by HEW. Paradoxically, southern districts in need of federal aid to support their struggling school systems were paid in federal dollars to not discriminate against African American schoolchildren, and this, in turn, was one factor that led to their access to schools with better resources and opportunities.

A policy report to the Educational Testing Services in 2010 by Paul E. Barton and Richard J. Coley offers additional historical context to explain the success of African Americans in the last three decades. Stressing the effectiveness of compensatory education programs, they contend that "at the top of the list of factors that may have contributed to progress in closing the gap," particularly in the 1970s and 1980s, "are the federal government's investments in Head Start and Title I of the 1965 Elementary and Secondary Education Act (ESEA)."[9] Their assessment is based on the positive results seen in the longitudinal evaluations of Head Start and Title I and the federal monies provided to the two programs. By 1970, the combined apportionments for Head Start and Title I were 1.7 billion dollars. By 1980, they were $3.9 billion and by 1985, $5.3 billion. Pointing to the importance of the combination of education and social welfare factors that former Head Start director Edward F. Zigler and others have emphasized, Barton and Coley concluded that the funds "went to feed infants and children who might have gone hungry, and research is clear that such deprivation has an impact on learning and cognitive development."[1]

The cumulative end result of these initiatives and developments alongside *Brown*, the 1964 Civil Rights Act, and many other equity initiatives of this era was a generation of African American youth, for the first time, attending school without the legal restriction and punitive enforcement of segregation.[11] Another end result was the "birth" of the achievement gap, as African American students, for the first time, were being directly compared with their White peers in some form of standardized assessment. The NAEP reading scores, particularly those from the 1970s, are a part of this history. Schoolchildren in 1971 would become parents in the 1990s and grandparents in the twenty-first century, and they—unlike their parents and grandparents—would be in a better position to help the next generation of African American schoolchildren advance their reading, writing, and mathematical skills. While African American progress in academic achievement has not been a steady linear change between 1971 and 2008, it is reasonable to assume that the increased access African American schoolchildren had to a quality education post-1970 led to an improvement in the group's NAEP average reading scores (as seen in Figures 12.1 and 12.2) in the proceeding years. It is also reasonable to speculate and reassess how compensatory education may have contributed to these gains over time.[12]

EDUCATIONAL ATTAINMENT

Another measure used to assess the achievement gap is educational attainment. The literature in the field is replete with examples of the gap between White and African American high school and college graduation rates. Notwithstanding, what is targeted in this section is the longitudinal progress African Americans have made in high school completion and college attendance independently of their peer groups. As Figure 12.3 illustrates,

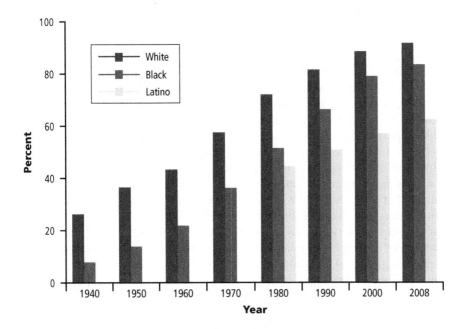

	White	Black	Latino
1940	26.1	7.7	N/A
1950	36.4	13.7	N/A
1960	43.2	21.7	N/A
1970	57.4	36.1	N/A
1980	71.9	51.4	44.5
1990	81.4	66.2	50.8
2000	88.4	78.9	57.0
2008	91.5	83.3	62.3

Figure 12.3 Percent of persons age 25 or older who completed high school, 1940–2008. *Source:* Adapted from: Table 8 Percent of Persons Age 25 and Over, by Years of School Completed, Race/Ethnicity, and Sex: Selected Years, 1910 to 2008, http://nces.ed.gov/programs/digest/d08/tables/dt08_008.asp?referrer=list

in 1940, only 7.7% of African Americans aged twenty-five years or older had a high school diploma. By the time of *Brown*, African Americans had a high school graduation rate of less than 20 percent. Notwithstanding, by 1980, the number of African Americans with a high school diploma—or its equivalent, the General Education Development (GED) degree—more than doubled; and by 2008, nearly 83.3% of all African Americans age twenty-five or older had completed their high school requirements. In this sixty-eight year period, the high school graduation rate for African Americans increased by 75.6%, and after the passage of the Elementary and Secondary Education Act (1965), the cornerstone of compensatory education, the high school graduation rate for African Americans nearly tripled.

Historians who have researched the origins of the comprehensive high school, or African American education in the first half of the twentieth century, document that the lack of secondary schooling opportunities for African Americans undermined any possibility of raising their high school completion percentages. In Mississippi, a state with a majority Black population well into the twentieth century, African Americans had virtually no opportunity to attend school beyond the elementary grades. In 1940, for example, "of the 115,000 educable black children of high school age, only 9,473 were enrolled in a high school. By contrast, there were 575 high schools for white adolescents and they enrolled 62,747 students." By 1950, just 261 schools throughout Mississippi were "doing some high school work," but only a handful of these schools were considered to be the equivalent of a comprehensive high school. Mississippi epitomized most southern states of this time period. It never developed a system of high schools for Blacks prior to the *Brown* decision because the role of high schools—to prepare young adults for citizenship, college, work, and leadership opportunities—remained antithetical to the expectations Whites had of African Americans.[13]

According to economist Derek Neal, by the 1970s, the "shock" the African American community suffered from being denied access to a quality high school education resulted in African American adults being underprepared to take advantage of their newfound freedoms and economic opportunities in a post-de jure segregated society. To Neal, African Americans without a quality education or high school diploma (a minimum requirement to be qualified for most job considerations post-1965) were caught in a vicious cycle of poverty and these combined realities may offer one explanation of the halted progress seen in NAEP average reading and math scores of African American schoolchildren in the late 1980s and 1990s. Many African Americans were unable to achieve economic mobility because of limited educational preparation or because they lacked a high school diploma and were forced to reside in impoverished neighborhoods with inferior schools and resources. All of these factors, and more, should be considered when assessing achievement gaps. Using a combination of data—educational attainment, test scores, graduation rates, and skill development—to assess what is needed for an individual to effectively compete in the contemporary marketplace, Neal concluded:

> Results based on convergence rates that represent best case scenarios for Black-youth suggest that even approximate Black–White skill parity is not possible before 2050, and equally plausible scenarios imply that the Black–White skill gap will remain quite significant throughout the twenty-first century. Absent changes in public policy or shocks to the economy that facilitate invest-

ment in Black children, there is little reason to be optimistic about the future pace of Black–White skill convergence.[14]

To state more plainly, if Neal is correct, African Americans in the twenty-first century will never gain economic parity or the skill sets needed to effectively compete in the workplace unless additional investments in the form of compensatory education are specifically targeted toward African American communities still impacted by the vestiges of past discrimination and harm.

If high school enrollment and completion rates were low or non-existent for African Americans prior to the passage of ESEA, logic dictates that college enrollment and completion rates were even lower. In 1903, W. E. B. Du Bois in his famed publication, *The Souls of Black Folk*, argued that at least 10 percent of the African American population should obtain a baccalaureate degree from a liberal arts college or university. Du Bois wanted to produce what he called the "Talented Tenth"; a cadre of classically trained college-educated African Americans who could serve as the leaders of their race.[15] As he so eloquently stated, "The Negro race, like all races, is going to be saved by its exceptional men. The problem of education, then, among Negroes must first of all deal with the Talented Tenth; it is the problem of developing the Best of this race that they may guide the Mass away from the contamination and death of the Worst, in their own and other races."[16] Nearly ninety years would elapse before Du Bois's vision of a "Talented Tenth" would be realized.

As Figure 12.4 illustrates, in 1940, almost thirty years after Du Bois's treatise, only 1.3% of African Americans aged twenty-five or older had a baccalaureate degree; in 1950, just 2.2%, and in 1960 only 3.5%. By 1980, fifteen years after the initiation of Title I and the Higher Education Act, the percentage doubled to 7.9% and by 2008, 19.7% of all African Americans twenty-five or older had a baccalaureate degree. What these data suggest is that as secondary education became more available to African Americans after 1970, so too did the likelihood of African Americans attending college at a rate competitive to their peers. What these data also illustrate (when assessed alongside high school completion data) is that in 1940, one in seven African Americans who graduated high school also graduated college; and in 2008, the percentage improved as one in four African Americans who graduated high school also graduated from college.

CONCLUSION

So what does all this mean? What these data demonstrate is that following the passage of the Elementary and Secondary Education Act, the main source of funding for what was then called compensatory education,

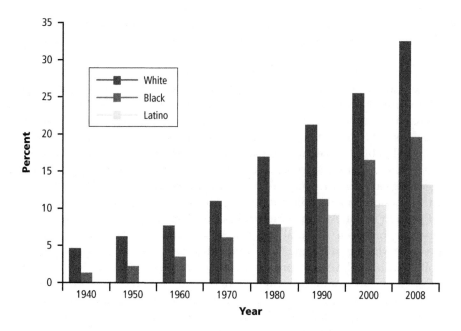

	White	Black	Latino
1940	4.6	1.3	N/A
1950	6.2	2.2	N/A
1960	7.7	3.5	N/A
1970	11.0	6.1	N/A
1980	17.0	7.9	7.6
1990	21.3	11.3	9.2
2000	25.6	16.6	10.6
2008	32.6	19.7	13.3

Figure 12.4 Percent of persons age 25 or older with a Baccalaureate degree. *Source:* Adapted from: Table 8 Percent of Persons Age 25 and Over, by Years of School Completed, Race/Ethnicity, and Sex: Selected Years, 1910 to 2008, http://nces.ed.gov/programs/digest/d08/tables/dt08_008.asp?referrer=list

African Americans, when given the chance to attend and receive schooling on a more equal basis, made tremendous strides in virtually every measureable category used to assess academic achievement. These data also illustrate that there is a need for historians to lend their expertise and training in assisting educators and policymakers in the re-articulating and addressing of this important quandary. The intergenerational comparisons offered in this short essay serve as a counter-assessment to the traditional modes of analysis that compare the achievement scores and educational outcomes of White students to minority students. By applying an historical analysis in assessing the academic achievement and educational outcomes of African Americans, one can gain a better understanding of both the unique challenges this group has faced and overcome in society, as well as the academic progress, from one generation to the next, they have made in school. The comparison is not relational to other races or ethnicities, but to African Americans themselves. In many ways, the methodology applied seeks to change the focus and emphasis of the debate over who is achieving or underachieving in school and in overall life outcomes.

As it is currently applied, discourse and analysis on the achievement gap (whether intentionally or not) inculcates in the minds of all involved that the performance and progress of students from minority or underrepresented backgrounds should be relational or in comparison to the majority population: Whites. This consideration offers a binary analysis that pits one group against another—Whites versus otherness—and it has the potential to instill in children who are underperforming a very negative perception of who they are and what they can become. Self-esteem, or a high regard for self, is one of the most important attributes a child needs in order to do well in all aspects of life. For instance, if people in society only hear what African Americans are *not* doing, rather than what they have conventionally done to advance themselves in the wake of progressive changes in American society, society-at-large (inclusive of African Americans) will accept as true a very negative perception of African Americans and their ability to effectively compete in society. During the *Brown* litigation, social psychologists Kenneth B. Clark and Mamie Clark illustrated this in astounding and painful detail in the "doll tests" they conducted on young African American children. The Clarks concluded that racial prejudice, segregation, and low expectations of African Americans caused countless African American children to develop an unhealthy self-image and to expect only inferior opportunities in life.[17]

The perceptions drawn from current discourse and analysis on the underachievement of African Americans to Whites, according to educational researcher Bruce Hare leads to a "differentiated" self-esteem and effort on the part of African American schoolchildren. He demonstrates that African American students, in order to maintain a healthy self-esteem in school, emphasize establishing peer-relations (making friends) over academic achievement (performing at their highest level). The choices these students made to ensure a healthy sense of self in school has had a ripple effect in how African American students who have adopted this strategy are viewed. To Hare, it has led to a low or lowered expectation of African Americans from society, their teachers, schools, peers, and, in many cases, their own communities.[18] Shifting the discourse on the achievement gap from what African American children are not doing in comparison to

Whites, to what they have accomplished, from one generation to the next over an extended period of time, provides an alternative way to frame the debate. It also provides an opportunity to highlight how African Americans have made tremendous strides in the classroom, to educate the nation on the education debt African Americans have accrued since their earliest experiences in the United States, and concurrently address the underperformance or limitations African American children have in school.

The reality is that African Americans have a very different history than Whites and despite nearly fifty years of federal reform and a collective effort on the part of African Americans to improve themselves, they still are not equal in society.[19] Many Americans assume that the initiatives of the 1950s and 1960s, such as *Brown*, The Civil Rights Act, and ESEA made African Americans equals, but this notion is based more on perception than reality and it sorely miscalculates the impact racism, discrimination, and segregation had (and continues to have) on this group's overall progression. The following formula illustrates this well: 246 years of enslavement (1619–1865) + 100 years of state-sanctioned segregation (1865–1965) – 46 years of something other than enslavement and state-sanctioned segregation does not = 0—that is, equality.[20] Put differently, the authors of this essay are among the first generation of American children born in a United States where slavery and state-sanctioned segregation does not exist. Laws may have been ratified which afford African Americans a chance to participate in mainstream society in ways they have not historically been able to do, but these laws do not require people to think differently about African Americans and their perceived place, existence, or *comparison to others* in the American social order. Only you and I, in learning about the strengths and limitations of each other, can do that.

In 1935, W. E. B. Du Bois, in his epic publication, *Black Reconstruction* asked, "If a poor, degraded, disadvantaged horde achieves sudden freedom and power, what could we ask of them in ten years?"[21] The question was addressed to the expectations the nation had of the African Americans who emerged from slavery in 1865, but who had not by 1875 achieved equality to the people who had hitherto held them in bondage. The authors of this article ask a slightly similar question to the one posed by Du Bois. "What can one ask of a people in a single generation?" In a single generation African Americans have more than doubled their high school graduation rates and tripled their college completion rates. In the last thirty years they have consistently raised their NAEP average reading scores to narrow gaps between themselves and their peer groups. Statistics of this nature are usually deemed progress and the people who achieved them, a success. These are scenarios of progress, when they are not presented as an objectionable comparison of one group to another. Rethinking compensatory education may help us see achievement gaps in a new way, in historical perspective across the generations. This rethinking may also help us reassess the effectiveness of compensatory education itself, despite the "deficit thinking" that initially accompanied it.[22]

As historians of African American education, we look forward to documenting what the next generations of Africans Americans, in relation to their predecessors, will achieve in school. Hopefully, additional measures of federal support, such as those established by ESEA and the compensatory education programs that emerged from the Act, will be created in the twenty-first century to aid and assist future generations of students in their educational advancement.

NOTES

This chapter is a reprint of an article published in *Teachers College Record* 114 (June 2012): 1–17. The authors extend an extremely warm and gracious thank you to *Teachers College Record* for permission to reprint this essay in this volume.

1. *Public Law 107–110 of the 107th Congress, An Act to Close the Achievement Gap with Accountability, Flexibility, and Choice, so that No Child is Left Behind* (Washington D.C.: Government Printing Office, 2002); *The Obama Education Plan: An Education Week Guide* (Hoboken, NJ: Jossey-Bass, 2009); Khadijah Rentas, "Study: Achievement Gap Narrows between Black, White Students," *CNN U.S.*, 16 July 2009, accessed 1 August 2001 from http://articles.cnn.com/2009-07-16/us/education.gaps_1_white-students-achievement-gap-african-american?_s=PM:US.

2. Gloria Ladson-Billings, "From the Achievement Gap to the Education Debt: Understanding Achievement in U.S. Schools," *Educational Researcher*, 35, no. 7 (October 2006): 3–12.

3. For literature that apply a similar historical analysis to assessing the achievement gap see, Paul Peterson, ed., *Generational Change: Closing the Test Score Gap* (Lanham, MD: Rowan & Littlefield Publishers, 2006); Mark Berends, Samuel R. Lucas, and Roberto V. Peñaloza, "How Changes in Families and Schools are Related to Black–White Test Score Trends," *Sociology of Education* 81 (2008): 313–344; Launor F. Carter, "The Sustaining Effects of Compensatory and Elementary Education," *Educational Researcher* 13, no. 7 (August–September 1984); James D. Anderson, "The Schooling and Achievement of Black Children: Before and After *Brown v. Topeka*, 1900–1980," in Martin L. Maehr and David E. Bartz, eds., *The Effects of School Desegregation on Motivation and Achievement* (Greenwich, CT: JAI Press, Inc., 1984); Paul E. Barton and Richard J. Coley, *The Black–White Achievement Gap: When Progressed Stopped* (Princeton, NJ: Education Testing Service, 2010); Chance W. Lewis, Marlon James, Stephen Hancock, and Valerie Hill-Jackson, "Framing African American Students' Success and Failure in Urban Settings: A Typology for Change,"

Urban Education 43, no. 2 (March 2008): 127–153; James D. Anderson, "The Historical Context for Understanding the Test Score Gap," *The National Journal of Urban Education & Practice* 1 (2007): 1–21. Anderson, "The Historical Context for Understanding the Test Score Gap," offers one of the best statements on applying an historical lense to the achievement of African Americans in society and the debate on the achievement gap when he states, "African Americans and educators have much to celebrate, yet currently muting the applause is the looming test score gap" (p. 14).

4. Rentas, "Study: Achievement Gap Narrows between Black, White Students."
5. For literature that detail a comparison of African Americans to Whites on the achievement gap see among others, Linda Hertert and Jackie Teague, "Narrowing the Achievement Gap: A Review of Research, Policies, and Issues," *EdSource* (2003), accessed 1 August 2011 from, http://www.edsource.org/pub_achgap1-03_report.html; Richard Rothstein, *Class and Schools: Using Social, Economic, and Educational Reform to Close the Black–White Achievement Gap* (New York, NY: Columbia University: Teacher's College Economic Policy Institute, 1994); Jay R. Campbell, Catherine M. Hombo, and John Mazzeo. *NAEP 1999 Trends in Academic Progress: Three Decades of Student Performance* (Washington, D.C.: OERI, U.S. Department of Education, 2000); National Governors' Association, *Closing the Achievement Gap* (2005), accessed 1 August 2011 from, http://www.subnet.nga.org/educlear/ achievement/; Rob Greenwald, Larry V. Hedges, and Richard D. Laine, "The Effect of School Resources on Student Achievement," *Review of Educational Research* 66, no. 3 (Fall 1996): 361–96; National Center for Education Statistics. *Education Achievement and Black–White Inequality* (Washington, D.C.: Department of Education., 2001); Barton and Coley, *The Black–White Achievement Gap*; David Grissmer, A. Flanagan, and S. Willamson, "Why Did the Black–White Score Gap Narrow in the 1970s and 1980s?," in Christopher Jencks and Meredith Phillips eds., *The Black–White Test Score Gap* (Washington, D.C.: Brookings Institution Press, 1998), 182–226; Christopher Jencks and Meredith Phillips, eds., *The Black–White Test Score Gap* (Washington, D.C.: Brookings Institution Press, 1998); Lee, Jaekyung, "Racial and Ethnic Achievement Gap Trends: Reversing the Progress toward Equity?," *Educational Researcher* 31, no. 1 (January/February 2002): 3–12.
6. Michael J. Klarmen, *From Jim Crow to Civil Rights: The Supreme Court and the Struggle for Racial Equality* (New York, NY: Oxford University Press, 2004), 362.
7. Ibid., 363.
8. Ibid.
9. Barton and Coley, *The Black–White Achievement Gap*, 9.
10. Ibid. On the importance of health care nutrition and other factors, see, among others, Edward Zigler and Susan Muenchow, *Head Start: The Inside History of America's Most Successful Educational Experiment* (New York, NY: Basic Books, 1992); Edward Zigler and Sally Styfco, *The Hidden History of Head Start* (New York, NY: Oxford University Press, 2010); Barbara Beatty and Edward Zigler, *"Reliving the History of Compensatory Education: Policy Tensions, Bureaucracy, and the Policiticized Role of Science in the Evolution of Head Start," Teachers College Record, Special Issue on "Rethinking Compensatory Education,"* 114, no. 6 (June

2012); and Matia Finn-Stevenson and Edward Zigler, *Schools of the 21st Century* (Boulder, CO: Westview Press, 1999).

11. *Brown, Brown II* (1955), The Civil Rights Act (1964), and ESEA (1965) were complementary to many other judicial and legislative reforms that would be ratified during the Kennedy-Johnson presidencies. In addition, the Higher Education Act (1965), the Voting Rights Act (1965), the 1965 signing by President Johnson of Executive Order 11246, which enforced affirmative action for the first time, and the Civil Rights Act of 1968, which prohibited discrimination in the sale, rental and financing of housing, all had a cumulative and positive impact on ensuring African Americans had access to resources and equity in ways unmatched in American history.

12. Progress in African American achievement has never been linear. NAEP average reading scores for African American fluctuated and declined somewhat between 1988 and 1999. For instance, nine-year old African Americans closed the achievement gap between 1971 and 1988 by thirty-two points only for this gap to fluctuate between 1988 and 1999. For thirteen-year old African Americans the gap closed by eighteen points between 1971 and 1988 only to drop and re-stabilize by 2004. Most studies on the African American/White achievement gap have difficulty explaining the movement of these gaps whether studied independently or to another peer group. For a source that offers one of the best assessments of the differing theories and explanations on this consideration see, Barton and Coley, *The Black–White Achievement Gap,* 14.

13. Christopher M. Span, *From Cotton Field to Schoolhouse: African American Education in Mississippi, 1862–1875* (Chapel Hill: University of North Carolina Press, 2009), 178.

14. Derek Neal, *Why Has Black–White Skill Convergence Stopped?* (University of Chicago and National Bureau of Economic Research, April 2005), 2.

15. W. E. B. Du Bois, "The Talented Tenth," in *The Negro Problem: A Series of Articles by Representative American Negroes of To-Day,* ed., Booker T. Washington (New York, NY: James Potts & Company, 1903), 33–75.

16. Ibid., 33.

17. Kenneth B. Clark, *Prejudice and Your Child,* 2nd enlarge edition (Boston, MA: Beacon Press, 1963); Kenneth B. Clark, *Dark Ghetto: Dilemmas of Social Power* (Hanover, NH: Wesleyan University Press, 1965).

18. Information on the research conducted by Bruce Hare is obtained from Claude M. Steele, "Race and the Schooling of Black Americans," *The Atlantic Monthly* 269, no. 4 (1992): 67–78. See also Bruce R. Hare, ed., *2001 A Race Odyssey: African Americans and Sociology* (Syracuse, NY: Syracuse University Press, 2002).

19. For an excellent account on the inequities between African Americans and Whites, see Shapiro, Thomas M. and Melvin L. Oliver, *Black Wealth/White Wealth: A New Perspective on Racial Inequality* (New York, NY: Routledge, 1996); Whoriskey, Peter, (Wealth Gap Widens between Whites, Minorities," *Washington Post,* 25 July 2011, accessed 1 August 2011 from, http://www.washingtonpost.com/business/economy/wealth-gap-widens-between-whites-minorities-report-says/2011/07/25/gIQAjeftZI_story.html; Kochhar, Rakesh, Fry, Richard, and Taylor, Paul, "Twenty-to-One: Wealth Gaps Rise to Record Highs

between Whites, Blacks, Hispanics," *Pew Social & Demographic Trends*, 26 July 2011, accessed from, http://pewsocialtrends.org/2011/07/26/wealth-gaps-rise-to-record-highs-between-whites-blacks-hispanics/.

20. This formula is adapted from Joe Feagin's article, "Documenting the Costs of Slavery, Segregation, and Contemporary Racism: Why Reparations Are in Order for African Americans," *Harvard BlackLetter Law Journal* 20 (2004): 49–81.

21. W. E. B. Du Bois, *Black Reconstruction in America, 1860–1880* reprint (New York, NY: Free Press, 1998), 637.

22. Richard R. Valencia, *Dismantling Contemporary Deficit Thinking: Educational Thought and Practice* (New York, NY: Routledge, 2010).

CHAPTER 13

FUTURE DIRECTIONS OF HISTORICALLY BLACK COLLEGES AND UNIVERSITIES

Marybeth Gasman
Felecia Commodore
University of Pennsylvania

Historically Black Colleges and Universities (HBCUs) are the only institutions in the United States that were created with the express purpose of educating Black citizens. Until the mid-1960s, HBCUs were, with very few exceptions, the only higher education option for most African Americans. With the push for the integration of historically White institutions during the Civil Rights Movement, enrollment dropped at HBCUs, and their role of educating the near entirety of the Black middle class shifted. Today, the 105 HBCUs enroll 11 percent of Black students in the United States, yet they represent less than 3 percent of colleges and universities in the country.[1] Moreover, great numbers of African Americans who pursue graduate and professional education receive their undergraduate degrees at Black colleges.[2] Based on existing literature and the opinions of HBCU experts, we draw conclusions of HBCUs major strengths and challenges. Looking towards the future of HBCUs we explore these strengths and challenges.

Using Past as Prologue, pages 325–339
Copyright © 2015 by Information Age Publishing
All rights of reproduction in any form reserved.

We also posit ways in which HBCUs can address their challenges and build upon their strengths to ensure not only their existence but their continued success. Although this chapter is future oriented, it is important for scholars to also consider the history of HBCUs, especially the history beyond the 1930s as very little has been written. A greater understanding of the experiences of faculty, students, and the institutions themselves would help us to understand the current situations that HBCUs find themselves in today. Many of the current issues faced by HBCUs are rooted in the past, such as problems with revolving leaders, low endowments and alumni giving, and problems with accreditation and performance outcomes. All of these issues are tied to a history of underfunding throughout the existence of HBCUs.

WHERE ARE WE?

Value Added versus Low Retention

HBCUs are an important piece of the tapestry of higher education. These institutions provide a unique space and contribution to the education of generations of African Americans, first generation, and low-income students. The value added nature of the education provided by HBCUs has aided in the building of a Black middle class as well as opportunities for students to access upward mobility and economic empowerment for themselves, their families, and their communities. HBCUs are willing to educate those that are deemed "at-risk" students. These students are often considered ill prepared for collegiate work and prime candidates to be unsuccessful in persisting towards and attaining a college degree. However, unlike many of their institutional counterparts, HBCUs are not only willing to accept these students, they are often successful in getting them up to speed, producing successful and strong college graduates. A myriad of anecdotal evidence supports these claims of a "value added" impact; what remains is to conduct more empirical research on the subject.

Several authors have examined the positive impact that HBCUs have in terms of increasing social equality for their future graduates.[3] Of direct importance to the "value-added" concept, many researchers have looked at the impact of HBCUs on student outcomes, including overall satisfaction with the collegiate experience, future success, career attainment, and potential salary.[4] From this research we learn that the academic climate at HBCUs has a significant impact on the intellectual and social gains of students compared to African American students at Historically White Institutions (HWIs).[5] In addition, research tells us that HBCUs offer unique support systems that promote high levels of student involvement.[6] Furthermore, research shows us that although the pre-college characteristics of students who attend HBCUs predict lower wages than the pre-college characteristics of students who attend HWIs, the value added in future wages from attending an HBCU is 38 percent higher than that from attending an HWI for the average Black student. When disaggregated by gender, the added value is even higher for Black men.[7]

Though this is the case, there are other issues that are present when risks are embraced. HBCUs are often brought under scrutiny and criticism for their low retention and graduation rates. In recent years, numerous media reports have lambasted HBCUs, calling into question the very existence of these institutions. Furthermore, some scholars have put forth research that interrogates the quality of education offered by HBCUs. The most recent example is the 2010 publication by Fryer and Greenstone. In this article, which received substantial media attention, the authors argue, with questionable evidence that by some measures "HBCUs retard Black progress."[8] Under federal and state administrations, such as the current ones, increases in accountability pressures create an environment in which HBCUs will be asked to justify increased state and federal expenditures. This justification will be difficult for some HBCUs in light of low graduation rates. HBCUs, on average, have a 30% graduation rate, a statistic for which they are often criticized.[9] The raw numbers may appear damning, but they do not tell the full story.

When considering graduation rates, it is important to keep in mind that the majority, but certainly not all, of HBCU students are low-income, first-generation, and Pell-Grant-eligible.[10] Students with these characteristics are less likely to graduate no matter where they attend college.[11] To be clear, HBCUs with a more selective admissions process do reflect higher retention and graduation rates. With federal and state funding policies becoming more connected to measures such as graduation rates, HBCUs will need to find a way to stay true to their mission of access yet address their challenges with the retention, persistence, and completion of students.

Gender

In the past few years there has been significant growth in the research related to gender on HBCU campuses, ranging from the Thurgood Marshall College Fund's report *Understanding Gender at Public Black Colleges and Universities* to work on gendered student success and engagement to issues of sexuality and HIV/AIDS.[12] This research has shown that HBCU student bodies are predominantly female while faculties are predominantly male. Lundy-Wagner and Gasman take a closer look at the body of HBCU research and find that gender is rarely discussed. Furthermore, when gender is addressed it is often focused on African American women—African American men receive little to no attention.[13] Female undergraduate students outnumber male undergrads at HBCUs at a slightly higher (3 percent) rate than the national average.[14] A more significant gap appears when considering Black undergraduate male enrollment compared to Black females at certain HBCUs. The lack of balance in overall HBCU enrollment results in a significant gender imbalance on individual HBCU campuses, with some Black colleges having female enrollments as high as 76 percent. Of note, five colleges have more men than women on their campuses: Arkansas Baptist College, Edward Waters College, Concordia College-Selma, Livingstone College, and Texas College.[15]

Affordability versus Lack of Financial Resources

Access is an important aspect of many HBCUs' missions. HBCUs strive to remain affordable options for students to pursue higher education. Most recently, an article by Valerie Wilson stated, "if a student is just as likely to persist and complete a degree at an HBCU as a TWI [traditionally White institution], then it is more economical to attend a[n] HBCU at a fraction of the cost of an education at a comparable TWI."[16] There have also been studies pointing out the relationship between the ability to attain financial aid and mental distress for African American students.[17] Yet, with increased media reports on financially strapped HBCUs, critics might ask if continuing to offer an education for much less than HWIs is advantageous to these struggling institutions. Of vital importance, this question must be balanced with HBCUs' long-standing commitment to educating low-income students.

It is a fact, however, that HBCUs have low endowments compared to their HWI counterparts. This should not be surprising considering the long history of subpar and unfair funding of these institutions for decades—fueled by systematic racism among other factors. When it comes to the area of funding, many of the states studied have tried to address decades of underfunding and unfair funding allocations with a lump sum amount. Funding appropriations for HBCUs are well below those of many of their HWI counterparts, but formulas including enrollment, large operations among other components seem to be used to justify this practice. For example, in North Carolina, the University of North Carolina (UNC) & North Carolina State (NC State) receive more funding than all five HBCUs combined. Some would argue this is a form of discrimination and in fact, institutional racism. When funding is considered on a per student basis, HBCU students in North Carolina are funded at 50 percent less than those at HWIs. Since their inception, HBCUs have been under-funded (in part due to segregation and systemic racism) and, with few exceptions, these institutions continue to suffer from low percentages of alumni giving, stretched operating budgets, and meager endowments. The proportion of federal research and development funding for research performing HBCUs is not balanced.[18] Though federal funding has increased over the years, that received by HBCUs is still a small fraction.[19] This trend in funding is often reflected on the state level as well.[20] Though the argument of underfunding continues and should continue to be made, HBCUs must simultaneously address how to make their institutions more financially sustainable. Withholding standout institutions such as Spelman College, many HBCUs have yet to find their steady stride in the world of fundraising and development. Fundraising is the most important factor for the long-term sustainability of HBCUs. Institutions with substantial endowments and vibrant alumni giving programs are less likely to have problems with accreditation, student retention, leadership, and faculty satisfaction.[18]

Community Engagement versus Lack of Marketing

Community engagement has recently become a buzzword in higher education circles and literature. But, far before it was trendy, HBCUs have been engaging in community engagement. Out of a deep commitment and necessity (due in part to the segregated nature of the United States), HBCUs were intensely involved in their communities, often providing housing, daycare services, nursing, and informal education. Perhaps the greatest example of civic engagement can be seen in the role that HBCUs played in the Civil Rights Movement.[19] Many HBCU leaders, faculty, and students were instrumental in pushing for equality and more significantly, these individuals trained community members in the ways of activism and civil disobedience. Gasman and McMickens found that a majority of HBCU mission statements still had a strong statement of commitment to community service on behalf of the institution.[20] In recent years, there have been some scholarly attempts to capture the community engagement of Black colleges, specifically their support of African American-owned businesses, economic impact in the community, exemplary service-learning programs, and Black colleges' role in increasing African American capital.[24]

Yet, with all of this great work, activism, and civic engagement, HBCUs struggle in conveying their current stories of contributions, relevancy, and successes. HBCUs need to become better at sharing their successes and marketing their institutions. Communicating HBCU success stories to the general public is essential. Two books that tell a convincing story of HBCUs, and are aimed at a general audience, are Williams and Ashley's *I'll Find a Way or Make One: A Tribute to Historically Black Colleges and Universities* and Drewry and Doermann's *Stand and Prosper: Private Black Colleges and their Students*.[25] Unfortunately, HBCU stories remain uncovered and spoken of only in intimate circles rather than shared and pushed to the forefront.

This leaves the negative narrative of these institutions and their constituencies to persist and to perpetuate.

Training Leadership versus Attaining Sustainable Leadership

HBCUs have played a large role in educating the nation's teachers, doctors, lawyers, judges, scientists, policymakers, professors, etc.[26] Silbulkin and Bulter found that Black doctorates were slightly more likely to have earned their B.S. from an HBCU than an HWI.[27] The fact that the proportion of Black doctorates originating from HBCUs was at least equal to, if not slightly higher than the proportion of available Black baccalaureates is noteworthy.[28] HBCUs are clearly producing leadership in their graduates. But there is much concern and criticism surrounding their ability to procure sustainable leadership for their institutions.

Ezzell and Schexnider point out that along with their unique culture, HBCUs tend to have issues recruiting talented leadership as presidential aspirants may be averse to dealing with the challenges of underfunding, limited resources, and legacies of conservative leadership found at many HBCUs.[29] On average, HBCU presidents serve six years, compared to 8.5 years nationally.[30] But a cadre of HBCU presidents has served very long terms—a full 16 percent have served between fifteen and twenty-five years. A long-term presidency has one major consequence that is often overlooked: when presidents are at an institution too long, staff and faculty may begin to rely too much on them and as a result, they do not take on leadership roles and problem-solving themselves.[31]

Along with the challenges of aging leadership comes the challenge of engaging with advancing technologies. This is not to imply that all that are higher in age are not technologically savvy. But, HBCU presidents tend to be behind the curve in this area. HBCU presidents lag behind their national counter-parts in their embrace of social media. According to a 2011 Pew survey of 1,055 college and university presidents throughout the country, over 50 percent of higher education leaders were active on Facebook and Twitter. For HBCU presidents, that rate drops to 13 percent for Facebook, and 12 percent for Twitter.[32]

Afrocentric, Challenging, Supporting Curriculum versus Challenges to Holding True to Mission

Research shows that African American students are empowered when the curriculum embraces their experiences, culture and history.[33] One unique aspect of many HBCUs is their Afrocentric focus in teaching and learning. Though not completely focused on Afrocentricity, one study that could serve as a model for evaluating the special boost of an HBCU curriculum is Perna and colleagues' article entitled, "The Contributions of HBCUs to the Preparation of African American Women for STEM Careers."[34] In this study, the authors showcase the exceptional strategies for learning used by HBCUs to promote the attainment of Black women in the graduate STEM fields, including the fostering of a competitive, yet supportive, environment for learning.[35] HBCUs have also been heralded for their student-focused, student-centered approach to teaching. Hargrove et al. explore the importance of understanding student learning styles to foster academic success in engineering students at Morgan State University.[36]

Innovative approaches towards curriculum at HBCUs are not limited to the undergraduate population. In an economic time that saw a dip in law school enrollment, HBCU law schools found a way to strengthen their niche by crafting relevant curriculum.[37] Staying true to their missions with a focus on social justice, the deans of the six HBCU law schools have taken strides to have curriculum that makes their students competitive in the marketplace—focusing on strengths and practical curriculum.[38] Recently, it was reported that Clark Atlanta University had significantly more graduates find jobs in academia than their counterparts—70 percent of their humanities doctoral graduates landing academic positions.[39] Clark Atlanta credits this mostly to their curriculum, which they feel is designed specifically towards higher education and teaching in higher education.[40]

Yet, with the many successes of their Afrocentric curriculum and approach, HBCUs find much pressure to alter their approaches. Handling the pressures of desegregation and trying to sustain the unique institutional mission of HBCUs is indeed a challenge in the twenty-first century. Many argue that the decrease in enrollment of African American students at HBCUs is the direct result of desegregation policies. Minor argues against that by pointing to the increase in students attending HBCUs. But some policies had indirect effects on the enrollment of African American students at HBCUs.[41] For instance, some of these policies have made it so that the cost of institutions has become very similar to that of HWIs. When this cost similarity among institutions occurs academic program offerings become more important. When looking at HBCU funding and its relationship to course and program offerings this leaves HBCUs at a disadvantage compared to their well-endowed HWI counterparts.[42] States have avoided enforcing desegregation settlements leading to settlements that have little effect on institutional capacity and as a result, institutional capacity is not being fully materialized.

Diversity versus Producing HBCU Scholars

Another strength of HBCUs is the diversity of their faculty and student bodies. Compared to their HWI counterparts, HBCUs offer a pluralistic academic environment. Although it is important to maintain their unique mission—that of educating African Americans—some scholars argue that HBCUs would benefit from stressing their great diversity to potential students, be they African American, Latino, or White. For students looking for a nurturing, challenging, and diverse environment, many HBCUs are ideal. HBCUs, as a universe of two and four-year colleges, universities, graduate and professional schools have, on average, 30 percent student diversity and in excess of 40 percent faculty diversity.[43] White students often find HBCUs to have welcoming environments.[44] Prominent scholars such as Walter Allen of University of California, Los Angles and Frances Bonner of Howard University, among others, have started to explore this topic and the changing role of HBCUs in American society.[45]

In 1950, Blacks made up nearly 100 percent of HBCU enrollment. In 1980, they represented 80 percent of total enrollment.[46] In the past thirty years, the proportion of Latino enrollment at HBCUs has increased, especially in regions of the country where the Latino population is growing rapidly.[47] In 2011, total Asian American enrollment at HBCUs was 4,311, a 60 percent increase from 2001.[48] The White enrollment at HBCUs has hovered between 10 and 13 percent in the past twenty years.[49] Today, a full quarter of HBCUs across the nation have at least a 20 percent non-Black student body. Some people worry that the changing composition of HBCUs endangers the very aspect of these institutions that makes them unique; others argue that diversity makes these institutions stronger, by fostering mutual respect and an appreciation for Black culture among a broader population.

The growing diversity at HBCUs is not limited to their student bodies but extends to their faculties as well.[50] White faculty reported experiencing a heightened self-awareness working at HBCUs. They have also learned much about the African American culture and had their false, misinformed assumptions challenged.[51] With more non-Black students and non-Black faculty, HBCUs find themselves expanding their educational goals and objectives while attempting to remain true to their core missions. Often HBCUs critics use an argument of the institutions lacking diversity. This comes from a lack of understanding diversity beyond the idea of racial identity. Even if campuses are composed of mainly Black students this does not indicate a lack of diversity as Blacks are not a monolithic group and should not be looked at as such.

HBCUs have produced the vast majority (studies show anywhere from 40 to 70 percent) of African American scholars working in academe today, especially those in tenured faculty positions. Perna found that more than 55 percent of African Americans who received their bachelor's degrees from HBCUs and become faculty members return to teach in HBCUs.[52] Additionally, over 70 percent of African Americans with doctoral degrees from HBCUs return to teach in the HBCU setting.[53] In order to secure the future of HBCUs, it is vital for these institutions to "grow their own" future faculty—faculty members that care about the needs of HBCUs and can bolster the nurturing environment purported by HBCU supporters.

Bettez and Suggs use the writings and personal accounts of current African American scholars who attended HBCUs to support their argument that HBCUs do well in preparing a generation for leadership.[54] These scholars all espoused a sentiment that their HBCU education and experiences provided an "unmatched capacity to build their educational foundations for continued academic success beyond completion of their undergraduate degrees."[55]

WHERE DO WE GO FROM HERE?

HBCUs have stood the test of time, firmly planted on the shoulders of centuries of a strong sense of mission and service to their students and communities. In order to continue to thrive and serve a new generation of students seeking access to higher education there are ways in which they can continue to build on their strengths and confront the challenges they face.

Graduation and Retention Rates

HBCUs must address their low retention and graduation rates. Michael T. Nettles, Senior Vice-President of the Educational Testing Service (ETS) states, "Retention is a sign of efficiency at colleges and universities and contributes to an institution's public image" (Gasman et al., 2013, p. 10). HBCUs should continue to seek out and develop alternative ways to measure success at their institutions. But, in the meantime, schools that take seriously the task of increasing student retention and developing programs and strategies that increase graduation rates will find themselves headed in the right direction. Along with graduation rates, HBCUs are primed to take the lead in being spaces to reclaim and revive the Black male college student population. John Wilson, president of Morehouse College, echoes this sentiment: "The idea of college as a special and essential gateway to a successful life is lost on far too many young Black men. More Americans need to join Morehouse College in adopting the urgency to change that (Gasman et al., 2013, p.7)," he states. Concerted efforts to develop relationships and construct pipelines for Black male students to aspire to and increasingly successfully enroll in college must be made. Institutions that have already been successful in this area must be more forthcoming and open to sharing their successful strategies with other institutions. Likewise, institutional leaders at HBCUs that struggle in the area of gender parity must be open to taking advice and learning lessons from their more successful sister institutions.

Fundraising and Finances

Looking to the future, HBCUs must firm up their financial foundation. There are a number of strategies these institutions can employ to move in that direction. To strengthen fundraising operations HBCUs can take the following actions. First, they can cultivate Black fundraisers by introducing fundraising as a career to students with an interest in the future of HBCUs. HBCUs would benefit from hiring more fundraisers of color and fundraisers who understand the HBCU environment and the needs of African American alumni. Second, HBCUs should teach students about philanthropy and giving back to their institution starting at new student orientation. Unless students and alumni understand the role that they play in sustaining the institution, they will not comprehend the importance of giving back financially. Third, HBCUs should form partnerships with community organizations, other HBCUs, other Minority Serving Institutions, and majority institutions. Corporations, foundations, and other funders value partnerships because they bring together common strengths and create opportunities for creative and innovative thinking. Fourth, HBCUs need to study the changing agendas of public and private funders and make connections to these agendas. Long gone are the days of HBCUs getting funding based on their admirable historic legacies; today funders want to see how HBCUs respond to and lead major trends in higher education. Funders, such as Kresge Foundation, are making substantial investments into HBCUs that are addressing concerns and educational issues that line up with those of the foundation. Having data that give concrete evidence of programmatic success gives funders the confidence that their investment of money will provide a high return. Therefore, HBCUs must be diligent in data collection. Not for the mere sake of evaluation but also to aid in securing funding.

Leadership

Funders and donors are more likely to give when they feel a school is stable and secure. High turnover and egregious errors build mistrust between constituents and the institutions with which they associate. Steady yet visionary leadership has to be a priority for HBCUs. It is vital to communicate examples of strong, successful leadership to the general public, the media, and policymakers. The representation of Black leadership, HBCU leadership in particular, is often unfairly skewed towards the negative in media outlets; there must be a more nuanced understanding of HBCU leadership.[56] Public confidence in HBCU administration is instrumental in generating much needed income from state, federal, and private funding sources. Walter Kimbrough, president of Dillard University, stated, "Boards are beginning to realize that they need progressive, innovative, and truly student-oriented leaders in these very challenging times" (Gasman et al., 2013, p.14). HBCUs may need to step out of familiar territory and comfort zones and look for leadership that may be new to the HBCU community. This is not to say there are not talented administrators within the HBCU community. These persons should also serve as models and mentors for aspiring HBCU leaders.

With only 30 percent of HBCU presidents being female, institutions will be served well not only by seeking out more qualified female candidates but also ensuring their campuses are places where women leaders feel they can be supported in leadership. HBCU presidents must also be open to new strategies, opportunities, and ways to market and push forward their respective institutions. This means embracing and using new technology. This involves having a presence in arenas such as Twitter, Facebook, LinkedIn, etc. Being active in social media not only creates a new level of accessibility to the president but also allows for the insertion of HBCU leadership's voice in conversations going on about higher education. Social media is also an avenue for sharing.

CONCLUDING THOUGHT

HBCUs have long legacies of doing great work. This legacy has been studied and documented in seminal works such as James D. Anderson's *The Education of Blacks in the South, 1865–1930*, William Watkins' *White Architects of Black Education*, and Joy Williamson-Lott's Radicalizing the *Ebony Tower: Black Colleges and the Freedom Movement in Mississippi*.[57] These stories have served as the foundation on which HBCUs stand on, fighting the battle of proving relevancy. As the higher education landscape sees increases in tuition prices, and dwindling resources and funding, these legacies, though great, will not be enough for HBCUs to deter naysayers, critics, and skeptics. Moving into this next age of higher education HBCUs cannot simply rely on their historical accomplishments. They must share the stories of the success they are currently engaging in and experiencing. Sharing may be in the form of increased participation in national studies and research.

Sharing may be bolstering the public relations operations and media presence of institutions. Sharing could be showing diligence and intentionality in the collection of robust and complete data. Sharing could also be imploring that board members, administrators, and alumni make concerted efforts not only to desire accountability for their respective institutions but to also take an active role in the promotion, fundraising, and the garnering of support and investments. No matter the manner, share these institutions must. HBCUs must tell the contemporary story of HBCUs; the history and legacy are formidable and essential, but the real story is what HBCUs are doing today and the potential they have to contribute.

NOTES

1. U.S. Department of Education, National Center for Education Statistics, NCES 2011- (Washington, D.C.: United States Government Printing Office, 2011)
2. U.S. Department of Education, National Center for Education Statistics, NCES 2011-(Washington, D.C.: United States Government Printing Office, 2011).
3. M. Christopher Brown, II and James E. Davis, "The Historically Black College as Social Contract, Social Capital, and Social Equalizer," *Peabody Journal of Education* 76 (2001): 31–49.
4. Walter R. Allen, "The Color of Success: African-American College Student Outcomes at Predominantly White and Historically Black Public Colleges and Universities," *Harvard Educational Review* 62 (1992): 26–444.
5. D. Jason DeSousa and George D. Kuh, "Does Institutional Racial Composition Make a Difference in What Black Students Gain from College?" *Journal of College Student Development* 37 (1996): 257–267.
6. Lemuel W. Watson and George D. Kuh, "The Influence of Dominant Race Environments on Student Involvement, Perceptions, and Educational Gains: A look at Historically Black and Predominantly White Liberal Arts Institutions," *Journal of College Student Development* 3 (1996): 415–424.
7. Fries-Britt, Sharon L. Fries-Britt, and Bridget Turner, "Uneven Stories: Successful Black Collegians at a Black and a White Campus," *Review of Higher Education* 25(2002): 315–330.
8. Roland G. Fryer Jr. and Michael Greenstone, "The Changing Consequences of Attending Historically Black Colleges and Universities," *American Economic Journal: Applied Economics* 123 (2010): 116–148.
9. U.S. Department of Education, National Center for Education Statistics, NCES 2011- (Washington, D.C.: United States Government Printing Office, 2011).
10. Charmaine J. Mercer and James B. Stedman, "Minority-serving Institutions: Selected Institutional and Student Characteristics," in *Understanding Minority-Serving Institutions,* ed. Marybeth Gas man et al. (Albany: State University of New York Press, 2008), 28–42.

11. Ibid.

12. Thurgood Marshall Scholarship Fund, *Understanding Gender at Publically Historically Black Colleges and* Universities, by Shirley M. Geiger (Washington, D.C.: Thurgood Marshall Scholarship Fund, 2007).

13. Valerie Lundy-Wagner and Marybeth Gasman, "When Gender Issues are Not Just About Women: Reconsidering Male Students at Historically Black Colleges and Universities," *Teachers College Record* 113(2011): 934–968.

14. U.S. Department of Education, National Center for Education Statistics, NCES 2011 (Washington, D.C.: United States Government Printing Office, 2011).

15. Marybeth Gasman, Ufuoma Abiola and Sydney Freeman, "Gender Disparities at Historically Black Colleges and Universities," *Journal of Negro Education* (forthcoming).

16. Valerie R. Wilson, "The Effect of Attending an HBCU on Persistence and Graduation Outcomes of African-American College Students," *Review of Black Political Economy* 34 (2007): 11-52.

17. Ronald J. Peters Jr., Kentya Ford, Mi-Ting Lin, Angela F. Meshack, Regina J. Johnson, & E. James Essien, "The Relationship Between Perceived Psychological Distress, Behavioral Indicators and African American Student Financial Aid Attainment Difficulty," *American Journal of Health Studies* 26 (2011).

18. Marybeth Gasman, "Historically Black Colleges and Universities in a Time of Economic Crisis," *Academe* 95(2009): 26–28.

19. Ibid.

20. Ibid.

21. Marybeth Gasman and Nelson Bowman III, "How to Paint a Better Portrait of HBCUs," *Academe* 97 (2011): 24–27.

22. Ibid.

23. Marybeth Gasman and Tryan McMickens, "Liberal or Professional Education?: The Missions of Public Black Colleges and Universities and Their Impact on the Future of African Americans," *Souls* 12 (2010) 286–305.

24. Arinola O. Adebayo, Adeyemi A. Adekoya, and O. Felix Ayadi, "Historically Black Colleges and Universities as Agents of Change for the Development of Minority Business," *Journal of Black Studies* 32 (2001): 166–183.

25. Henry N. Drewry and Humphrey Doermann, *Stand and Prosper: Private Black Colleges and their Students* (Princeton: Princeton University Press, 2001).

26. Ibid..

27. Amy E. Sibulkin and J. S. Butler, "Differences in Graduation Rates between Young Black and White College Students: Effect of Entry into Parenthood and Historically Black Universities," *Research in Higher Education* 46 (2005): 327–348.

28. Ibid.

29. Jack L. Ezzell Jr. and Alex J. Schexnider, "Leadership, Governance, and Sustainability of Black Colleges and Universities," *TrusTeeship* (2010).

30. Marybeth Gasman, *The Changing Face of Historically Black Colleges and Universities.* Philadelphia, PA: Penn Center for Minority Serving Institutions, 2013.

31. Robert Birnbaum and Paul D. Umbach, "Scholar, Steard, Spanner, Stranger: The Four Careers Paths of College Presidents," *Review of Higher Education* 24 (2001): 203–215.

32. Marybeth Gasman, "HBCU Presidents and Social Media," *Huffington Post*, September 5, 2012, http://www.huffingtonpost.com/marybeth-gasman/hbcu-social-media-use-_b_1856214.html; Marybeth Gasman, "Vacancies in the Black College Presidency," *Chronicle of Higher Education*, April 12, 2012, http://chronicle.com/blogs/innovations/vacancies-in-the-Black-college-presidency-whats-going-on/32204

33. Marybeth Gasman, "Historically Black Colleges and Universities in a Time of Economic Crisis," *Academe* 95 (2009): 26–28.

34. Laura Perna, Valerie Lundy-Wagner, Noah Drezner, Marybeth Gasman, Susan Yoon, Enakshi Bose, and Shannon Gary, "The Contributions of HBCUs to the Preparation of African American Women for STEM Careers: A Case Study," *Research in Higher Education* 50(2008): 1–23.

35. Ibid.

36. S. Keith Hargrove, John A. Wheatland, Duowen Ding, and Cordelia M. Brown, "The Effect of Individual Learning Styles on Student GPA in Engineering Education at Morgan State University," *Journal of STEM Education: Innovations & Research* 9 (2008): 9.

37. Lekan Oguntoyinbo, "Social Justice," *Diverse: Issues in Higher Education* 29 (2012): 12–13. (2012).

38. Ibid.

39. Marybeth Gasman and Nelson Bowman III, "How to Paint a Better Portrait of HBCUs," *Academe* 97 (2011): 24–27.

40. Ibid.

41. James T. Minor, "Groundwork for Studying Governance at Historically Black Colleges and Universities," in *Understanding Minority-Serving Institutions*, eds. Marybeth Gasman et al. (Albany: State University of New York Press, 2008), 169–182.

42. Ibid.

43. J. K. Pierre and C. R. Welch. "Why Historically Black Colleges and Universities are Needed in the 21st Century." *Journal of Race Gender & Poverty*, no. 1 (2009), 101, 105.

44. Brighid Dwyer, "Framing the Effect of Multiculturalism on Diversity Outcomes among Students at Historically Black Colleges and Universities," *Educational Foundations* 20 (2006): 37–59; Rosemary B. Closson and Wilma J. Henry, "The Social Adjustment of Undergraduate White Students in the Minority on an Historically Black College Campus," *Journal of College Student Development* 49 (2008): 517–534.

45. Walter R. Allen, "A Forward Glance in a Mirror: Diversity Challenged—Access, Equity, and Success in Higher Education," *Educational Researcher* 34 (2005): 18–23.

46. Marybeth Gasman, *Envisioning Black Colleges: A History of the United Negro College Fund* (Baltimore: Johns Hopkins University Press, 2007); U.S. Department of Education, National Center for Education Statistics, NCES 1980(Washington, D.C.: United States Government Printing Office, 1980).

47. Taryn G. Ozuna, "Examining the First-Year Experience and Perceptions of Sense of Belonging among Mexican American Students Enrolled in a Texas HBCU" (PhD diss., University of Texas, Austin, 2012).
48. U.S. Department of Education, National Center for Education Statistics, NCES 2011(Washington, D.C.: United States Government Printing Office, 2011),
49. Ibid.
50. Lenoar Foster, "The Not-So-Invisible Professors: White Faculty at the Black College," *Urban Education* 36 (2011): 611–629.
51. Rosemary B. Closson, & Wilma J. Henry, "The Social Adjustment of Undergraduate White Students in the Minority on an Historically Black College Campus," *Journal of College Student Development* 49 (2008): 517–534.
52. Laura Perna, Valerie Lundy-Wagner, Noah Drezner, Marybeth Gasman, Susan Yoon, Enakshi Bose, and Shannon Gary, "The Contributions of HBCUs to the Preparation of African American Women for STEM Careers: A Case Study," *Research in Higher Education* 50 (2008): 1–23.
53. Ibid.
54. Silvia C. Bettez and Vickie L. Suggs, "Centering the Educational and Social Significance of HBCUs: A Focus on the Educational Journeys and Thoughts of African American Scholars," *The Urban Review* 44 (2012): 303–310.
55. Ibid.
56. Marybeth Gasman, "Truth, Generalizations, and Stigmas: An Analysis of the Media's Coverage of Morris Brown College and Black Colleges Overall," *Review of Black Political Economy* 34(2007): 111–135; Marybeth Gasman, "HBCU Presidents and Social Media," *Huffington Post*, September 5, 2012, http://www.huffingtonpost.com/marybeth-gasman/hbcu-social-media-use-_b_1856214.html
57. James D Anderson, *The Education of Blacks in the South, 1865–1930* (Chapel Hill, NC: University of North Carolina Press, 1988); William Watkins, *White Architects of Black Education: Ideology and Power in America, 1865–1954* (New York, NY: Teachers College Press, 2001); and Joy Ann Williamson, *Radicalizing the Ebony Tower: Black Colleges and the Black Freedom Struggle in Mississippi* (New York, NY: Teachers College Press, 2008).

CHAPTER 14

CONNECTING THE DOTS

Reflecting on Pedagogy and African American Educational History

Michelle A. Purdy
Washington University in St. Louis

As historians of African American educational history, we attempt to help connect the dots between what we know historically and the current manifestations of African Americans' educational successes, challenges, and dilemmas. We contemplate how our historical digging, siphoning, uncovering, analyzing, contextualizing, and storytelling provides a deeper, fuller interpretation of the past and how our work will aid others more focused on the contemporary better connect the dots as they make their next move. In this chapter, I posit that the teaching of African American educational history aids students with making connections among larger themes related to education and schooling in the United States and general U.S. history. African American educational history provides an opportunity for students to consider the enduring reality of unequal education in U.S. society and how those marginalized seek quality education. Often as scholars, we do not write about our teaching, but as mentors have shared and philosophers

Using Past as Prologue, pages 341–352
Copyright © 2015 by Information Age Publishing
All rights of reproduction in any form reserved.

have stated, one learns through teaching.[1] Therefore, it seems plausible that writing about teaching can be transformative. Educational historian Jack Dougherty noted, "Through scholarly journals, we can transform the private act of teaching into a more public form of academic work, subject to critical review by our peers, so that innovations may be thoughtfully considered and perhaps modified and used by others in both scholarly and general communities."[2] This final chapter focuses on key texts used in educational courses not specifically focused on educational history or the study of history. These texts have engaged students and helped them connect the dots among the past, present, and future of the U.S. educational system. Together, these texts and the chapters in this volume offer instructors, with varied research and teaching interests, possibilities for interrogating more fully education and schooling in the United States through the inclusion of African American educational history.

As evident by the authors in this volume, scholars of African American educational history teach in a variety of higher education institutions, including schools and departments of education and history. We may find ourselves teaching undergraduate or graduate students who take our courses either because they are specifically interested in education and/or history or to satisfy general course requirements. Beyond those courses specific to African American educational history and U.S. educational history, those of us in colleges or departments of education may teach any number of courses related to K–12 education or higher education. We may teach undergraduate courses that introduce students to the history of U.S. schooling, the debates about the purposes of education and schooling over time, and the relationship between schooling and society. We may be instructors for teacher education courses in which students critically examine the social construction of race, social class, gender, sexual orientation, disability, and language, and how power, privilege, and oppression operate in U.S. society and U.S. public schools. We may also lead doctoral seminars intended to introduce students to seminal texts in educational research and/or the history of U.S. education and schooling. While the courses we teach have different purposes and audiences, some lend themselves to making connections between the past and the present in order to deliberate deeply the underpinnings of contemporary educational success, issues, and challenges. In doing so, students should be pushed to avoid presentism and to think historically and learn important historical knowledge. As one considers the relationship among education, schooling, and society, including contemporary issues such as the resegregation of schools, challenges faced by marginalized communities in urban, suburban, and rural schools, and the achievement gap or more aptly identified as "the education debt" by educational scholar Gloria Ladson-Billings, African American educational history remains central to U.S. history and continued structural inequalities.[3]

Yet, many students, whether at the undergraduate or graduate level, have limited knowledge about the role of race and racism in the U.S. educational system; in fact, they have limited knowledge of the general history of race and racism in the United States. They should not be faulted for this, but met where they are. Therefore, while not at the "expense" of other marginalized groups nor by creating a hierarchy of oppression, introducing students to Black educational history, even in education classes that address a range of topics and include multiple modes of inquiry, is essential for understanding race and racism presently in U.S. schooling and for informing the choices and actions they will make as future teachers, researchers, policymakers, professionals, and citizens.

To address the relationship between the past and present, one may elucidate such themes and tensions that include power and oppression, agency and resistance, policy and practice, access and denial, micro and macro, and individual and collective. Including African American educational history in education courses illuminates the political, economic, social, and ideological realities underlying educational pursuits by African Americans and the relationship between education and society. With this knowledge, students will hopefully continue to make connections beyond class about the complexities and contradictions inherent in the U.S. educational system.

INTRODUCING RACE AND RACISM

One approach to including African American educational history in education courses is not to begin with actual African American educational history texts or even the past. Beginning with the present and/or the importance of stories and history allows students to contemplate what they know about contemporary issues and their historical knowledge and how they learned about those issues and that knowledge. Acclaimed author Chimamanda Adiche's "The Danger of a Single Story" is helpful for sparking discussion about the power of story.[4] In this TED Talk, Adiche addressed single stories she learned from books, single stories others have had of her, and the single stories she once had. Towards the conclusion of the talk, she stated, "Many stories matter. Stories have been used to dispossess and to malign. But stories can also be used to empower, and to humanize. Stories can break the dignity of a people. But stories can also repair that broken dignity."[5] Through a critical discussion of Adiche's talk, students learn why it is necessary to consider multiple stories and perspectives when learning about the U.S. educational system, past and present.

Gloria Ladson-Billings' 2006 American Educational Research Association Presidential Address, "From the Achievement Gap to the Education Debt: Understanding Achievement in U.S. Schools" couples the present and the past and helps to frame contemporary U.S. educational inequalities. For many students, whether at the undergraduate or graduate level, education majors or non-education majors, they have heard and/or interrogated the term "achievement gap." As Ladson-Billings noted, "The term produces more than 11 million citations on Google. "Achievement Gap," much like certain popular culture music stars, has become a crossover hit."[6] Ladson-Billings argued, however, "that our focus on the achievement gap is akin to a focus on the budget deficit, but what is actually happening to African American and Latina/o students is really more like the national debt. We do not have an achievement gap; we have an education debt." And this debt is an accumulation of "historical, economic, sociopolitical, and moral decisions and policies that characterize our society."[7] Through her discussion of these four debts, Ladson-Billings incorporated examples from U.S. history to show the impact of the debt on "past education progress," "past education research findings," and "the potential for forging a better educational future." Through reading this piece, especially at the beginning of the semester, students realize that the playing field has never been equal and that the achievement gap is not new nor solely based on test scores.

UNDERSTANDING SLAVERY AND EDUCATION

One starting point in courses for including African American educational history is a focus on the relationship between the institution of slavery and the development of U.S. schooling. Historian Allison Davis contended, "For the American story simply cannot be told without discussion and analysis of the experiences of black people whose labor created the nation's wealth, whose enslavement undergirded and undermined the concepts of democratic freedom, and whose civil exclusion sparked the political revolutions of the twentieth century."[8] This quote also aptly relates to the development of U.S. schooling as education was used as a tool to disenfranchise and stifle those of African descent both enslaved and free. Several texts may prove useful whether courses are addressing education in the colonial period, the rise of common schools in the nineteenth century, and the changing role of family and religion in education or the construction of race alongside larger themes of identity, power, privilege, and oppression and other socially constructed categories.

Frederick Douglass' *Narrative of the Life of Frederick Douglass: An American Slave* is very telling about the power of education for those enslaved. Through this work, students grapple with the harshness of the institution of slavery and the use of Christianity to justify slavery. Such a text serves as a springboard for considering the multiple reasons why southern states outlawed education for those enslaved in the 1800s. Students glean one reason as noted by one of Douglass' masters, Mr. Auld, when he learns that his wife, Mrs. Auld, is teaching Douglass the ABCs. Douglass recounted Mr. Auld stating, "Learning would *spoil* the best nigger in the world. Now if you teach that nigger (speaking of myself) how to read there would be no keeping him. It would forever unfit him to be a slave."[9] *Narrative* also illuminates that schooling was not for all in nineteenth century United States and the ways in which education was conceived to support the political, economic, and social development of the United States. Simultaneously, *Narrative* provides a perspective on what it means for those marginalized to receive an education. After learning to read and write, Douglass stated, "As I writhed under it, I would at times feel that learning to read had been a curse rather than a blessing. It had given me a view of my wretched condition without the remedy. It opened my eyes to the horrible pit, but to no ladder upon which to get out."[10] This dilemma of learning—understanding what it means to be oppressed and then having the power of literacy and education to critique one's oppression and society—is a theme applicable to studying the history of education for other groups including women, European and Asian immigrants, Native Americans, and Mexican Americans.

Heather Andrea Williams' *Self Taught: African American Education in Slavery and Freedom* augments Douglass' narrative because it broadens the narrative beyond one individual and addresses the power of literacy and education for those enslaved and newly freed. Williams stated, "Despite laws and custom in slave states prohibiting enslaved people from learning to read and write, a small percentage managed through ingenuity and will, to acquire a degree of literacy in the antebellum period."[11] *Self-Taught* tells the multiple ways in which enslaved and freed people acquired education: hiding spelling books under their hats, turning to White children or poor Whites for instruction, trading money and food for letters and words, taking advantage of masters being away on Sundays, and willing mistresses who would teach. Moreover, *Self-Taught* examines how African Americans taught themselves and the relationships they navigated with northern Whites who came South to educate them. Through Douglass and Williams, students become aware of the risks taken by various groups (i.e., slaves, free people of color, Whites) for African Americans to secure education in the nineteenth century. Moreover, Williams' work allows students to analyze a historical text in which African American voices' are foregrounded.

James Anderson's *The Education of Blacks in the South, 1860–1935* is a third text that changes students' knowledge and perceptions about African Americans. Students come to understand that while common schools were established in the Northeast and Midwest, the South had no system of public schools until after the Civil War, and former slaves were the individuals who sought "universal, state-supported public education" in the South.[12] As he wrote, "Indeed, a central theme in the history of the education of black

Americans is the persistent struggle to fashion a system of formal education that prefigured their liberation from peasantry."[13] Moreover, Anderson examines the ideological tensions that shaped Black education in the South, the development of different schooling levels (i.e., common schools, normal schools, high schools, and higher education), and the double taxation African Americans endured to secure and support Black schooling options. *Narrative, Self-Taught,* and *The Education of Blacks* signify what Anderson noted in his introduction:

> The history of American education abounds with themes that represent the inextricable ties between citizenship in a democratic society and popular education. It is crucial for an understanding of American educational history, however, to recognize that within American democracy there have been classes of oppressed people and that there have been essential relationships between popular education and the politics of oppression. Both schooling for democratic citizenship and schooling for second-class citizenship have been basic traditions in American education.[14]

Including African American educational history provides students with a deeper understanding of slavery. The reading of these texts compels students to contend with the purposes of education in relationship to the development of the United States as both a democracy and capitalistic society and the intertwinement of slavery, the construction of race and racism, and educational opportunity.

UNDERSTANDING JIM CROW, *BROWN V. BOARD,* AND SCHOOL DESEGREGATION

The twentieth century provides much to consider with respect to U.S. education, and African American educational history is central to the contours of change. First, both the rise of the high school from the mid-nineteenth century to the mid-twentieth century and the Progressive Era in the early twentieth century overlap with significant junctures in African American educational history. Simultaneously occurring are the Jim Crow era of "separate but equal" schooling, *de facto* separate schooling in other parts of the country, the increased presence of both pedagogical progressives and administrative progressives, the professionalization of teaching and the challenge for more equity by female teachers, curriculum debates, and the increased Americanization of immigrants, including the second wave of European immigrants and Asian immigrants, and Mexican Americans.

Students can consider these overlapping histories through a variety of perspectives including that of curriculum and educational leadership. For example, instructors can render more complicated an analysis of the debate between Booker T. Washington and W. E. B. Du Bois concerning vocational education and liberal arts education. Whether drawing on Anderson and/or Washington's *The Future of the American Negro* and Du Bois' "Of Mr. Booker T. Washington and Others" in *The Souls of Black Folk*, students should be asked to consider each man's personal context and life story, their interactions, and the benefits and drawbacks of both types of education given the context.[15] Students need to discern that African Americans (or for that matter any group of people) are not monolithic and that individuals had differing strategies and modes of operation, contextualized in part by their own lives, experiences, and beliefs. As Dorsey noted about her teaching, "I place great emphasis on the diversity of the black experience. To disrupt the assumption of a monolithic, universal black experience, I instruct students to pay careful attention to the impact that time, location, and occupation had on the lives of black people in the past."[16] Moreover, the Washington and Du Bois debate provides an additional angle by which to consider the overarching vocational education and liberal arts education debate as the U.S. population, its world position, and industrialization continued to grow in the early twentieth century.

Understanding the realities of the Jim Crow South is also important for students to contemplate educational opportunity and all-Black schools in the early to mid-twentieth century. Vanessa Siddle Walker's *Their Highest Potential* causes students to ponder the following: "some evidence suggests that the environment of the segregated school had affective traits, institutional policies, and community support that helped black children learn in spite of the neglect their schools received from white school boards."[17] While *Their Highest Potential* acknowledges the discrepancy in funding between Black and White schools, it provides a window into the value and promise of Black schools with ethics of care. Through Du Bois' "Does the Negro Need Separate Schools?" students are introduced to the type of education Black students might receive in White institutions and his challenge to African Americans about their own thinking about Black institutions. As Du Bois stated,

> Does the Negro need separate schools? God knows he does. But what he needs more than separate schools is a firm and unshakable belief that twelve million American Negroes have the inborn capacity to accomplish just as much as any nation of twelve million anywhere in the world ever accomplished, and that this is not because they are Negroes but because they are human.[18]

Examining Black education during this era allows for students to consider the educational dilemmas facing African Americans who were legally, politically, economically, and socially disenfranchised throughout the nation.

Moving to the mid-twentieth century, the U.S. federal government intervened more directly in education. Therefore, whether through considerations of the multiple federal acts ranging from the 1958 National Defense Education Act to the 1975 Education for All Handicapped Children Act or the "War on Poverty," school desegregation becomes integral to the national story. Having students study the landmark 1954 *Brown v. Board of Education* decision provides the necessary context for students to comprehend the relationship between education and the law and the current resegregation of schools.

Although scholars continue to debate *Brown* including the NAACP strategy, *Brown's* overall effect on the Civil Rights Movement, and the ensuing desegregation battles that followed, students should still be knowledgeable about the actual case. As educational historian Joy Ann Williamson stated, "To teach *Brown* is to deconstruct simple notions of Civil Rights Movement triumphs and visions of a country eager to right historical wrongs."[19] Through a focus on *Brown*, students conceptualize and understand the gravity of the work that made the case(s) a reality, including previous cases such as *Roberts v. Boston* (1849) and *Mendez v. Westminster* (1946), the agency and risk of the plaintiffs, the legal strategy of the NAACP to overturn *Plessy v. Ferguson* and undo Jim Crow, and the relationship of the case to the United States' world position following World War II.

Richard Kluger's *Simple Justice* either taught in its entirety or by specific chapters, along with the actual *Brown I* and *Brown II* decisions, is an essential text. In particular through Kluger's Chapter 26, "Simple Justice," students learn the importance of the Court, the timeline of the case, how the judges deliberated, and the difference between *Brown I* and *Brown II*. As Williamson indicated, "few [students] have ever read the original court documents and even fewer realize there were two separate decisions, that four states and the District of Columbia were involved, and that the South fought aggressively for years to nullify their effect on school attendance." [20] By reading *Brown I* and *Brown II* students interrogate the ways in which the decision was written, the use of social science research, and the characterization of Black students. For example, discussing such quotes from *Brown I* as "To separate them from others of similar age and qualification solely because of their race generates a feeling of inferiority as to their status in the community that may affect their hearts and minds in a way unlikely ever to be undone," gives students pause. Coupled with the role of the doll test performed by Kenneth and Mamie Clark and the ways in which such language perpetuates deficit theories about Black children, students learn to consider the complexities of the case itself and its legacy.[21]

African American educational history also provides a lens for students to engage substantially with the resistance to *Brown* in the South and school desegregation in those states not legally affected by *Brown*. Another Ladson-Billings' piece, "Landing on the Wrong Note: The Price We Paid for Brown," overviews the complexities of *Brown*, the decision's place in U.S.

history and international relations, and the "costs" of *Brown* including the dismissal and demotion of Black educators, the closing of Black schools, and White flight and the establishment of segregationists academies.[22] To delve deeper into the narrative of school desegregation and reform following *Brown*, instructors may want students to read two different books simultaneously as suggested by Doughtery. David Cecelski's *Along Freedom Road*, which chronicles the 1968–1969 school boycott in Hyde County, North Carolina to oppose the closure of two historically Black schools, and Jerald Podair's *The Strike that Changed New York*, which details the well-known community control story of Ocean Hill-Brownsville.[23] Cecelski's book allows students to contemplate what it would mean to lose one's school and whether or not they could imagine boycotting school for a year or their parents encouraging it. On the other hand, Podair's book calls them to wrestle with understanding the multiple dynamics among union leaders, teachers, and community members. Examining the arc of educational opportunity for African Americans in the twentieth century alongside major changes in U.S. educational history yields an understanding of the unevenness of equal educational opportunity, those who fought for the possibility of equal education, and the shifting priorities of the federal government.

CONCLUSION: COMING FULL CIRCLE

Whether students are considering contemporary issues involving the resegregation of schools, urban education reform, the role of local property taxes in funding schools, the relationship between the federal government and schooling, high stakes testing and accountability, curriculum and pedagogy, or collective impact strategy to solve educational issues, having an introduction to some of the defining moments in Black educational history underlines their knowledge of continued inequities in education and the complexities of these debates. Moreover, they recognize that their own educational experiences are a part of a much larger continuum and system than they have previously considered. Consequently, when students, in particular those desiring to be teachers, read more contemporary research such as Lisa Delpit's "The Silenced Dialogue," they are able to offer a layered understanding of Black educational pursuits and needs.[24] Building on both historical and contemporary discussions, students are able to engage in discussion about how teachers of color can be silenced in schools, the culture of power, and the importance of knowing and acknowledging one's power in order to have open dialogue. This reading not only stimulates questions about teacher interaction and the power of teachers in schools, but also the effects of educating students to navigate the culture of power.

Through the inclusion of African American educational history, students can also more fully contemplate the state of urban education. For example, students are more keenly able to discuss a present-day issue in their communities such as the school transfer issue in the St. Louis metropolitan area. When the state deemed Normandy and Riverview school districts unaccredited in summer 2013, students in those districts had the option to transfer to another school district. Yet, some school districts, including the predominantly White Francis Howell school district, resisted. Moreover, there has been controversy about the spending of funds in the transfer districts that come from the original districts.[25] After gaining a better understanding of school desegregation struggles, including those in St. Louis, students are more apt to recognize that challenges continue for urban school districts, which are often home to African Americans and other people of color or recent immigrants, who are disproportionally impoverished.[26] Further, students recognize that the challenges are multi-faceted; they are political, economic, and social, and they are historically rooted in the purposes of education that differ for different groups.

As I conclude, I must acknowledge that the inclusion of African American educational history is not always welcomed, as evident from students' body language, hesitancy to participate in large group discussions, and anonymous student comments on evaluation forms. Yet, other students, from all backgrounds, have appreciated learning about African American educational history alongside other histories. As evident from positive student comments, e-mails, and their final assignments, once students confront their own understanding of race and racism, as not biological and as part of a system of power and oppression that is sustained by policy, practice, and ideology, they are willing to engage in their readings, class discussions, and in conversation with their professor—an African American female.

As professors, may we constantly seek ways to improve our pedagogy and the connections we make for students among the past and present. Reflecting on our teaching allows us to aim for even clearer examples of intersections of educational pursuits by those marginalized and in power. As one considers their pedagogy, the pieces in this volume are additional historical texts to be included in education and history courses as well as courses concerned with urban issues, gender, and American culture. These chapters help to illuminate dimensions of the African American educational experience and will help students to consider particular stories that are part of a larger African American tradition of pursuing educational equity and the multiple forces that influence and undermine that pursuit. Collectively, our work on this volume is one means by which all of us concerned with the African American educational experience—past, present, and future—can connect the dots for our students and one another.

NOTES

1. I have been fortunate to have mentors who have inspired my approach to teaching and exceptional colleagues and students to work alongside at Emory University, Michigan State University and Washington University in St. Louis; these mentors, colleagues, and students have informed my teaching through their examples, provided constructive feedback on my syllabi and teaching, and allowed me to share pedagogical ideas. In particular, I am grateful for my colleague, Dr. Vera L Stenhouse, with whom I have discussed teaching and learning for a number of years and who reviewed initial drafts of this chapter.

2. Jack Dougherty, "Introduction," *History of Education Quarterly* 44, no. 1 (Spring 2004): 97.

3. Gloria Ladson-Billings, "From the Achievement Gap to the Education Debt: Understanding Achievement in U.S. Schools," *Educational Researcher* 35, no. 7 (October 2006): 3–12.

4. I owe a debt of gratitude to my colleague Dr. Terry Flennaugh for introducing me to Adiche's *The Danger of a Single Story.*

5. Chimamanda Adiche. *The Danger of a Single Story* (TED, 2009), 18 min., 49 sec, http://www.ted.com/talks/chimamanda_adichie_the_danger_of_a_single_story (accessed July 8, 2014).

6. Ladson-Billings, "From the Achievement Gap to the Education Debt," 3.

7. Ibid., 5.

8. Allison Dorsey, "Black History is American History: Teaching African American History in the Twenty-First Century," *The Journal of American History* 93, no. 4 (Mar. 2007): 1172.

9. Frederick Douglass, *Narrative of the Life of Frederick Douglass: An American Slave, Written by Himself with Related Documents,* ed. David W. Blight (Boston, MA: Bedford/St. Martin's), 63–64.

10. Ibid., 68.

11. Heather Andrea Williams, *Self-Taught: African American Education in Slavery and Freedom* (Chapel Hill, NC: The University of North Carolina Press, 2005), 7.

12. James Anderson, *The Education of Blacks in the South, 1860–1935* (Chapel Hill, NC: The University of North Carolina Press, 1988), 4.

13. Ibid., 3.

14. Ibid., 1.

15. Booker T. Washington, "The Future of the American Negro, 1899," in *The School in the United States: A Documentary History,* ed. James W. Fraser (New York, NY: Routledge, 2001), 118–124; W. E. B. Du Bois, "Of Mr. Booker T. Washington and Others," in *The School in the United States: A Documentary History,* ed. James W. Fraser (New York, NY: Routledge, 2001), 124–136.

16. Dorsey, 1172–1173.

17. Vanessa Siddle Walker, *Their Highest Potential: An African American School Community in the Segregated South* (Chapel Hill, NC: The University of North Carolina Press, 1996), 3.

18. W. E. B. Du Bois, "Does the Negro Need Separate Schools?" *The Journal of Negro Education* 4, no. 3 (July 1935): 333.

19. Joy Ann Williamson, "*Brown,* Black, and Yellow: Desegregation in a Multi-Ethnic Context," *History of Education Quarterly* 44, no. 1 (Spring 2004): 109.
20. Ibid.
21. U.S. Supreme Court, *Brown, et al. v. Board of Education of Topeka, et al., No. 1,* Supreme Court of the United States, 347 U.S. 483; 1954.
22. Gloria Ladson-Billings, "Landing on the Wrong Note: The Price We Paid for *Brown,"* Educational Researcher 33, no. 7 (October 2004): 3–13.
23. Jack Dougherty, "Making Sense of Multiple Interpretations," *History of Education Quarterly* 44, no. 1 (Spring 2004): 105–108; David Cecelski, *Along Freedom Road: Hyde County, North Carolina and the Fate of Black Schools in the South* (Chapel Hill, NC: The University of North Carolina Press, 1994); and Jerald Podair, *The Strike That Changed New York, NY: Blacks, Whites, and the Ocean Hill-Brownsville Crisis* (New Haven, CT: Yale University Press, 2002).
24. Lisa Delpit, "The Silenced Dialogue: Power and Pedagogy in Educating Other People's Children," *Harvard Educational Review* 58, no. 3 (August 1988): 280–298.
25. Elisa Crouch and Jessica Bock, "Money Being Paid by Normandy, Riverview Gardens to Other Districts Not Being Spent," *St. Louis Post Dispatch,* February 10, 2014.
26. Kimberly Jade Norwood, "Minnie Liddell's Forty-Year Quest for Quality Public Education Remains a Dream Deferred," *Washington University Journal of Law and Policy* 40 (2012): 1–66.

EPILOGUE

FROM FREEDOM SCHOOLS TO FREEDOM SCHOOLING?

V. P. Franklin
University of California, Riverside

In his final book before his assassination, Dr. Martin Luther King, Jr. asked the question: Where do we go from here? And he posed two alternatives: "Chaos or Community." *Using the Past as Prologue* offers well-documented assessments of the educational experiences of African Americans histori- cally at the elementary, secondary, and higher education levels, public and private, since the mid-nineteenth century. These analyses build upon and expand the analysis of African American educational history included in *New Perspectives on Black Educational History*, published in 1978.[1]

Since that time, there has been a huge expansion in the research on the history of African American education; however, the efforts begun the 1950s and 1960s to increase the diversity in U.S. classrooms through the integration of children of color into all-White schools has ended, and accountability and increased standardized testing were introduced to try and close the gap in academic achievement between children of color and White students.[2] For many years the poor performance of U.S. students on international tests on academic progress was blamed on children of color, but by the beginning of the twenty-first century, it became clear that the

Using Past as Prologue, pages 353–360
Copyright © 2015 by Information Age Publishing
All rights of reproduction in any form reserved.

level of performance of middle and upper income White students in the United States was on par only with the lowest performing students in South Korea, Japan, Finland, and most other western industrialized nations.[3] As is clear from the chapter by Sharon Pierson in *Using the Past as Prologue*, educational excellence was found in all-Black schools in the South even under the Jim Crow conditions. This chapter and many other studies have demonstrated that historically the absence of educational resources did not prevent the delivery of high quality schooling to African American students.[4]

Beginning in the 1980s, having swept aside even the possibility of public school desegregation, voluntary or court-ordered, conservative businesspeople and educational administrators decided to fund the introduction of systems of accountability into public schools, and this new emphasis was advanced greatly by the federal government's "No Child Left Behind" and "Race to the Top" mandates. And unfortunately, while regular standardized testing in reading and math was required of all public school students, there were few resources made available to improve the educational outcomes at public schools where students consistently performed poorly on standardized tests. Instead, these public schools were closed and educational entrepreneurs were given contracts and substantial funding to open "charter schools" that attempted to improve the academic achievement levels for poor children of color. Thus far, while thousands of these publicly funded, but privately operated schools have been opened in urban school districts, with very few exceptions, the performance on standardized tests of students of color enrolled in charter schools has been no better than those attending traditional public schools.[5]

At the same time, the new emphasis on accountability and standardized testing has greatly damaged the overall educational experiences for children of color and others by driving out of the curriculum the courses and programs in art, music, athletics, science, and even history—areas not tested in the accountability systems. Educational historian Diane Ravitch in *The Death and Life of the Great American School System: How Testing and Choice Are Undermining Education* (2011) and *Reign of Error: The Hoax of the Privatization Movement and the Danger to America's Schools* (2014) has argued that the movement toward public education being dominated by profit-driven business enterprises and wealthy capitalists has greatly harmed the schooling of American children. Ravitch demonstrates that through the guidelines issued to school districts seeking "Race to the Top" funding, Secretary of Education Arne Duncan was able to use hundreds of millions of dollars to advance the interests of educational entrepreneurs who decide to open charter schools. The financial and political groups supporting the "privatization" of U.S. public education view the bodies of African American and other children of color as valuable for increasing corporate wealth. Since the exploitation of children of color has been so advantageous in the past, why not profit from the exploitation of children in urban public schools as well. Concerned mostly about the students' performance on standardized tests, opening charter schools is viewed as a business opportunity facilitated and funded by the federal government. The same federal officials, who have allowed the bankers and finance capitalists, in league with university administrators, to saddle 40 million U.S. college graduates with debts averaging $30,000, paved the way for wealthy capitalists to profit from the "privatization" of urban public education.[6] At the same time, rates of academic failure and dropping out remain high for African American and other children of color.

So, where do we go from here? What can we learn from the study of African American educational history about how to create alternatives to failure, underachievement, and exploitation in the education of African American children in the twenty-first century? In the past African American communities raised "collective cultural capital" to support both public and private schooling for African American children and adults. We have numerous case studies of rural and urban schools in the South and other regions supported financially by the local African American communities.[7] The hundreds of Rosenwald schools built throughout the South between 1912 and 1932 would not have been opened without the financial commitment—in writing—from the local Black community, agreeing to provide money, resources, and labor.[8] It was the collective cultural capital of African Americans in the South that supported public and private education for African American children and adults throughout the Jim Crow era.

Following the 1954 *Brown v. Board of Education* decision, African American parents in both the North and the South were promised equal opportunity for high quality public education, but "massive resistance" to public school integration in the South and political resistance nationwide to "busing" for school desegregation were strong enough to remove, with the assistance of the U.S. Supreme Court, existing school desegregation orders, and to prevent future lawsuits.[9] African American higher educational history between 1970 and 2004 was dominated by debates over the goals of "Affirmative Action" and while hundreds of thousands of women benefited, it came under attack because it was portrayed as damaging to some Whites who considered themselves more deserving. African Americans were again targeted and scapegoated, and by the second decade of the twenty-first century Affirmative Action was no longer a strategy for achieving "diversity" in the workplace or U.S. higher education.[10]

Perhaps we should look to the history of the African American educational experience to try and address the narrowing of African American children's formal schooling to test preparation. Throughout long periods of their experience in the United States, African American children and adults were denied access to public education and thus they created and funded their own educational institutions. Some of the earliest were the classrooms set up at the beginning of the nineteenth century by African Methodist and other Protestant churches, and African American women who opened private-venture schools. Because African Americans paid taxes that supported public education, they sought state funding for separate Black public schools beginning in northern cities before the Civil War.[11] During and after the war, African Americans opened "Freedom Schools" for the freedpeople, and hundreds of others were sponsored by northern missionary societies and the federal government's Freedmen's Bureau. Many of the Freedom Schools opened during the Civil War and Reconstruction eras eventually became the first public schools funded partially by southern state governments.[12]

In the wake of the *Brown* decision in the 1960s and 1970s, one of the approaches used to desegregate predominantly African American and Latino urban public school systems was the opening of public "magnet schools" in hopes that the innovative curriculum and programs in music, art, science, business, technology, and other content areas would attract White students. The reports on the magnets schools opened in the 1970s revealed that they not only attracted White students, their innovative and exciting curricula decreased dropout rates and improved academic levels. Given the early success of the magnet schools, arts educator Ronald Batchelor and I called for the expansion of magnet schools, not just to promote school integration, but to improve the academic achievement and retention rates of African American and other children of color in urban public schools. In 1978 we argued that the introduction of "Freedom Schooling" into U.S. public education would allow students to learn reading, writing, mathematical, and other skills as they mastered the particular subject matter—art, music, science—in the new "Freedom Schools."[13]

Unfortunately, in the early 1980s following the publishing of the 1983 federal government report *A Nation at Risk*, the thrust of campaigns for educational reform focused not on the successful model offered by the public magnet schools, but on the gaps in academic achievement levels between Whites and children of color. The next two decades witnessed the implementation of "accountability systems" in public school systems to measure the effectiveness of teachers and schools in preparing elementary and secondary students to take standardized tests.[14] Over those same three decades, however, public school districts that opened magnet schools reported high levels of academic achievement and low dropout rates for Whites and children of color. Reports and studies appeared praising the magnet schools as "The Forgotten Choice" and "The Overlooked Model" that have been successful in improving the educational achievement levels of both minority and majority students in urban public schools.[15]

In the 1860s and 1870s Freedom Schools were opened in the South to provide literacy training for the freedpeople. In the 1960s, Freedom Schools were opened in Chicago, New York City, Milwaukee, and other northern cities to provide instruction to those students participating in school boycotts demanding "quality integrated education" as part of larger civil rights campaigns taking place in those cities.[16] In 1964, in the Mississippi civil rights protests as part of the "Freedom Summer" campaign, Freedom Schools were opened throughout the state to instruct African American students in their rights and duties as U.S. citizens and to prepare them for their future roles as participants in the Civil Rights Movement.[17]

Freedom Schooling has been introduced as a form of "supplementary education" in the form of summer enrichment programs in Detroit in the 1990s; and more recently, through the "Freedom School Summer Program" organized by the Children's Defense Fund.[18] More importantly, given their historical roots in the African American experience and the success of the magnet school model over the last forty years, there is a need to introduce Freedom Schooling into urban public schools as an alternative to the current emphasis on privatization, profit-making, and standardized testing.[19] We need to use the African American past as prologue for the advancement of U.S. public education for both majority and minority students in the twenty-first century.

NOTES

1. Martin Luther King, Jr., *Where Do We Go From Here: Chaos or Community?* (1968; reprinted Boston, MA: Beacon Press, 2010); V. P. Franklin and James D. Anderson, eds., *New Perspectives on Black Educational History* (Boston, MA: G.K. Hall, 1978).

2. There have been numerous books published in the "achievement gap," see, for example, Richard Rothstein, *Class and Schools: Using Social, Economic, and Educational Reform to Close the Black–White Achievement Gap* (New York, NY: Teachers College Press, 2004); Mani Singham, *The Achievement Gap in U.S. Education: Canaries in the Mine* (San Francisco, CA: R & L Education, 2005); Pedro Noguera and Jean Y. Wing, eds. *Unfinished Business: Closing the Racial Achievement Gap in Our Schools* (San Francisco, CA: Jossey-Bass, 2008); Joseph Murphy, *The Educator's Handbook for Understanding and Closing the Achievement Gap* (New York, NY: Corwin Press, 2009); Tyrone Howard, *Why Race and Culture Matter in Schools: Closing the Achievement Gap in America's Classrooms* (New York, NY: Teachers College press, 2010); Wade Boykin and Pedro Noguera, *Creating Opportunity to Learn: Moving from Research to Practices in Closing the Achievement Gap* (Washington, DC, ASCD Press, 2011).

3. Yong Zhao, *Catching Up or Leading the Way: American Education in the Age of Globalization* (Washington, DC: ASCD Press, 2009): Tony Wagner, *The Global*

Achievement Gap: Why Even Our Best Schools Don't Teach Our Children the Skills They Need (New York, NY: Basic Books, 2010.

4. Vanessa Siddle Walker, *There Highest Potential: An African American School Community in the Segregated South* (Chapel Hill: University of North Carolina Press, 1996); and *Hello Professor: A Black Principal and Professional Leadership in the Segregated South* (Chapel Hill: University of North Carolina Press, 2009); V. P. Franklin, "Recent Books on African American Educational History," *Journal of African American History* 87 (Fall 2002): 446–450; Alison Stewart, *First Class: The Legacy of Dunbar, America's First Black Public High School* (Chicago, IL: Lawrence Hill Books, 2013); and Sharon Gay Pierson, *Laboratory of Learning: HBCU Laboratory Schools* and *Alabama State College Lab High in the Era of Jim Crow* (New York, NY: Peter Lang, 2014).

5. Paul E. Peterson and Matthew West, *No Child Left Behind? The Politics and Practice of School Accountability* (Washington, D.C.: Brookings Institution, 2003); Deborah Meier and George Wood, eds. *Many Children Left Behind: How the No Child Left Behind Act Is Damaging Our Children and Our Schools* (Boston, MA: Beacon Press, 2004); W. James Popham, *America's Failing Schools: How Parents and Students Can Cope with No Child Left Behind* (New York, NY: Routledge, 2005); Patrick J. McGuinn, *No Child Left Behind and the Transformation of Federal Education Policy, 1965–2005* (Lawrence: University Press of Kansas, 2006); Lee W. Anderson, *Congress and the Classroom: From the Cold War to No Child Left Behind* (State College: Penn State Press, 2008); Jesse Rhodes, *An Education in Politics: The Origins and Evolution of No Child Left Behind* (Ithaca, NY: Cornell University Press, 2014).

6. Diane Ravitch, *The Death and Life of the Great American School System: How Testing and Choice Are Undermining Education* (New York, NY: Basic Books, 2011); and *Reign of Error: The Hoax of the Privatization Movement and the Danger to America's Schools* (New York, NY: Basic Books, 2014).

7. V. P. Franklin and Carter Savage eds., *Cultural Capital and Black Education: African American Communities and the Funding of Black Schooling, 1860 to the Present* (Greenwich, CT: Information Age Publishing, 2004).

8. Mary Hoffschwelle, *Rosenwald Schools of the South* (Gainesville: University Press of Florida, 2006).

9. Clive Webb: *Massive Resistance: Southern Opposition to the Second Reconstruction* (New York, NY: Oxford University Press, 2005); George Lewis, *Massive Resistance: The White Response to the Civil Rights Movement* (London: Bloomsbury Publishing, 2006); John K. Day, *Southern Manifesto: Massive Resistance and the Fight to Preserve Segregation* (Oxford: University Press of Mississippi, 2014); Lillian Rubin, *Busing and Backlash: White against White in an Urban School District* (Berkeley: University of California Press, 1973); Robert Formisano, *Boston against Busing: Race, Class, and Ethnicity in the 1960s and 1970s* (Chapel Hill: University of North Carolina Press, 2004); Joyce Baugh, *The Detroit Busing Case: Milliken v. Bradley and the Controversy over Desegregation* (Lawrence: University Press of Kansas, 2011).

10. See, Charles Lawrence and Mari Matsuta, *We Won't Go Back: Making the Case for Affirmative Action* (New York, NY: Houghton-Mifflin, 1997); Terry H. Anderson, *The Pursuit of Fairness: A History of Affirmative Action* (New York Oxford

University Press, 2004): Faye J. Crosby, *Affirmative Action Is Dead, Long Live Affirmative Action* (New Haven, CT: Yale University Press, 2004); Tim Wise, *Affirmative Action: Racial Preference in Black and White* (New York, NY: Routledge, 2005); Randall Kennedy, *For Discrimination: Race, Affirmative Action, and the Law* (New York, NY: Pantheon Books, 2013).

11. Carter G. Woodson, *The Education of the Negro Prior to 1861* (Washington, DC: Associated Publishers, 1915); Carleton Mabee, *Black Education in New York State: From Colonial to Modern Times* (Syracuse, NY: Syracuse University Press, 1979) ; V. P. Franklin, *The Education of Black Philadelphia: The Social and Educational History of a Minority Community, 1900-1950* (Philadelphia: University of Pennsylvania Press, 1979); Hilary J. Moss, *Schooling Citizens: The Struggle for African American Education in Antebellum America* (Chicago. IL: University of Chicago Press, 2009).

12. Ronald E. Butchart, *Northern Schools, Southern Blacks, and Reconstruction: Freedmen's Education, 1862–1875* (Westport, CT: Greenwood Press, 1980); and *Schooling the Freed People: Teaching, Learning, and the Struggle for Black Freedom, 1861–1875* (Chapel Hill: University of North Carolina Press, 2013); James D. Anderson, *The Education of Blacks in the South, 1860–1935* (Chapel Hill: University of North Carolina Press, 1988); Heather A. Williams, *Self-Taught: African American Education in Slavery and Freedom* (Chapel Hill: University of North Carolina Press, 2007); Christopher Span, *From Cottonfield to Schoolhouse: African American Education in Mississippi, 1865–1875* (Chapel Hill: University of North Carolina Press, 2009).

13. Ronald Batchelor and V. P. Franklin, "Freedom Schooling: A New Approach to Federal–Local Cooperation in Public Education," *Teachers College Record* 62 (December 1978): 225–48.

14. Maris A. Vinovskis, *From a Nation at Risk to No Child Left Behind: National Education Goals and the Creation of Federal Education Policy* (New York, NY: Teachers College Press, 2008).

15. E. Frankenberg and G. Siegel-Hawley, *The Forgotten Choice: Rethinking Magnet Schools in a Changing Educational landscape* (Los Angeles, CA: The Civil Rights Project, 2009), and "The Overlooked Model," *American School Board Journal* (November 2009): 34–35; Susan Eaton, "Special Issue—A New Vision of School Reform: The Pull of Magnets," *The Nation* (14 June 2010): 30–35; V. P. Franklin. "Commentary: Teachers Unions Strike Back? No Need to Wait for `Superman' Magnet Schools Have Brought Success to Urban Public School Students for Over Thirty Years," in *Black Educational Choice*, ed. Diane Slaughter-Defoe and Howard Stevenson (New York, NY: Praeger Books, 2013), 217–219.

16. Alan Anderson and George Pickering, *Confronting the Color Line: The Broken Promise of the Civil Rights Movement in Chicago* (Athens: University of Georgia Press, 1987); Clarence Taylor, *Knocking at Our Own Door: Milton A. Galamison and the Struggle to Integrate New York City Schools* (New York, NY: Columbia University, 1997); Jack Dougherty, *More than One Struggle: The Evolution of Black School Reform in Milwaukee* (Chapel Hill: University of North Carolina Press, 2003).

17. Doug McAdam, *Freedom Summer* (New York, NY: Oxford University Press, 1988); Bruce Watson, *Freedom Summer: The Savage Season That Made Mississippi Burn and Made America a Democracy* (New York, NY: Viking Press, 2010); and

Jon Hale, "'The Student as a Force for Social Change': The Mississippi Freedom Schools and Student Engagement," *Journal of African American History* 96 (Summer 2011): 325–348.

18. E. Gordon, B. Bridgall and A. S. Moroe, eds. *Supplementary Education: The Hidden Curriculum of High Academic Achievement* (Lanham, MD: Rowman and Littlefield, 2004).

19. V. P. Franklin, "Freedom Schools and Mastery Learning: Providing Alternatives to Failure in Urban Public Education in the United States," in *Living on the Boundaries: Urban Marginality in National and International Contexts,* ed. Carol Camp Yeakey (London: Emerald Publishing, 2012), 159–177.

ABOUT THE EDITORS

Dionne Danns is an associate professor at Indiana University in the Department of Educational Leadership and Policy Studies. Her research focuses on the history of education, particularly African American education. Her 2003 book *Something Better for Our Children: Black Organizing in Chicago Public Schools, 1963–1971* examined student, teacher and community activism around school reform. She recently completed her second book, *Desegregating Chicago's Public Schools: Policy Implementation, Politics, and Protest, 1965–1985*, which focuses on the federal government's use of public policy to eliminate racial segregation and discrimination in public institutions in the United States through the 1964 Civil Rights Act.

Michelle A. Purdy is an assistant professor in the Department of Education in Arts & Sciences at Washington University in St. Louis. She earned her PhD in educational studies at Emory University, and her research focuses on the history of U.S. education, the history of African American education, and the history of school desegregation. She is presently working on a book manuscript that examines the interplay of politics and race in historically White elite K–12 private schools in the mid-twentieth century. She is the author of forthcoming articles in *History of Education Quarterly* and *The Journal of African American History*.

Christopher M. Span is the Associate Dean for Academic Programs in the College of Education and an Associate Professor in the Department of Education Policy, Organization, and Leadership (EPOL) at the University of Illinois at Urbana-Champaign. He is a historian of African American education and a co-editor of *History of Education Quarterly* (the number one journal in his field). In 2007, he participated on a "Brief of Historians" as *amicus curiae* for the Supreme Court consolidated *Parents* and *Meredith* (2007) school desegregation case. He has authored numerous book chapters and articles on the educational history of African Americans and in 2009, his book, *From Cotton Field to Schoolhouse: African American Education in Mississippi, 1862–1875,* was published through the University of North Carolina Press. It details the first schooling opportunities of African Americans in the state during and after the Civil War.

ABOUT THE CONTRIBUTORS

James D. Anderson is the Edward William and Jane Marr Gutgsell Professor of Education; the Head of the Department of Education Policy, Organization and Leadership; and affiliate Professor of History. His scholarship focuses broadly on the history of U.S. education, with specializations in the history of African American education in the South, the history of higher education desegregation, the history of public school desegregation, and the history of African American school achievement in the twentieth century. He is senior editor of the *History of Education Quarterly.* Anderson has served as an expert witness in a series of federal desegregation and affirmative action cases, including *Jenkins v. Missouri, Knight v. Alabama, Ayers, v. Mississippi,* and *Gratz v. Michigan.* He served as an adviser for and participant in the PBS documentaries *School: The Story of American Public Education* (2001), *The Rise and Fall of Jim Crow* (2002) and *Forgotten Genius: The Percy Julian Story.* He was elected to the National Academy of Education in 2008. In 2012, he was selected as a Fellow for Outstanding Research by AERA and received the Lifetime Achievement Award from the American Association of Colleges for Teacher Education. In 2013, he was appointed Center for Advanced Study Professor at the University of Illinois.

R. Scott Baker is associate professor of education at Wake Forest University where he teaches courses on educational history and policy and directs the program in Schools, Education, and Society. He has written extensively on the history of African American education, school desegregation, and the origins of contemporary accountability systems. His publications include "Testing Equality," *Paradoxes of Desegregation,* "Pedagogies of Protest," and

Using Past as Prologue, pages 363–366
Copyright © 2015 by Information Age Publishing
All rights of reproduction in any form reserved.

"Deconstructing Desegregation." He is currently working on a history of African American education since 1954.

Eddie R. Cole is an assistant professor of education at the College of William and Mary. His research focuses on college presidents' public speeches and student unrest in the 1960s, which in 2012 earned him a one-year appointment as a fellow at the Randall L. Tobias Center for Leadership Excellence. He also has interest in the scholarship of teaching and learning and explores differences in faculty teaching practices across different institutional contexts (e.g., HBCUs). He teaches the history of higher education, special mission colleges and universities, and academic life courses in the higher education program.

Felecia Commodore earned her PhD in higher education at the University of Pennsylvania's Graduate School of Education, where she served as a research assistant at the Penn Center for Minority Serving Institutions. She has a background working as an admissions counselor and academic advisor at Trinity University, Washington, D.C. and University of Maryland, College Park, respectively. Felecia obtained an MA in Higher Education Administration from the University of Maryland, College Park, MD and a B.S. in Marketing with a minor in Sociology from Drexel University in Philadelphia, PA. Felecia was recently a 2013 intern for the Southern Education Foundation. Felecia's research focus area is HBCU leadership, governance, and administrative practices.

V. P. Franklin, PhD, holds a University of California Presidential Chair and is Distinguished Professor of History and Education at the University of California, Riverside. He is the author of over sixty scholarly articles and five books on African American history and education; the co-editor of five books, and is currently documenting the roles and contributions of children and young people to the Civil Rights Movement. Since 2002 he has served as the Editor of *The Journal of African American History* (formerly *The Journal of Negro History*).

Marybeth Gasman is a professor of higher education in the Graduate School of Education at the University of Pennsylvania. She also serves as the Director of the Penn Center for Minority Serving Institutions. Her latest book is *Educating a Diverse Nation: Lessons from Minority Serving Institutions,* (Harvard University Press, 2015).

Jon N. Hale is an assistant professor at the College of Charleston in South Carolina. His research focuses on the history of resistance through education during the Civil Rights Movement. His manuscript, *The Freedom Schools: A History of Student Activists During the Civil Rights Movement,* is forthcoming

(Columbia University Press, 2016). His research has also been published in *The Journal of African American History, History of Education Quarterly* and the *Journal of Social Studies Research.* His service focuses on civil rights education initiatives connected to Quality Education as a Constitutional Right and the Southern Initiative of the Algebra Project.

Worth Kamili Hayes is an assistant professor of History at Tuskegee University. Prior to joining Tuskegee he served as an Assistant Professor of History and Chair of the Department of Social Sciences and Criminal Justice at Benedict College. He received his MA and PhD in history from Emory University. His research centers on the histories of Black education, the African diaspora, twentieth century U.S. urbanization, and post-world War II Black activism. His current project illuminates "the golden age of black private education" in Chicago from 1940–1990 and reveals the critical role alternative institutions played in African Americans' pursuit of quality education.

Alisha Johnson received a master's degree in education history from the University of Washington and is currently working toward her PhD at the University of Illinois at Urbana-Champaign, where she is recognized as a Graduate College Distinguished Fellow. Her research interests focus on historical spaces of non-interference in Black education. Her work is particularly attentive to the anomalous spaces for liberal movement in Black education, or what she calls "the holes in the net."

Donna Jordan-Taylor holds a doctorate from the University of Washington in Educational Leadership and Policy Studies, with a focus in African American educational history. She also holds a master's degree in Spanish, and teaches courses in Spanish, Educational Foundations, and African American history and culture at the University of Washington, Tacoma.

Sharon G. Pierson is an adjunct professor at Ramapo College of New Jersey. She earned her PhD in History and Education, and MA in Curriculum & Teaching at Teachers College, Columbia University, where her studies of the equalities in schooling and social justice in education ignited her research interests in African American educational history. In addition to presentations and journal articles, *Pierson's Laboratory of Learning: HBCU Laboratory Schools and Alabama State College Lab High in the Era of Jim Crow,* Peter Lang Publishers, was released in 2013.

Ishwanzya D. Rivers received her PhD in Educational Policy Studies from the University of Illinois at Urbana-Champaign. Her research interests focus on college access, choice, recruitment, and retention for underrepresented students, with an emphasis on the community college. Particularly, she examines relationships between higher education institutions, legislative policy, institutional policy, and social and economic outcomes for historically underrepresented and underserved students. She authored "If They Don't Make a Place for Us, We Should Make a Place for Ourselves": African American Women and Nursing at State Community College" in *Black Women in Leadership: Their Historical and Contemporary Contributions* (2013). She is also the co-author of "Dear Mr. Kozol..." Four African American Women Reauthoring Savage Inequalities (2013), published in *Teacher's College Record*.

Katrina M. Sanders is an associate professor at The University of Iowa in the department of Educational Policy and Leadership Studies. She is a historian of American education whose research interests are situated within African American education, Catholic education, and American race relations. She is the author of *"Intelligent and Effective Direction": The Fisk University Race Relations Institute, 1944–1969 and the Struggle for Civil Rights.* She is currently working on her second book that examines a southern Black Catholic school community from 1894 to 1971.

Elizabeth Todd-Breland is an assistant professor of History at the University of Illinois at Chicago. She earned her PhD in History at the University of Chicago. Her teaching and research focuses on twentieth-century U.S. urban and social history, African American history, and the history of education. She is currently finishing a book manuscript that analyzes transformations in Black politics, shifts in modes of education organizing, and the racial politics of education reform from the 1960s to the present. Todd-Breland has organized professional development workshops and courses for K–12 teachers on critical pedagogy, African American history, urban education, and college readiness.

CPSIA information can be obtained
at www.ICGtesting.com
Printed in the USA
LVOW04*2233311215

468675LV00001B/4/P